Nonprofits and Government

**ELIZABETH T. BORIS
AND
C. EUGENE STEUERLE,
EDITORS**

NONPROFITS AND GOVERNMENT

Collaboration and Conflict

THE URBAN INSTITUTE PRESS
Washington, D.C.

THE URBAN INSTITUTE PRESS
2100 M Street, N.W.
Washington, D.C. 20037

Library of Congress Cataloging in Publication Data

Nonprofits and Government: Collaboration and Conflict
[Elizabeth T. Boris and C. Eugene Steuerle, editors].

Includes bibliographical references and index.

1. United States—Politics and Government—1993–2. Democracy—United States. I. Boris, Elizabeth T.

JK271.G723   1998   98-6761
320.973'09'049—DC21   CIP

ISBN 0-87766-687-3 (paper, alk. paper)
ISBN 0-87766-686-5 (cloth, alk. paper)

Printed in the United States of America.

Distributed in North America by:
University Press of America
4720 Boston Way
Lanham, MD 20706

THE URBAN INSTITUTE is a nonprofit policy research and educational organization established in Washington, D.C., in 1968. Its staff investigates the social and economic problems confronting the nation and public and private means to alleviate them. The Institute disseminates significant findings of its research through the publications program of its Press. The goals of the Institute are to sharpen thinking about societal problems and efforts to solve them, improve government decisions and performance, and increase citizen awareness of important policy choices.

Through work that ranges from broad conceptual studies to administrative and technical assistance, Institute researchers contribute to the stock of knowledge available to guide decision-making in the public interest.

Conclusions or opinions expressed in Institute publications are those of the authors and do not necessarily reflect the views of staff members, officers or trustees of the Institute, advisory groups, or any organizations that provide financial support to the Institute.

ACKNOWLEDGMENTS

This book would not have been possible without the assistance and advice of many people. We would like to thank the authors who contributed to this volume. They were engaged partners in this project, participating in an authors' conference and delivering their papers at the June 1998 "Nonprofits and the Government: The Challenge of Civil Society" conference in Washington, D.C. We also wish to thank the panelists, discussants, and participants at that conference who gave us feedback and suggestions on those papers. The advisory committee of the Urban Institute's Center on Nonprofits and Philanthropy provided comments and suggestions on the book outline, helping us refine the focus of the manuscript. We extend our thanks to the authors, researchers, and Urban Institute staff who reviewed the book, and to Joseph Cordes and Dan Oran for help with several chapters. We are deeply indebted to Rachel Mosher-Williams, whose support and coordination throughout the project were invaluable. Joseph Pickard also provided administrative aid while the book was being written and produced, as did Mildred Woodhouse and interns Karin Willner, Bob Grim, and Steve Dyson. Our thanks also go to Scott Forrey and Blair Potter at the Urban Institute Press for their patience and hard work on this book.

Elizabeth T. Boris
C. Eugene Steuerle

CONTENTS

There is a nonprofit organization to fill almost every imaginable human need or interest: health care, education, religion, social services, civil rights, community development, legal aid, art, recreation, politics, public policy, labor unions, international peace, environmental protection, social clubs, and so on. Regardless of their individual origins, these organizations create relationships and networks that connect people to each other and enable them to work toward mutual goals. Nonprofits also provide services, whether to members only or to the larger community.

These goals and activities bring nonprofits into contact with the government in a complex, dynamic relationship. In *Nonprofits and Government: Collaboration and Conflict*, a group of distinguished authors from many disciplines analyzes the nature and extent of both aspects of the relationship.

As providers of services, nonprofits frequently act as partners of government. Medicare and Medicaid are prime examples: These government programs pay nonprofit hospitals and other organizations to provide health services to eligible individuals. Government use of nonprofits to deliver social services burgeoned in the 1960s and 1970s and has remained at significant levels since then. Nonprofits may also act in lieu of government, providing accreditation or consumer protection.

Conflict as well as cooperation is built into the relationship. Many nonprofit organizations working with poor, homeless, or minority groups, for example, seek to influence public policy on behalf of these groups. Other nonprofits, such as religious or political groups, may engage in advocacy to promote the beliefs or views of their members. While participation in civic activity is essential to democracy, these activities can put nonprofits at odds with the government. For its part, the government bestows or denies tax-exempt status and oversees the charitable activities and finances of nonprofits.

Nonprofit organizations have been called the glue that holds civil society together. As such they are a natural area of interest and research for the Urban Institute. Publication of *Nonprofits and Government: Collaboration and Conflict* is particularly exciting to us because it is the first book to appear from the Institute's new center on nonprofits and philanthropy. With their exploration of a broad range of policy issues, the authors add to our understanding of the nonprofit-government relationship. Moreover, their insights will stand us in good stead as we analyze the effects on this relationship of recent changes in funding for social services.

William Gorham
President
The Urban Institute

AN OVERVIEW OF THE NONPROFIT-GOVERNMENT RELATIONSHIP

NONPROFIT ORGANIZATIONS IN A DEMOCRACY: VARIED ROLES AND RESPONSIBILITIES

Elizabeth T. Boris

THE NONPROFIT ORGANIZATIONS OF CIVIL SOCIETY

The nonprofit organizations of civil society are separate from, but deeply interactive with, both the market and the state. Nonprofits have in common that they are voluntary and self-governing, may not distribute profits, and serve public purposes as well as the common goals of their members. These organizations are even more diverse than the titles we use for them: nonprofit, nongovernmental, civil society, philanthropic, tax-exempt, charities, voluntary associations, civic sector organizations, third sector organizations, independent sector organizations, and social sector organizations.

"Nonprofit organization" is the generic term used in this chapter. The nonprofit sector includes religious congregations, universities, hospitals, environmental groups, art museums, youth recreation associations, civil rights groups, community development organizations, labor unions, political parties, social clubs, and many more. Nonprofits play prominent social, economic, and political roles in society as service providers, employers, and advocates. They also play the less visible, but increasingly recognized, roles of fostering community engagement and civic participation, enhancing the quality of life, and promoting and preserving civic and religious values.

Scholars are beginning to document the central role that formal and informal nonprofit organizations play in creating the glue that holds communities together and the avenues they provide for civic participation (Etzioni 1993; Verba, Schlozman, and Brady 1995). Voluntary associations are identified as central to prosperous and successful democracies. They help to build the networks of trust and reciprocity, the social capital, that allows democratic societies to function effectively (Putnam 1993; Walzer 1991). Cooperative activities may bring together people with divergent opinions who learn to work together on issues of mutual interest or for the common good. Citizens participate in democratic governance by joining together to accomplish public purposes, voice their concerns to government, and monitor the impact of business, government, and nonprofit activities on the public. Nonprofits also serve to mediate opposing social forces—in the arts and religion, for example, as described in chapter eight, "Clash of Values: The State, Religion, and the Arts," by Robert Wuthnow. All of these activities require the freedom to associate, deliberate, and act in the public sphere.

Voluntary entities exert a profound cumulative effect on the quality of life and play a variety of roles in most countries where they are permitted to operate. Chapter ten, "Government-Nonprofit Relations in International Perspective," by Lester Salamon, examines the ongoing debate over the appropriate roles of government and nongovernmental, voluntary organizations overseas. Nonprofits are also significant actors at the global level in areas such as environmental protection, human rights, conflict resolution, relief, economic development, and religious activities.

As a group, nonprofits are heterogeneous. They reflect common aspirations but sharp differences as well. Their impacts can be positive or negative, confrontational or conciliatory, depending on their activities and the perspective of the analyst. Thus, the interaction between government and nonprofit organizations in civil society is complex, but it is also dynamic, ebbing and flowing with shifts in policy, political administrations, and social norms.

What Are Nonprofit Organizations?

Nonprofit organizations in the United States are defined and regulated primarily under the federal tax code. They are formal organizations that do not distribute profits and are exempt from federal taxes by virtue of being organized for public purposes described in the revenue code. All nonprofit organizations with revenues of $5,000 or more, except religious groups, are required to register with the Internal Revenue Service (IRS). Organizations with revenues of more than $25,000 are required to file an annual Form 990 (or Form 990PF for private foundations) with the IRS. Form 990 provides the basis for most financial data on nonprofit organizations.

Those nonprofit organizations that serve broad public purposes and are organized for educational, religious, scientific, literary, relief of poverty, and other activities for the public benefit are eligible to apply for charitable status under section 501(c)(3) of the tax code. Charitable status permits organizations to receive tax-deductible contributions. This group of nonprofits serves the broad public, accounts for the majority of tax-exempt organizations, and is the focus of most chapters in this book. Mutual membership organizations such as labor unions, recreation clubs, credit unions, and political parties are also tax-exempt, nonprofit organizations that play important roles, but they are not central to this book.

Even within the charitable portion of the nonprofit sector, the organizations are extremely diverse. They vary greatly in missions, origin, structure, size, and financial means. Their diversity confounds attempts to understand them and build adequate theory. Research over the past two decades has made progress in measuring the scope of the formal organizations, but little has been accomplished in measuring the informal groups, coalitions, and religious organizations. There is also a dearth of information on the direct and indirect contributions of nonprofit groups to society.

Scope of Nonprofit Organizations in the United States

The nonprofit sector in the United States is characterized by the diversity of organizations and activities, the concentration of resources in a small number of organizations, and the fragmented nature of activities that vary in scale and by geographic area.

There were approximately 1.5 million tax-exempt nonprofit organizations in 1996. Among them are 1.2 million organizations registered with the Internal Revenue Service and an additional 266,000 religious congregations of all types (see table I.1). There are probably millions more small formal and informal associations (with less than $5,000 in revenues) that are not required to register with the IRS (Smith 1994).

Among registered nonprofits in 1996 were 654,000 "charitable" organizations eligible to receive tax-deductible contributions. This group includes traditional charities—hospitals, universities, soup kitchens, etc.—that make up over half of registered nonprofit organizations.

In addition to the "charitable" organizations, there are approximately 140,000 public-serving social welfare organizations that are tax exempt under IRS section 501(c)(4). Most of those organizations may not receive tax-deductible gifts; many elect to do substantial lobbying. In chapter nine, "Nonprofit Advocacy and Political Participation," Elizabeth Reid discusses nonprofits as politically active

Table I.1 NUMBER OF NONPROFIT ENTITIES IN THE UNITED STATES, 1989–1996
(Numbers in Thousands)

	1989 Number	1989 Percent	1992 Number	1992 Percent	1996 Number	1996 Percent	1989–96 % change
Total private nonprofit organizations	**1,262**	**100.0**	**1,351**	**100.0**	**1,455**	**100.0**	**15.3**
Tax-exempt orgs. registered with the I.R.S.	993	78.7	1,085	80.3	1,189	81.7	19.7
Total 501(c)(3) charitable organizations[a]	464	36.8	546	40.0	654	44.9	40.9
Total public charities	422	33.4	500	37.0	600	41.2	42.2
Reporting with financial data	138	10.9	165	12.2	200	13.7	44.9
Out-of-scope organizations	0.5	0.0	0.5	0.0	1	0.1	100.0
Reporting public charities	137	10.9	165	12.2	199	13.7	45.3
Operating	124	9.8	148	11.0	178	12.2	43.5
Supporting	13	1.0	16	1.2	21	1.4	61.5
Mutual benefit	0.5	0.0	0.5	0.0	0.6	0.0	20.0
Nonreporting[b]	284	22.5	335	24.8	400	27.5	40.8
Private foundations	42	3.3	46	3.4	54	3.7	28.6
501(c)(4) social welfare organizations	141	11.2	143	10.6	140	9.6	-0.7
Other reporting tax-exempt organizations	388	30.7	396	29.3	395	27.1	1.8
Religious congregations not reporting[c]	269	21.3	266	19.7	266	18.3	-1.1

Sources: U.S. Internal Revenue Service Return Transaction File, 1997; Stevenson, David, Thomas H. Pollak, and Linda M. Lampkin, *State Nonprofit Almanac 1997; Nonprofit Almanac 1996–1997* as updated by Independent Sector, 1998.

a. Includes public charities and private foundations. All section 501(c)(3) entitles are not included because certain organizations, including congregations and conventions or associations of churches, need not apply to the IRS for recognition of exemption unless they desire a ruling.

b. Includes nonfilers and organizations reporting with gross receipts below $25,000.

c. Estimates of the number of religious congregations in Independent Sector's *Nonprofit Almanac 1996–1997* and 1998 update to the Almanac were 341,000 in 1992 and 1996 and 344,000 in 1989 (number imputed from 1987 and 1992 estimations). The figures above were adjusted to exclude the 75,000 religious congregations that have registered with the IRS and are counted under Total 501(c)(3) charitable organizations.

organizations, highlighting the representative and participatory functions of nonprofit advocacy.

Other types of tax-exempt organizations primarily serve their members; for example, business leagues, social and recreational clubs, war veterans' organizations, cemetery companies, labor unions, benevolent life insurance associations, and credit unions. Donations to those organizations are not tax-deductible. While all of these groups potentially contribute to the social fabric of the country, we know most about the "charitable" 501(c)(3) organizations and the "social welfare" 501(c)(4) organizations that make up the majority of formal nonprofit organizations. I focus on them because of their public-serving nature (see table I.2).

Types of Organizations

The variety of nonprofit organizations is evident in the categories of the National Taxonomy of Exempt Entities (NTEE) developed by the National Center for Charitable Statistics to classify all nonprofit organizations (Stevenson 1997). The NTEE includes 9 major groups, 26 categories, and over 600 subcategories. The major groups are:

- Arts, culture, humanities (e.g., art museums, historical societies)
- Education (e.g., private schools, universities, PTAs)
- Environment and animals (e.g., Humane Societies, the Chesapeake Bay Foundation)
- Health, hospitals (e.g., nonprofit hospitals, the American Lung Association)
- Human services (e.g., Girl Scouts, YMCA, food banks, homeless shelters)
- International, foreign affairs (e.g., CARE, the Asia Society, International Committee of the Red Cross)
- Public societal benefit (e.g., Rockefeller Foundation, the Urban Institute, civil rights groups, United Ways)
- Religion-related (e.g., interfaith coalitions, religious societies)
- Mutual membership/benefit (e.g., nonprofit credit unions, labor unions, fraternal organizations)

The number of nonprofits is growing more quickly than the population, and there is tremendous variation in the size, resources, scope, and capacity of the different types of nonprofit organizations (see table I.3). Most are extremely small entities with meager resources that operate locally with modest budgets and volunteer labor. Some organizations are large and professional, with hundreds of employees

Table I.2 TAX-EXEMPT ORGANIZATIONS REGISTERED WITH THE IRS, 1996

Section	Description	Number
501(c)(1)	Corporations organized under act of Congress	20
501(c)(2)	Titleholding corporations	7,100
501(c)(3)	**Charitable and religious***	**654,186**
501(c)(4)	Social welfare	139,512
501(c)(5)	Labor, agricultural organizations	64,955
501(c)(6)	Business leagues	77,274
501(c)(7)	Social and recreational clubs	60,845
501(c)(8)	Fraternal beneficiary societies	91,972
501(c)(9)	Voluntary employees' beneficiary associations	14,486
501(c)(10)	Domestic fraternal beneficiary societies	20,925
501(c)(11)	Teachers' retirement funds	13
501(c)(12)	Benevolent life insurance associations	6,343
501(c)(13)	Cemetery companies	9,562
501(c)(14)	State-chartered credit unions	5,157
501(c)(15)	Mutual insurance companies	1,212
501(c)(16)	Corporations to finance crop operations	23

501(c)(17)	Supplemental unemployment benefit trusts	565
501(c)(18)	Employee-funded pension trusts	2
501(c)(19)	War veterans' organizations	31,464
501(c)(20)	Legal service organizations	131
501(c)(21)	Black lung trusts	25
501(c)(22)	Multiemployer pension plans	0
501(c)(23)	Veterans' associations founded prior to 1880	2
501(c)(24)	Trusts described in Section 4049 of ERISA	1
501(c)(25)	Holding companies for pensions, etc.	794
501(d)	Religious and apostolic organizations	113
501(e)	Cooperative hospital service organizations	54
501(f)	Cooperative service organizations of operating educational organizations	1
521	Farmers' cooperatives	1,773
Total		**1,188,510**

Source: Internal Revenue Service, *1996 Annual Data Book*, Publication 55B.

*All section 501(c)(3) organizations are not included because certain organizations, such as congregations, integrated auxiliaries, subordinate units, conventions or associations of churches, and organizations with less than $5,000 in gross receipts, need not apply for recognition of exemption unless they desire a ruling.

Table I.3 GROWTH IN NUMBER OF NONPROFITS,* 1989–1996

Type	1989	1996	Increase	Percent Increase
Arts/culture	13,817	19,509	5,692	41.2
Education	16,939	28,235	11,296	66.7
Environment and animals	3,305	5,799	2,494	75.5
Health	23,039	28,234	5,195	22.5
Human services	45,156	66,514	21,358	47.3
International	1,196	1,816	620	51.8
Public/societal benefit	8,352	13,615	5,263	63.0
Religion related	5,764	8,846	3,082	53.5
Unknown	6,119	5,036	−1,083	−17.7
Total	**123,687**	**177,604**	**53,917**	**43.6**

Source: U.S. Internal Revenue Service Return Transaction File, 1997, as adjusted by the National Center for Charitable Statistics.

*Includes nonprofit organizations classified as operating public charities that report to the IRS (file Form 990) and are required to do so. Excludes private foundations, foreign organizations, government-associated organizations, and organizations without state identifiers.

and many millions of dollars in expenditures. Resources are concentrated in the largest organizations.

The active charitable nonprofits (excluding private foundations) include only about 4 percent with expenses of more than $10 million a year. This group of approximately 6,770 organizations holds more than three-quarters of the assets and is responsible for almost 80 percent of the expenditures of the nonprofit sector. In contrast, almost 41 percent of organizations (72,447) have expenses of less than $100,000, only 0.6 percent of the total expenses for the field (see figure I.1). The assets of philanthropic foundations are also highly concentrated in the largest foundations.

Hospitals and higher education institutions account for a disproportionate share of the assets, expenses, and employment in the nonprofit sector. Hospitals make up 2.8 percent of organizations but more than 46 percent of expenditures. Private colleges and universities are about 1.4 percent of organizations but account for over 12 percent of expenses. Human service organizations, in contrast, account for over a third of active charities but expend only about 13 percent of the resources (see figure I.2). Aggregate national statistics do not reveal a great deal about the majority of nonprofit organizations.

Regional Variation

There are regional and state differences in the numbers, types, finances, and growth of nonprofit organizations. The numbers tend to

Figure I.1 NONPROFIT* FINANCES BY TOTAL EXPENSE LEVEL, 1996

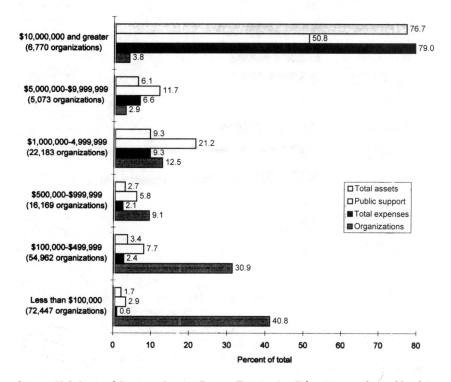

Source: U.S. Internal Revenue Service Return Transaction File, 1997, as adjusted by the National Center for Charitable Statistics.
*Only operating public charities are included. See table I.3 for definition.
Note: Numbers are preliminary.

vary with the population levels. California, Texas, and New York have the largest numbers of nonprofits. The growth rates for nonprofits tend to be higher for states that have rapidly growing populations. Sparsely populated states, however, have among the highest density levels of nonprofits. Vermont, for example, had a density of 15 organizations per 10,000 people compared to five for Texas and almost seven nationally (see figure I.3).

The Northeast has proportionately more arts, culture, and humanities organizations; the Midwest more human services; and the West more environmental groups. The Northeast, with about one-fifth of the population, is home to almost a quarter of nonprofit organizations that account for almost a third of the expenditures of the sector (see table I.4). These data are suggestive of the varied regional cultures of

Figure I.2 DISTRIBUTION OF NONPROFITS* AND TOTAL EXPENSES BY
ACTIVITY, 1996

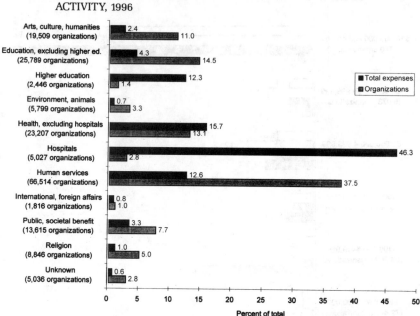

Source: U.S. Internal Revenue Service Return Transaction File, 1997, as adjusted by the
National Center for Charitable Statistics.
*Only operating public charities are included. See table I.3 for definition.
Note: Numbers are preliminary.

philanthropy described by Julian Wolpert in his research. Some areas
have higher rates of giving and stronger civic and nonprofit infrastructure than others. Wealthier areas have larger numbers of nonprofit
organizations that provide amenities such as recreation, private
schools, and art activities (Wolpert 1993). Cultural differences appear
to affect the types of organizations and their financial strength in each
region.

The portrait of the nonprofit sector that emerges is one of disparate
groups, thinly and unevenly spread across the states with a great
range of missions and activities. As a whole, their increasing economic strength raises their visibility, but most are community-based
and not well known outside of their neighborhoods. They are growing
in number, but they are still only a small fraction (about 5 percent) of
the approximately 24 million business, government, and nonprofit
entities in the country. Because the fiscal capacity of states and cities
varies just as widely as the nonprofit sector, the effect of future shifts

Figure I.3 NUMBER OF NONPROFIT ORGANIZATIONS* PER 10,000 RESIDENTS, 1996

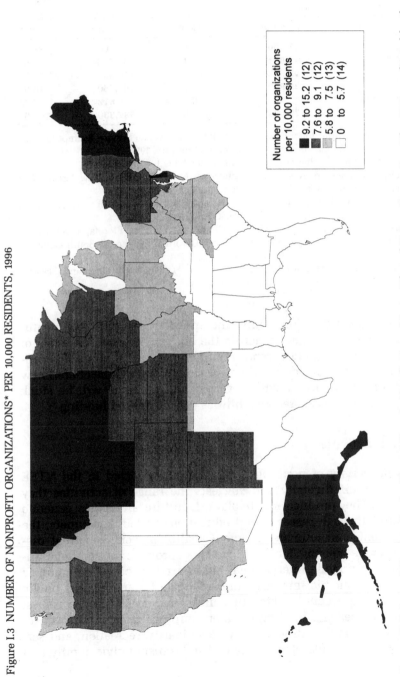

Number of organizations
per 10,000 residents

9.2 to 15.2 (12)
7.6 to 9.1 (12)
5.8 to 7.5 (13)
0 to 5.7 (14)

Source: U.S. Internal Revenue Service Exempt Organizations/Business Master File and Return Transaction File, 1997, as adjusted by the National Center for Charitable Statistics.

*Only operating public charities are included. See table I.3 for definition.

Table I.4 NUMBER OF NONPROFITS* AND TOTAL EXPENSES, BY REGION, 1996
(Dollars in Millions)

Region	Organizations	Percent	Expenses	Percent
Northeast[a]	41,766	23.5	167,100	31.1
Midwest[b]	42,801	24.1	131,760	24.5
South[c]	52,982	29.8	140,903	26.2
West[d]	39,900	22.5	96,760	18.0
U.S. Territories	155	0.1	812	0.2
Total	**177,604**	**100.0**	**537,336**	**100.0**

Source: Urban Institute 1998, based on U.S. Internal Revenue Service Exempt Organizations/Business Master File and Return Transaction File, 1997.
*Only operating public charities are included. See table I.3 for definition.
a. Includes: Connecticut, Maine, Massachusetts, New Hampshire, New Jersey, New York, Pennsylvania, Rhode Island, Vermont.
b. Includes: Illinois, Indiana, Iowa, Kansas, Michigan, Minnesota, Missouri, Nebraska, North Dakota, Ohio, South Dakota, Wisconsin.
c. Includes: Alabama, Arkansas, Delaware, District of Columbia, Florida, Georgia, Kentucky, Louisiana, Maryland, Mississippi, North Carolina, Oklahoma, South Carolina, Tennessee, Texas, Virginia, West Virginia.
d. Includes: Alaska, Arizona, California, Colorado, Hawaii, Idaho, Montana, Nevada, New Mexico, Oregon, Utah, Washington, Wyoming.

in governmental decisionmaking and spending on charitable organizations cannot be projected across the board. Likewise, the effect of devolution or other policy trends on different types of nonprofits cannot be uniformly considered. Some organizations will be offered new opportunities to partner with government, and some will be stuck with expanded service responsibilities and decreased funding.

Nonprofit Activities

The wide variety of nonprofit organizations reflected in the NTEE highlights their diversity and suggests the range of activities they undertake. They produce and display art, culture, and music; generate knowledge through research and education; protect consumers, the environment, and animals; promote health; prevent and treat diseases; provide housing, food, and clothing; promote international understanding; provide international aid and relief; create community social and economic infrastructure; advocate for and against public policies that affect civil rights, gun control, abortion, and other issues; provide services and funding to other nonprofit groups; transmit religious values and traditions; provide solidarity, recreation, and services to members and others; promote and transmit civic, family, and economic values; educate and register voters; and try to meet virtually every human need.

This long laundry list gives some sense of the difficulty of defining and describing the nonprofit sector. It also makes clear that voluntary organizations do many things that are also done by governments and businesses. There are no sharp boundaries between the sectors. There are, however, some distinctive activities, including religious worship, membership activities, and government monitoring, that are overwhelmingly accomplished in the nonprofit sector, as well as activities more likely to be undertaken by nonprofits than by either government or business. Eighty-six percent of museums, botanical gardens, and zoological gardens, for example, are nonprofit. Some activities are more evenly divided between government and nonprofits, for example, social services, where approximately 58 percent of providers are nonprofits.

Business, government, and nonprofits sometimes undertake the same or similar programs or services, such as child care, hospital care, and research. They collaborate or cooperate in providing services such as low-income housing. Some small businesses fear incursions by nonprofits into commercial areas, while nonprofit leaders voice concern about the conversions of nonprofit hospitals and health maintenance organizations into for-profit businesses. Nonprofits have a long history of pioneering programs that were subsequently taken over by the other sectors. In chapter two, "Meeting Social Needs: Comparing the Resources of the Independent Sector and Government," C. Eugene Steuerle and Virginia Hodgkinson illustrate the overlap of service functions in an analysis of the capacity of nonprofits and the government to serve the public. Chapter three, "The Nonprofit Sector and the Federal Budget," by Alan Abramson, Lester Salamon, and C. Eugene Steuerle, demonstrates the similar roles of the nonprofit and government sectors, outlining how changes in federal spending since the 1980s have affected areas of interest to nonprofit organizations.

Primary education, kindergartens, and disease control were popularized by nonprofits and taken over by government when demand outpaced the ability of nonprofit providers to supply services. Recreation programs pioneered by nonprofits were picked up by businesses and developed into profitable enterprises.

Some nonprofits have the characteristics of business corporations or of government programs, and a small number of organizations do change from one type of organization to another. Governments set up nonprofit corporations to carry out some public programs, for example, the Corporation for Public Broadcasting. Nonprofits may create profit-making subsidiaries (which pay taxes on earned income) to subsidize their charitable activities. A few give up their tax-exempt status when their missions can be accomplished more effectively as business corporations or when economic incentives make it profitable for them to become businesses. The conversion of nonprofit hospitals to for-profit businesses is a recent example. Conversions raise questions about whether it is in the public interest for businesses to take over hospitals and certain other types of services, but as long as the assets are reserved for charitable purposes and some form of community service is maintained, the current barriers to conversion are minimal. John Goddeeris and Burton Weisbrod discuss in chapter seven, "Why Not For-Profit? Conversions and Public Policy," the growing trend toward conversion of organizational form.

The overlapping and complementary nature of the three sectors provides useful flexibility for American society. Public-serving activities are not restricted to government but can be undertaken through multiple avenues. Diverse publics with different tastes and needs organize to meet perceived needs. Social entrepreneurs implement their visions through nonprofit organizations, but the alternatives they develop sometimes find their way into the public or business sectors.

ROLES OF NONPROFIT ORGANIZATIONS

Why do nonprofits exist? Scholars answer that question in different ways, depending on their disciplines and orientations. Economic theories include the notions of "market failure," "government failure," and "nonprofit failure," as ways of explaining the public services delivered by nonprofits, and the partnership of the government with the nonprofit sector in financing a variety of public services.

Market failure is based on the concept that there are desired services or collective "goods" that do not have sufficient potential for profit to attract business providers. Market failure is also precipitated by insufficient information on the quality of services, which may lead consumers to turn to nonprofit providers that are perceived as trustworthy because they do not have a profit motive. Similarly, government failure implies that there are public services that government will not provide for reasons that may include the cost or the limited constituency that desires the service (Weisbrod 1988; Hansman 1987).

"Nonprofit failure" explains the nonprofit-government partnership as resulting from the need of nonprofits to finance services demanded by the public through governments. In this theory, nonprofits are the preferred providers of services, and government action only becomes necessary when nonprofits are unable to meet perceived needs (Salamon 1995). In chapter one, "Complementary, Supplementary, or Adversarial? A Theoretical and Historical Examination of Nonprofit-Government Relations in the United States," Dennis Young reviews current economic theories as they relate to the historical relationship between government and nonprofit organizations.

Scholars also look to history and to the religious roots of charity, altruism, and social justice to explain the giving and volunteering that characterize involvement in nonprofit organizations and rights-oriented social movements as well as the helping behaviors so evident in religious organizations (Payton 1988; Wuthnow 1991; O'Connell 1997).

Political scientists view the role of the nonprofit sector in terms of providing avenues of civic participation and representation of interests in the pluralistic, political system of a heterogeneous society. Diverse values and interests are aggregated through associations and represented to the political system through political advocacy and lobbying of the government by many nonprofit groups (Berry 1984; Douglass 1987; Verba, Schlozman, and Brady 1995). Roger Lohmann builds on the idea of the Commons as the civic arena in his book on the nonprofit sector (Lohmann 1992).

Communitarians view voluntary associations in more organic terms, as the precursors of government and the market and thus as among the most basic of social relationships that connect people and create communities. Those relationships became more complex over time and evolved into the state and the market (Etzioni 1993). Robert Putnam and others use the concepts of social capital and civil society in a basically communitarian framework (Putnam 1993; Walzer 1991).

The variety of explanations and approaches is appropriate for this multifaceted array of organizations. Each theory brings insights and facilitates clearer understanding of nonprofit organizations. The following chapters will borrow from these approaches to provide a broad, descriptive look at some of the major roles played by nonprofit organizations.

We use a civil society approach to look at the role of nonprofits in generating the social capital that links people to their communities and to others. The social capital role includes fostering civic values and participation, monitoring government, and informing public policy through education, research, and analysis. We use an economic perspective to look at the creation of income, jobs, and knowledge, as well as service provision and economic development. We employ a religious perspective to look at the role of nonprofits in alleviating poverty and promoting and maintaining religious values and beliefs.

Social Capital

Nonprofit organizations, regardless of origin, create networks and relationships that connect people to each other and to institutions quite apart from the organization's primary purposes. Those relationships build social capital, the cooperative networks that permit individuals to work together for mutual goals. Recent research by Robert Putnam and others suggests that relationships such as those fostered by choral societies, bowling leagues, and other community associations build the trust and cooperation that is essential for the effective functioning of society, politics, and economy (Putnam 1993). Other research shows that political and civic engagement is related to feelings of efficacy and the belief that participation in community activities leads to worthwhile outcomes (Pew Research Center for the People and the Press 1997).

Nonprofit organizations use volunteers as members of boards of directors, in staff management and service positions, as fundraisers, and in many other capacities. Volunteers bring expertise from business, government, and the community to bear on local, national, and international problems. Volunteer experiences enhance civic engagement and diffusion of expertise as people of various backgrounds learn about the needs of their communities and others, and act together to solve them. Volunteering also harnesses the enthusiasm of young and old and adds meaning to their lives. People who are involved in youth groups, churches, and other voluntary activities when young are more likely to give, volunteer, and be engaged in civic life in adulthood (Hodgkinson and Weitzman 1996a). Those who are involved in their communities are also more likely to be healthy and happy (Seligman 1991). Of genuine concern is whether there is a participation gap in the United States, particularly among poor people, who are generally not as involved in voluntary associations and often do not have the resources, opportunities, and skills to make their needs known in the political system (Verba, Schlozman, and Brady 1995).

Some of the most profound social changes of this century have been promoted through a combination of research, public education, advocacy, legislation, and litigation fostered by nonprofit organizations, usually working in coalitions with religious and other groups, sometimes in cooperation with government and business interests. Civil rights groups, in collaboration with religious and other organizations, attacked racial segregation in this country through direct action, lobbying, advocacy, litigation, and public education. Environmental groups used research, public education, advocacy, and litigation in their pioneering efforts to reduce air and water pollution and protect the environment and wildlife. Mothers Against Drunk Driving used a variety of tools, including public education, to create a major change in public perception about the consequences of drinking and driving. Anti-smoking groups fostered research and used the results to educate the public about the negative impacts of tobacco smoking on health. The women's movement continues to use public education and advocacy to promote equity and rights for women in the workplace and control over reproductive choices, while the anti-abortion movement focuses public attention on the religious and ethical values that they feel should guide those choices. Groups in California successfully organized to collect signatures and put on the ballot measures to cut public spending and overturn affirmative action in that state.

Not all civic activities are designed to introduce change. Some groups aim to conserve or protect from outside forces values that they espouse, or try to prevent the erosion of values they cherish or advantages they enjoy. The National Rifle Association, for example, promotes gun ownership and lobbies against legislation that would limit the availability of guns. As Wuthnow's chapter illustrates, the most deeply felt controversies over values are played out in the nonprofit sector—around religious beliefs, artistic expression, personal responsibility, and individual rights. Nonprofits express conflicts over competing values long before they reach the political system. In extremely divisive cases such as racial segregation and access to abortion, the issues involve legislative and judicial battles at the national, state, and local levels over long periods of time.

Policy

Many nonprofit efforts inform and influence domestic social and economic policies as well as international affairs. Much policy activity involves nonpartisan research, writing, evaluation, and demonstration projects. Some groups try to influence executive agencies; others, the legislative branch. Think tanks and universities conduct research and evaluations and make that information available to policymakers through publications, news media, forums, and individual conversations. Nonprofit advocacy groups try to educate the public and encourage individuals to contact their representatives directly or to sign petitions for or against certain positions. Some nonprofits also try to influence public policy through demonstrations, sit-ins, parades, and boycotts.

Grantmaking foundations and other nonprofits try to influence public policy by demonstrating the efficacy of alternative approaches to public issues such as economic development or teen pregnancy. They may conduct experimental programs, evaluate the results, and communicate them to public authorities.

Religious

Religious organizations serve the spiritual needs of their members and promote and preserve the group's religious doctrines and values. Sacramental activities and membership serving activities such as child care and counseling are often supplemented by social services, crisis care, and advocacy activities (Printz 1997; Hodgkinson and Weitzman 1993; Cnaan 1997). Religious congregations also impart civic skills to members who learn to organize and collaborate for common ends. Black churches are well known for their political work, particularly around civil rights (Harris 1994). Catholic churches are vocal in opposition to birth control and abortion. Certain Christian churches support conservative political positions on issues such as abortion, gay rights, and family values. Religious congregations are also among the most forceful advocates for peace, social justice, and policies that protect the poor.

The separation of church and state in the United States results in most religious entities falling outside of the government regulatory framework for nonprofit organizations. Houses of worship and closely aligned entities enjoy the benefits of tax exemption and deductible contributions but are not required to register or report to the IRS, although many do for a variety of reasons. A preliminary sorting of the IRS files indicates that a substantial proportion of nonprofits have religious roots or affiliations (Pollak 1997).

Faith-based nonprofits and religious congregations are caught in a political crossfire right now. At the same time that they are being touted by both liberals and conservatives as ideal vehicles for assessing and serving the public's needs, the convergence of religion and government in new partnerships and new (as well as old) funding patterns is making many groups uncomfortable.

Service

Nonprofits of all types provide services that may be offered to the whole community, to members only, to governments, to businesses, and to other nonprofits. The services may be free or require a fee, such as a tuition payment. Voluntary labor, donations, direct and indirect government grants, and payments provide a complex mix of revenues for nonprofits (see table 2.3, chapter two, this volume). Nonprofits overlap with business and governments as service providers, for example, in education and medical care. They may be contractors to governments and businesses (providing preschool programs or drug abuse treatment), be collaborators with governments (maintaining national and regional parks or preventing diseases), or act in lieu of government (accreditation or consumer protection). In chapter five, "Government Financing of Nonprofit Activity," Steven Rathgeb Smith examines the many ways in which government funds nonprofit activity and considers the potential impact of this financing on the organizational culture of nonprofits and the services that they provide.

Government may use nonprofits to undertake activities that require reaching local populations with culturally sensitive materials or to avoid building up staff for short-term projects. Nonprofits provide a way for governments to devolve programs to state and local authorities and provide services without incurring government salary scales and bureaucratic red tape. Chapter six, "Nonprofits and Devolution: What Do We Know?" by Carol De Vita, summarizes the current research on devolution and its probable effects on nonprofit organizations.

Nonprofits also interact with and provide a variety of services for the business sector. They collaborate with businesses in promoting quality of life in areas where firms operate. Donations to and contracts with cultural organizations, child care, and recreation groups underwrite amenity services that attract and hold corporate employees. Support through gifts and contracts also enables universities to undertake research, develop technology, and train current and future employees. Environmental groups help to level the playing field for socially responsible behavior by demanding, for example, that all competitors within an industry clean up pollutants. Collaboration between voluntary groups and businesses develops when industries benefit from the educational and advocacy campaigns of nonprofits, as in disease prevention and anti-smoking campaigns that benefit life insurance companies.

Nonprofit business associations provide information, research, and advocacy services for member corporations. They monitor the health of industries and the impact of legislation and regulation on corporate activities. They may provide low-cost insurance or cooperative buying opportunities. Similar nonprofit associations provide such services for groups of nonprofits, health-related nonprofits, philanthropic foundations, colleges and universities, symphonies, museums, and others.

While nonprofit organizations have historically played the role of service providers for the public, competition with for-profit companies is becoming an increasingly serious issue for them. As government turns more to the market to contract out for (what it assumes will be) more efficient sources of service, nonprofits may be excluded from new opportunities resulting from welfare reform and other shifts in government spending.

Economic

Nonprofits also play an economic role that is becoming better known through research that documents the contributions to the economy of nonprofit employment and the goods and services produced. The growing number of nonprofit organizations with their increased role as employers (especially in hospitals, private universities, and multipurpose organizations like the American Red Cross, Catholic Charities, and others) adds significantly to the national income. The nonprofit sector employs over 10 million people plus another 5.5 million full-time equivalent volunteers. It generated annual funds estimated at $550 billion in 1996. An estimated 6.5 percent of national income originates in the nonprofit sector (Hodgkinson and Weitzman 1996b).

This economic role, however, is disproportionately concentrated in the largest organizations. As in other parts of the economy, the resources of the nonprofit sector are highly concentrated. More than one-third of nonprofit employees work in hospitals. A study of nonprofits that report to the IRS shows that the top 1 percent of organizations in 1995 are responsible for 28 percent of income, and the top 10 percent for 68 percent of income (Pollak and Pettit, forthcoming).

Nonprofits are the entry point into the labor force for many women and minorities. About two out of three workers in the nonprofit sector are women. Major nonprofit hospitals and universities also anchor whole inner-city neighborhoods or small towns with employment opportunities, services, and amenities like arts, culture, and recreation opportunities. They pay payroll taxes and generate taxable income through employment. Because most do not pay property taxes or sales taxes, they may be perceived as a drain on the local economy. A growing number of large nonprofits, including foundations, make payments in lieu of taxes to city governments. The city of Philadelphia now requires payments in lieu of taxes from the larger nonprofits within its jurisdiction, after a series of stories in *The Philadelphia Inquirer* criticized nonprofits for not contributing to the city's coffers (Borowski and Gaul 1993). In chapter four, "Tax Treatment of Nonprofit Organizations: A Two-Edged Sword?" Evelyn Brody and Joseph Cordes discuss the special tax treatment of nonprofit organizations, a primary area of government regulation of the nonprofit sector.

Studies of the economic impact of nonprofits, however, reveal significant economic contributions to local economies. In Baltimore, for example, a study of the nonprofit sector conducted by the Merrick School of Business at the University of Baltimore showed a fast-growing part of the local economy that provided enough full-time equivalent jobs for 18 percent of the workforce and generated $5.4 billion in economic activity in the city. The Baltimore city government received an estimated $41 million in "piggy back" state income tax, real estate tax, and sales tax revenues traceable to spending by nonprofits, their vendors, and employees. Visitors to Baltimore's nonprofit tourist attractions spent over $303 million in the city. Nonprofit elementary and high schools and community service organizations spent an estimated $900 million annually on behalf of the city's residents, more than half of Baltimore city government spending on similar programs and services (Maryland Association of Nonprofit Organizations 1997).

NEGATIVE IMPACTS

Nonprofits have the potential for positive as well as negative impacts on society and are subject to the failings of the people who lead them. The regulatory framework is designed to protect the public from malfeasance, but other types of potential negative impacts are not as easily regulated. Some are obvious: nonprofits can be a divisive and fragmenting influence on the political system. They may undermine political parties (or support them), and well-funded groups can manipulate public opinion and promote ideological positions or have a disproportionate impact on public policy. Low-income populations may be at a disadvantage in the policy process because they may not have access to groups that can represent their interests. Although there is little confirming evidence, nonprofits may have an edge over businesses in the same markets because of their tax-exempt status.

Other potentially negative consequences are not as obvious. The use of nonprofits by governments to deliver services may separate governments from direct credit or blame for services funded, thus undermining popular support for public financing of programs or promoting cynicism toward nonprofits if programs do not work. Nonprofits can provide a "cop-out" for political leaders who wish to curtail government responsibilities. Nonprofits can also be used by wealthy communities to provide for their needs while they fail to provide tax revenues for public education and other public health and human services for low-income residents. Hopefully, the already significant role of nonprofit organizations in human service provision and the well-established but sometimes hidden relationship between government and nonprofits will be uncovered as welfare reform, devolution, and other shifts play out.

CONCLUSION

We must understand the variety of roles played by the nonprofit sector before we can thoroughly explore its relationship with government. Because the spheres of activity undertaken by nonprofits and government intersect in so many ways, the nature and scope of nonprofit organizations will be sensitive to changes in public policy. For example, budget policy affects the demand for services provided by nonprofits, as well as the ability of agencies to supply those services. Similarly, tax policy affects the resources available to nonprofits in fulfilling their missions.

It is important to remember that interaction between nonprofits and government in a civil society is dynamic. Therefore, while studying the past can be useful, mechanically projecting the future from the past can be misleading. Simplistic assumptions about what nonprofit organizations can do and how they affect society may lead to public policies that are ineffective or have unintended negative consequences both for the organizations and for society.

Note on Data Sources

During the past 15 years, researchers (Virginia Hodgkinson, Lester Salamon, and others) have made great progress in assessing the dimensions of the nonprofit sector in the United States and in other countries. This has been difficult because governments do not collect and maintain data about nonprofit organizations as they do for businesses. In 1981, a group of researchers started the National Center for Charitable Statistics (NCCS) to collect information derived from IRS reporting forms, classify organizations by purpose, and produce periodic statistics. Through the years, NCCS has developed and refined a classification system (the National Taxonomy of Exempt Entities) for nonprofits and issued regular reports.

To date, the most comprehensive source of data on the nonprofit sector in the United States is the *Nonprofit Almanac 1996–1997*, published by Independent Sector and updated in May 1998. Its companion volume, *The State Nonprofit Almanac 1997*, published by NCCS at the Urban Institute, contains more refined data at the state level.

A pathbreaking analysis of the IRS data on nonprofit organizations is also included in The Charitable Nonprofits: An Analysis of Institutional Dynamics and Characteristics, by William G. Bowen, Thomas I. Nygren, Sarah E. Turner, and Elizabeth A. Duffy (San Francisco: Jossey-Bass Publishers, 1994).

While such data on nonprofits have improved greatly over the past several years, data on the sector as a whole are limited. One problem is the absence of many nonprofits from the IRS data sets, the gaps being greatest for small social service and advocacy organizations (Gronbjerg 1994). There is also little information on nonprofits with less than $5,000 annually in gross receipts that are not required to register or file information returns with the IRS. While estimates vary, there may be several million such formal and informal groups in existence (Smith 1994). There are virtually no data available on most unstaffed coalitions or civic and community groups that do not meet the threshold for reporting. In addition, some organizations may be unaware of the reporting requirements, and others may choose not to report.

References

Abramson, Alan J., Lester M. Salamon, and C. Eugene Steuerle. Forthcoming. "The Nonprofit Sector and the Federal Budget: Recent History and Future Directions."
Berry, Jeffrey M. 1984. *The Interest Group Society.* Boston: Little, Brown.

Boris, Elizabeth T. 1997. "Civil Society: The Foundation of Democratic Participation." Dissemination Paper #7. Washington, D.C.: Inter-American Development Bank.

————. 1999. "The Nonprofit Sector in the 1990s." In *The Future of Philanthropy in a Changing America*, edited by Charles Clotfelter and Thomas Erlich.

Boris, Elizabeth T., with Rachel Mosher-Williams. 1997. "Nonprofit Advocacy Organizations: Assessing the Definitions, Classifications, and Data." Paper presented at annual meeting of ARNOVA, Indianapolis, IN, December 4–6.

Borowski, Neill A., and Gilbert M. Gaul. 1993. *Free Ride: The Tax-Exempt Economy.* Kansas City: Andrews and McMeel.

Chambré, Susan. 1994. "Voluntarism in the HIV Epidemic: Raising Resources for Community-Based Organizations in New York City and Sullivan County." NSRF Working Paper Series. Washington, D.C.: Nonprofit Sector Research Fund.

Cnaan, Ram. 1997. "Social and Community Involvement of Local Religious Congregations: Findings from a Six-City Study." Paper presented at annual meeting of ARNOVA, Indianapolis, IN, December 4–6.

Cnaan, Ram, Amy Kasternakis, and Robert J. Wineburg. 1993. "Religious People, Religious Congregations, and Volunteerism in Human Services: Is There a Link?" *Nonprofit and Voluntary Sector Quarterly* 22: 33–51.

Coleman, James S. 1990. *Foundations of Social Theory.* Cambridge: The Belknap Press of Harvard University Press.

Conference Board. 1997. *Corporate Contributions in 1996.* New York: The Conference Board, Inc.

Cortes, Michael. 1997. "A Statistical Profile of Latino Nonprofit Organizations in the U.S." Paper presented at annual meeting of ARNOVA, Indianapolis, IN, December 4–6.

Dees, J. Gregory. 1998. "Enterprising Nonprofits." *Harvard Business Review* (Jan.–Feb.): 55–67.

De Vita, Carol, and Eric Twombly. 1997. "Nonprofit Organizations in an Era of Welfare Reform." Paper presented at annual meeting of ARNOVA, Indianapolis, IN, December 4–6.

Douglass, James. 1987. "Political Theories of Nonprofit Organization." In *The Nonprofit Sector: A Research Handbook*, edited by Walter W. Powell (43–54). New Haven: Yale University Press.

Drucker, Peter F. 1992. *Managing the Non-Profit Organization: Practices and Principles.* New York: HarperCollins Publishers.

Etzioni, Amitai. 1993. *The Spirit of Community: Rights, Responsibilities, and the Communitarian Agenda.* New York: Crown Publishers, Inc.

Flynn, Patrice. 1995. "Responding to Changing Times." Catholic Charities USA 1994 Annual Survey, Washington, D.C.

Gelles, Erna. 1993. "Administrative Attitudes and Practices of For-Profit and Nonprofit Day Care Providers: A Social Judgment Analysis." Paper presented at annual meeting of ARNOVA, Toronto, October 28–30.

Gillman, Todd J. 1987. "Health Clubs Hit YMCAs' Tax Breaks." *Washington Post*, June 30.

Gray, Bradford H., ed. 1986. *For-Profit Enterprise in Health Care*. Washington, D.C.: National Academy Press.

Gronbjerg, Kirsten A. 1993. *Understanding Nonprofit Funding*. San Francisco: Jossey-Bass Publishers.

———. 1994. "Using NTEE to Classify Non-Profit Organizations: An Assessment of Human Service and Regional Applications." *Voluntas* 5 (3): 301–28.

Guterbock, Thomas M., and John C. Fries. 1997. "Maintaining America's Social Fabric: The AARP Survey of Civic Involvement." Report prepared for American Association of Retired Persons, Washington, D.C.

Hansmann, Henry. 1987. "Economic Theories of Nonprofit Organization." In *The Nonprofit Sector: A Research Handbook*, edited by Walter W. Powell (27–42). New Haven: Yale University Press.

Harris, Frederick C. 1994. "Something Within: Religion as a Mobilizer of African-American Political Activism." *Journal of Politics* 56: 42–68.

Hodgkinson, Virginia. 1996. *Volunteering and Giving among Teenagers 12 to 17 Years of Age*. Washington, D.C.: Independent Sector.

Hodgkinson, Virginia, and Murray Weitzman. 1986. *Nonprofit Almanac 1986–1987*. Washington, D.C.: Independent Sector.

———. 1993. *From Belief to Commitment: The Community Service Activities and Finances of Religious Congregations in the United States*. Washington, D.C.: Independent Sector.

———. 1996a. *Giving and Volunteering in the United States*. Washington, D.C.: Independent Sector.

———. 1996b. *Nonprofit Almanac 1996–1997*. Washington, D.C.: Independent Sector.

Hopkins, Bruce R. 1992. *The Law of Tax-Exempt Organizations*. New York: John Wiley & Sons, Inc..

Kaplan, Ann E. 1997. *Giving USA 1997*. New York: AAFRC Trust for Philanthropy.

Lohmann, Roger. 1992. *The Commons*. San Francisco: Jossey-Bass Publishers.

Maryland Association of Nonprofit Organizations. 1997. "The Baltimore City Nonprofit Sector: A Study of Its Economic and Programmatic Impacts in the City of Baltimore." Report prepared by the Jacob France Center. Baltimore: University of Baltimore.

McCarthy, Kathleen. 1993. *Women's Culture: American Philanthropy and Art, 1830–1930*. Chicago: University of Chicago Press.

Minkoff, Debra C. 1997. "Producing Social Capital: National Movements and Civil Society." *American Behavioral Scientist* 40 (5, April): 606–19.

National Commission on Philanthropy and Civic Renewal. 1997. "Giving Better, Giving Smarter: Renewing Philanthropy in America." Washington, D.C.: National Commission on Philanthropy and Civic Renewal.

O'Connell, Brian. 1997. Powered by Coalition: The Story of Independent Sector. San Francisco: Jossey-Bass Publishers.

O'Neill, Michael. 1989. The Third America: The Emergence of the Nonprofit Sector in the United States. San Francisco: Jossey-Bass Publishers.

Oster, Sharon M. 1995. Strategic Management for Nonprofit Organizations: Theory and Cases. New York: Oxford University Press.

Payton, Robert L. 1988. Philanthropy: Voluntary Action for the Public Good. New York: American Council on Education/Macmillan Publishing Company.

Pew Research Center for the People and the Press. 1997. "Trust and Civic Engagement in Metropolitan Philadelphia: A Case Study." Study report. Philadelphia, PA: Pew Research Center for the People and the Press.

Pollak, Thomas H. 1997. "A Profile of Religious Organizations in the IRS Business Master File and Return Transaction Files." Paper presented at annual meeting of ARNOVA, Indianapolis, IN, December 4–6.

Pollak, Thomas H., and Kathryn L. S. Pettit. Forthcoming. "The Finances of Operating Public Charities, 1989–1995." Washington, D.C.: National Center for Charitable Statistics.

Printz, Tobi J. 1997. "Services and Capacity of Faith-Based Organizations in the Washington, D.C., Metropolitan Area." Paper presented at annual meeting of ARNOVA, Indianapolis, IN, December 4–6.

Putnam, Robert D. 1993. Making Democracy Work: Civic Traditions in Modern Italy. Princeton: Princeton University Press.

Reid, Elizabeth. 1997. "Participation of Low-Income People and Organizations in Welfare-to-Work Coalitions and Networks." Paper presented at annual meeting of ARNOVA, Indianapolis, IN, December 4–6.

Renz, Loren, Crystal Mandler, and Trinh C. Tran. 1997. Foundation Giving. New York: Foundation Center.

Salamon, Lester M. 1987. "Partners in Public Service: The Scope and Theory of Government-Nonprofit Relations." In The Nonprofit Sector: A Research Handbook, edited by Walter W. Powell (99–117). New Haven: Yale University Press.

———. 1989. "The Changing Partnership between the Voluntary Sector and the Welfare State." In The Future of the Nonprofit Sector, edited by Virginia A. Hodgkinson and Richard Lyman (41–6). San Francisco: Jossey-Bass Publishers.

———. 1992. America's Nonprofit Sector: A Primer. New York: Foundation Center.

———. 1995. Partners in Public Service: Government-Nonprofit Relations in the Modern Welfare State. Baltimore: Johns Hopkins University Press.

Seligman, Martin E. P. 1991. *Learned Optimism: How to Change Your Mind and Your Life*. New York: Alfred A. Knopf.

Skloot, Edward, ed. 1988. *The Nonprofit Entrepreneur: Creating Ventures to Earn Income*. New York: Foundation Center.

Skocpol, Theda. 1995. *Protecting Mothers and Soldiers: The Political Origins of Social Policy in the United States*. Cambridge: Harvard University Press.

Smith, David H. 1994. "The Rest of the Nonprofit Sector I: The Nature of Grassroots Associations in America." Paper presented at annual meeting of ARNOVA, Berkeley, CA, October 20–22.

Stevenson, David R. 1997. *The National Taxonomy of Exempt Entities Manual*. Washington, D.C., and New York: National Center for Charitable Statistics and Foundation Center.

Stevenson, David R., Thomas H. Pollak, and Linda M. Lampkin. 1997. *State Nonprofit Almanac 1997*. Washington, D.C.: The Urban Institute Press.

U.S. Congress. 1996. House Committee on Small Business. *Government-Supported Unfair Competition with Small Business*. 104th Cong., 2d sess., July 19.

Verba, Sidney, Kay Lehman Schlozman, and Henry E. Brady. 1995. *Voice and Equality: Civic Voluntarism in American Politics*. Cambridge: Harvard University Press.

Walzer, Michael. 1991. "The Idea of Civil Society: A Path to Social Reconstruction." *Dissent* (Spring): 293–304.

Weisbrod, Burton A. 1978. *The Voluntary Nonprofit Sector*. Lexington: Lexington Books.

———. 1988. *The Nonprofit Economy*. Cambridge: Harvard University Press.

Wolff, Edward. 1999. "Economy and Philanthropy." In *The Future of Philanthropy in a Changing America*, edited by Charles Clotfelter and Thomas Erlich.

Wolpert, Julian. 1993. "Patterns of Generosity in America: Who's Holding the Safety Net?" Twentieth Century Fund Paper. New York: Twentieth Century Fund.

Wuthnow, Robert. 1991. *Acts of Compassion*. Princeton: Princeton University Press.

———. 1997. "The Role of Trust in Civic Renewal." Working Paper #1. College Park, MD: National Commission on Civic Renewal.

Chapter One

COMPLEMENTARY, SUPPLEMENTARY, OR ADVERSARIAL? A THEORETICAL AND HISTORICAL EXAMINATION OF NONPROFIT-GOVERNMENT RELATIONS IN THE UNITED STATES

Dennis R. Young

INTRODUCTION

From time to time, public policymakers in the United States take an oversimplified view of the nonprofit sector and its relationship with government. In the 1980s, the Reagan administration argued that, as government cut back on its expenditures for public services, the nonprofit sector would simply fill the vacuum through volunteer effort and charitable contributions (Bremner 1988; Salamon 1995). In the 1990s, House Speaker Newt Gingrich expressed a similar view through his program *Contract with America* (U.S. Congress 1995), while members of Congress proposed the Istook amendment, which would have curtailed lobbying by nonprofit organizations receiving federal funds. According to these perspectives, nonprofits were simply service organizations, capable of running on voluntary resources and with no legitimate role in public policy formation.

The left has made similar errors of oversimplification that have disparaged private philanthropy and implicitly extolled governmental solutions to public needs:

> Philanthropy remained in bad repute in liberal and radical circles throughout the 1930s. . . . Eduard C. Lindeman . . . whose *Wealth and Culture* (1936) was a study of the operation of one hundred foundations during the 1920s, offered an economic interpretation of modern philanthropy: it was disintegrating capitalism's way of distributing, in its own interests, wealth which could not be spent on luxuries, was not needed for reinvestment, and could not profitably be employed for speculation. Foundations, and by implication, all large-scale benefactions, denoted the development of a rudimentary social consciousness

in the donors, but they also represented the donors' determination to control social thought and expression (Bremner 1988, 152).

The reality of government–nonprofit sector relations in the United States is far richer and more complex than such one-dimensional views suggest. Nonprofit organizations interact with government in several different ways; these patterns of interaction vary over time and among different fields of service. In various contexts, nonprofits have served as privately supported supplementary service providers of public goods, as complementary partners with government in public service provision, and as advocates and adversaries in the process of public policy formulation and implementation. Often, two or three of these roles are manifested simultaneously.

In this chapter, we trace the historical evolution of these three modes of government-nonprofit relations. Various strands of economic theory pertaining to nonprofit organizations illuminate the circumstances under which we can expect nonprofits to fulfill different roles vis-à-vis government—supplementary, complementary, and adversarial. These three theoretical modes of government-nonprofit relationships are first explained and then applied as conceptual screens for examining the history of government–nonprofit sector relationships in the United States, from colonial times to the present. Each theoretical cut reveals new insights into the complex of relationships between nonprofits and government, and no single view provides a full understanding.

Finally, we consider how the alternative views of government-nonprofit relations can inform the present debate on the roles of government, nonprofits, and business in the United States. Recent developments, including governmental retrenchment and devolution, privatization of public services, restructuring in the business sector, and commercialization in the nonprofit sector, have dislocated extant patterns of government–nonprofit sector relationships. Government no longer takes comprehensive responsibility for social welfare; corporations have become more narrowly strategic in their philanthropic programs; substantial new private wealth has been created among business entrepreneurs; and nonprofits have become more competitive and market-oriented in their quests to remain financially viable and to address growing social needs. This shuffling of institutional conditions leaves open to question how the sectors will continue to divide responsibilities and work together to solve social problems and meet public needs in the future. Our review of the history of government-nonprofit relations through the three theoretical lenses suggests that a new "social contract" between government, nonprofits, and business must emerge if public needs are to be met.

STRANDS OF THEORY

Different strands of economic theory support alternative notions of the nonprofit sector as supplementary, complementary, or adversarial to government. (This taxonomy is similar to that postulated by Najam (1997) for relations between government and nongovernmental organizations internationally.) In the supplementary model, nonprofits are seen as fulfilling demand for public goods left unsatisfied by government. In this view, the private financing of public goods can be expected to have an inverse relationship with government expenditure. As government takes more responsibility for provision, less needs to be raised through voluntary collective means.

In the complementary view, nonprofits are seen as partners to government, helping to deliver public goods largely financed by government. In this perspective, nonprofit and government expenditures have a direct relationship with one another. As government expenditures increase, they help finance rising levels of nonprofit activity.

In the adversarial view, nonprofits prod government to make changes in public policy and to maintain accountability to the public. Reciprocally, government attempts to influence the behavior of nonprofit organizations, by regulating their services and responding to their advocacy initiatives as well. The adversarial view does not posit any specific relationship between the levels of nonprofit and governmental activity. For example, nonprofits can advocate for smaller or more efficient government operations, or they can advocate for new programs and regulations that would increase government activity.

The three perspectives are by no means mutually exclusive. Nonprofits may simultaneously finance and deliver services where government does not, deliver services that are financed or otherwise assisted by government, advocate for changes in government policies and practices, and be affected by governmental pressure and oversight. For example, Kramer (1981) observed that nonprofits' reliance on public funds to deliver services did not necessarily constrain their advocacy activity.

Moreover, while the three views frame our discussion of nonprofit-government relations as if nonprofits and government were distinct entities from one another, in fact, the boundaries are often blurred.

For example, the governing boards of some nonprofit community development agencies have members appointed by government officials, and many state universities and public libraries incorporate private fundraising associations or foundations within their structures. To a certain extent, such hybrids can be understood as forms of government-nonprofit collaboration vis-à-vis the complementary view of nonprofit-government relations. More generally, however, we abstract from some of the messy detail of the real world in the following discussion and proceed under the assumption that government-nonprofit boundaries can be recognized without undue difficulty in most instances.

In the same vein, we note that the three analytical views developed here all derive essentially from rational choice models in the economics tradition. Other schools of thought (e.g., behavioral and sociological theory) also contribute much to the understanding of institutional relationships such as those between government and nonprofit organizations, as well as to an appreciation of the limitations of the economic approach (see Powell and DiMaggio 1991, chapter 1, for an excellent discussion of these issues).

Nonprofits as Supplements to Government

The thesis that nonprofit organizations provide collective goods on a voluntary basis was first advanced by Burton Weisbrod in his seminal work on government failure (Weisbrod 1977). The basic premise is that citizens have individual preferences about the levels, qualities, and types of public goods they desire and how much they are willing to pay for them. Governments decide on the level of public goods provision based on citizens' preferences and are constrained by considerations of equity and bureaucratic procedure to tax and to offer levels of public good in a uniform way (Douglas 1987). Given democratic voting and policymaking procedures, governments follow preferences of the median voter or of a dominant political coalition (Buchanan and Tullock 1962) in choosing those uniform tax rates and levels, types, and qualities of services. If citizen preferences are not homogeneous, some citizens (e.g., those whose preferences vary substantially from those of the median voter) will be left unsatisfied, either paying for and receiving more (of various types of) public goods than they want, or paying less and receiving less than they want. Citizens in the latter group are presumed willing to provide additional levels of public good by mobilizing on a voluntary collective basis through the nonprofit sector.

Weisbrod (1977) points out that nonprofits are not the only solution to the problem of public goods provision where the preferences of the citizenry are heterogeneous. Various private market substitutes for public goods may be purchased by citizens instead (e.g., guard dogs to supplement public policing). Moreover, where multiple local political jurisdictions exist, as they do in the United States, people may move to communities where tax rates and public goods levels best match their preferences (Tiebout 1956). These solutions, however, all have their limitations. Exercising mobility is costly. Political jurisdictions package multiple public goods together so that citizens cannot make perfect matches between communities and personal preferences for services and taxes. And private goods are usually imperfect substitutes for public goods. Hence, substantial room is left for nonprofits to fill the role of supplementer of government services.

In light of this theory, we can expect substantial variation in nonprofit sector–government relationships among fields of activity. In areas such as the arts where citizen preferences vary widely, private nonprofit provision can be expected to be substantial. In areas such as policing and defense where preferences may be relatively homogeneous, we can expect the nonprofit role to be less substantial. In areas such as social services, where citizens' preferences can be volatile, we can expect nonprofit provision to respond to ebbs and flows of public sentiment and consensus.

The supplementary model also suggests an interesting dynamic when people's preferences change over time. In particular, public decisions to expand the role of government in areas traditionally served by nonprofits can be viewed as a threat by the latter. Commenting on government activism in the 1960s, for example, Bremner (1988) notes:

> To some observers government intrusion into areas formerly the preserve of voluntary activity comprised a more serious threat to philanthropy than internal rivalries (184).

Alternatively, however, the supplementary view also illuminates the notion that private action is often actually intended to prod government into action. For example, the Ford Foundation's Public Affairs Program in the 1960s funded "demonstration" programs "addressing education and delinquency in the slums and mobilizing the electoral strength of minority communities" (Bremner 1988, 187).

Nonprofits and Government as Complements

Lester Salamon (1995) has been the principal advocate for the view that nonprofits and government are engaged primarily in a partnership or contractual relationship in which government finances public services and nonprofits deliver them. Aspects of both economic theory of public goods and economic theory of organizations help clarify the rationale behind this thesis. First, the theory of collective action as advanced by Mancur Olson (1965) highlights the phenomenon of "free riding," when people attempt to provide collective goods on a voluntary basis. Where the good to be provided is "nonrival" (i.e., can be consumed by one party without reducing the amount available to others) and "nonexcludable" (i.e., the good cannot be made available to one party without making it simultaneously available to others), then people have the incentive to avoid contributing to its provision but to consume it once it is provided by others. As a result, such goods will not be provided at efficient levels through voluntary collective effort. The problem of free riding is exacerbated where groups are large and relatively homogeneous in their preferences (so that no one party is tempted to provide the good on its own). Solutions to the public goods problem include social pressure (e.g., appealing to conscience, peer-to-peer solicitations, etc.), tying together of private incentives with public goods support (e.g., bonuses given to members of public radio stations), and coercion (e.g., using the police power of the state to collect taxes). It is the latter solution that suggests that government should undertake to finance public goods, either directly or through tax incentives, while not necessarily becoming the vehicle for their delivery.

Economic theory of organizations, specifically several aspects of the theory of the firm and transactions-cost theory, help illuminate why, in many instances, it may be more efficient for government to delegate delivery of services to private organizations (e.g., nonprofits) than to deliver those services itself. Coase (1988) addresses the question of why a business firm, for example, would choose to carry out a marginal transaction through the market rather than internally. For example, why might a firm contract out for a particular task rather than hire or direct its current employees to do it? One part of Coase's explanation is that as an organization gets larger, the costs of administering additional transactions, such as enlarging the bureaucracy, rise. At some point it becomes cheaper to contract outside rather than expand work internally, i.e., there are "diminishing returns to management" as well as possible differences in direct production costs inside versus outside the organization. Such an explanation appears relevant to government provision of public services. Complaints about the cost and inefficiencies of public bureaucracies are common. Despite the costs of arranging and monitoring external contracts (see

Gronbjerg 1997), it may be cheaper for governments to contract out for certain services than perform them internally. In addition, labor costs may be lower in the private sector if the latter is not unionized, and private suppliers may be better able to exploit economies of scale for certain services by producing them for more than one jurisdiction. (See Ferris 1993 for a comprehensive discussion of government's decision to contract out.)

It is not clear that governments always try to minimize their production costs (see Niskanen 1971 for one explanation of why they presumably do not). Assuming that they do sometimes try to reduce costs, however, the Coase argument helps explain why governments sometimes contract for service delivery with private suppliers. This explanation does not distinguish between nonprofit and for-profit contractors, however. Some additional considerations apply to this issue. Another aspect of transactions-cost theory pertains to the information an organization requires in order to carry out a market transaction efficiently. In the case of public services, two aspects related to the quality of services delivered appear relevant. First, government may choose to contract out, not only because it is cheaper but also because it may be unable to differentiate its services in response to the heterogeneous preferences of its citizens. There would be too much information to gather in order to do so. By contracting with nonprofits that are knowledgeable about the individual communities in which they are based, however, government can overcome the information problem and, within limits, allow those delivery agents to customize their services to local constituents.

To a certain extent, such differentiation would be possible if government contracted with for-profit businesses as well, so long as those businesses were community-based or conscientious about monitoring the preferences of their customers. Without its own data, however, how could government verify such responsiveness? Here is where another aspect of the transaction-cost literature comes into play in favor of nonprofits. Nonprofits operate under different incentives than for-profits. In particular, they do not face the same imperatives to skimp on quality, renege on promised service parameters, or lower the costs of production by homogenizing services in order to increase profits (see discussion of contract failure, below). Hence, government presumably faces lower monitoring and contract enforcement costs associated with ensuring differentiated, responsive community services, by contracting with nonprofits rather than with for-profits.

Steinberg (1997) points out that the arguments for nonprofits as less costly contractors for government are subject to a number of caveats and subtleties associated with donor reactions to government financing, the internal motives of nonprofit agents, the level of competition, and the structure of the contracts themselves. Nonetheless he concludes that:

> Non-profit organisations deserve some preference in bidding because they provide benefits to the government (reduced opportunistic behavior and reduced transaction costs of negotiating, monitoring and enforcing a contract) that cannot be enforceably written into a contract with for-profits (Steinberg 1997, 176).

In all, the theory of public goods coupled with the theory of transactions costs provides a plausible explanation for why government and nonprofits often engage in a complementary relationship in which government finances and nonprofits deliver services. This relationship is more likely to be observed in areas such as social services where free riding is a significant problem, where direct public production is likely to require a large bureaucratic operation, and where differences in local preferences favor some differentiation of services to alternative locales and consumer groups.

Finally, a curious but historically important variation of government-nonprofit complementary relationships occurs where the government and nonprofit-sector roles are reversed in terms of financing and service delivery. Interestingly, there are many instances throughout U.S. history where government has been the recipient of private largesse for the purpose of carrying out public projects such as the care of public monuments (see below). A theoretical explanation of such behavior seems more consistent with the supplementary than complementary view but with a slight twist: Private parties raise funds for activities that would not be supported by public demand. Moreover, the private givers find it more efficient, given the costs of private supply, to "contract" with government for their production rather than produce the goods themselves. (This would occur, for example, where the projects represent marginal additions to public-sector operations and where private supply would have to start from scratch.) Additionally, the public values these activities, accepts implementation within the public domain, and may even contribute something to their financing. In this sense, private financing of governmental projects needs to be understood through both the supplementary and complementary lenses.

Nonprofits and Government as Adversaries

To date, the advocacy role of nonprofit organizations in public policy and the role of government in controlling nonprofit organizations have not been explicitly addressed by economic theories of nonprofit organizations. To a certain extent, nonprofit advocacy and government pressure on nonprofits can be understood through the complementary lens of nonprofit-government relations. Often, nonprofits and government are collaborators in passing legislation or changing public attitudes. Similarly, government sometimes encourages, prods, and stimulates private, voluntary activity in support of social goals (see below). But advocacy activity suggests that there is also a third way of characterizing the relationship between nonprofit organizations and government—as adversaries in policymaking and service delivery.

Again, however, bits and pieces of economic theory help to illuminate the adversarial relationship. On the issue of nonprofit advocacy, Weisbrod's (1977) theory of government failure is again helpful. In heterogeneous communities, where minority views are not well reflected in public policy, minorities will organize themselves on a voluntary collective basis, not only to provide public services for themselves but also to press government to more adequately serve their interests. In the basic Weisbrod model, government would have no incentive to respond since it simply follows the preferences of the majority. More nuanced analyses of public choice, however, which allow for logrolling, vote trading, and concentration of minority efforts on particular issues, demonstrate that organized minorities can be effective in having their public policy concerns addressed (Buchanan and Tullock 1962). Such minorities mobilize themselves through voluntary associations or interest groups, becoming an important component of the government–nonprofit sector constellation of relationships.

The Weisbrod model is also helpful for understanding how new public services come into being through advocacy. Proposals for new programs will at first be favored only by a minority of voters and hence not immediately adopted by government. A minority of citizens may promote the idea through advocacy and demonstrate its efficacy with voluntary contributions. Nonprofit "think tanks" may play a role in such efforts (Hall 1994) or, as noted above, foundations may fund "demonstration projects" (Bremner 1991). Such promotional efforts may be successful in securing pilot funding from government. Eventually the concept may be proven and receive the support of a majority, at which point government may undertake full-scale provision.

Economic theory is also helpful for understanding why government is motivated to oversee nonprofit organization behavior and performance and sometimes to press nonprofit organizations to change. In particular, the theory of contract failure first developed by Henry Hansmann (1980) postulates that nonprofit organizations are chosen as efficient vehicles for delivering services where there is a condition of "information asymmetry" between consumers and producers that would allow a profit-making firm to exploit consumer ignorance to its advantage. Nonprofits are seen to be more efficient in this circumstance because the nondistribution constraint (which precludes the distribution of "profits" to those who control the organization), as Hansmann argues, or the internal governance structure of nonprofit organizations, as Ben-Ner (1986) suggests, reduces the incentives and opportunities for nonprofits to cheat consumers; this makes them more "trustworthy."

Why then, if nonprofits are more trustworthy, does government need to regulate them? Two reasons are implicit in the theory of contract failure. First, the trustworthiness of nonprofit organizations depends in part on the credibility of the nondistribution constraint and the integrity of the nonprofit governance structure. These, in turn, must be policed, and that is government's role. Government must ensure that the nondistribution constraint is indeed observed (Young 1983) and that appropriate principles are followed for constituting governing boards, to ensure nonprofits' trustworthiness.

Second, contract failure may be seen as a broad phenomenon subject to a variety of approaches and solutions, including licensure, accreditation, competition, and other means. Utilization of nonprofits is one weapon in the arsenal—and not necessarily a perfect or complete solution to the problem. Nonprofits also violate the trust put in them on occasion, and some of the same oversight mechanisms that government uses to oversee for-profit providers in various markets can be applied to nonprofits as well.

Finally, it is interesting to return to Weisbrod's (1977) model in the context of the nonprofit advocacy role and explore its implications for government behavior. If nonprofits advocate for minority positions in the policy arena, it follows that government may react by trying to defend majority interests. One form that reaction may take is attempted restriction of nonprofit advocacy. In the guise of regulation, government can become the adversary of nonprofits in the policy arena. Recent deliberations over the Istook amendment, which proposed to curtail advocacy by nonprofits receiving any federal funds, or the various deliberations leading to the restrictions on foundations in the 1969 Tax Act (Bremner 1991; Hall 1994) may be partially understood in that light.

Finally, it is worth observing that nonprofits and government may oppose one another for the simple reason that these parties independently pursue objects whose impacts are felt differently by the two parties. For example, public-sector initiatives to reduce taxes and simplify the tax code, although not intended to harm nonprofits, have the effect of doing so. In such instances, the actions of the government reflect Weisbrod's model of public-sector decisionmaking in which the majority approves what it sees as a public good, and minority (nonprofit) interests are forced to oppose what they view to be a public bad.

HISTORICAL PERSPECTIVES

The supplementary, complementary, and adversarial theories, taken as a cluster, themselves bear witness to the overall complexity of non-profit-government relationships. These are not mutually exclusive ways of understanding those relationships but rather overlapping models that each capture important elements of reality. History may be examined in layers by asking sequentially: What do each of the models reveal about the nature of government-nonprofit relationships as they have evolved in the United States?

We proceed by reviewing, through each of the three theoretical lenses, the history of the nonprofit sector in the United States at various stages—colonial times, the early republic, post–Civil War, late nineteenth and early twentieth century, and modern times—as documented by several contemporary nonprofit-sector scholars. History is examined here in a necessarily cursory fashion through secondary and tertiary sources. This approach does not do justice to the work of serious nonprofit historians, but it does suggest the utility of the proposed theoretical framework in probing for a comprehensive understanding of government-nonprofit relations and how they are changing over time. Hopefully it partially addresses Hall's (1992) complaint:

> The shortcomings of the social sciences have stemmed primarily from their ahistoricity and their tendency to fragment and thereby distort the continuum of collective action (109–110).

Finally, it must be acknowledged that the very concept of nonprofit as a sector is a modern construct that we must impose somewhat awkwardly to analyze earlier historical periods. Like the blurring of the boundaries between sectors in the modern era, this ambiguity of institutional definitions requires a certain amount of license in making observations on the essence of historical fact using the crude instruments at hand.

History through the Supplementary Lens

On one level, the relative roles of government and nonprofit organizations in the United States may be appreciated by examining how nonprofits have attended to collective needs left unaddressed by government:

> Americans had a long experience in founding voluntary agencies to perform tasks which individuals could not accomplish alone and which public bodies, for one reason or another, were not able to undertake (Bremner 1988, 176).

While documentation is spotty, it is clear that nonprofit activity supplementary to government predates the U.S. republic. A review by Lohmann (1992) suggests that colonists brought with them religion-based traditions of mutual aid:

> Scottish immigrants to Boston formed the first ethnic mutual aid society in 1657, initiating a trend that continues today for virtually every ethnic, racial, or nationality group. . . . A French religious order founded the first American orphanage in New Orleans in 1718. . . . Residents of Williamsburg, Virginia and Philadelphia founded early mental hospitals (121).

Lohmann goes on to note that:

> New England Puritans, Virginia planters, and Dutch colonists in New York and New Jersey all adopted church-based relief committees as the basis of colonial welfare systems. Only gradually did the New England Puritan towns move to civil welfare administration. Although religious voluntary associations date from the earliest settlement of New England, more secular associations of charitable and mutual aid societies, fire brigades, lodges, and professional societies emerged later, mainly in Boston (122).

O'Neill (1989) emphasizes the point that religion dominated what we now think of as the nonprofit sector in colonial times and the early period of the republic:

> . . . religion was by far the most important part of what would come to be known as the nonprofit sector. Arts and culture organizations were nonexistent, health care was primitive and family based, formal education was far less extensive than it is now, social services were minimal, and somewhat frowned upon, and there was nothing even vaguely re-

sembling grant making or international assistance organizations. As far as the incipient nonprofit sector went, religion was virtually the only game in town (25).

Interestingly, while religion and government were sometimes intertwined during the colonial period, specifically in New England and the South, O'Neill argues that the diversity of religious beliefs in the colonies ultimately made necessary the separation of church and state, hence reinforcing the development of the nonprofit sector as supplementary to government:

> What started to emerge almost immediately in the English colonies was the notion that allegiance to one country, culture, language and tradition could coexist with sharp diversity in religious ideas and practices . . . the English colonists simply had to deal with the fact of religious diversity; the economic, political, social, and military realities of the New World left them no choice. It was principally this variety of religious experience in colonial New England that prepared the way for religious liberty. That idea and reality, in turn, played a critical role in the development of the American third sector, since organized religion not only was a major part of the sector but also spawned much of the rest. Without religious diversity and state neutrality toward religion, the American nonprofit experience would have been very different (26– 27).

Bremner (1988) notes that in the early period of the republic, private initiative in higher education was a particularly important area of nonprofit activity as a supplement to government:

> The field of higher education, neglected by the federal government and very poorly supported by the states, gave philanthropists their greatest opportunity for service. A nation growing rapidly in population and wealth possibly needed more colleges than the twenty-odd in existence at the start of the century (48).

O'Neill (1989) describes one of many examples where privately based initiatives ultimately led to adoption by government in the first half of the nineteenth century:

> In 1813 . . . Quakers . . . founded the first private psychiatric hospital in the United States. . . . With a revolutionary set of practices, the Quakers released the insane from their chains, gave each a private room with a window, allowed them to walk around the wooded grounds and work in the hospital gardens, and made caring conversation the basis of treatment. When the State Lunatic Hospital at Harrisburg was opened in 1851, the Pennsylvania General Assembly declared that the quality of care should be the highest and should be based on the Quaker model (72–73).

In both the nineteenth and twentieth centuries, the traditions of self-help, both religious and secular but largely separate from government, continued to be very important:

> Most nineteenth century U.S. residents immigrated from cultures with broad repertoires of associational and common practices. . . . Culturally, these immigrants were already armed with many organizational skills. . . . From the start these skills were used in organizing fire companies, mutual aid societies, local governments, and an array of other associations. . . . During much of the nineteenth and early twentieth century, fraternal organizations serving both civic and quasi-religious functions were an important means of social integration for the middle and lower classes, particularly in predominantly rural areas (Lohmann 1992, 123).

Bremner (1988) observes that "The twenty-five or thirty years after the Civil War seemed, to Americans living at the time, an era of stunning achievement in all fields of philanthropy" (85). Nielsen (1979) claims that the late nineteenth and early twentieth century was the period in which private initiative peaked in its prominence:

> . . . in the last decades of the nineteenth century and the first decades of the twentieth century, many Third Sector institutions—in addition to the churches—developed private sources of support and simultaneously an ideology of separateness which affected the policies of both private agencies and government (14).

The surge of private, nonprofit initiative supplemental to government in this period was fueled by a combination of new and enormous private, concentrated industrial wealth and political progressivism stemming from industrialization, urbanization, and immigration. According to Hall (1992):

> . . . the use of private nonprofit organizations grew enormously in the last decades of the nineteenth century. Big business and private wealth underwrote the growth of universities, libraries, hospitals, museums, social-welfare organizations, professional societies, and private clubs. At the same time, the middle and lower classes supported labor unions, mutual-benefit societies, fraternal organizations, volunteer fire companies, building and loan associations, and even cooperatively owned nonprofit businesses. Growing awareness of urban poverty among the middle and upper classes encouraged the establishment of charitable organizations of every sort, ranging from traditional funds for the relief of the sick, poor, and disabled to new forms of nonprofit activity, such as settlement houses and charity organizations. . . . No less important than the private organizations directed to the reform of society was the rise of new kinds of cultural organizations whose pri-

mary constituencies were the rich. The establishment and professionalization of museums and symphony orchestras . . . played a major role in recasting the nature of urban culture (39).

Andrew Carnegie's *Gospel of Wealth* was influential in this period and supportive of the concept of philanthropy as a substitute for government programming:

> According to the gospel of wealth, philanthropy was less the handmaid of social reform than a substitute for it. Wise administration of wealth was an antidote for radical proposals for redistributing property and a method of reconciling the poor and the rich (Bremner 1988, 102).

The role of women was especially important in creating voluntary associations that addressed social needs in this era of weak government:

> While wealthy businessmen such as John D. Rockefeller and Andrew Carnegie lavished massive donations on growing crops of foundations, universities, museums, and think tanks created in the corporate image of their business ventures, women—even very wealthy women—continued to build their own organizations through an economy of time, rather than cash . . . [These] voluntary associations were unusually influential in weak governmental systems, such as that of the United States in this era . . . (McCarthy 1997, 145–146).

Of great long-term significance in this period was the invention of the modern foundation, which institutionalized the ability of private interests to fund nonprofit-sector activity in a focused manner:

> . . . credit for establishing the first foundation of the modern type—an open-ended endowment devoted "to the good of mankind," which carried out its charitable purposes by giving money to institutions rather than operating them, and which entrusted decision making to staffs of experts . . . went . . . to Margaret Olivia Slocum Sage, the widow of Wall Street buccaneer Russell Sage. . . . Mrs. Sage decided to establish a philanthropic trust "elastic in form and method to work in different ways at different times" for "the permanent improvement of social conditions" (Hall 1992, 47).

As Hall notes, the Russell Sage Foundation was followed by the major foundation initiatives of Andrew Carnegie, John D. Rockefeller, and other industrial giants. Those initiatives were but one aspect of a broader strategy of "welfare capitalism" that allowed private initiative and wealth to underwrite a variety of programs supplemental to government's own efforts:

> Sometimes welfare capitalism involved direct corporate subsidies of charitable organizations, as with the massive support by the railroad

> industry of the Young Men's Christian Association (Y.M.C.A.). . . .
> Companies also contributed to the creation of parks and playgrounds,
> schools, and libraries . . . (50).

Other institutional innovations, including the community foundation and the community chest, also emanated from the era of business and private social activism in the late nineteenth and twentieth centuries, as means to coordinate the development and allocation of private resources to community needs (Hall 1992, 51).

While much of the twentieth century witnessed the growing role of government in the provision of public services of all varieties, supplemental provision by nonprofit-sector institutions has persisted and indeed grown. Early in the depression of the 1930s, for example, President Hoover perhaps unduly emphasized charity as a substitute for potential government relief. Partially as a consequence of this experience, charity fell into some public disrepute between the 1930s and the 1960s (Bremner 1988). But measurements made since then (in the 1980s) of the size and scope of the sector reveal the substantial character and continued growth of churches, foundations, trade and professional associations, and other subsectors that support themselves without government help and that provide collective goods essentially supplemental to that of the government sector. Indeed, the number of foundations has continued to grow over the course of the century, along with the real value of assets they hold and the allocations they dispense (Hodgkinson and Weitzman 1996). Moreover, the measured part of the supplemental nonprofit sector may indeed represent only a fraction of the total picture. If David Horton Smith (1997a) is correct, existing quantitative research has missed a substantial fraction of the grassroots organizations that provide great magnitudes of self-help, communal, relief, and other services, essentially on a volunteer basis without significant exchange of funds, and supplemental to government. These organizations trace back even further than formalized nonprofit organizations and have been part of the American scene since the beginning (Smith 1997b).

Finally, the end of the twentieth century may be witness to a resurgence of the supplemental model, not just in the United States but internationally. Weisbrod (1997) notes:

> . . . the growing importance of nonprofits everywhere, as population migration and the flow of information through television and computers have the effect of magnifying diversity in country after country. . . . This growing diversity of societies is bringing, everywhere, retrenchment of government and increased reliance on the nonprofit sector (542–543).

The supplementary lens identifies an important component of the history of nonprofit sector–government relations in the United States. In various contexts, private citizens, rich as well as those of limited means, have often provided for themselves and for others. In some cases, such activity is supplemental to existing government provision; in other cases, the nonprofit sector creates and supports new forms of collective activity not previously undertaken by government. History shows as well that such activity is undertaken by minorities, including ethnic and religious groups, as well as by business leaders with their own social preferences and agendas, different from the political majority, in a manner that appears consistent with the supplemental theory of voluntary collective action.

Some scholars argue, however, that the supplemental mode of nonprofit-government relations is not the dominant stream. For example, Hall (1992) claims that voluntary associations were relatively sparse and subservient to government in the eighteenth and early nineteenth centuries. And Nielsen (1979) considers the period of private-sector vigor in the late nineteenth and early twentieth centuries to have been an aberration from the more pervasive mode of nonprofit sector–government interpenetration. Thus, the supplementary lens gives only a partial view, and we need to take another look through the complementary lens.

History through the Complementary Lens

Several scholars, including Hall (1992), Nielsen (1979), Bremner (1991), McCarthy (undated, 1997), and Salamon (1987), have observed that governmental partnerships with private philanthropy and nonprofit organizations have been a part of the American scene from colonial times. No less prominent a figure than Benjamin Franklin was a proponent of public/private collaboration:

> His political talents were never better displayed than in his ability to unite public and private support behind municipal improvements. He played a leading part in the establishment of both the Pennsylvania Hospital (1751) and the academy which became the University of Pennsylvania (Bremner 1988, 17–18).

The case of Harvard University is often cited as the earliest example of public support and nonprofit provision:

> The situation of Harvard College, the oldest eleemosynary corporation in the colonies, illustrates well the anomalous status of all colonial corporations. Although chartered as a corporation, the college was gov-

erned by boards composed of ministers of the tax supported
Congregational church and government officials sitting ex officio. Although Harvard possessed a small endowment, given partly by benevolent colonists and partly by British friends, it was regarded as a public
institution because most of its revenues came from legislative grants
and from tuitions and fees (Hall 1992, 16–17).

Parallel situations characterized Yale vis-à-vis the state of Connecticut
(Salamon 1987) and Williams College (Massachusetts), Columbia
(New York), and the University of Pennsylvania (Nielsen 1979).

Similar arrangements were found in the health and social services
in colonial and postrevolutionary times:

> Early hospitals such as Pennsylvania Hospital, founded in 1752, of-
> fered health care for indigent patients with their expenses paid by local
> or colonial governments. Private institutions for the mentally ill such
> as the Hartford (Ct.) Retreat and McLean Hospital in Boston used state
> and local government funds to provide care for indigent mentally ill
> patients (Smith and Lipsky 1993, 47).

Governmental involvement and financial support of private, nonprofit organizations providing higher education, hospital care, and
social services, begun in the early republic, continued unabated
through the nineteenth and twentieth centuries. For example, Nielsen
(1979) cites Massachusetts General Hospital, Louisville General Hospital, University Hospital in Baltimore, and Natchez Charity Hospital
as examples of private, nonprofit institutions established or supported
with state government funds in the years between 1820 and 1840.
McCarthy (undated) documents similar activity in the arts after the
civil war. And Salamon (1987) observes that toward the end of the
nineteenth and beginning of the twentieth centuries, government support of hospitals and nonprofit social service organizations was fairly
common:

> A survey of seventeen major private hospitals in 1889 . . . revealed that
> 12 to 13 percent of their income came from government . . . [and] . . . a
> 1901 survey of government subsidization of private charities found that
> "except possibly two territories and four western states, there is proba-
> bly not a state in the union where some aid [to private charities] is not
> given either by the state or by counties and cities" (100, 101).

Observers seem to agree, however, that governmental support of nonprofit organizations did not become extensive until the mid-twentieth
century. According to Smith and Lipsky (1993):

> . . . government funding of private service organizations was not exten-
> sive by today's standards. A 1914 survey revealed that "22 states made

no appropriations whatever to privately managed charities, fifteen make such appropriations sparingly, and nine place no apparent restrictions on their grants" (49).

In the 1930s, however, the federal Works Progress Administration promoted an especially important example of government-nonprofit collaboration in the arts, helping important institutions such as Chicago's Art Institute, the Cincinnati Museum, and New York's Metropolitan Museum survive financially:

> Although Federal One and the Treasury arts program are the most familiar examples of Depression Era government patronage, the influence of the WPA extended to local cultural institutions as well, adding a new slant to the practice of third party government. . . . By 1933, the [Metropolitan] Museum's investment income was diminishing as well, generating salary cuts. By 1936, however, staff costs were being offset by workers seconded from the WPA. Clerical staff, carpenters, painters, masons, lecturers, even guards were provided with support from the public till (McCarthy, undated, 18–19).

Government-nonprofit collaboration picked up some lost steam in the 1960s. The public/private partnership in public service, never dissolved but in abeyance during and for some years after the New Deal, took on new life in the 1960s and 1970s (Bremner 1988, 210). And Salamon, writing in 1987, observed that "although government support of the voluntary sector has deep historical roots in this country . . . this support has grown considerably in scope and depth over the past thirty years" (101).

The magnitude and scope of governmental support and contracting with nonprofits began to grow dramatically in the 1960s because of expansion in federal programs. For example:

> Federal expenditures for social welfare services almost tripled between 1965 and 1970. . . . The federal role continued to expand throughout the 1970s. . . . A big percentage of the increase in public funding of social services was expended through nonprofit agencies. . . . Faced with public pressure to expand social services, particularly for the poor, Congress enacted the 1967 Amendments to the Social Security Act. . . . which specifically encouraged states to enter into purchase-of-service agreements with private agencies. . . . A 1971 study indicated that 25 percent of state spending on social services was for purchased services. . . . By 1976 this expenditure had risen to 49% (Smith and Lipsky 1993, 55).

In addition, in 1961, the establishment of the Combined Federal Campaign allowed certain charities to solicit charitable contributions from federal employees (Bremner 1988, chapter 13). Nor was the experience of expanded government financial support for nonprofits limited to the social services. In a study of 16 local communities in 1982, government reliance on nonprofit organizations to deliver public services was found to be extensive in social services, housing and community development, health care, and the arts. In each of these fields, more than 40 percent of government expenditures were allocated to private, nonprofit organizations (Salamon 1987). In the arts, the creation of the National Endowment was a particularly important element in the developing public/private partnership:

> According to Senator Claiborne Pell, who helped to draft the enabling legislation, the notion of using the Endowment "as a catalyst . . . [to] help spark nonfederal support . . . was the key to the entire proposal." With the creation of the NEA, the notion of public/private partnerships emerged full blown (McCarthy, undated, 32).

International relief was another area where public support of nonprofit efforts became important:

> The engines of cooperation between public and private sector efforts in overseas aid were the Food for Peace Program, originating in 1954, and the Agency for International Development (AID), founded in 1961 . . . people to people groups such as Catholic Relief, CARE, Church World Service, and the American Joint Distribution Committee distributed 70 percent of the donations. . . . In addition to supplying surplus commodities, mostly food, the government paid the overseas freight costs of clothing, medicine, and other material purchased by or given to voluntary agencies by their members (Bremner 1988, 196–7).

While the expansion of contractual arrangements between government and nonprofits was dramatic in the 1960s and 1970s, Bremner (1988) stresses its continuity with earlier periods in American history:

> In some respects purchase of service agreements marked a return, although on a much larger scale, of the nineteenth-century practice of granting subsidies from public funds to private orphanages, hospitals, and relief societies. Had advocates or critics of privatization chosen to do so they might have cited examples in earlier periods of American history when towns, counties, and states delegated responsibility for the care of the poor and criminals to private contractors (202).

The reverse model of private financing and public provision has also appeared throughout U.S. history. In the early republic, for example, Stephen Girard made bequests to the city of Philadelphia for improvement of certain streets and to the state of Pennsylvania for the development of canals (Bremner 1988, 39). Later examples include

James Smithson's gift to the federal government for what became the Smithsonian Institution, Andrew Mellon's gift of the National Gallery, and Andrew Carnegie's gifts of public libraries to many communities (Bremner 1988). This tradition is also reflected in various voluntary campaigns to raise charitable funds for government monuments, including the building of the Washington Monument and the refurbishing of the Statue of Liberty; foundations' contributions to fund drives during and after World Wars I and II; the establishment of the Sanitary Commission during the Civil War to improve conditions in military camps; and various other organized voluntary efforts to financially assist government in wartime from revolutionary times to the present era (Bremner 1988). Indeed, the tradition continues unabated:

> Private givers further supported their part of the public-private part-
> nership by contributing to mainly tax-supported institutions such as
> state colleges and universities, public radio and television stations, and
> public or endowed museums, libraries, parks and zoos. Nearly every
> public educational, civic, or cultural institution cultivated "Friends"
> whose gifts supplemented appropriations from federal, state, or local
> government. In New York City in 1987 twenty public monuments in
> need of costly repair were put up for "adoption" by private donors; in
> Washington, D.C., the National Park Service, operating on a tight
> budget, asked private individuals to donate money to replace aging and
> dying cherry trees around the Tidal Basin (Bremner 1988, 211).

Finally, the complementary relationships of government and non-profits extend to more subtle instances where government has acted as an encourager and cheerleader of nonprofit-sector efforts. In the early years of the depression, for example, President Hoover "enlisted the services of one hundred leaders of business, industry, finance and philanthropy" in the "task of mobilizing and coordinating the charitable resources of the country" (Bremner 1988, 139). National administrations exerted similar efforts during wartime, and in the 1990s we have witnessed such efforts as the Points of Light program and the President's Summit aimed at stimulating volunteerism and engaging business in the solution of social issues.

The early 1980s was a high-water mark in the partnership between government and nonprofit organizations in the delivery of public services, at least in terms of funding. Beginning in the Reagan administration, however, policy initiatives shifted toward cutbacks in government funding and encouragement of private organizations to take up the slack not only in terms of service delivery but resource support as well. Still, funded partnership arrangements between government and nonprofits persist and even continue to be the norm. With the acceleration of federal devolution in the 1990s, however, much depends on the propensity of state and local governments to compensate for federal budget cuts and exploit the flexibility of new block-granting arrangements to expand and diversify contracting with private providers. That prospect is by no means certain:

> The federal money machine is turned off. This is not just a fiscal event. It shifts the social policy agenda to others—mainly to state governments—when it comes to defining social needs, determining how to meet them, and deciding who should have the responsibility for doing so. Nonprofit organizations have every reason to be very nervous about these budget reductions (Nathan 1996, 49).

The complementary lens reveals a very different overlay of nonprofit-government relations than does the supplementary lens. Through the complementary lens we see one sector engaging the other in order to get the public's business done together. At various times and places in American history, private philanthropy has been a supportive force, helping government with financing to get its work done. More generally, government has been the driver, looking to nonprofits as means of delivering mainstream public services under mandates of public policy. That orientation was particularly apparent in the post–World War II period when the federal government allocated massive new funding for social services, health care, education, and the arts but largely resisted the creation or expansion of new government bureaucracies to deliver those services. In terms of theory, the transactions and production costs associated with contracting with or subsidizing existing nonprofits, as well as creating many new nonprofit organizations, were apparently more reasonable than those associated with administering a greatly expanded governmental delivery system.

While efficacious for government, the partnership model, under which government finances and nonprofits deliver the services, may have looked more ominous for nonprofits. As noted, this mode of government-nonprofit relations clearly gained prominence in the 1960s and 1970s. And it would appear that nonprofits could hardly have resisted its momentum. Given mandates for expanded public services and facing internal fiscal problems, many nonprofits had the choice of joining the parade or being swept aside:

> As demands for social services burgeoned with the mobilization and social ferment in American cities in the 1960s, traditional agencies experienced pressures from within and without to expand their activities. . . . Federal funding . . . pushed up revenues throughout the sector. . . . The growth of government funding clearly bailed out many

financially troubled traditional agencies. . . . With these public funds agencies enter into a new relationship to government. Agencies which for decades had relied on private contributions or small government subsidies were now primarily dependent on government funds. . . . The traditional agencies had now become instrumentalities of government funding, expanding beyond niches supported by private funds (Smith and Lipsky 1993, 58–60).

History through the Adversarial Lens

As nonprofit organizations became more dependent on government funding in the 1960s and 1970s, the nature of the relationship between government and nonprofits changed in other ways as well:

> Historically, government purchased services from charitable organizations and attached few strings beyond those common to many other service purchasers. Today governments contract for whole programs, and even create providers where they otherwise do not exist. There is more contracting today than ever before, and the terms of contracting are more demanding. If in the past government went to the private sector for limited services, today its purchasing power is such that it is often in a position to shape the sorts of services offered by private providers (Smith and Lipsky, 9–10).

Thus, public funding has been accompanied by greater governmental control and regulation of nonprofits. Some of this regulation derived from failures similar to those that occur in the profitmaking marketplace:

> During the 1950s standards of care in some of the traditional service areas started to come under criticism . . . for example . . . systems of adoption placement dependent upon sectarian community agencies. . . . Social welfare advocates attacked the larger traditional agencies for neglecting the needs of the poor and racial and ethnic minorities. Meanwhile, government officials exerted greater regulatory oversight over private social programs, especially on public safety and staffing issues (Smith and Lipsky, 53).

Another form of reaction took place in the arts, where government officials sought to censor artistic endeavor and restrict funding for controversial projects:

> Questions of censorship, state control, and ideology surrounded the demise of the Federal Writers and Theater Projects in the 1930s, only to reemerge in more vitriolic form at century's end. . . . Led by Senator Jesse Helms, conservatives balked at what they deemed the use of pub-

lic monies to display works that they considered obscene (McCarthy, undated, 43–44).

While government oversight, regulation, and control of nonprofit-sector services grew considerably in the mid- and late twentieth century in the United States, those functions, too, have long historical roots. The earliest manifestations of government control of nonprofits predate the republic and center on the debate concerning the very existence of nonprofits as corporate entities. In colonial times, the status of nonprofits was unclear. Recall that Harvard College was governed by boards composed of ministers and government officials (Hall 1992, 16–17). In the early days of the republic, government-nonprofit relations differed by state, depending on the state's position on the issue of incorporation of private organizations:

> In the South, a forcefully expressed body of anticorporate doctrine began to emerge, largely under the tutelage of Thomas Jefferson. Although favoring the freedom of individuals to associate for common purposes, Jefferson worried that such groups, if incorporated and empowered to hold property, would become the basis for new kinds of tyranny . . . he believed that all [organizations]—governmental and nongovernmental—should be restricted in their powers and privileges (Hall, 22–23).

A crucial turning point was the Dartmouth College case, which:

> . . . involved New Hampshire's efforts to take over Dartmouth College. When Jeffersonians took control of the legislature in 1816, they reorganized the college, changed its name, and replaced its twelve-member self-perpetuating board with twenty-one gubernatorially appointed trustees and a board of twenty-five legislatively appointed overseers, who enjoyed veto power over the trustees. The president of the college was required to report annually to the governor on its management, and the governor and his council were empowered to inspect the college every five years and report on its condition to the legislature (Hall, 28–29).

Dartmouth College ultimately won its case in the Supreme Court in 1818, on the grounds that the college's charter constituted a contract between trustees and donors that could not be violated without contravening the Constitution. This set the precedent that has allowed nonprofit corporations in the United States to maintain their corporate integrity without threat of arbitrary governmental intervention.

Still, government regulation of nonprofits continued to evolve. For example, at the time of the Civil War, the U.S. Freedmen's Bureau attempted to discourage duplication in the efforts of voluntary societies devoted to the needs of freed slaves. Around the same period, several states established state charity boards "to inspect, report upon, and make recommendations for improving public welfare institutions and such private ones as received state assistance" (Bremner 1988, 91).

National emergencies sometimes required unusually heavy control of nonprofits by government. Just prior to World War II, the Neutrality Act of 1939 required "voluntary agencies which wished to engage in civilian war relief in belligerent countries to register with and submit monthly reports to the Department of State" (Bremner 1988, 158). And during World War II, the Roosevelt administration established the War Relief Control Board:

> The board now had the power to control all solicitations for voluntary war relief. . . . It had power to license and withdraw licenses from war relief agencies and, in the interest of economy and efficiency, to eliminate or merge organizations. The board scheduled the various national fund appeals and prevented competing campaigns during the periods set aside for the Red Cross National War Fund, United Jewish Appeal, and War Bond drives. The staff of the Control Board sharply scrutinized overhead costs and made reasonable economy of operation a requirement for continued licensing (Bremner 1988, 159–160).

In the 1970s, charitable solicitation gained prominence as an issue for state and local governmental regulation:

> Just as conduct of foundations had seemed to require corrections in the 1960s so, in the 1970s, according to many state and local officials, the activities of charities that solicited money from the public needed to be brought under closer scrutiny. By the end of the decade twenty states and numerous county and local governments had adopted laws or ordinances limiting charity solicitations to organizations that could prove a sizable proportion of the collection went for charitable purposes rather than for salaries and administrative costs (Bremner 1988, 190).

As Bremner hints in the above quotation, perhaps the most vociferous efforts at government regulation of nonprofits have been those directed toward foundations. Here the issue has been the concentration of private power under nonprofit auspices, and the public influence of that power. These concerns were apparent in the Jeffersonian era and became prominent again in the late nineteenth and early twentieth centuries with the blossoming of the large industrial enterprises and the concentration of private wealth in the large foundations of Carnegie, Rockefeller, Ford, and others. It was no secret that these institutions intended to influence public affairs:

The new foundations, particularly Russell Sage and Rockefeller, were unusual for not only the broad discretion granted their trustees but also their explicit goals of reforming social, economic, and political life. These lofty ends were to be achieved not by direct political action, but by studying conditions, making findings available to influential citizens, and mobilizing public opinion to bring about change. This relationship between academic experts, influential private parties, and government would become the paradigm of a new kind of political process—one based on policy rather than politics (Hall 1992, 48).

Although concerns about the power of foundations were expressed in the 1930s and 1940s, the issue intensified in the 1950s:

In April 1952, the Select (Cox) Committee for the House of Representatives began an investigation of "educational and philanthropic foundations and other comparable organizations which are exempt from federal taxation to determine whether they are using their resources for the purposes for which they were established . . . (Hall 1992, 68).

This began a series of congressional inquiries into foundations, picking up steam in the 1960s when foundations such as Field, Ford, and others were becoming particularly active on social issues such as voter registration, school decentralization, and urban poverty. Ultimately, the 1969 Tax Reform Act put new restrictions on foundations and other tax-exempt organizations:

The 1969 Tax Reform Act created a large number of new regulations for private foundations, mainly aimed at keeping foundations out of politics, preventing them from controlling large business interests, and making them more open and accountable (O'Neill 1989, 146).

Governmental efforts on restricting foundations can be seen as part of a wider effort by government to limit advocacy by nonprofit organizations. As Simon (1987) notes:

The federal tax code limits the channels through which nonprofits can participate in public affairs activities, here defined as "those activities which seek to study, criticize, inform people about, and modify the actions of government at all levels" (90).

In the 1990s, conservatives in Congress made several attempts to pass the Istook amendment, which would ban lobbying by any nonprofit organization receiving federal funding. This issue, too, has a historical pedigree. As Bremner (1988) recounts:

Rules against lobbying by tax-exempt organizations . . . went back to 1934 and had been reiterated in 1954 and strengthened in 1969. Efforts at relaxation of the rules began in the latter year when the American

Bar Association . . . charged that the neutrality of the tax laws with
respect to lobbying had been upset in favor of business interests
against charitable organizations. . . . In addition to the fairness issue
advocates of relaxation questioned the constitutionality of the restrictions and charged the Nixon administration used IRS audits to harass
groups that criticized or opposed its policies (194).

Indeed, during the 1970s the pressure from government to suppress
advocacy cut a broad swath, extended to grant-making:

During the Nixon administration the tax-exempt status of civil rights,
welfare rights, environmental, and antiwar groups, and public interest
law firms received censorious attention from the Internal Revenue Service. In 1974 Alan Pifer, president of the Carnegie Corporation of New
York, called the situation "paradoxical": foundations were advised they
could engage in activities bearing on public policy development but
given to understand that it would be unwise to do so (Bremner 1988,
191).

Nor was the Nixon administration the last in pressing to restrict nonprofit advocacy prior to the 1990s. In the 1980s, for instance, the
Reagan administration worked to exclude advocacy organizations
from the Combined Federal Campaign (Bremner 1988).

It appears that, through various regulations and restrictions, government has attempted to restrict the activities of nonprofits and hold
them accountable to the public. Reciprocal efforts by private interests,
through the ongoing formation and development of voluntary associations, have served to hold government to account, to influence the
direction of public policy, and ultimately to protect the nonprofit
sector itself from government attack. Hall (1992) provides a summary
of Tocqueville's observations in the early nineteenth century:

Tocqueville . . . view[ed] private voluntarism . . . as a fundamental part
of a national power system. . . . At its core there was, as he observed,
"a natural and perhaps a necessary connection" between the civil associations and the political associations through which citizens combined to influence the state. And this connection was of no small
significance. First, it was the basis for organizing *political* opposition
to the power of elected officials. . . . Second, this connection was the
basis for formulating the conceptual agenda on which political opposition necessarily had to be based. Tocqueville's belief that the ability of
an organized political opposition to diminish the moral authority of
the majority came not from its numerical strength, but from the pecul-
iar relation of political and civil associations, through which "those
arguments that are most fitted to act on the majority" are discovered in

the hope of ultimately "drawing over the majority to their own side, and then controlling the supreme power in its name" (85–86).

O'Neill (1989) ties these developments back to religious diversity in the colonies and early republic, leading to the first amendment to the Constitution as a fundamental pillar of the nonprofit sector in its advocacy role:

> ... the First Amendment, which deals with freedom of religion, freedom of speech, freedom of assembly, and the right to petition government over grievances, can without exaggeration be seen as the Magna Carta of the nonprofit sector in American life. These First Amendment freedoms guarantee not only to individuals but also to groups the right to assemble, speak out, and proclaim values and beliefs. The independence of the independent sector finds its strongest legal support in the First Amendment, including its religious liberty clause (30).

Since colonial times social reformers have been active in pushing government to take action or institute programs in such areas as prison reform, help for the poor and homeless, care of neglected children, opposition to slavery and assistance to freedmen, and improvement of schools. Such activity has extended to the improvement of governance itself. In the context of the settlement house movement of the late nineteenth and early twentieth centuries, Bremner (1988) observes a host of voluntary associations were at work or organizing to strengthen the social framework of democracy and to restore and extend the principles of self-government (109). Women's movements have been a very important strand of public policy advocacy:

> A growing number of scholars have set about to analyze the connections between activism of women's groups and government policy in the late nineteenth and early twentieth centuries. . . . They have stressed the relationship between women's voluntary associations and the creation of social services and political programs that in the United States culminated in the New Deal and the welfare state. . . . Women's efforts to establish playgrounds, libraries, and public health programs and their activism in state and local government contributed to the development of federal programs like Social Security and Aid to Dependent Children. . . . Their voluntary associations constituted a link between grassroots women's groups and those women who gained national power and recognition, for example, Frances Perkins, the first female cabinet member. These women were able to build on small, local issues to lay the groundwork for the campaigns for social justice that ultimately shaped national policy (Robertson 1998, 193).

Overall, social action movements, manifested largely though voluntary organizations, have been aimed at changing public policy across a broad spectrum of issues:

> America from the start has been a hotbed of social, economic, religious, and political reformism. . . . The revolution, the Civil War, Populism, Progressivism, and the New Deal have been among the earlier surges. The years since World War II have seen the eruption of a combination of powerful thrusts of dissent and demands for change. The most notable of these have been the civil rights movement, the anti–Vietnam War movement, the student rebellion, the environmental movement, the consumer protection movement, the women's liberation movement, and the movement for greater responsiveness and accountability of institutions, both government and corporate (Nielsen 1979, 157).

Bremner (1988) notes that the 1970s were an exceptionally active period for advocacy organizations in the United States:

> The same period that saw government and voluntary service agencies working in closer cooperation also witnessed the rise of a great many advocacy organizations monitoring the performance of government and seeking to influence public policy by lobbying, demonstrations, litigation, and empowerment of beneficiaries of social programs (203).

While Nielsen characterizes social movement organizations as the "soft" part of the nonprofit sector, he acknowledges that the boundary is fuzzy between this part of the sector and the highly structured "hard," service-oriented part of the sector:

> These distinctions are more clear in concept than in practice. Nonprofit organizations do not break neatly into two distinct segments . . . rather they are arranged as points along a spectrum according to the particular mix of service orientation and reformism which gives each its distinctive personality (156).

Still, the distinction is important because in it lies a fundamental tension in the contemporary nonprofit-government relationship—to what extent should organizations that receive tax benefits or direct governmental support be allowed to spend that money to influence public policy? Despite the different tax-exemption categories (for example, 501(c)3 versus 501(c)4), the virtual impossibility of segmenting nonprofits neatly into those that do and do not attempt to influence public policy promulgates a tension between government and nonprofits that continues unabated to the present day.

Interestingly, the blurring of nonprofit categories in the public policy dimension is mirrored by blurring in the commercial sphere as well, and this, too, has ramifications for the adversarial relationship with government. Looking toward the end of the twentieth century and the beginning of the next millennium, Weisbrod (1997) predicts:

> . . . that the increased fiscal pressure on nonprofits will lead them to generate new, more creative forms of commercial activities, and that these new forms will further blur the distinctions between nonprofit organizations and private firms. In the process, I expect reconsideration of many existing public policies regarding nonprofits: their subsidization and restrictions on their freedom to lobby government; to engage in joint ventures with private firms; and to compete with private firms. I also expect increased pressure from government to require nonprofits to disclose more publicly their compensation of executives, and I anticipate the applicability of antitrust laws to nonprofits to emerge as a political issue (547).

The congressional attack on foundations of the 1950s and 1960s galvanized foundations and other parts of the sector into unprecedented collective action, first through exercises of self-study via the Peterson and Filer Commissions, and ultimately to the organization of Independent Sector, a comprehensive umbrella organization designed to increase public understanding about the sector and to advocate for its interests at the national level. Thus, instead of continuing to present itself in a fragmentary manner, the sector would for the first time have a vehicle to speak as one vis-à-vis government in addressing public policy that affects nonprofit organizations. That voice has been used subsequently to address major national policy initiatives of the 1980s and 1990s affecting the welfare of the sector, including the Reagan budget cuts; the federal budget cuts proposed in connection with the Contract with America (U.S. Congress 1995); changes in the tax code such as above-the-line deductibility of contributions by non-itemizers, the proposed flat tax, and reductions in tax rates that would reduce incentives to give; and the issue of intermediate sanctions for disciplining nonprofits in violation of federal law, as well as the very question of restrictions on lobbying by nonprofit organizations.

Governments have severely challenged nonprofits at the state and local level in recent years as well, especially in connection with property tax exemptions. In the 1990s challenges to property tax exemptions have been pursued in many states, including Colorado, Maine, New Hampshire, New York, Oregon, Pennsylvania, Utah, and Wisconsin (Salamon 1997). Mirroring its efforts at the national level, the nonprofit sector has also begun to mobilize at the state and local levels, especially through state associations of nonprofit organizations, which now exist in three dozen states. In the new environment of devolution, these associations are intended to give the nonprofit sector a stronger voice in the local policy process, especially in state capitols. The free-rider tendencies that characterize the large and diverse nonprofit sectors at the state and local levels hamper efforts to mobilize these state associations. Federal devolution initiatives may, however, ultimately prove to be the same kind of catalyst for organizing nonprofits at the state level in the 1990s that congressional attacks on foundations in the 1960s were for galvanizing collective action by the sector at the national level.

THE CHANGING SOCIAL CONTRACT

The foregoing discussion suggests that, while each conceptual lens offers substantial insight in every period, different views of the non-profit sector–government relationship have prevailed at different times in U.S. history. The adversarial lens is especially helpful in understanding the early republic, when public and private spheres of autonomy were first being sorted out, and the mid- to late twentieth-century period, when government sought to redress the balance of power of government and private interests. The supplementary lens helps especially to illuminate the late nineteenth and early twentieth centuries, when private interests asserted themselves in providing for social needs. The complementary lens is particularly useful in explaining the post–World War II era, when government sought to address social needs without unduly expanding its own bureaucracy.

In each of these periods, there appears to have been an implicit, though dynamic, understanding of the relative roles of government, business, and the nonprofit sector in addressing the overall needs of society. Before the period of rapid industrial growth, the "social contract" consisted of a division of responsibilities between very modest government efforts to provide for social needs and multiple, autonomous private efforts. With massive changes following the Civil War, including industrialization and immigration, the private sector—through new social welfare associations and underwriting of various forms of welfare capitalism by the business sector—assumed new levels of responsibility for collective needs. In the mid-twentieth century, an American version of the welfare state emerged, with government, partnered with nonprofit organizations, providing for public needs not only in human services but extending to the arts, education, health, the environment, and other fields. While there is substantial variation among areas of public service activity, these chronological patterns are remarkably similar from field to field over the past three centuries (O'Neill 1989). There is nothing permanent, however, about the pattern of intersector relations from era to era:

> Relations between responsibilities assigned the three sectors are neither rigidly defined nor permanently fixed but shift from time to time to meet changing circumstances and needs (Bremner 1991, 216).

The present era of the 1980s and 1990s is manifesting another sea change in which the social contract is implicitly being rewritten. Seen through the three lenses of government-nonprofit relations, however, the new contract appears to be substantially incomplete. One principal emphasis appears again to be most visible through the supplementary lens, where government is seen as taking a relatively passive, fiscally conservative role in public service provision, and the private, nonprofit sector is expected to move to the fore with new levels of charitable funding and volunteering. Unlike the turn-of-the-century period 100 years ago, however, which also witnessed the rapid growth of new industrial enterprise and amassing of private wealth, it is not clear what contemporary economic engines are able or willing to power new private initiatives of requisite strength. Certainly there are impressive new industrial enterprises now, especially in the technology and communications areas, but these are embedded in a highly competitive international economy that leads them to downsize and shed employees rather than take care of them. And while there have been massive gifts by corporate titans such as George Soros and Ted Turner, these have been isolated instances; corporate philanthropy generally is becoming more of an exercise in strategic marketing and employee morale-building than corporate social responsibility (Burlingame and Young 1996). Certainly there is massive new private individual and corporate wealth, but tax reform policy initiatives, such as tax simplification and lowering of tax rates, threaten to undermine rather than strengthen incentives for charitable giving (Steinberg 1996). Additionally, concerns about "unfair competition" voiced by the business sector and more general anxieties about corruption of nonprofits as a consequence of their involvement in market enterprises may eventually limit the ever-increasing dependence of nonprofit organizations on commercial sources of income (Weisbrod 1998).

The complementary lens reveals an arena in which government-nonprofit partnerships could evolve very differently. The numbers and variety of arrangements through which government and nonprofits collaborate are no doubt increasing—as government seeks ways of squeezing more out of its limited resource base—but such collaboration could no longer be the main event if government, at least at the federal level and possibly at all levels, removes itself from bottom-line financial responsibility for providing public services.

Viewed through the adversarial lens, the changing social contract is even more in flux. While extolling the virtues of private, charitable initiative, many legislators seem more willing now both to challenge the tax exemptions of nonprofit organizations and to limit the voice of nonprofits in the policy arena. Thus, while reducing its own resource commitments to social needs, government appears also to be hampering the ability of nonprofits to function successfully, both in raising their own resources and in speaking out for those who may be ill-served under a new regime of limited government responsibility.

While the current changes derive from various political agendas as well as economic forces, the incompleteness of the pending new social contract may be more a matter of inattention than ill intention. Examination of the contemporary scene through the three lenses reveals gaps and inconsistencies that need to be brought to consciousness and resolved through some holistic concept of what the new contract ought to be. What are the roles of nonprofits and government, absolutely and in relation to one another, and what is the social role of business and private wealth? If nonprofits are to assume new levels of public responsibility, how can resources be mobilized for them to do so? How can they do so if government limits tax incentives to give, questions the legitimacy of nonprofit commercial enterprise, and suppresses nonprofits' voice in the public policy arena? And if private wealth is to drive new levels of voluntary initiative, how can that wealth be mobilized? In particular, how can businesses and individuals of means be encouraged to contribute at a level that compensates for governmental withdrawal? Or will we live in a society in which great inequalities of wealth and welfare persist and grow, and social problems fester without amelioration or resolution?

Nonprofit organizations appear to be caught in the middle of this perplexing uncertainty over the pending social contract. Contemporary government policy toward the nonprofit sector is inconsistent, at once encouraging the growth of voluntarism and private initiative and at the same time limiting its resource base. And the role of the economy's largest and arguably most important sector—business—remains anomalous, again largely due to the absence of an overall concept of the social contract underlying public policy. On the one hand, business is reducing its explicitly philanthropic efforts. In addition, segments of the business community object to expansion of nonprofits into commercial arenas, while other parts of the business sector expand into areas of health care, social services, and education that once were more exclusive domains of nonprofit activity. On the other hand, businesses have discovered partnerships with nonprofits as a lucrative marketing strategy, and employee voluntarism as an efficient means of building morale and maintaining good relations in the communities where they are located. Overall, however, the social role of business remains in flux and is not clearly articulated as part of an overall consensual social arrangement.

Benjamin Franklin was a great social reformer who was driven by his own holistic concepts of society applicable to the times:

> Self-reform through voluntary mutual-benefit associations led before long to voluntary associations directed to public benefit. These would eventually include subscription libraries, volunteer fire companies, a hospital, and an academy, the latter of which received charters of incorporation from the Pennsylvania legislature (Hall 1992, 19).

Franklin also invented bifocals. He knew how important it was to use appropriate lenses in order to see things clearly at different distances. For government-nonprofit relations and the issue of the social contract, Franklin might have prescribed trifocals. We need all three conceptual lenses—supplementary, complementary, and adversarial—to bring the issues into full view and proper focus.

Note

I would like to thank Elizabeth Boris, Eugene Steuerle, Robert Wuthnow, Kathleen McCarthy, Waldemar Nielsen, Robert Bremner, Richard Steinberg, and Stuart Mendel for their helpful comments and suggestions.

References

Ben-Ner, Avner. 1986. "Nonprofit Organizations: Why Do They Exist in a Market Economy?" In *The Economics of Nonprofit Institutions*, edited by Susan Rose-Ackerman (94–113). New York: Oxford University Press.

Bremner, Robert H. 1988. *American Philanthropy*, 2nd ed. Chicago: University of Chicago Press.

Buchanan, James M., and Gordon Tullock 1962. *The Calculus of Consent*. Ann Arbor: University of Michigan Press.

Burlingame, Dwight F., and Dennis R. Young. 1996. *Corporate Philanthropy at the Crossroads*. Indianapolis: Indiana University Press.

Coase, Ronald H. 1988. *The Firm, the Market and the Law*. Chicago: University of Chicago Press.

Douglas, James. 1987. "Political Theories of Nonprofit Organizations." In *The Nonprofit Sector: A Research Handbook*, edited by Walter W. Powell (43–54). New Haven: Yale University Press.

Ferris, James M. 1993. "The Double-Edged Sword of Social Service Contracting: Public Accountability Versus Nonprofit Autonomy." *Nonprofit Management and Leadership* 3 (4): 363–76.

Gronbjerg, Kirsten A. 1997. "Transaction Costs in Social Service Contracting: Lessons from the U.S.A." In *The Contract Culture in Public Services*, edited by Jeremy Kendall (99–118). London: Ashgate Publishing Limited.

Hall, Peter Dobkin. 1992. *Inventing the Nonprofit Sector*. Baltimore: The Johns Hopkins University Press.

———. 1994. "Historical Perspectives on Nonprofit Organizations." In *The Jossey-Bass Handbook of Nonprofit Leadership and Management*, edited by Robert D. Herman and Associates (3–43). San Francisco: Jossey-Bass Publishers.

Hansmann, Henry. 1980. "The Role of Nonprofit Enterprise." *Yale Law Journal* 89 (3): 835–901.

Hodgkinson, Virginia A., and Murray S. Weitzman. 1996. *Nonprofit Almanac 1996–1997*. San Francisco: Jossey-Bass Publishers.

Kramer, Ralph M. 1981. *Voluntary Agencies in the Welfare State*. Berkeley: University of California Press.

Lohmann, Roger. 1992. *The Commons*. San Francisco: Jossey-Bass Publishers.

McCarthy, Kathleen D. Undated. "Twentieth Century Cultural Patronage." Working Paper, Center for the Study of Philanthropy, City University of New York.

———. 1997. "Women, Politics, Philanthropy: Some Historical Origins of the Welfare State." In *The Liberal Persuasion: Arthur Schlesinger, Jr., and the Challenge of the American Past*, edited by John Patrick Diggins (142–50). Princeton: Princeton University Press.

Najam, Adil. 1997. "The 3 C's of NGO-Government Relations: Confrontation, Complementarity, Collaboration." Boston University, draft.

Nathan, Richard P. 1996. "The 'Nonprofitization Movement' as a Form of Devolution." In *Capacity for Change?* edited by Dwight F. Burlingame, William A. Diaz, Warren F. Ilchman, and Associates (23–55). Indianapolis: Indiana University Center on Philanthropy.

Nielsen, Waldemar A. 1979. *The Endangered Sector.* New York: Columbia University Press.

Niskanen, William A. 1971. *Bureaucracy and Representative Government.* Chicago: Aldine-Atherton.

Olson, Mancur. 1965. *The Logic of Collective Action.* Cambridge: Harvard University Press.

O'Neill, Michael. 1989. *The Third America.* San Francisco: Jossey-Bass Publishers.

Powell, Walter W., and Paul J. DiMaggio, eds. 1991. *The New Institutionalism in Organizational Analysis.* Chicago: University of Chicago Press.

Robertson, Nancy M. 1998. "Kindness or Justice? Women's Associations and the Politics of Race and History." In *Private Action and the Public Good,* edited by Walter W. Powell and Elisabeth S. Clemens (193–205). New Haven: Yale University Press.

Salamon, Lester M. 1987. "Partners in Public Service: The Scope and Theory of Government-Nonprofit Relations." In *The Nonprofit Sector: A Research Handbook,* edited by Walter W. Powell (99–117). New Haven: Yale University Press.

———. 1995. *Partners in Public Service.* Baltimore: The Johns Hopkins University Press.

———. 1997. *Holding the Center.* New York: Nathan Cummings Foundation.

Simon, John G. 1987. "The Tax Treatment of Nonprofit Organizations: A Review of Federal and State Policies." In *The Nonprofit Sector: A Research Handbook,* edited by Walter W. Powell (67–98). New Haven: Yale University Press.

Smith, David Horton. 1997a. "Grassroots Associations Are Important: Some Theory and a Review of the Impact Literature." *Nonprofit and Voluntary Sector Quarterly* 26 (3, September): 269–306.

———. 1997b. "The International History of Grassroots Associations." *International Journal of Comparative Sociology* 27: 3–4.

Smith, Steven Rathgeb, and Michael Lipsky. 1993. *Nonprofits for Hire.* Cambridge: Harvard University Press.

Steinberg, Richard. 1996. "Can Individual Donations Replace Cutbacks in Federal Social Welfare Spending?" In *Capacity for Change?* edited by Dwight F. Burlingame, William A. Diaz, Warren F. Ilchman, and Associates (57–79). Indianapolis: Indiana University Center on Philanthropy.

———. 1997. "Competition in Contracted Markets." In *The Contract Culture in Public Services,* edited by Jeremy Kendall (161–79). London: Ashgate Publishing Limited.

Tiebout, Charles. 1956. "A Pure Theory of Public Expenditure." *Journal of Political Economy* 64 (October): 416–24.

U.S. Congress, House Committee on Ways and Means. 1995. *Contract with America: Overview: Hearings before the Committee on Ways and Means.* House of Representatives, 104th Congress, first session, January 5, 10, 11, and 12, 1995. Washington, D.C.: U.S. Government Printing Office.

Weisbrod, Burton A. 1977. *The Voluntary Nonprofit Sector.* Lexington: D.C. Heath and Company.

————. 1997. "The Future of the Nonprofit Sector: Its Entwining with Private Enterprise and Government." *Journal of Policy Analysis and Management* 16 (4): 541–55.

Weisbrod, Burton A., ed. 1998. *To Profit or Not to Profit: The Commercialism Dilemma of the Nonprofit Sector.* New York: Cambridge University Press.

Williamson, Oliver E. 1975. *Markets and Hierarchies.* New York: The Free Press.

Young, Dennis R. 1983. *If Not for Profit, for What?* Lexington: D.C. Heath and Company.

THE FLOW OF MONEY BETWEEN
GOVERNMENT AND NONPROFITS

Chapter Two

MEETING SOCIAL NEEDS: COMPARING THE RESOURCES OF THE INDEPENDENT SECTOR AND GOVERNMENT

C. Eugene Steuerle and Virginia A. Hodgkinson

INTRODUCTION

The role of the nonprofit sector is often compared with that of government, in no small part because both sectors provide social benefits to the public. Comparisons between nonprofits and government are also invoked in political debates over whether government is too large or small, whether nonprofit organizations should assume greater responsibility for tackling public problems, or whether nonprofit organizations are failing to separate their political efforts from their charitable, religious, or other nonprofit missions. Closely related to those political debates is the question of whether growth in government tends to displace the nonprofit sector, or vice versa.

Other chapters in this volume address many of those issues. Here we provide an overview of the resources for meeting social needs that are available in the nonprofit sector relative to government. Our focus is generally on that portion of the nonprofit sector identified as the "independent sector," which includes not only organizations that qualify under section 501 (c)(3) of the Internal Revenue Code for a tax deduction because they are devoted to religious, educational, charitable, scientific, cultural, health, and similar purposes but also civic leagues and organizations operated exclusively for the promotion of social welfare under section 501(c)(4). This group excludes other 501(c)(4) nonprofits, such as cemeteries, labor unions, clubs, and other forms of mutual benefit societies.

Our definition of social needs focuses on social welfare functions such as health, welfare, and education that have traditionally been supported by both nonprofit organizations and the government. In the not very distant past, government spent only small proportions of its revenue on social welfare. Today, the majority of public expenditures fall into that category. In recent decades, the percentage of total government spending directed toward social welfare has continued to rise as spending on the "physical" side of government—defense, highways, energy, buildings—has declined in relative importance (see figure 2.1). Defense itself has declined from about 60 percent of federal spending in the mid-1950s to around 15 percent today.

As we shall see, the government has dramatically influenced the character of the independent sector. The new focus on devolution in the context of welfare reform in the 1990s has caused fresh attention to be directed to the role of nonprofit organizations in the social welfare system, but devolution of service responsibilities to the nonprofit sector has been occurring in some subsectors for decades. A driving force behind many recent changes in the size and scope of the nonprofit sector is the extent to which some of its subsectors have increasingly come to serve as intermediaries or contractors in providing the services being financed by government.

In focusing on resources, we do not pretend to provide more than a statistical snapshot of a more complex picture of the relative role of government and nonprofits. Government enforces order and contracts, while nonprofit organizations provide individuals and communities with a voice and a means for participation. Those and many other very important activities cannot be measured adequately by a simple focus on measures of resources such as budget outlays, contributions, or volunteer time. Nonetheless, examining trends in resources reveals much about the extent to which the public relies on these two sectors to meet a range of different social needs, how priorities have changed over time (often by subsector), and the degree to which the two sectors exert control over the delivery of social services. By comparing the two sectors, we can also roughly assess the extent to which their activities complement or substitute for each other.

THE INEVITABLE INADEQUACY OF BOTH SECTORS

Any discussion of resources must recognize that both the nonprofit and the government sectors face limits on their ability to satisfy all social needs. This follows from the unavoidable problem of (economic) scarcity, which recognizes that, although needs are infinite, the resources available to satisfy those needs are not. Thus, no single nonprofit organization, nor group of organizations, nor government agency can prevent all death, suffering, and pain, nor educate each

Figure 2.1 TRENDS IN FEDERAL SPENDING

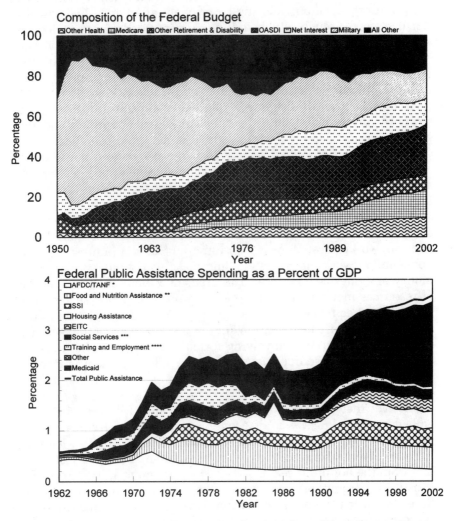

Sources: For top figure: Calculations based on data from the *Budget of the United States Government Fiscal Year 1998*. OMB (1997). For bottom figure: Based on historical data from the Budget of the United States Government Fiscal Year 1997 and unpublished projections from the Congressional Budget Office. *Before 1997 this includes AFDC, AFDC child care, AFDC job training (JOBS), Emergency Assistance, net Child Support Enforcement, and the Child Care and Development Block Grant. From 1997 outward, this includes TANF, the new child care block grant, and net Child Support Enforcement. **Includes Food Stamps. Child Nutrition, and the Supplemental Nutrition Program for Women, Infants, and Children. ***Includes Social Services Block Grant, Foster Care and Adoption Assistance, Children and Family Services Programs, Aging Services Program, and the National Service Initiative. ****Not including AFDC job training (JOBS).

one of us to our full potential. Moreover, it should also be noted that nonprofit organizations and the government are merely two institutional means through which *individuals* act to address a variety of social needs. Despite all the power of institutions, our individual efforts at being good parents, neighbors, spouses, friends—and, yes, citizens of the state and participants in the efforts of nonprofit organizations—form the base on which a "civil society" is built.

As noted above, this chapter explores the capacity—measured in terms of physical and budgetary resources—of nonprofits and the government for meeting social needs. It is not a philosophical essay on the attributes of a good society. Nonetheless, only by considering the vast scope of what we do in total can we place in perspective the activities of government and the independent sector, and their relationship to each other.

What we do through government and nonprofits is moderate when compared to what we accomplish as individuals, in our households and our workplaces. Why is this important to our inquiry? It is at home and at work that we spend and make use of most of our time, money, and physical resources. Hundreds of billions of dollars' worth of resources may flow through the nonprofit and public sectors, but as important as those resources are, they are small in relation to the economy at large. Moreover, the sum of measured economic activity includes only activities involving formal exchanges in the marketplace. Thus, the resource snapshot we are able to present is limited to those formal exchanges, plus some adjustments for volunteer activity.

The fact that the activities of nonprofits and the government are embedded in a larger web of economic and other activities has an important implication. When government expands it is at least as likely to divert resources from the household and business sectors as it is from the nonprofit sector. Why? There is simply greater room for substitution from those sectors with the largest quantity of resources. Similarly, when the nonprofit sector expands it often substitutes for activities undertaken in the home or by businesses instead of government. For example, as formal schooling and child-care arrangements have expanded, government and the nonprofit sector have increased their efforts simultaneously. The substitution was often for labor that otherwise might have been employed in private business or in home-provided education and caretaking.

A corollary is that if substitution can take place elsewhere, then the nonprofit sector and government often complement rather than substitute for each other. Expanded or changing government services may

create a demand for more nonprofit organizations to act as intermediaries, and conversely, a larger independent sector may demand more
government services.

Nonprofit organizations also alternate roles between complement-
ing and substituting for what government does, depending upon the
social needs to be met. Government programs may displace private
assistance for old age, for instance, or they may expand the need for
new types of organizational assistance to the retired by expanding the
numbers and proportion of the population who are encouraged to drop
out of the workforce at younger ages even though they are living
longer.[1]

In any event, we should expect the size of the nonprofit sector or
government—whether measured by income produced, assets, workers, or other attributes—to change over time not only relative to each
other but also relative to the business and household sectors. The
relative "size" will vary in no small part with the relative efficacy
with which nonprofits and government help achieve various goals,
including those of greater equity and well-being for parts of the population. Large swings in the relative importance of the independent
and government sectors can come about through an expansion of
defense needs or of government contracts to nonprofit organizations,
through tax revolts, or through the transformation of large nonprofits
into profit-making institutions. There is, therefore, no basis for the
common view that an ever-growing or ever-declining government or
nonprofit sector is somehow good or bad in and of itself. Swings in
relative size may represent either gains or losses to society, but they
are not *inherently* bad or good because there is no unchanging ideal
size for these sectors over all time periods.

Constraints on Both Sectors

If the challenge of meeting infinite needs with finite resources were
not enough, government and nonprofits also face significant constraints on their ability to collect and use resources. Government does
not obtain its resources in the same way as nonprofit organizations.
For example, there are relatively few contributions by individuals to
government (although there are exceptions, as in the case of purchases
of war bonds and volunteering in public schools). It may instead appear that government has an easier time raising resources than do
nonprofits because of its legal power to tax. Yet the ability to tax is
limited because the act of taxation exacts a variety of costs. The most
visible is that taxes reduce the amount of income that people and

businesses have to spend. Less visible but equally important is the fact that taxes are costly to administer and enforce, and also distort people's economic decisions about working and saving.

The need to treat individuals fairly—which is essential when compulsory forces of the state are at play—can also have the unintended consequence of discouraging experimentation and limiting flexibility in government programs. Norms of fair taxation and equitable distribution of benefits tend to push government toward uniform treatment of citizens in equal situations. But that may also make it administratively difficult to respond to the particular needs of individuals (Douglas 1987; Steuerle, Gramlich, Heclo, and Nightingale 1998, appendix).

In contrast, the nonprofit sector often can better respond to individual situations, but seldom in any uniform manner.[2] Such responses depend upon the nature of the organization and the cohesion of the community (Wolpert 1993). People often express their generosity through a community or church or other voluntary or citizen association in which they are involved, leaving aside other communities and groups that may have equal or greater needs. The definition of community and church is at once both inclusive (it encourages identity and mission) and exclusive (it excludes those who do not belong and ignores issues to which the organizational mission is not directed). Nonprofit organizations often do not have the time and resources to worry about standards such as equal treatment, so they select on the basis of membership or geography (see, for instance, Printz 1997). Similarly, even when individuals give beyond the immediate family, it is usually to relatives and friends. In 1995, for instance, 56 percent of respondents in a national survey indicated that their household gave an average of $1,527 (3.3 percent of average household income) to assist relatives and friends who did not live with them. That compared with an average household charitable contribution of $902 (2 percent of average household income) for those same respondents (Hodgkinson and Weitzman, Giving, 102).

MAJOR FINDINGS

With that background, we now provide some data on the size, capacity, and employment of the nonprofit sector, often comparing it with the government sector or to wider measures of economic output. We start with two caveats. First, one should avoid the temptation to project the future based on the recent past. Some of the trends we will

discuss are sustainable, some are not, and some of the measures themselves are affected by the interaction between government and the
nonprofit sector, especially when the former pays the latter to carry
out its functions.

Second, one should not confuse statistical measures of resources
with "importance." Resources such as revenues often are counted
twice. For example, one dollar of government spending through a
contract with the nonprofit sector may result in only one dollar of
output to the economy, despite being counted in both sectors' revenues
and expenditures.

By the same token, measures of resources can understate the impact
of the activities of government and nonprofits. Regardless of size, the
presence of good government allows individuals to act without fear
of repression or anarchy and with trust that legal obligations will be
fulfilled. The presence of nonprofits can provide unity within diversity, enhance goodwill in society, or encourage a "civil society," in
which social interaction more easily transpires among individuals
and with their government. Some measures of resources are also incomplete; for example, there is no way to account for the added output
that is made possible when individuals work for nonprofits at lower-
than-market wages.

With those cautionary notes, the following broad conclusions can
be drawn about the resources of the independent sector.

The Independent Sector in Relation to the Economy

The independent sector is a large part of the American economy:

- It produces almost 7 percent of gross domestic product.
- It owns about 5 percent of private sector net worth.
- It employs close to 12 percent of the labor force, if volunteers are
  counted.

Figure 2.2 displays three measures of the size of the independent
sector and its relationship to other sectors of the economy. The nonprofit sector produces 6.7 percent of national income, about one-third
of which is an estimate of the value of volunteer time. As might be
expected, it is still much smaller than the business sector, which
dominates the production of goods and services. When calculations
of output are made, they reflect mainly the places where production
occurs, not who finances it. Thus, federal, state, and local government
production in figure 2.2 is much lower than the amount of taxes they
collect or expenditures they make, which are in excess of one-third

Figure 2.2 THE NONPROFIT SECTOR IN THE U.S. ECONOMY

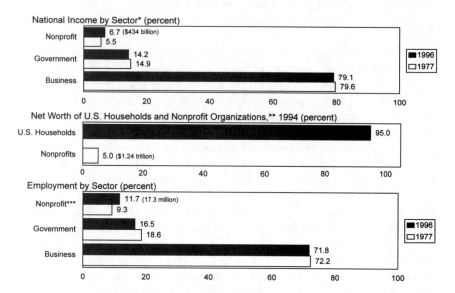

Sources: Hodgkinson and Weitzman, *Nonprofit Almanac, 1996–1997* and Interim Update through p. 140; Board of Governors of the Federal Reserve System, Flow of Funds Accounts of the United States (Washington, D.C., 1998).
*The independent sector itself accounted for 4.9 percent of national income in 1996, which includes assigned value of volunteers.
**Excludes net worth of organizations not reporting to government—mainly churches and organizations with less than $25,000 in annual receipts. Measures of assets and liabilities are not calculated in precisely the same way for nonprofits as part of household sector and for nonprofits standing alone.
***Includes volunteers, full- and part-time employment for the nonprofit sector. Independent sector employment was: 1977: 8.5, 1996: 10.8.

of personal income. The largest sources of difference are transfers, such as Social Security, which involve very little outright production, and services such as health care, which are purchased from other sectors that are credited with their production. Over the last couple of decades, government has increasingly spent larger shares of its expenditures and revenues on transfers and produced less within the sector itself.

The nonprofit sector now holds about 5 percent of the combined net worth of U.S. households and nonprofit organizations (business assets are included in household net worth and, therefore, not counted separately).[3] There are many valuation problems that on net probably cause that estimate to be low; for instance, the nonprofit sector totals shown in figure 2.2 exclude the assets of churches and some small organizations.

Employment by the nonprofit sector, including volunteers, is about 11.7 percent of total employment in the United States. That figure, which has grown over the past couple of decades, is higher than the sector's share of gross national product (GNP), at least partly because of the way that national income is measured. It values the output of many services at the rate of payment to the factors of production or at the cost of sale of the product. Consider a child-care center in which paid workers might earn less than they could in other jobs. As one consequence, charges for the services of the center will also be lower than they might otherwise be. In effect, the value of the lower-than-market wages accrues to the children and families using the center. But that value will not be counted in national income.[4] The services of a $5,000-a-year child care worker who could make $20,000 elsewhere will be counted as $5,000, not $20,000. Hence, it is not surprising that nonprofit labor would make up a larger percentage of the total labor force than nonprofit output would of total output.

Relative Size of Monetary Contributions to Nonprofits

Although the independent sector is economically important, charitable contributions are a rather small share of total income and are dwarfed by the government's social welfare spending.

- The independent sector receives about 2 percent of personal income as contributions, which is about one-twelfth of the government's social welfare spending.

Figure 2.3 shows that monetary contributions to the independent sector are about 2 percent, perhaps a little less, of personal income. That can be contrasted to social welfare spending supported by the government at all levels, which has been in excess of 20 percent of personal income since the early 1970s and is close to 25 percent today. By far the largest part of that spending is on retirement assistance and health care (social insurance) for the near-elderly and elderly, followed by education and then public aid.

Outright charitable giving of money has always been moderate relative to the total monetary resources and assets of households and relative to the economy's output. For better or worse, that is one reason why government has stepped in to provide many social welfare benefits. Some would argue that relying on government means greater distortions of behavior because of costs such as those associated with

Figure 2.3 GOVERNMENT* SOCIAL WELFARE SPENDING AND CHARITABLE CONTRIBUTIONS (1960–96)

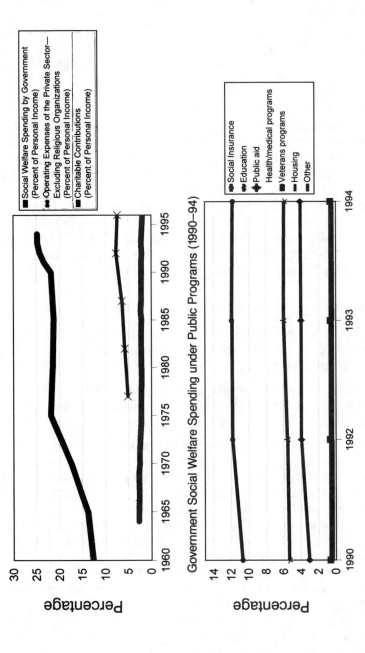

Government Social Welfare Spending under Public Programs (1990–94)

Sources: *Economic Report of the President,* February 1998; *Annual Statistical Supplement to the Social Security Bulletin,* Social Security Administration, 1994 and 1997; *Giving USA 1997, The Annual Report on Philanthropy for the Year 1996,* AAFRC Trust for Philanthropy, 1997.

*Includes federal, state, and local social welfare spending.

enforced taxation. Others, however, argue that only government can ensure that people who would otherwise free-ride—that is, benefit from others' efforts without sharing in the cost—pay their "fair share" of the cost for social welfare efforts.

No matter who is right, individuals have shown more willingness to pay higher taxes than to contribute voluntarily out of their own pockets. That immediately calls into question the notion that non-profits could take on all social welfare roles if they had to rely upon private contributions. It might be nice to hope that voluntary effort could rise to that level—some individuals do give a substantial portion of their income to charity—but no historical precedent for such widespread generosity exists, no matter how much the nation's various religions and mores might espouse the values associated with giving. It is highly doubtful, therefore, that the nonprofit sector could, in the foreseeable future, rely upon voluntary giving to take over all or even most social welfare functions, such as providing health care or minimum cash benefits to the elderly, universal education for the young, or widespread opportunity for college attendance.

Growth in Public Social Welfare Spending

Public social welfare spending, which affects much of the independent sector in some way, has grown quite rapidly in the postwar period.

- Between 1960 and 1994, the share of personal income devoted to public sector social welfare spending almost doubled, rising from just over 12.5 percent of gross domestic product (GDP) to close to 25 percent (figure 2.3).

Especially worth noting is the large and significant growth in social welfare spending between the mid-1960s and mid-1970s. Indeed, almost one-third of the nation's growth in domestic spending over its entire history, measured relative to the size of the economy, occurred during Richard Nixon's presidency (Steuerle, Gramlich, Heclo, and Nightingale 1998). Public social welfare spending relative to national income leveled off from the mid-1970s to the late 1980s, and then resumed its growth in the late 1980s and early 1990s, mainly due to rises in health care spending. Note also that much of that growth at the federal level was accomplished without increases in average tax rates, as peace dividends continually allowed shifts toward social welfare spending (see figure 2.1).

No peace dividend was available to state and local governments, but they nonetheless also show moderate growth in domestic and social welfare spending that exceeded the economy's real growth rate. In the past, some of that growth may have been induced by federal matching grant formulas, which might lead one to speculate that state and local growth in welfare spending could slow in the future if enough federal matching grants are converted into block grants.

Yet, as noted by Mermin and Steuerle (1997), recent devolution of "welfare" to the states so far has actually *increased* federalization of the financing of cash welfare, that is, the federal government has taken on a bigger *share* of its total financing. One reason is that the incentives for states to spend are reduced under the new block grants, as opposed to matching grants,[5] while at the same time, 1996 legislation temporarily boosted federal funding during a period of both economic expansion and declining welfare roles. In the longer term, it is reasonable to expect lower state spending on cash welfare as a percent of personal income and as a percent of their own revenue. That may be partially offset by the effect of Medicaid sharing formulas as health costs continue to rise, which so far has meant large and rising portions of state budgets spent on health care.

Constancy of Private Giving

In contrast to rising public social welfare spending, private contributions have been almost constant as a percent of personal income, although apparently declining a bit in recent years.

- Total private contributions of money and assets have fallen somewhat as a percent of personal income in recent years.
- The share of income given to health organizations has declined over the past 20 years, and religious institutions have claimed a declining income share for a longer period of time.
- More recently, rates of giving among higher-income individuals have fallen.

In 1996, charitable giving stood at 1.9 percent of personal income, slightly below its post-1964 average of 2.3 percent (Hodgkinson and Weitzman, *Almanac*, 86). One needs to be a bit careful here, as there are problems of both overreporting and underreporting on tax returns and surveys, and changes in survey techniques or IRS audit practices could produce different types of error over time. Still, the rate of giving today is probably somewhat below the levels witnessed in the 1960s and early 1970s.

Most donations are made by individuals rather than organizations (figure 2.4). When one adds up all sources of private contributions, the annual rate of growth in real (inflation-adjusted) private contributions equaled 2.9 percent from 1977 to 1996 (figure 2.5). Giving, however, has shifted among subsectors. Over the same period, private giving to health services increased only very slightly, by about 1 percent per year. The increasing amounts of federal spending on health care and research probably did result in a decline in the private supply of giving to this subsector.

Private contributions to religious organizations were also below the average for all independent sectors over this period, although only slightly. Religious giving declined through the 1960s and early and mid-1970s, however, so it has at best stabilized in recent years, rather than being restored to its former status (Hodgkinson and Weitzman, *Almanac* and *Interim Update*).

There is also some indication that high-income taxpayers are not contributing the same percentage of their annual income in 1990 as they did a decade earlier (see table 2.1). At least two other changes are

Figure 2.4　PHILANTHROPIC GIVING BY SOURCE, 1996 (Percent)

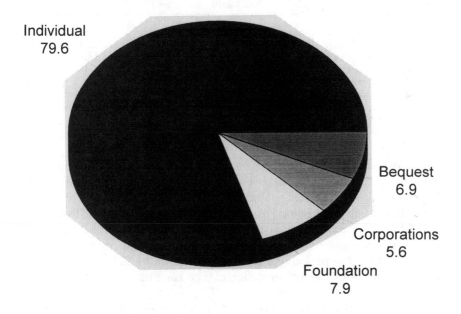

Individual
79.6

Bequest
6.9

Corporations
5.6

Foundation
7.9

Source: Ann E. Kaplan, *Giving USA 1997*, pp. 32–38.

Figure 2.5 ANNUAL RATES OF CHANGE IN PRIVATE CONTRIBUTIONS: 1977–96

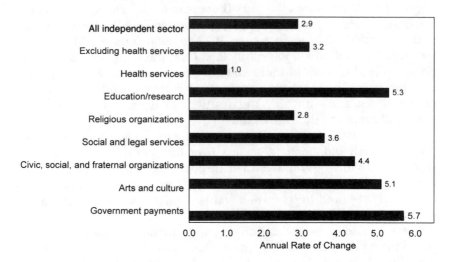

Source: Hodgkinson and Weitzman, *Nonprofit Almanac 1966–1997* and Interim Update (Washington, D.C.: Independent Sector, 1998).

Table 2.1 GIVING BY WEALTHY INDIVIDUALS, 1979–1994**

	1979	1984	1991	1994
Rate of giving (percent)	3.6	3.1	3.1	3.3
Top 1 percent share of total income (percent)	9.4	11.2	12.8	13.7
Top 1 percent share of total giving (percent)	14.0	14.1	14.1	16.6

Source: Gerald Auten, Charles Clotfelter, and Richard Schmalbeck, "Taxes and Philanthrophy among the Wealthy," University of Michigan Working Paper, 1998, table 5.
**Note: From 1979 to 1994, the share of total giving by the wealthy increases at a slower rate than their share of income and, therefore, their overall rate of giving decreases.

occurring among this group. First, there has been an increased concentration of income at higher-income levels since the late 1970s (Steuerle, Gramlich, Heclo, and Nightingale 1998). Meanwhile, the same group has experienced many changes in tax law, including lower tax rates (see, for instance, Auten, Cilke, and Randolph 1992 and Auten, Clotfelter, and Schmalbeck 1997). Recall that the top tax rate declined over that period, going from 70 percent to 50 percent in 1981 to 28 percent or 33 percent in 1988 and then back up to about 41 percent after 1993.

Despite those modest recent declines, charitable giving as a whole still shows a relative constancy that is surprising in two respects.

First, a series of changes in tax policy, mainly in the 1980s (see next chapter), significantly increased the net cost of charitable giving, leading many analysts to expect a sharp drop in private giving. Second, if it is true that government spending on social needs displaces private charity, one might have expected the substantial increase in public spending described above to have displaced more private giving than appears to be the case.

One needs to be rather cautious in interpreting the results of data from any particular time period. Individuals adjust their behavior only gradually in response to a change, such as an increase in the after-tax cost of giving. For example, when tax rates change, individuals may take years to fully respond. Randolph (1995) finds that people are much more likely to adjust their giving up or down in response to what they believe to be temporary changes in their tax rates, and hence in the after-tax cost of giving, than they are to changes that they believe to be permanent.[6]

Apart from changes in tax rates, a further complication is that the more uneven income distribution in the last couple of decades has been attributed to a variety of factors that may separately influence giving. Those include an increase in the number of two-earner couples where both spouses earn significant incomes, and, at the very top, the appearance of a "winner-take-all" economy with large rewards to those who obtain, through publicity or other means, status or unique monopolylike positions (Frank and Cook 1995). Here, too, individuals may react to large increases in (relative) income only gradually with a lag; and if so, those who move into much higher income levels may delay giving away many of their newfound gains until they get older.

Moreover, almost all previous estimates of the determinants of giving examine only the supply side of giving, but the demand for giving—that is, the needs of churches and research and educational institutions—may be more invariant (inelastic in economists' terms). In effect, if we start to respond to lower incentives by giving less, then the demand for our giving becomes more pressing and offsets some of the decline in giving that might otherwise occur. That would explain how changes in incentives might shift who gives while at the same time resulting in little or no changes in total giving. Kent Smetters (1998) was the first to develop a formal model that predicts behaviors that are consistent with some of the patterns we currently see in the data.[7]

Even before the increase in the after-tax cost of giving and shifts in the distribution of income that took place in the 1980s, there was a small drop from the higher level of giving in the mid-1960s. Yet it bears repeating that the drop was remarkably small (perhaps one-third of one percent of personal income) when compared with the growth in social welfare spending of more than 10 percent of personal income that took place between the mid-1960s and the late 1990s.

If one were to use those data to make a naive case that government social welfare spending displaces charitable giving, it would imply at most that $100 of additional social welfare spending displaces $3 of charitable giving in aggregate. That is consistent with Richard Steinberg's (1993) estimate that the rate of displacement ranges from 1 to 10 percent. A problem with any aggregate estimate, of course, is that the effect may vary over time, by subsector, and even by charity. If a government activity displaces one type of charitable effort but enhances another, for instance, the combined effect may show up as no net displacement of total charitable activity even though each separable change may be substantial.

Importance of Volunteer Time

Contributions of volunteer time significantly leverage the resources available to the independent sector.

- When contributions of time and foregone earnings are added, donations made to the independent sector are about double the size they appear when only monetary contributions are taken into account.

Volunteer effort is expended largely, if not entirely, in the independent sector. Although estimation requires using a variety of simplifying assumptions, the value of volunteer effort has been measured as close to the value of actual cash contributions. Thus, as of 1996, the worth of volunteer effort to the independent sector is estimated at $128.7 billion (table 2.2), while total giving of money or assets was $117.5 billion, of which individual giving outside of bequests is about four-fifths (Hodgkinson and Weitzman, *Almanac*).[8]

In assigning a value to volunteer time, there is a potential for both underestimation and overestimation. The time contribution of volunteers is estimated based upon the average wage rate, which is then applied to unpaid volunteer time. Yet many of those who work for pay in the nonprofit sector also contribute, but in the form of lower wages instead of unpaid time. For example, teachers in many religiously affiliated schools are paid much less than teachers in public schools, but there is no evidence that they are less qualified or produce less quality and quantity of educational services. We, therefore, underes-

Table 2.2 EMPLOYMENT AND VOLUNTEERING IN THE INDEPENDENT SECTOR

	1977	1987	1992	1996(p)
Paid employees, full- and part-time (percent of labor force)	5.3	5.7	6.6	7.4
Volunteers, full-time employee equivalent (percent of labor force)	3.1	3.9	4.0	4.3
Total assigned dollar value of volunteer time, excluding informal volunteering (in billions of constant 1996 dollars)	$76.0	$114.8	$121.7	$128.7

Sources: Hodgkinson and Weitzman, *Nonprofit Almanac 1996–1997* and Interim Update (Jan. 1998), Independent Sector; *Giving and Volunteering in the United States*, Independent Sector, 1996.
(p) = preliminary

timate the value of their services by valuing their time at the wage actually paid, instead of the wage that they could earn. The difference between what employees of nonprofits are paid and what they *could* earn is not counted in the estimates of the value of volunteers.[9] The best that has been attempted so far has been to readjust national income accounts to include the value of volunteer time and nonpaid family workers since 1984 (Hodgkinson and Weitzman 1993).

On the other hand, many volunteers and low-paid workers in the nonprofit sector enjoy the camaraderie, fellowship, and autonomy associated with their work and are less concerned with their "productivity" as volunteers. That makes valuation of their actual output more difficult. In any event, when the value of volunteering is added to direct charitable contributions, the output of the independent sector rises relative to government.

That is not to imply that the government does not receive volunteer support. In fact, it typically receives about one-quarter of total volunteer time, primarily from efforts made in conjunction with public schools (Hodgkinson and Weitzman, *Almanac*, 75). Still, the vast bulk of volunteer effort—about two-thirds—is transmitted through nonprofits. Moreover, some 93 million persons report either working for or volunteering with nonprofit organizations at least some of the time during a year (Hodgkinson and Weitzman, *Almanac*).

Given the assumptions that are needed in order to value volunteer time, one should interpret trends cautiously. Nonetheless, volunteer efforts appear to have increased from about 1977 to 1987 and to have leveled out since then.

Several issues pertaining to volunteers are not addressed here.[10] For example, surveys have noted that certain groups in the population (blacks, young people, Hispanics, other ethnic groups, low-income individuals, and older people) are not asked to volunteer at the same rates as more affluent whites between the ages of 25 and 64, thus resulting in a lower rate of volunteering among those demographic groups (Hodgkinson and Weitzman, *Giving*).

Comparability of the Two Sectors in Terms of Spending

Measuring resources in terms of total spending brings the relative size of the independent sector and government closer together.

- Spending by nonprofits and government appears more comparable in size, in part because the nonprofit sector is a major contractor or intermediary for both government and for other parts of the private sector.
- Due partly to this contracting, employment by the nonprofit sector as a share of total employment increased by almost exactly the amount as the decline in government employment from 1977 to 1996.

As opposed to spending financed by private contributions, total spending by the nonprofit sector comes somewhat closer in size to government (see figure 2.3). What accounts for this magnified measure of nonprofit sector activity? The nonprofit sector does not finance its activities exclusively from charitable donations of money and time; it also charges for many of its activities, especially in such areas as health and education. In turn, the government often works through other sectors to achieve its goals. Perhaps the best examples of government money flowing through nonprofit organizations are Medicare and Medicaid or grants for higher education.

One of the more interesting and telling recent institutional changes has been the growth in nonprofit sector employment, from 9.3 percent to 11.7 percent of all employment between 1977 and 1996 (see figure 2.2). Interestingly, that growth is almost of the same order of magnitude as the decline in the government sector from 18.6 percent to 16.5 percent of all employment. Many of our government officials like to proclaim their success at reducing the size of government and point in particular to the decline in the direct employment of individuals. In truth, what has occurred in large part is that the government has increasingly paid others to perform the work it finances.

That outsourcing or contracting for services has not simply been a result of "reinvention" of government—e.g., finding private garbage disposal companies to displace public employees. Instead, the figures are dominated by the very large growth in government spending for services, particularly health care. Doctors, nurses, and others increasingly have had to view themselves as service providers for government insurance payments. Their work for the government has in a sense displaced others' work in areas where government activity has declined—defense being the most obvious example.

Government payments to nonprofit organizations have been growing much faster than private sector payments and contributions (see the chapter by Smith in this section). Table 2.3 shows the growth in both aggregate sources for various subsectors of the independent sector during the period from 1977 to 1996. As can be seen, only in civic, social, and fraternal organizations has the growth in private sector payments and contributions been significantly in excess of government payments. For education and research the rate of growth of each has been about the same, although both have grown significantly faster than the economy as a whole. Payments for social and legal services have also grown fairly rapidly, with government payments still growing 20 percent faster than private payments. Between 1977 and 1996, government and private payments in virtually all of the independent sector grew faster than the cumulative real growth in GDP of 62 percent (table 2.3). The sole exception was government payments to civic, social, and fraternal organizations.

It is hard to determine the extent to which these past trends will continue. The amount that can be produced under government contracts by its very nature must be less than total production in the economy, so the growth rate in the former cannot forever exceed the latter.[11] Some slowdown in government support of nonprofits may have been experienced recently. While it grew by 5.7 percent annually from 1977 to 1992, for instance, it dropped to 2.9 percent from 1992 to 1996 (Hodgkinson 1998). On the other hand, the social and legal services subsector have continued to grow more recently. Such growth might come from activities such as state and federal efforts to engage nonprofit organizations in efforts to help low-income households with job search activities.

Diversity of the Independent Sector

Measures of resources available to all nonprofit organizations disguise the great diversity of the independent sector.

- The nonprofit sector is diverse and heterogeneous; its characteristics are hidden in aggregate figures dominated by the large health

Table 2.3 GOVERNMENT PAYMENTS AND INDEPENDENT SECTOR CONTRIBUTIONS BY NONPROFIT SUBSECTOR
(Billions of Constant 1996 Dollars)

Subsector	Government Payments 1977	Private-Sector Payments and Contributions 1977	Government Payments 1996	Private-Sector Payments and Contributions 1996	Change 1977–96 (%) Government Payments	Change 1977–96 (%) Private-Sector Payments and Contributions
Health services	$38.60	$67.9	$127	$159.6	229	135
Education/research	11.60	39.4	23.1	81.7	100	107
Religious organizations	—	39.6	—	71.4	—	81
Social and legal services	13.00	10.0	39.9	28.3	207	183
Civic, social, and fraternal organizations	4.80	4.0	5.4	10.0	13	150
Arts and culture	0.44	2.9	1.5	6.7	241	131
Addendum: GDP					62	

Sources: Hodgkinson and Weitzman, Nonprofit Almanac 1996–1997 and Interim Update (Jan. 1998), Independent Sector; Bureau of Economic Analysis, National Income & Product Accounts, 1929–1996 Summary (Aug. 1997).

and education subsectors and/or by the largest organizations in terms of expenses and assets.

There are a variety of ways of disaggregating the independent sector to get a better view of its component parts. Figure 2.6 shows the distribution of employment and of total funds received by different

Figure 2.6 EMPLOYMENT AND SHARE OF TOTAL FUNDS FOR SELECTED
SUBSECTORS IN THE INDEPENDENT SECTOR: 1977 AND 1996

Distribution of Employment for Selected Subsectors in the Independent Sector (Percent)

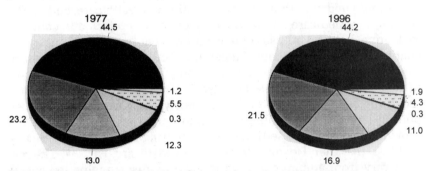

Share of Total Funds for Selected Subsectors in the Independent Sector (Percent)

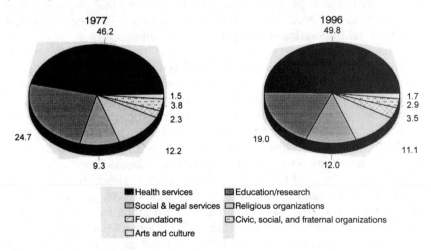

■ Health services   ▨ Education/research
▢ Social & legal services ▢ Religious organizations
▨ Foundations   ▨ Civic, social, and fraternal organizations
▢ Arts and culture

Source: Hodgkinson and Weitzman, *Nonprofit Almanac 1966–1997* and Interim Update (Washington, D.C.: Independent Sector, 1998).

subsectors. Health services has about 44 percent of total independent sector employment; education and research about 21 percent. Similarly, health services garner about one-half of all funds received by the independent sector; education a little less than one-fifth.

Those numbers warn us to be careful in distinguishing claims made about the entire sector from claims about its various subsectors. What may happen to social services, for example, may be very different from what happens to health services.

Trends in government and nonprofit spending on health care demonstrate the different ways in which shifts in government policy can affect nonprofit organizations. Rising government payments for health have dominated growth in overall spending on health care, and, under current law, Medicare and Medicaid growth are projected to continue to dominate almost all uses of new government revenues (see the next chapter in this volume, and Steuerle, Gramlich, Heclo, and Nightingale 1998). But those payments go not only to nonprofit organizations, mainly nonprofit hospitals, but also to profit-making organizations, including doctors' offices. In the past few years, government has been putting larger shares of its money into doctor services that are not provided in a hospital setting (e.g., by putting money into Medicare, Part B, rather than Hospital Insurance or Medicare, Part A). The reasons vary from attempts to save money (by discouraging expensive hospital stays) to reactions to arbitrary budget accounting rules. (Medicare hospital payments are paid out of a fund that depends upon Social Security Health Insurance taxes and thus is threatened with a shortfall, while Medicare outpatient care is paid mainly out of general revenues.)

The consequence of a simple shift to outpatient care, even if the same services and personnel are involved, is that fewer funds flow through nonprofit hospitals and more funds flow directly through doctors' offices. Thus, growth from 1992 to 1996 in government payments to the nonprofit health subsector has slowed considerably from the earlier 1977 to 1992 period (Hodgkinson 1998). Another shift has occurred as more hospitals have moved to profit-making status. It does not follow, however, that there will be a net loss in "charitable" activity simply because fewer receipts flow through nonprofit hospitals. Such activity could fall, however, if somehow the levels of charitable contributions or free care given to low-income patients decline when there is a movement out of hospitals into doctors' offices or other settings defined as "profit-making" (for a more elaborate discussion of the conversion issue, see Goddeeris and Weisbrod, this volume).

Finally, nonprofit organizations exhibit a phenomenon common to modern organizational life: the dominance of larger organizations. Among public charities that report information about their finances and operations on the IRS 990 form, organizations with more than $10 million in expenses make up a mere 3.8 percent of total organizations but have more than two-thirds of total assets and expenses. Correspondingly, more than 70 percent of organizations (those with less than $500,000 in expenses) have only 4.5 percent of total expenses and 5.4 percent of total assets (see figure I.1 in Boris, this volume). Indeed, much nonprofit activity may not be reflected here at all. If a group of volunteers organizes and has little or no financing, it may not even establish itself as a legal organization, much less file with any administrative or statistical agency. Note also that subsectors with larger institutions, such as the education and health sector, show up with smaller percentages of total organizations than their percentages of total expenses and assets, whereas other subsectors, such as environment and animals or human services, have a much larger share of total organizations than they do of total expenses or assets (see figure I.2 in Boris, this volume).

CONCLUSION

In recent decades the government and the nonprofit sector have often acted more as complements than substitutes in many of their activities. When one considers the relatively constant rate of charitable contributions out of personal income and the growth in shares of total output and employment by the nonprofit sector—all of which occurred during a period of rising social welfare spending by government—it is hard to argue that increased government activity has displaced private nonprofit activity in any aggregate sense. Indeed, one of the most important aspects of the modern relationship between the sectors is the way that the government has increasingly turned to the nonprofit sector to serve as an intermediary or contractor in providing many public services.

Although more government social welfare spending does not appear to have crowded out nonprofit activity in the aggregate, there has nonetheless been both significant displacement and reorientation of specific nonprofit activities over time. For example, the very large government role in programs for the elderly probably has displaced much cash or housing assistance to the old that would have otherwise occurred. The movement toward foster care helped reduce the use of orphanages. Large government subsidies for health care have probably reduced charitable contributions to hospitals. The expansion of public schooling coincided historically with the decline in the percentage of children attending religiously based schools. In each of those cases, of course, other factors are also at play, but, clearly, when government meets a need, private efforts often shift focus within the independent sector at large.

In many cases, what is observed can be better described as "replacement" rather than "displacement." That follows from the observed constancy of the share of personal income that is contributed to charitable activities. A constant share of income that is earmarked for contributions implies that the activities financed by such contributions will rise at about the rate of growth in the economy. Since the nature of charitable activities is changing, that implies that the public will "replace" support for some "old" activities with support for new efforts. In other words, a decrease in the rate of giving to one activity may often mean an increase in another.

Returning to a point made at the start of this chapter, one should not be surprised to find that what looks like "crowding out" of nonprofits is apt to represent a shifting of priorities within the independent sector. Recall that theoretically there is no *a priori* reason why government activity should necessarily displace nonprofit activity. The two sectors are merely means for satisfying a range of social needs identified by individuals. The two sectors can act as both substitutes and complements in fulfilling that role. More spending by government on education, for instance, could either substitute for private and nonprofit spending, or add to the demand for scholarship funds.

It would also be a mistake to think that all past trends, whether of short or long duration, will continue. For example, the federal government's social welfare budget may continue to grow faster than the economy, but social security and health care are scheduled to garner the lion's share of that growth. If cash assistance in Social Security grows enough, it may displace other government social welfare efforts that use nonprofit organizations as intermediaries. Within health care, there are significant pressures to subsidize health maintenance organizations, or insurance groups, or profit-making organizations— almost any approach that will help to control costs. There is also less emphasis on hospitals and more on outpatient care, which tends to take place in profit-making settings. The latter movement could reduce the relative size of nonprofit hospitals simply because more dollars flow directly to doctors.

As another example, devolution of welfare to the states has been accompanied by significantly larger amounts of money being spent on child care and job search and transportation even as cash assistance is reduced. Those welfare reform shifts could expand different service roles for nonprofits and public institutions alike, both of which might spend more on early childhood care, education, and career counseling.

Each of these examples illustrates one of the basic themes of this chapter: that the growth of the nonprofit sector, no matter how measured, is likely to vary over time relative to growth in government and the economy as a whole. Whether the consequence is positive or negative cannot be determined without specific examination of each change and a much broader concept of social welfare that takes account of the combined changes in all sectors—nonprofit, government, business, and household.

Notes

1. By not adjusting age of retirement as people live longer while providing higher levels of annual benefits, Social Security and Medicare encourage individuals to retire for almost a decade more than they did around 1950. That is, the average individual both retires about five years earlier and lives about five years longer. This creates a new and different type of demand for services by individuals who are not "old" by more traditional standards of short remaining life spans.

2. Admittedly, government often makes exceptions to a uniformity standard, but only at the cost of inequity and a disgruntled citizenry. For example, queues, which define who is the "next" eligible beneficiary in a precise legal fashion, are used in housing and other programs even though they are extraordinarily arbitrary in their application.

3. Household net worth also includes the value of government bonds; because of the large value of that debt, the government sector would actually show up as a negative value if presented under that set of accounts.

4. Similarly, national income accounts exclude the value of all services and goods produced in the home and not sold in the market.

5. These changes in incentives are not examined here in any depth. On the one hand, removal of matching grants may make states more efficient in spending their money. With no match, when they spend a dollar, it will cost them a dollar. On the other hand, some would argue that fear of having too high a tax rate relative to neighbors creates a "race to the bottom" where states bow out of providing any social welfare themselves. Still another issue is whether any federal minimum—such as might be provided by the earned income tax credit, food stamps, and Medicaid—might not already deal with many of these interstate equity and efficiency issues.

6. The expected difference in response is similar to how people might be expected to act if, say, Macy's announced it would offer a 50 percent discount on all purchases made between Christmas and New Year's, but offered no discount thereafter. Shoppers could be expected to respond to this "once in a lifetime" chance by shifting purchases of goods they might have made in future years to the "sale year." That would magnify their spending in the sale year and cut into sales in the subsequent year. Economists believe that people will respond to temporary changes in tax incentives in similar fashion. For example, if people believe that their tax rate in one year is likely to be unusually high, they would be advised (and are by tax planners) to shift charitable contributions and other deductions into that year. That produces an exaggerated increase in charitable contributions in the year in which the tax rate is temporarily high (and hence the net cost of giving is temporarily low).

7. Still another recent study using cross-section data, but using a new econometric technique, also argues that taxpayer responses to tax rates are much lower than many former studies tended to find (see Bradley and McClelland 1998).

8. Note that these figures relate to the independent sector and are slightly lower than the figures used for employment in the entire nonprofit sector shown in figure 2.1.

9. Note that national income accounting traditionally leaves out most nonmarket valuation. Adding in the value of volunteer time logically leads to adding in the value of volunteer effort that comes in the form of lower pay, which logically leads to adding in the value of all nonmarket production. Such comprehensive estimation has never been performed.

10. Longer-term forces are not investigated here. It is worth noting, however, how larger societal factors can affect the availability of volunteers. For example, not too long ago, a nation of farmers simply had limited time and resources to gather together in formal volunteer activity even though interfamily cooperation may have been intensive. With urbanization came many demands, often met by generous increases in volunteer efforts of women who were not always working at paid jobs, but worked instead through the home and volunteer associations. (See, for example, McCarthy 1982 and Ann Firor Scott 1992.) On the other hand, recent decades have seen a greater concentration of work, especially by women, in the formal marketplace and a lesser concentration of work among the many near-elderly and elderly who now typically retire almost two decades before expected year of death.

11. There is an exception if one is counting payments rather than production: if layers of intermediation continually increase, so that each payment moves through more and more organizations before reaching its end use, then growth in gross payments can continually exceed GDP growth.

References

Auten, Gerald E., James M. Cilke, and William C. Randolph. 1992. "The Effects of Tax Reform on Charitable Contributions." *National Tax Journal* 45: 267–90.

Auten, Gerald E., Charles Clotfelter, and Richard Schmalbeck. 1998. "Taxes and Philanthropy among the Wealthy." Working Paper Series 98-15.

Ann Arbor: Office of Michigan Tax Policy Research, University of Michigan School of Business.

Bradley, Ralph, and Robert McClelland. 1998. "A Robust Estimation of the Effects of Taxation on Charitable Contributions." Bureau of Labor Statistics, Washington, D.C.

Douglas, James. 1987. "Political Theories of Nonprofit Organization." In *The Nonprofit Sector: A Research Handbook*, edited by Walter Powell (43–54). New Haven: Yale University Press.

Frank, Robert H., and Philip J. Cook. 1995. *The Winner-Take-All Society*. New York: Free Press.

Gronbjerg, Kirsten A. 1993. *Understanding Nonprofit Funding*. San Francisco: Jossey-Bass Publishers.

Hodgkinson, Virginia. 1998. "Updates and Revisions for the Nonprofit Almanac." Unpublished.

Hodgkinson, Virginia, and Murray Weitzman. 1992, 1994, and 1996 editions. *Giving and Volunteering in the United States*. Washington, D.C.: Independent Sector.

————. 1993. "Measuring the Nonprofit Sector in the United States Economy: Conceptual Framework and Methodology." *Voluntas* 4 (2): 141–62.

————. 1996. *Nonprofit Almanac 1996–1997*. Washington, D.C.: Independent Sector.

Kaplan, Ann E. 1997. *Giving USA 1997*. New York: AAFRC Trust for Philanthropy.

McCarthy, Kathleen. 1982. *Noblesse Oblige*. Chicago: University of Chicago Press.

Printz, Toby J. 1997. "Services and Capacity of Faith-Based Organizations in the Washington, D.C., Metropolitan Area." Paper presented at the annual meeting of ARNOVA, Indianapolis, IN, December 4–6.

Randolph, William. 1995. "Dynamic Income, Progressive Taxes, and the Timing of Charitable Contributions." *Journal of Political Economy* 103 (4): 709–38.

Rathgeb Smith, Steven, and Michael Lipsky. 1993. *Nonprofits for Hire: The Welfare State in the Age of Contracting*. Cambridge: Harvard University Press.

Renz, Loren, Crystal Mandler, and Trinh C. Tran. 1997. *Foundation Giving*. New York: Foundation Center.

Salamon, Lester M. 1995. *Partners in Public Service: Government-Nonprofit Relations in the Modern Welfare State*. Baltimore: Johns Hopkins University Press.

Salamon, Lester M., and Helmut K. Anheier. 1996. *The Emerging Nonprofit Sector: An Overview*. Manchester: Manchester University Press.

Scott, Ann Firor. 1992. *Natural Allies: Women's Associations in American History*. Urbana: University of Illinois Press.

Smetters, Kent. 1998. "A Free-Rider Explanation of the Charitable Giving Puzzles of the 1980s and an Application to Fundamental Tax Reform." Unpublished paper.

Steinberg, Richard. 1989. "The Theory of Crowding Out: Donations, Local Government Spending, and New Federalism." In *Philanthropic Giving: Studies in Varieties and Goals*, edited by Richard Magat (143–56). New York, NY: Oxford University Press.

———. 1990. "Taxes and Giving: New Findings." *Voluntas* (1): 61–79.

———. 1996. "Can Individual Donations Replace Cutbacks in Federal Social Welfare Spending?" In *Capacity for Change: The Nonprofit World in an Age of Devolution*, edited by Dwight F. Burlingame, William A. Diaz, Warren F. Ilchman, and Associates (57–79). Indianapolis: Indiana Center on Philanthropy.

Steuerle, C. Eugene, and Gordon Mermin. 1997. "Devolution as Seen from the Budget." Policy Brief, Series A, No. A-2. Washington, D.C.: Urban Institute Press.

Steuerle, C. Eugene, Edward N. Gramlich, Hugh Heclo, and Demetra Smith Nightingale. 1998. *The Government We Deserve: Responsive Democracy and Changing Expectations.* Washington, D.C.: Urban Institute Press.

Stevenson, David R., Thomas H. Pollak, and Linda M. Lampkin. 1997. *State Nonprofit Almanac 1997.* Washington, D.C.: Urban Institute Press.

Verba, Sidney, Kay Lehman Schlozman, and Henry E. Brady. 1995. *Voice and Equality: Civic Voluntarism in American Politics.* Cambridge: Harvard University Press.

Weisbrod, Burton A. 1988. *The Nonprofit Economy.* Cambridge: Harvard University Press.

Wolpert, Julian. 1993. "Patterns of Generosity in America: Who's Holding the Safety Net?" A Twentieth Century Fund Paper. New York: The Twentieth Century Fund Press.

Chapter Three

THE NONPROFIT SECTOR AND THE FEDERAL BUDGET: RECENT HISTORY AND FUTURE DIRECTIONS

Alan J. Abramson, Lester M. Salamon, and C. Eugene Steuerle

INTRODUCTION

Government spending and tax policies are central in shaping the role of the nonprofit sector. Government spending policies affect the levels of need in society and hence the extent of the problems that nonprofit organizations might be called upon to address. Moreover, since government has become an important financier of nonprofit activity, these same policies can enhance or circumscribe the ability of nonprofits to respond to these needs. Government tax policies, in turn, affect the levels of private charitable support to which nonprofits have access and thereby their ability to make up from private sources what they lose from governmental ones.

During the past two decades, important changes have taken place in both spending and tax policies at the federal level. The purpose of this chapter is to examine these changes and to gauge the impact that they have had on nonprofit organizations. In addition, the chapter also looks ahead at how possible changes in government spending and tax policies over the next several years may affect nonprofits.

FEATURES OF THE ANALYSIS

Underlying the analysis in this chapter are several key methodological features that we have used in our earlier work on this subject (Abramson and Salamon 1986; Salamon with Abramson 1981; Salamon and Abramson 1982).

In the first place, we focus here only on a subset of federal government actions that affect nonprofit organizations, namely federal spending and federal tax policies. Federal credit programs, which consist of direct loan and loan guarantee programs, including student loan programs, are excluded from this analysis, as are regulatory policies.

Second, we examine the impact of federal spending on both the *demand* for and the *supply* of nonprofit services. The demand impact is measured by changes in the overall levels of federal spending in fields where nonprofits are active, on the theory that, as federal spending in these fields declines, the demand for services from private nonprofits increases. For example, when federal food stamp spending declines, more needy individuals may turn to nonprofit soup kitchens for assistance.

But federal spending changes also affect the supply of nonprofit services. This occurs because many nonprofit organizations receive a significant portion of their income from federal sources. For example, federal grants to nonprofit health clinics increase the resources available to these organizations to provide services.

In most federal social programs, only a portion of the program's total expenditures is channeled through nonprofits. Thus, the absolute size of the demand effect is likely to be greater than the absolute size of the supply effect. Both effects of spending changes are important, however, as reflections of the impact of federal budget decisions on nonprofits.

Unfortunately, no comprehensive federal statistical data sources track the flow of federal support to nonprofits. To remedy that situation, we have developed estimates of the share of program resources flowing to nonprofit organizations under each program through which nonprofits receive support. These estimates were based on detailed examination of programmatic data, scrutiny of existing program evaluations, and extensive discussions with program managers at the federal, state, and local levels. Our estimates of federal support flowing to nonprofits include funds that flow directly from the federal government to nonprofit organizations, as well as federal funds that flow indirectly through state and local government or other entities to nonprofits. We estimated that, in fiscal year (FY) 1997, more than 30 percent of overall federal spending in programs of interest to nonprofits was channeled through nonprofits for delivery of services.[1]

A third feature of the approach adopted here is that it takes the level of social need as given and analyzes the availability of public and private resources to meet this need. In fact, however, as indicated in table 3.1, needs change over time. Between 1980 and 1995, the poverty population increased by 24 percent, from 29.3 million

Table 3.1 SELECTED INDICATORS OF DEMAND FOR NONPROFIT SERVICES, 1995 VS. 1980 (In Millions of Persons, Except Where Indicated)

| Program Area | Amount | | Change, 1995 vs. 1980 | |
	1980	1995	Amount	Percent
Social Welfare				
Persons below poverty level	29.3	36.4	+ 7.2	+ 24
Children below poverty level	11.1	14.0	+ 2.9	+ 26
Persons 65 and over below poverty level[a]	3.7	3.3	− 0.4	− 10
Total population	227.7	263.2	+ 35.4	+ 16
Persons 65 and over[b]	25.6	33.9	+ 8.3	+ 33
Persons 85 and over[b]	2.2	3.8	+ 1.5	+ 68
Births to teenagers (thousands)[c]	552.2	505.5	− 46.7	− 8
Immigrants (thousands)	531.0	720.0	+ 189.0	+ 36
Education and Research				
High school dropouts	5.2	4.0	− 1.2	− 24
Health				
Persons without health insurance[d]	31.0	40.6	+ 9.6	+ 31
Fetal and infant deaths (thousands)[e]	78.9	55.4	− 23.5	− 30
AIDS deaths (thousands)[f]	12.5	31.3	+ 18.8	+ 150
Income Assistance				
Unemployed workers	7.6	7.4	− 0.2	− 3
Criminal Justice				
Juvenile arrests for drug abuse (thousands)	86.7	143.3	+ 56.6	+ 65
Child abuse cases (thousands)[g]	690.7	1,000.5	+ 309.8	+ 45
Social Welfare Spending by State and Local Governments (FY 1998 dollars in billions)[e,h]	$317.1	$493.8	+ $176.7	+ 56
Education	$208.5	$348.6	+ $140.1	+ 67
Medicaid and other hospital and medical care	$77.7	$105.3	+ $27.6	+ 35
Other[i]	$30.8	$39.9	+ $9.1	+ 29

Source: U.S. Bureau of the Census 1997.

a. Data for 1979 and 1995.

b. Data for 1980 and 1996.

c. Data for 1980 and 1994.

d. Data for 1987 and 1995.

e. Data for 1980 and 1993.

f. Initial data for all deaths 1985 and before.

g. Data for 1990 and 1995.

h. "Social welfare" expenditures as defined by the U.S. Social Security Administration, excluding social insurance programs (e.g., unemployment insurance, workers compensation, public employee retirement). See U.S. Bureau of the Census 1997, p. 373.

i. Includes Aid to Families with Dependent Children (AFDC), Supplemental Security Income (SSI), child nutrition, institutional care, social services, etc.

persons to 36.4 million persons. While increased state and local social welfare spending may have helped to meet some of these new
demands, 80 percent of the rise in state and local spending was in the
area of education, and an additional 15 percent went for Medicaid and
other health-related purposes, leaving only a relatively small portion
of the increase to meet other needs related to the growth in the poverty
population. If anything, therefore, the data reported here likely understate the extent of change.

Fourth, we focus here on "outlays" as our measure of spending.
This can be confusing because when Congress allocates money to a
program, it formally makes an "appropriation" or grant of "budget
authority" to the program. Ultimately, however, it is not the grant of
budget authority but the actual outlays of money that make the difference on the ground. This therefore seemed the appropriate measure
to use, even though it often takes well over a year for changes in budget
authority to show up as changes in outlays.

Fifth, we measure changes in federal outlays against FY 1980 as the
base year. We have used FY 1980 as the base year in part because it
falls near the end of one presidential administration (Jimmy Carter's)
and the beginning of another (Ronald Reagan's). When interpreting
the numbers in this report, however, it is important to bear in mind
that FY 1980 was not the high point in spending for many of the
programs considered here. For many of the social service programs,
that high point actually occurred several years earlier. Thus, some of
the reductions reported here would be higher if we had used an earlier
base year.

With the FY 1980 base year, we employed two methods to measure
changes. First, we compared spending in the outyears to actual FY
1980 levels, adjusted for inflation. The gross domestic product (GDP)
implicit price deflator was used for adjusting all programs except the
health finance programs, such as Medicare and Medicaid, for which
we used the Consumer Price Index (CPI) for medical services.

In addition to measuring outyear spending levels against FY 1980
in absolute terms, we also measured them in relative terms, as a
percentage of GDP. In particular, we used an index method that involves setting the percentage of GDP devoted to federal spending in
areas of nonprofit activity in FY 1980 equal to 100 and then computing
the appropriate index values for other years based on spending and
GDP levels in those years. An index value of 60 for FY 1997 means
that the portion of GDP devoted to federal spending in areas of nonprofit activity in FY 1997 is only 60 percent of the share of GDP that
was allocated for the same purposes in FY 1980.

Finally, our chapter focuses on spending of federal funds only and not spending from state and local governments' own source revenues. As indicated above, however, the data do include federal dollars that flow indirectly through state or local governments or other entities to nonprofit organizations.

OVERALL FEDERAL SPENDING IN PROGRAM AREAS OF CONCERN TO NONPROFIT AGENCIES, FY 1980–97

As noted above, federal budget decisions affect the demand for non-profit services by increasing or decreasing the resources that government is putting into certain kinds of activities. Federal spending changes also affect revenues of nonprofit agencies and their consequent ability to supply services to meet that demand.

This section takes up the first of these effects. The following section then analyzes the effects of the same budget decisions on the *revenues* of nonprofit agencies.

Federal Activity in Fields Where Nonprofits Are Active

Federal spending might reasonably be expected to affect the demand for services from nonprofit organizations in seven principal areas: (1) social welfare, including social services, employment and training, and community development; (2) education and research, consisting of elementary and secondary education, higher education, and research and development; (3) health care, including health finance and health services; (4) income assistance, including housing, cash, food, and other income assistance programs; (5) international relief and assistance; (6) culture and the arts; and (7) conservation and the environment. Throughout the chapter, we identify these fields as "program areas of interest to nonprofit organizations."

Baseline Spending: FY 1980

Within these broad areas we identified well over 100 federal programs of particular importance to the nonprofit sector. As reflected in table 3.2, these programs accounted for FY 1980 federal outlays of $345.4 billion, expressed in FY 1998 dollars. By comparison, total federal expenditures in that year amounted to $1.2 trillion. In other words, programs identified here as being especially relevant to nonprofit or-

Table 3.2 FEDERAL SPENDING IN PROGRAM AREAS WHERE NONPROFITS ARE ACTIVE, FY 1980–97 BY YEAR
(In Billions of Constant FY 1998 Dollars)

| Fiscal Year | All Programs | | Excluding Medicare and Medicaid | | Excluding Medicare, Medicaid, and Income Assistance | | Federal Spending as a Percentage of GDP (FY 1980 = 100) |
| | Outlays | Change from FY 1980 | Change from FY 1980 | | Change from FY 1980 | | |
			Amount	Percent	Amount	Percent	
1980	$345.4						100
1982	339.1	−$6.3	−$25.9	−14	−$26.9	−24	76
1983	342.5	−2.9	−25.7	−14	−31.6	−28	70
1984	345.6	+0.2	−27.1	−15	−31.8	−28	65
1985	365.2	+19.8	−20.9	−11	−27.6	−24	66
1986	363.0	+17.7	−23.0	−12	−30.0	−26	62
1987	361.7	+16.3	−26.2	−14	−32.6	−29	58
1988	371.7	+26.3	−19.8	−11	−30.6	−27	57
1989	382.3	+36.9	−16.1	−9	−29.1	−26	56
1990	402.1	+56.7	−8.4	−5	−25.1	−22	58
1991	426.9	+81.5	+8.7	+5	−17.9	−16	63
1992	464.0	+118.6	+24.4	+13	−13.6	−12	64
1993	488.7	+143.3	+38.5	+21	−8.6	−8	66
1994	514.9	+169.5	+51.6	+28	−5.9	−5	65
1995	537.3	+191.9	+59.6	+32	−4.1	−4	65
1996	543.5	+198.1	+56.4	+31	−6.1	−5	62
1997	554.1	+208.7	+59.0	+32	−4.6	−4	60
Total 1982–97	6,802.6	+1,276.4	+105.1	+4	−$325.8	−18	63

Source: See appendix A.

ganizations represented approximately one-fourth of all federal expenditures in FY 1980.

Of that amount, by far the largest share, representing almost half of all federal outlays in these fields, consisted of health care expenditures, chiefly for Medicare and Medicaid. Another 20 percent of the total represented income assistance payments. Spending for social welfare and for education and research accounted for about 15 percent and 12 percent of the total, respectively. Outlays for foreign aid, arts and culture, environment and conservation, and the nonprofit postal subsidy made up the remaining 4 percent of federal spending in these areas.

Aggregate Changes: FY 1982–97 vs. FY 1980

Overall federal spending in program areas of interest to nonprofits fell below FY 1980 levels during the early years of the Reagan administration but then recovered so as to be substantially above FY 1980 levels by FY 1997. As shown in table 3.2, the total inflation-adjusted value of federal spending in these fields declined from $345.4 billion in FY 1980 to a low of $339.1 billion in FY 1982 before climbing to $554.1 billion in FY 1997.

This aggregate picture is somewhat misleading, however, because it is heavily affected by the inclusion of the two large federal health programs, Medicare and Medicaid, which grew substantially during this period. By contrast, major reductions in spending occurred in many of the other areas of interest to nonprofit organizations, including employment and training, community development, and higher education. Thus, while overall spending in all of the areas of interest to nonprofits registered a cumulative gain of $1.3 trillion over the FY 1982–97 period compared with FY 1980 levels, outside of Medicare and Medicaid the aggregate gain was a much smaller $105.1 billion. And if income assistance is also excluded, the remaining programs experienced a cumulative 16-year reduction of $325.8 billion.

Expressed somewhat differently, the percentage of GDP devoted to federal spending in areas of interest to nonprofits, outside of Medicare, Medicaid, and income assistance, declined some 40 percent between FY 1980 and FY 1997, so that by FY 1997 it was only 60 percent of what it had been in FY 1980.

Breakdown by Functional Areas

As shown in table 3.3, the direction and level of federal spending changes varied considerably by program area between FY 1980 and FY 1997.

Table 3.3 CHANGES IN FEDERAL SPENDING IN PROGRAM AREAS WHERE NONPROFIT ORGANIZATIONS ARE ACTIVE, FY 1982–97 VS. FY 1980, BY PROGRAM AREA (In Billions of Constant FY 1998 Dollars)[a]

Program Area	Outlays		Change, FY 1997 vs. FY 1980		Cumulative Change, FY 1982–97 vs. FY 1980 Level	FY 1997 Outlays as a Percent of GDP (FY 1980 = 100)
	FY 1980	FY 1997	Amount	Percent		
Social Welfare	**$50.1**	**$38.3**	**−$11.8**	**−24**	**−$303.3**	**50**
Social services	14.6	23.3	+8.6	+59	+15.2	103
Employment and training	20.0	7.0	−13.1	−65	−201.8	23
Community development	15.5	8.0	−7.4	−48	−116.7	34
Education and Research	**40.0**	**41.8**	**+1.8**	**+5**	**−59.6**	**68**
Elementary and secondary	13.5	15.4	+1.9	+14	−12.1	74
Higher education	17.2	10.7	−6.5	−38	−110.4	40
Research and development	9.2	15.7	+6.5	+70	+62.9	110
Health	**169.8**	**325.6**	**+155.8**	**+92**	**+1,192.1**	**203**
Health finance[b]	163.2	316.0	+152.8	+94	+1,192.6	211
Health services	6.7	9.6	+2.9	+44	−0.5	93

Income Assistance	**70.5**	**134.1**	**+63.6**	**+90**	**+430.9**	123
Housing	10.6	28.2	+17.6	+166	+152.9	172
Cash	28.5	65.6	+37.0	+130	+214.1	149
Food	27.2	36.7	+9.6	+35	+78.8	88
Other	4.2	3.6	−0.6	−14	−14.8	56
Foreign Aid	10.4	12.8	+2.4	+24	+51.9	80
Arts and Culture	1.7	1.2	−0.5	−31	−7.2	44
Environment	1.4	0.2	−1.2	−86	−15.4	9
Other	1.5	0.1	−1.4	−94	−13.1	4
Total	$345.4	$554.1	+$208.7	+60	+$1,276.4	128
Total, excluding Medicare and Medicaid	$184.2	$243.2	+$59.0	+32	+$105.1	84
Total, excluding Medicare, Medicaid, and income assistance	$113.7	$109.1	−$4.6	−4	−$325.8	60

Source: See appendix A.
a. Excludes federal credit programs.
b. Excludes Medicare premiums and collections.

The social welfare category, which includes the subareas of social services, employment and training, and community development, absorbed the largest amount of budget cuts in dollar terms between FY 1980 and FY 1997. During this period, the real value of federal spending in this area dropped from $50.1 billion in FY 1980 to $38.3 billion in FY 1997, a decline of $11.8 billion, or 24 percent, as shown in table 3.3. As this table also shows, the share of GDP devoted to social welfare programs by FY 1997 was only half of what it had been in FY 1980. Altogether, the value of federal spending in this area declined by a total of $303.3 billion over the entire 16-year period, FY 1982–97, compared with what would have been spent had FY 1980 spending levels been maintained.

The largest portion of this reduction resulted from massive cuts in federal employment and training programs. As of FY 1997, spending on these programs was 65 percent below what it had been in FY 1980. Significant cuts also occurred in the field of community development. Social service spending was below FY 1980 levels for much of the FY 1982–97 period but ended up 59 percent above the base year by the end of the period.

EDUCATION AND RESEARCH

Education and research programs registered the second largest amount of cumulative cuts during the FY 1982–97 period, with reductions totaling $59.6 billion over the 16 years.[2] Spending on education and research as a percentage of GDP was reduced by one-third between FY 1980 and FY 1997. Within this broad area, the reductions were concentrated in the subareas of higher education and elementary and secondary education. By comparison, spending for research grew over the period.

HEALTH

Largely as a result of increased spending for Medicare and Medicaid, federal health outlays rose substantially over the FY 1982–97 period. While Medicare and Medicaid spending rose sharply, however, outlays for the smaller health service programs increased by a smaller amount. By FY 1997, health finance outlays were up 94 percent over FY 1980 levels and absorbed more than twice their former share of GDP. Health service spending increased 44 percent over the same period. Taken together, over the period FY 1982–97 health spending rose by $1.2 trillion beyond what would have been spent had FY 1980 funding levels remained in effect.

INCOME ASSISTANCE

Spending on income assistance also increased over the FY 1982–97 period. Housing, cash, and food assistance programs registered increases while several other income assistance programs, including the low-income home energy assistance program (LIHEAP) and refugee and entrant assistance, had their funding reduced. As of FY 1997, the value of federal spending on income assistance was $134.1 billion, or 90 percent, higher than it had been in FY 1980. Altogether, these programs experienced a cumulative increase of $430.9 billion in funding over the FY 1982–97 period, compared with FY 1980 spending levels. The spending increase in this category resulted in part from increases in the poverty population and in part from the automatic adjustment of many of the income assistance programs to economic trends, which were negative at several key points during FY 1982–97.

INTERNATIONAL ASSISTANCE

Spending on international assistance programs, excluding credit programs, also registered increases over FY 1982–97. By FY 1997, foreign aid spending was $12.8 billion, 24 percent above FY 1980.

ARTS AND CULTURE

In contrast, federal spending on arts and culture programs fell substantially over the FY 1982–97 period. In this smaller area, federal spending declined 31 percent between FY 1980 and FY 1997, or by a cumulative total of $7.2 billion.

ENVIRONMENT AND CONSERVATION

In percentage terms, environment and conservation programs registered the biggest drop of all program areas between FY 1980 and FY 1997. By FY 1997, spending for these programs was 86 percent below FY 1980 levels. As a percentage of GDP, environmental spending in FY 1997 was only 9 percent of what it was in FY 1980.[3]

Summary

Overall federal spending in the program areas of concern to nonprofits declined in the early 1980s but subsequently recovered, so that by FY 1997 federal outlays in these areas were 60 percent above FY 1980 levels. This overall trend hides the very different spending histories of different programs, however. Medicare, Medicaid, and many other income assistance programs expanded rapidly throughout much of the FY 1980–97 period, in part because of rising health costs and to address the needs of an expanding poverty population (see table 3.1). Excluding these programs, total spending for the other program areas was actually still below FY 1980 levels in FY 1997, and the share of GDP devoted to these activities was also significantly lower. Thus, over the period FY 1980 to FY 1997, many nonprofits likely experienced greater demand for their services due to reduced federal spending in their program areas.

FEDERAL SUPPORT OF NONPROFITS, FY 1980–97

Changes in overall federal spending during FY 1982–97 in programs of interest to nonprofits not only affected demand on nonprofits for services but also affected their ability to meet this demand because of the impact of the changes on the revenues that nonprofit organizations received from federal programs.

Aggregate Changes: FY 1982–97 vs. FY 1980

Table 3.4 shows that, overall, federal support of private nonprofit organizations grew both in absolute terms and as a share of GDP. These aggregate data, however, mask two strikingly different trends in federal support.

On one hand, growth in federal Medicare and Medicaid programs significantly boosted federal support to private nonprofit health institutions—principally hospitals—and some human service agencies. Over the FY 1980–97 period, real federal support of nonprofit health institutions almost tripled in real terms and almost doubled as a share of GDP.

At the same time, federal funding of many other types of nonprofit organizations either grew much less or fell sharply in the early part of the FY 1982–97 period before recovering somewhat by the end of the period. As shown in table 3.4, by FY 1997 federal support of nonprofits outside of Medicare and Medicaid was 10 percent above FY 1980 levels, but the share of GDP devoted to federal support of nonprofits in FY 1997, excluding support flowing through the Medicare and Medicaid programs, was only 71 percent of what it had been in FY 1980. Moreover, because the increases occurred late in the period and followed a lengthy period during which spending was

Table 3.4 ESTIMATED FEDERAL SUPPORT OF NONPROFIT ORGANIZATIONS BY TYPE OF ORGANIZATION, FY 1982–97
(In Billions of Constant FY 1998 Dollars)

Type of Organization	Amount		Change, FY 1997 vs. FY 1980		Cumulative Change, FY 1982–97 vs. FY 1980	FY 1997 Support as a Percentage of GDP (FY 1980 = 100)
	FY 1980	FY 1997	Amount	Percent		
Social service	$13.2	$16.1	+$2.9	+22	–$35.1	79
Community development	3.2	3.2	0.0	–1	–11.2	64
Education and Research	**10.5**	**11.8**	**+1.2**	**+12**	**–0.2**	**72**
Elementary and secondary	0.7	0.7	–0.1	–8	–3.3	60
Higher education	4.8	2.9	–1.8	–39	–28.2	40
Research and development	5.0	8.2	+3.1	+62	+31.3	105
Health	**48.0**	**136.7**	**+88.7**	**+185**	**+664.9**	**185**
Health finance	45.8	133.8	+88.1	+192	+667.9	190
Health services	2.2	2.9	+0.7	+30	–2.7	84
Foreign aid	1.2	1.5	+0.2	+18	+4.2	77
Arts and culture	0.7	0.4	–0.3	–45	–3.7	35
Total	$76.9	$169.6	+$92.7	+121	+$619.0	143
Total excluding Medicare and Medicaid	$31.4	$34.6	+$3.1	+10	–$55.3	71

Source: See appendix A.

depressed, nonprofits lost a cumulative total of $55.3 billion, or about $3.5 billion per year, in the inflation-adjusted value of federal support from programs other than Medicare and Medicaid, compared to what would have been available had FY 1980 levels been maintained. This represents an 11 percent decline in the value of the federal support. The following sections describe the kinds of changes that lie behind these aggregate shifts.

SOCIAL SERVICE

Social service organizations—including agencies that provide day care, counseling, and related services to children, families, the elderly, and others; legal services; and employment and training services— were the biggest losers in dollar terms over the FY 1982–97 period. These agencies lost a cumulative total of $35.1 billion in federal support during the period, or about $2.2 billion a year. Because of spending increases in the 1990s, however, by FY 1997 the income that social organizations received through federal programs, including Medicaid, was actually 22 percent above what it had been in FY 1980. At the same time, though, as a share of GDP, federal support of social service agencies in FY 1997 was only 79 percent of what it had been in FY 1980.

COMMUNITY DEVELOPMENT

Organizations involved in housing, housing rehabilitation, economic development, neighborhood improvement, land acquisition, and historic preservation also suffered large reductions in federal support over FY 1982–97, with cumulative losses of $11.2 billion. By FY 1997, federal support of community development organizations was still 1 percent below what it had been in FY 1980, and it accounted for only 64 percent of the share of GDP allocated to these organizations in FY 1980.

EDUCATION/RESEARCH

Overall, federal funding of nonprofit education and research organizations fell by a cumulative total of $0.2 billion over FY 1982–97 compared to FY 1980 levels. Outside of student loan and loan guarantee programs, which are excluded from this analysis, assistance to higher-education institutions fell, with the amount of federal support of private colleges and universities declining from $4.8 billion in FY 1980 to $2.9 billion in FY 1997. Federal funding of private elementary and secondary schools, which received little federal assistance to begin with, declined slightly during FY 1982–97. In contrast, the level of federal research support of private nonprofit institutions, including private universities, rose a significant 62 percent between FY 1980 and FY 1997.

HEALTH

The varying impacts of federal funding changes are evident in the health area as well. Federal funding of all nonprofit health institutions rose by a cumulative total of $664.9 billion during the FY 1982–97 period. While federal support of nonprofit hospitals, nursing homes, and other providers through the Medicare, Medicaid, and other health finance programs increased sharply during the period, support for outpatient clinics and other nonprofit health service organizations showed little net change, falling below FY 1980 levels at the beginning of the Reagan administration but then climbing above the base year by the end of the Bush administration.

INTERNATIONAL ASSISTANCE

Federal support of nonprofit organizations in the foreign assistance area rose from $1.2 billion in FY 1980 to $1.5 billion in FY 1997, yielding a cumulative increase of $4.2 billion during the FY 1982–97 period.

ARTS AND CULTURE

Federal support to nonprofit arts and culture organizations, such as museums, art galleries, symphonies, community arts facilities, and theaters, was 45 percent lower in FY 1997 than it was in FY 1980. A significant portion of that loss resulted from the elimination of the public service employment program, which provided important support to numerous community arts agencies. In FY 1997, the share of GDP devoted to federal support of arts organizations was only 35 percent of its FY 1980 level.

Summary

Outside of the health finance, research, and foreign aid fields, federal support of nonprofits thus experienced cumulative declines over the FY 1982–97 period. Because of spending increases in the latter part of the period, however, by FY 1997 federal support of nonprofits was above FY 1980 levels in social services and health services as well as health finance, research, and foreign aid. In the remaining areas— community development, elementary and secondary schools, higher education, and arts and culture—federal support of nonprofit organizations was still lower in FY 1997 than it had been in FY 1980, in some cases by 35 percent or more. Overall, outside of Medicare and Medicaid, the amount of federal support flowing to nonprofits declined 29 percent as a share of GDP from FY 1980 to FY 1997.

More and more during this period, the support available to nonprofits flowed through the Medicare and Medicaid programs. In FY 1980, funding of nonprofits through these two programs already accounted for almost 60 percent of total federal support of nonprofits. By FY 1997, it made up nearly 80 percent of federal support of nonprofits, with the largest portion going to voluntary hospitals and private nonprofit nursing homes and a smaller portion flowing to nonprofit human service agencies.

TAX CHANGES AND CHARITABLE GIVING

The 1980s and 1990s were a period not only of significant shifts in federal spending but also of major changes in tax policy. Tax provisions are important because they affect private giving in a number of ways.

First, tax rates affect the "price of giving" to charity. The price of giving reflects the net, out-of-pocket cost of giving to charity. As an example, for an individual itemizing deductions and in the 45 percent tax bracket, the cost of giving $100 to charity is $55, since the government would have taken $45 more in tax if that income were not given away. The individual is given a choice between consuming $55 himself or giving $100 to charity. When the tax rate falls to 35 percent, the cost of the gift will rise to $65, which is the amount of consumption that the giver could undertake rather than give the $100 to charity. Conversely, when the tax rate rises, the cost of giving decreases and the incentive to give to charity increases.

Changes in tax policy also can affect charitable giving by increasing or decreasing the amount of income people have to spend. For instance, a reduction in tax rates might initially increase the income of individuals, thereby leading to a rise in giving through what economists call an "income" effect. One complication is that a reduction in current taxes must be paid for either by cutting government spending or by raising future taxes to pay for current borrowing. Those changes have their own income effects that may offset the initial effect. During the period examined here, however, average tax rate changes were generally implemented in a "revenue-neutral" fashion, which meant that tax collections as a proportion of total income ended the period fairly close to where they began.[4] Thus, income effects due to tax changes should have had only modest effects on the percent of income given to charity.

Expansions in the income tax *base* were also important, especially in the 1980s. Broadening the base of income subject to tax tended to increase the amount of reported, taxable income against which charitable contributions could be deducted. Moreover, by removing many tax shelter opportunities in the 1980s, tax-base broadening essentially elevated the relative status of the charitable deduction so that today it is one of the few significant ways that taxpayers can reduce taxes through discretionary action, especially at the end of the year.

Finally, there were a number of more moderate changes, such as the provision and elimination of a charitable deduction for non-itemizers, and the treatment of capital gain property donated to foundations.

Tax Changes: 1980–97

The 1980–97 period saw constant revision in the tax code. Most important for charitable giving, the price of giving was altered as tax rates were first lowered and then raised, although not back to their original levels. Because net income tax rates were lowered, individuals and corporations had less incentive to give to charity. In addition, a variety of changes were made in such areas as the treatment of appreciated assets, maximum deductible gifts to foundations, and corporate charitable giving. Some increased the incentive to give; some decreased it. This section highlights those changes and their effects.

ECONOMIC RECOVERY TAX ACT OF 1981

Perhaps the most important of the tax changes affecting charitable giving occurred at the beginning of this period. The Economic Recovery Tax Act of 1981 (ERTA) reduced marginal tax rates by approximately 23 percent between 1981 and the end of 1984. Indexing of tax brackets for inflation was introduced after 1984. This indexing checked future rises in tax rates, thereby also slowing the increase in the incentive to give.

The effect of these individual tax rate reductions on changes in giving is sometimes exaggerated, however. Tax rates had risen dramatically at the end of the 1970s, due largely to inflation-related "bracket creep." The 1981 tax cuts represented a return to lower real tax rates. Thus, when viewed from the perspective of a single point in time, the 1981 tax reductions seemed to signal a sharp increase in the price of giving. When viewed with a somewhat longer time horizon, however, the increase in the cost of giving in 1981 was in part a return to prior levels, after an unusually sharp fall in the late 1970s.

In addition, there has been some bracket creep since the early 1980s,[5] which has resulted from two factors. First, indexing was only for inflation, so real growth in incomes still pushes individuals gradually into higher brackets. Second, the period from the mid-1970s to the mid-1990s witnessed greater inequality of income. Some of this inequality was due to disparities in individual incomes, some to rising numbers of two-earner couples with good incomes for both spouses at one end and rising numbers of single heads of households at the other. As a consequence, more individuals would face higher tax rates today than in 1984, for example, regardless of later legislative changes in 1990 and 1993 that also increased tax rates.

The 1981 tax cut also established for the first time a charitable deduction for non-itemizers, thereby increasing their incentive to give. Starting at a very low level in 1982, when only 25 percent of contributions were deductible up to a maximum of $100, this deduction grew until 1986, when 100 percent of charitable contributions were to be deductible with no limit. The 1981 provisions, however, gave no allowance for deductions for non-itemizers beyond 1986, and the law was never extended. Since individuals probably lag in response to changes in tax provisions, many economists believe that the full impact of such a deduction, and its ability to increase charitable giving, was probably never fully tested. After all, there was a full deduction for non-itemizers in only one year, 1986.

Corporate tax changes also reduced tax incentives for corporate charitable giving. The 1981 act significantly increased tax write-offs for depreciation, which allowed many corporations to reduce their taxable income toward zero. A charitable deduction is of little immediate value to a corporation with little or no taxable income.

The incentive to give at time of death was also weakened because estate tax rates were lowered significantly. The allowance of a complete spousal benefit within the estate—before 1981, transfers to spouses could be taxable—also reduced incentives to give. In effect, no tax was assessed on the first spouse to die, and it became less important to plan for charitable giving before the death of the first spouse.[6]

DEFICIT REDUCTION ACT OF 1984

The Deficit Reduction Act of 1984 also affected charitable giving, but only slightly. Compliance was strengthened by the requirement for qualified written appraisals for contributions of property valued at $5,000 or more, excluding property with readily quotable market prices such as stocks and bonds. The limit on gifts to private foundations was increased from 20 to 30 percent, but overall limits on all giving at 50 percent of charitable giving were not altered. Although the net impact on charitable giving was small, the step did help simplify the treatment of gifts to foundations.

TAX REFORM ACT OF 1986

The Tax Reform Act of 1986 again lowered marginal tax rates substantially. The top rate was reduced to 33 percent for those with moderately high incomes and to 28 percent for those with the highest levels of taxable income. The corporate rate was reduced from 46 percent to 34 percent. At the same time, this act attacked a variety of tax shelters and mechanisms by which individuals had been able to reduce taxes through manipulation of portfolios and purchase of tax shelters. Although the rate reduction again pared the tax incentive to give, the reduction in tax shelter opportunities increased incentives. That is, those individuals who avoided tax through tax shelters probably never had much incentive for charitable giving, regardless of the tax rate, because they had much lower taxable income because of the shelters.

By increasing the standard deduction that can be taken in lieu of itemizing deductions (including charitable gifts), the 1986 Tax Reform Act also weakened the incentive to give. Again, the effect of this change is exaggerated by looking only at a point in time. The late 1970s and early 1980s, in particular, had eroded the value of the standard deduction and, accordingly, boosted the number of itemizers significantly. The 1986 act in many ways only restored a balance that had existed in prior years and followed a tradition of many postwar acts. As noted above, there has also been real bracket creep, so that the standard deduction and personal exemptions have generally risen more slowly than have real wages. Another relevant side effect has been an increase in the number of itemizers (although other changes such as declines in interest rates reduced deductions that could be itemized and tended to mitigate the size of the increase).

The 1986 act also reduced the incentive for charitable giving by strengthening the use of the Alternative Minimum Tax (AMT). This tax essentially establishes a second tax base and a second set of tax rates as an alternative to the regular income tax. The taxpayer is then required to pay the higher of regular tax or AMT. While the tax rates for AMT are lower, the base is broader. Indeed, many individuals would argue that the AMT base includes items that do not really belong in any tax base (e.g., the AMT does not allow for a personal exemption, and the "preferences" that are most likely to evoke AMT liability are the deduction for state income taxes and miscellaneous deductions like work expenses).

A change in the AMT of special relevance to charities was the addition to the AMT base of unrealized capital gains on gifts of appreciated property. The rationale for that change was that the income on such gains was never recognized for tax purposes. To allow it to be deducted as a charitable contribution, therefore, created a double deduction. As a simplified example, if one person earned $100 of additional wages and gave that $100 to charity, her taxable income would be $0 thanks to the charitable deduction—the $100 in income would be offset by a charitable deduction of $100. If another person earned $100 in additional accrued capital gains and gave the asset containing those gains to charity (the simplest example would be an asset that initially was almost worth nothing and grew in value to $100), his additional taxable income would equal minus $100; income would be zero before the deduction, as unrealized capital gains are not taxable, and the deduction would allow $100 to be subtracted from other taxable income.

One difficulty with including appreciated property in the tax base, however, was that there was no change in the treatment of appreciated assets at death. Accordingly, a person who held an appreciated asset could still forgo the tax on the appreciation and also give cash away to charity during life. That person would still benefit from both the nontaxation of the appreciation and the charitable deduction, just as in the example above. The 1986 law, therefore, actually provided a disincentive to giving away appreciated property instead of cash for those taxpayers likely to hold appreciated property until death.

OMNIBUS RECONCILIATION ACT OF 1990

In the Omnibus Reconciliation Act of 1990, Congress sought to induce more charitable giving by excluding from the AMT for 1991 capital gains on contributions of tangible personal property.[7] Museums, for example, experienced significant declines in gifts during the late 1980s. The 1990 legislative change was designed mainly to deal with museums' great difficulty in generating donations of art work and other collectibles when an AMT might be levied on that amount.

The 1990 act also saw some slight movement toward raising tax rates, thereby increasing the incentive to give. Tax rates were raised directly for a few individuals at the top of the income distribution. The top rate of 28 percent was increased to 31 percent, although some offset occurred through a lowering of an effective 33 percent rate for upper-middle-income taxpayers back to 31 percent.

Some other tax rate increases, however, provided no added incentive for more charitable giving. Health insurance (HI) tax rates were raised in Social Security by increasing significantly the cap on which the HI tax would be paid. Since Social Security allows no deductions for charitable contributions, there was no immediate effect, at least in terms of the price of giving, but a negative income effect could actually result from a higher tax bill. Any trend toward non–income tax sources reduces the potential incentive that would apply if the same additional revenues were to be collected from the income tax. The greater the reliance upon non–income tax sources, the smaller the relative incentive to give.

In a similar vein, the 1990 act restored and redesigned some provisions intended to increase tax rates indirectly. Personal exemptions were to be phased out, that is, reduced in value as income increased. A phaseout of itemized deductions was also created for taxpayers with incomes over $100,000. The phaseout effectively reduced itemized deductions by three cents for each dollar of income earned above this base. At a 31 percent tax rate, the phaseout was equivalent to a 0.96 percent additional tax rate.

Although the itemized deduction phaseout resulted in a small increase in the effective tax rate, the effects of the change on charitable giving were rather different from those that would have resulted from directly increasing the marginal tax rate by the same amount. What matters is that the effective tax rate on an extra $1 of income was increased by scaling back the amount of *itemized deductions*. Thus, while an extra $1 of income would raise taxable income by more than $1 and hence be taxed at an effective rate of 31.96 percent instead of 31 percent, an extra $1 of charitable contributions would still be deductible at the statutory rate of 31 percent because it usually lowers taxable income by exactly $1.[8]

Thus, the itemized deduction phaseout created a modest negative income effect by raising taxes, while usually keeping the marginal incentive to give the same. Symbolically, the itemized deduction phaseout also may have signaled that itemized deductions generally are not fully justifiable, and that charitable deductions are deemed no more worthy than deductions for interest expense or state and local taxes. Overall, then, the effect of raising tax rates indirectly in this manner was to weaken the tax incentive for charitable giving.

Perhaps most important, however, is that the itemized deduction phaseout tends to displace the income tax with other "taxes" for which no deduction is allowed. In the above example, the itemized deduction limitation effectively created an additional 0.96 percent tax rate for someone in the regular 31 percent bracket. This additional rate, however, was not added directly to the tax rate schedule. If it were, the taxpayer would receive a deduction worth 31.96 percent rather than one worth only 31 percent. As Congress moves back and forth—raising rates indirectly, then lowering them directly—the more likely it becomes that the net impact will be to reduce the importance of the charitable deduction.

OMNIBUS RECONCILIATION ACT OF 1993

In the Omnibus Reconciliation Act of 1993, tax rates for the highest-income taxpayers were raised significantly—from 31 percent to 39.6 percent at the very top (taxable incomes greater than $250,000) and to 36 percent at lower income levels ($140,000 of taxable income for a joint return). The higher rates again increased the incentive to give, as the relative cost of consuming out of that income, rather than giving the money away, was raised.

Gains on appreciated property were totally eliminated from the AMT tax base in this act, thereby restoring incentives to give away appreciated property. The preference was extended beyond tangible property to include gifts of stock, bonds, and other intangible assets.

To pay for the change in the AMT rules, the 1993 act moved to discourage noncompliance in the area of charitable giving. It required written substantiation from charities for gifts of $250 or more and also tightened the disclosure requirements for quid pro quo contributions, where the taxpayer receives some benefit for the gift made. In the former case, even canceled checks of taxpayers would be deemed insufficient evidence for a deduction. How these requirements will play out over time, and to what extent charities and taxpayers can implement them fully, remains to be seen.

TAXPAYER BILL OF RIGHTS ACT II OF 1996

As part of a "taxpayer bill of rights," Congress decided that certain abuses by charities should not cause outright repeal of their exempt status but instead should lead to penalties and excise taxes called "intermediate" sanctions. It also increased the responsibility of exempt organizations to provide copies of their returns. Better availability of returns through organizations such as the National Center for Charitable Statistics at the Urban Institute, plus the electronic transmission of scanned returns or the data on them, is likely soon to make the additional return availability requirements in the Taxpayer Bill of

Rights Act II unnecessary. Nonetheless, as information on nonprofits becomes much more easily accessible, public scrutiny of their activities is likely to intensify and even revolutionize the sector itself (Steuerle 1998).

SMALL BUSINESS TAX BILL OF 1996

In 1969, Congress enacted a number of antiabuse provisions against private foundations. It also denied deductions equal to fair market value for contributions of appreciated property to those foundations. In 1984, it reinstated full deductibility for such gifts (still subject to limits on gifts as a percent of income) for 10 years until the end of 1994. Then, in the Small Business Tax Bill of 1996, it temporarily extended full deductibility again, but only for 11 months from July 1, 1996, to May 31, 1997. Because only foundations were affected, the effect on overall charitable giving was less than for foundations, especially as public charities (and now mutual funds such as Fidelity and Vanguard) have increasingly been able to serve as partial substitutes and acquire some of the characteristics of foundations. Nonetheless, the constant change in the law, and some of the arbitrary distinctions between foundations and other charities, added to legal and planning costs and affected the timing of gifts unnecessarily.

TAX ACT OF 1997

In 1997, Congress enacted the first significant legislative tax reduction since 1981, although its aggregate size was much smaller. Among the more important provisions affecting charities was a reduction in the rate of tax on capital gains property and an increase in wealth exempt from the estate tax. The latter was not all that great, especially when compared with increases in societal income and wealth since the early 1980s. The capital gains tax reduction mainly reduced the price of consumption out of capital gains property and, consequently, raised the *relative* price of giving, rather than consuming, for a few individuals. The act also continued the practice of temporarily restoring (in this case, to June 30, 1998) the deduction for gifts of qualified stock to private foundations.

Net Effect on Charitable Giving

On balance, the overall thrust of tax policy in the 1980s and 1990s appears to have weakened the financial incentive for charitable giving. The net effect of these changes, however, depends on how individuals and corporations react to changes in such financial incentives, and the jury is still out on this issue.

When tax rates were cut in 1981 and 1986, the rise in the price of giving was widely expected to cut charitable contributions sharply. This expectation was based on econometric studies predicting that a 1 percent increase in the price of charitable giving would reduce charitable giving by at least 1 percent. Thus, some authors predicted that giving would fall by 15 percent in response to the rate cuts enacted in the 1986 act, and the same models had predicted that total giving in the 1980s would be cut by as much as 40 percent as a result of the 1981 act.[9]

These predictions, however, only partially fit the facts. Wealthy individuals, for example, experienced sharp increases in the after-tax cost of giving between 1980 and 1994, when the after-tax price of giving $1 rose from 30 cents to 69 cents between 1980 and 1991 and then fell back to about 60 cents in 1994 and beyond.[10] Consistent with predictions, giving has dropped significantly at the very high end of the income distribution (see previous chapter by Steuerle and Hodgkinson), but not by as much as might have been expected. Moreover, outside of that group, predicted drops in giving were not observed. Indeed, Steuerle and Hodgkinson note, giving as a percent of income has remained remarkably constant in the face of increases in the cost of giving.

Analysts have debated why the predictions of econometric models of giving have failed to materialize. Possible reasons include the fact that individuals may adjust to changes both in incomes and tax rates only slowly over time, until they are sure that their circumstances have changed permanently.

More recent econometric work has also raised questions about the results from earlier econometric studies. For example, the availability of panel data has allowed analysts to examine the behavior of the same taxpayers over several years—how they react to changes that they perceive to be temporary and to those that are permanent. A widely cited study using these data has found that people tend to react less sharply to changes in the price of giving that they believe to be permanent than they do to changes in the price of giving that result from temporary tax changes (Randolph 1995).

Still, there is a great deal of uncertainty as to how to interpret the data. For example, although the *rate* of giving by wealthy individuals has fallen, the *share* of giving by the highest-income taxpayers has gone up.[11] In effect, their giving simply has not gone up as fast as the income of the top group (which admits many newcomers over time).

If these individuals also have not fully adjusted to their higher relative status on the income scale—in the language of the studies, if they have not yet fully adjusted to their "permanent" income—then we may not yet have witnessed the rate of giving to which higher-income individuals will eventually adjust.

Another issue of special concern is that all these models predict what happens to giving by individuals while ignoring the possible feedback between donors' behavior and the ability of charities to meet social needs. If givers start to contribute less because incentives are reduced, the unmet needs of charities would rise immediately because support had fallen. These higher needs may reverberate back to induce individuals to give more. As an example, the fixed cost of running a church or a school may be invariant to the price of giving. It is the intersection of demand for giving (relative to other consumers' wants) and supply of needs that leads to the actual quantity of giving at different prices, at least if the economic model of giving is extended fully. Note that the combined demand and supply effects could also change the distribution of giving—e.g., reducing the share given by higher-income individuals as tax rates fall—even when total giving is unchanged. Kent Smetters has developed a model where individuals meet needs according to both the benefits from the charitable activity (a portion of which comes back to the individual in, say, better communities in which to live or other "externalities") and the price of giving as set in the tax code. That model yields some hypothetical response rates that can be made to roughly duplicate the historical shift in giving from higher- to lower-income households.[12]

Compliance effects are also hard to sort out. For instance, reporting on noncash contributions became stricter in 1985, but fewer individuals were audited as the 1980s progressed. Even numbers on the amount of charitable giving are partially suspect because of misreporting.

In sum, tax changes since 1980 have significantly affected the price of charitable giving and have almost certainly reduced incentives to give (see table 3.5). Tax rate decreases and some later increases were the most important among these changes. Independently of statutory rate changes, however, Congress has also tended increasingly to turn to tax sources other than the income tax or to charge a different tax rate on income earned than on deductions made. Over time, these tendencies reduce incentives for charitable giving, both by preventing a dollar of giving from offsetting a dollar of income subject to tax and, when taxes on net income increase, by reducing after-tax income. Changes in compliance rules and efforts, although unmeasured, also

Table 3.5 MAJOR TAX CHANGES SINCE 1980 AFFECTING CHARITABLE
CONTRIBUTIONS

Change in Incentive to Give	Major Tax Laws and Provisions Affecting Charitable Contributions
	Economic Recovery Tax Act of 1981
−	• Reduced individual marginal income tax by about 23% between 1981 and 1984; maximum rate reduced to 50% and capital gains rate to 20%.
−	• Top estate taxes rate scheduled to be reduced from 70% to 50%, exempt amounts raised, and a complete marital deduction allowed.
+	• Introduced charitable deduction for non-itemizers for 1982–86. Amount deductible rose from 25% of contributions up to $100 in 1982, to 100% of all contributions in 1986.
+	• Increased limit on corporate contributions from 5% to 10% of net income (effective 1982).
+	• Allowed deduction for scientific property used for college or university research on its basis plus 50% of the capital gain (previously only for medical equipment).
	Deficit Reduction Act of 1984
?	• Required signed qualified written appraisals for contributions of property valued at $5,000 or more (except securities with prices quoted on exchanges).
−	• Increased penalties for inflated appraisals.
+	• Increased limit on gifts to private foundations from 20% to 30% of adjusted gross income.
+	• Increased mileage allowance for use of passenger cars in performing services for charities from 9 cents to 12 cents per mile.
	Tax Reform Act of 1986
−	• Reduced individual marginal income tax rates by 1988 to range of 15% to 33%, with rate at highest income levels equal to 28%.
+	• Reduced opportunities to shelter income.
−	• Reduced corporate tax rate from 46% to 34%.
−	• Reduced number of itemizers by increasing standard deduction and reducing certain itemized deductions.
−	• Capital gains in gifts of appreciated property included as a preference under the Alternative Minimum Tax (AMT).
+	• Capital gains tax rates increased by elimination of exclusion; maximum rate equal to 28%.
−	• Charitable deduction for non-itemizers allowed to expire.
	Omnibus Budget Reconciliation Act of 1990
+	• Excluded capital gains on contributions of tangible personal property (such as art or antiques) from the AMT for 1991. Capital gains on stock, real property, conservation easement, etc., still subject to AMT. Exclusion extended to June 1992 in the Tax Extension Act of 1991.
+	• Increased individual income tax rate to 31% and altered "bubble" rates.

Table 3.5 MAJOR TAX CHANGES SINCE 1980 AFFECTING CHARITABLE
CONTRIBUTIONS (*continued*)

Change in Incentive to Give	Major Tax Laws and Provisions Affecting Charitable Contributions
–	• Introduced phaseout of itemized deductions for taxpayers with incomes over $100,000. Equivalent approximately to a 0.93% tax rate against which no charitable deductions are allowed.
+	• Increased alternative minimum tax rate to 24%.

Omnibus Budget Reconciliation Act of 1993

+	• Raised 31% top rate to 39.6% (36% when taxable income is less than $250,000).
+	• Made permanent the top estate tax rate of 55% (rather than 50% as scheduled as a final drop from 1981 act but continually delayed).
+	• Eliminated from the AMT all gains on appreciated property given to charity.
?	• Required written substantiation from charities for deductions of gifts of $250 or more, and increased disclosure requirements for quid pro quo contributions.

Taxpayer Bill of Rights Act II of 1996

+	• Imposed "intermediate sanction"—in lieu of outright removal of tax exemption—on certain self-dealing and excessive benefits for disqualified persons.

Small Business Tax Bill of 1996

+	• Temporarily restored, from July 1, 1996, to May 31, 1997, a deduction equal to fair market value for "qualified" appreciated stock contributed to a private foundation (previously denied in 1969 legislation, then allowed from 1985 to 1994 in 1984 legislation).
?	• Increased responsibilities of charities to provide copies of tax returns to the public.

Tax Act of 1997

–	• Lowered capital gains tax rate to a maximum of 20% (and for some average-income taxpayers to 10%). The maximum rate is lowered again to 18% for property held or owned more than five years and purchased after December 31, 2000.
+	• Temporarily restored again, from June 1, 1997, to June 30, 1998, a deduction equal to fair market value for "qualified" appreciated stock contributed to a private foundation.
–	• Increased the estate and gift tax unified credit from $600,000 to $1 million by 2006. Also allowed an exclusion for some qualified family-owned businesses from the estate tax.
+	• Increased the standard mileage rate to 14 cents per mile for computing charitable deductions.
?	• Eliminated certain abuses with respect to charitable remainder trusts.

Sources: Auten, Cilke, and Randolph 1992; Steuerle 1992, with revisions and updates.

seem to be important. The temporary inclusion of gifts of appreciated property in the AMT base did seem to reduce giving, but mainly at the top of the income distribution with respect to tangible property, and some of the decline was certainly a response to a stimulus that some regarded as temporary.

Many of the annual changes in giving detected throughout this period of tax revision must be interpreted with caution. Constant changes in the tax code itself may confuse tax planners and charities. Any particular year's giving may reflect several lagged responses to legal changes that occurred over time. Some individuals, moreover, change the timing of their giving in response both to past and expected tax changes.

Outlook

What does all this imply as we near the end of the century? Roughly speaking, half of the budget is taxes, half expenditures. We can no more expect Congress to leave the tax code alone than we can expect it to leave spending laws constant. Recent years have witnessed debates over income tax cuts, fundamental tax reform (e.g., a "flat" tax), and tax increases to deal with fiscal imbalance in programs for the elderly. As Congress increasingly turns toward paying for government from sources outside the income tax—through other taxes or through mandates—the immediate direct impact on total charitable giving is likely to be minimal. Over time, however, eroded support for the income tax as a means of financing will reduce charitable incentives. For example, cycles of tax increases and tax decreases might substitute non–income tax financing for income taxes. Disguised tax rate increases, such as limits on itemized deductions, raise similar concerns.

Closer scrutiny of charities themselves is also likely in the future. Unrelated business activity, salaries of top officials, the use of advertising, and the use of "foundation-like" charities without the restrictions of foundations (e.g., run through mutual fund companies) will probably receive renewed government attention. One potentially revolutionary change—more public scrutiny of tax forms filed by charities—is just around the corner. All this attention, in turn, may well induce charities to find improved private mechanisms for monitoring themselves. Depending upon how any or all of these changes are implemented, they could either increase or decrease giving, and they could either improve or reduce the efficiency of giving.

FEDERAL BUDGET CHANGES AND PRIVATE GIVING

The impact of tax changes on private giving is so important because one of the major arguments advanced by advocates of budget cuts in the early 1980s was that these cuts could easily be offset by growth in private giving. It is therefore appropriate to ask to what extent this hopeful expectation was actually met.

As reflected in the previous discussion, this question involves two separate issues: first, the extent to which private giving offset the reductions that occurred in overall federal spending in fields where nonprofits are active; and second, the extent to which this giving offset the direct revenue losses to nonprofit agencies in these fields.

In making this comparison, we do not suggest that everything the federal government has supported is worthy of continued support by the private sector or anyone else, or that private charity should be used for the same things as government funds. Nor do we suggest here that private support is in some sense "better" than public support, or vice versa. Rather the intent is to put the cuts that occurred into some perspective and to shed some light on a comparison that has too often been a subject of casual speculation.

Did Private Giving Offset the Budget Changes in FY 1982–95?

In FY 1980, private giving from all sources totaled about $87.6 billion, adjusted for inflation and expressed in terms of FY 1998 dollars.[13] Of that amount, about $48.1 billion went to churches and synagogues for sacramental religious activities; to health organizations that did not experience reductions in either the overall level of federal activity or in their levels of federal support; or to foundation endowments that were not available to defray the costs of service provision in the year in which the gift was given. That leaves a base of about $39.5 billion in private giving as of FY 1980 that flowed to the types of organizations that were negatively affected by subsequent federal budget cuts of the early 1980s.

Private Giving and the Service Gap

Federal spending in fields where nonprofits were active, excluding health and income assistance, was below FY 1980 levels through the 1980s and 1990s. As shown in column 2 of table 3.6, between FY 1982 and FY 1995, overall federal spending in these fields dropped a cu-

Table 3.6 CHANGES IN FEDERAL SPENDING COMPARED TO CHANGES IN PRIVATE GIVING, FY 1980–95, EXCLUDING HEALTH AND INCOME ASSISTANCE (In Billions of Constant FY 1998 Dollars)

FY	Change from FY 1980 Levels in:			Private Giving Change as Percentage of:	
	Federal Spending in Areas of Interest to Nonprofits[a]	Federal Support of Nonprofits[b]	Private Giving[c]	Change in Federal Spending in Areas of Interest to Nonprofits	Change in Federal Support of Nonprofits
1982	−$26.4	−$6.7	−$1.3	5	20
1983	−30.1	−7.6	+2.7	9	35
1984	−30.9	−7.6	+4.3	14	56
1985	−26.1	−6.5	+5.5	21	85
1986	−27.2	−6.4	+10.8	40	169
1987	−32.0	−6.8	+11.6	36	171
1988	−30.1	−5.9	+13.1	43	221
1989	−26.5	−4.2	+15.4	58	365
1990	−25.0	−4.4	+18.2	73	416
1991	−19.4	−2.0	+18.6	96	933
1992	−16.7	−0.7	+19.9	119	3,024
1993	−12.7	+1.1	+22.2	176	—
1994	−10.9	+2.2	+22.5	207	—
1995	−9.3	+3.3	+26.1	281	—
Total	−$323.2	−$52.2	+$192.2	59	369

Source: Data on private giving are adapted from calendar year data in Hodgkinson et al. (1996) and unpublished estimates by Independent Sector. Independent Sector, in turn, relies in part on giving data in AAFRC Trust for Philanthropy (1996). See also appendix A.
a. Excludes health and income assistance programs.
b. Excludes health programs.
c. Private giving to other than health or sacramental religious activities. Includes 20 percent of religious giving; excludes a one-time gift to the arts of $1.3 billion in calendar year 1982.

mulative total of $323.2 billion below what it would have been had FY 1980 levels been maintained.

Compared to the $323.2 billion cut in federal support, private giving for other than sacramental religious purposes and health increased by $192.2 billion during the same period, after adjusting for inflation, as shown in column 4 of the same table. In other words, the growth in private giving during those 14 years offset only 59 percent of the reduction in federal government spending that occurred. Only in the field of arts and culture did increased private giving make up for overall federal budget cuts throughout the FY 1982–95 period. Since overall federal international affairs spending was not cut during this period, there was no gap for private giving to fill in this field. In the areas of human services, housing and community development, and education, however, private giving failed to offset federal budget cuts for all or nearly all the FY 1982–95 period (see table 3.7, column 5).[14]

If private giving growth was not sufficient to offset the absolute declines in federal spending on programs of interest to nonprofits outside of health and income assistance, it did even worse in maintaining such spending at the share of GDP it had achieved as of 1980. The cumulative private giving increase of $192.2 billion during the period was enough to offset only 28 percent of the amount needed to maintain the share of GDP going to these programs as of 1980, as also shown in table 3.8.

Private Giving and Past Changes in Nonprofit Revenues

If private giving was not sufficient to offset the overall reduction in federal spending in fields between 1982 and 1995, however, it was at least able to make up for the reductions in federal support of non-profits. As shown in table 3.6, column 3, the losses in federal support totaled an inflation-adjusted $52.2 billion during FY 1982–95. The $192.2 billion in real growth in private giving that occurred in these areas during the same period was thus 3.7 times the revenue losses experienced by nonprofits. Indeed the growth in giving was more than enough to offset the decline in the share of GDP representing federal support to nonprofits during this period. In both cases, however, this favorable outcome did not materialize until the early 1990s. This means that from FY 1982 through FY 1992 cumulative reductions in federal support outpaced the cumulative increases in private giving.

Table 3.7   CHANGES IN PRIVATE GIVING COMPARED TO CHANGES IN FEDERAL SPENDING IN AREAS OF CONCERN TO NONPROFITS AND FEDERAL SUPPORT OF NONPROFITS, BY FIELD, FY 1982–95 VS. FY 1980, EXCLUDING HEALTH AND INCOME ASSISTANCE (In Billions of Constant FY 1998 Dollars)

Field	Cumulative Change, FY 1982–95 vs. FY 1980			Period in Which Cumulative Change in Giving Is Less Than Cumulative Change in:	
	Private Giving	Federal Spending in Areas of Concern to Nonprofits[a]	Federal Support of Nonprofits[b]	Federal Spending in Areas of Concern to Nonprofits	Federal Support of Nonprofits
Human Services[c]	+$48.0	−$175.7	−$39.1	1982–95	1982–93
Housing and Community Development[d]	+34.5	−114.9	−11.2	1982–95	1982–89
Education	+66.9	−63.0	−2.5	1982–94	1982–85
International Affairs	+6.5	+47.0	+3.7	No years	1982–83
Arts and Culture	+38.9	−6.2	−3.1	No years	No years

Source: Data on private giving are adapted from calendar year data in Hodgkinson et al. (1996) and unpublished estimates by Independent Sector. Independent Sector, in turn, relies in part on giving data in AAFRC Trust for Philanthropy (1996). See also appendix A.

a. Excludes health and income assistance.

b. Excludes health.

c. Includes social services and employment and training.

d. Includes public benefit and environment.

Table 3.8 CHANGE IN GIVING REQUIRED TO MAINTAIN FEDERAL SPENDING IN NONPROFIT AREAS AND FEDERAL SUPPORT OF NONPROFITS AT THEIR FY 1980 SHARE OF GDP VS. ACTUAL CHANGE IN PRIVATE GIVING, FY 1980–95, EXCLUDING HEALTH AND INCOME ASSISTANCE (In Billions of Constant FY 1998 Dollars)

FY	Private Giving Change Required to Maintain FY 1980 Share of GDP in:		Actual Change from FY 1980 Level in Private Giving[c]	Private Giving Change as Percentage of Change in:	
	Federal Spending in Areas of Interest to Nonprofits[a]	Federal Support of Nonprofits[b]		Federal Spending in Areas of Interest to Nonprofits	Federal Support of Nonprofits
1982	$26.8	$6.9	$1.3	5	19
1983	32.5	8.3	2.7	8	32
1984	41.1	10.4	4.3	10	41
1985	40.9	10.6	5.5	13	52
1986	46.4	11.7	10.8	23	92
1987	54.1	12.9	11.6	21	90
1988	57.3	13.4	13.1	23	98
1989	58.5	13.0	15.4	26	118
1990	59.7	13.9	18.2	30	131
1991	52.4	11.1	18.6	36	168
1992	52.4	10.5	19.9	38	190
1993	52.1	9.8	22.2	43	228
1994	55.0	9.9	22.5	41	227
1995	57.1	9.8	26.1	46	266
Total	$686.3	$152.1	$192.2	28	126

Source: Data on private giving are adapted from calendar year data in Hodgkinson et al. (1996) and unpublished estimates by Independent Sector. Independent Sector, in turn, relies in part on giving data in AAFRC Trust for Philanthropy (1996). See also appendix A.

a. Excludes health and income assistance programs.

b. Excludes health programs.

c. Private giving to other than health or sacramental religious activities. Includes 20 percent of religious giving; excludes a one-time gift to the arts of $1.3 billion in calendar year 1982.

Summary

As of FY 1995, increased private giving had failed to compensate for overall federal spending cuts in areas of concern to nonprofits, outside of health and income assistance. Moreover, only in FY 1993 did increased giving offset the cumulative nonprofit revenue gap resulting from reduced federal support. Thus, throughout much of the 1980s and 1990s, many nonprofits were at best only partially successful at replacing lost federal dollars with new, private charitable support.

THE FUTURE OF FEDERAL-NONPROFIT RELATIONS

Nor does it appear likely that this situation will change in the foreseeable future. To the contrary, despite the appearance of a budget surplus, the budget proposals put forward in President Clinton's FY 1999 budget would continue the past two decades' pattern of boosting health and income assistance spending while restraining or reducing spending in most other areas of concern to nonprofit organizations.[15] Thus, while overall federal spending in budget functions of concern to nonprofits would be higher in FY 2003 than it is in FY 1998 under the president's proposed budget, most of that increase is concentrated in the areas of health and income assistance (see table 3.9). Outside these two areas, federal spending under the president's budget will actually decline by another 2 percent between FY 1998 and FY 2003. These further reductions are mostly concentrated in community development and international aid, with modest increases projected in education, social services, and employment and training. Even these increases, however, were largely dependent on the successful conclusion of the failed "tobacco settlement," at least that version which would have brought the federal government substantial new revenues through higher taxes on cigarette sales.

Even with the tobacco revenues, therefore, the budget available as of this writing would still as of FY 2003 have left the inflation-adjusted value of federal spending on programs of interest to nonprofits, outside of health and income assistance, approximately 26 percent below the level reached in FY 1980. This means that approximately $136.4 billion in spending will be cut out of the stream of resources available for purposes in which nonprofits have a special interest over the next five years, compared with what would be available if FY 1980 spending levels were in place (see table 3.9, last figure excluding tobacco

Table 3.9 FEDERAL SPENDING IN BUDGET FUNCTIONS OF INTEREST TO NONPROFIT ORGANIZATIONS, PROPOSED FY 2003 OUTLAYS UNDER PRESIDENT CLINTON'S FY 1999 BUDGET VS. PROJECTED FY 1998 AND ACTUAL FY 1980 SPENDING LEVELS (In Billions of Constant FY 1998 Dollars)

Budget Function	Proposed FY 2003 vs. FY 1998		Proposed FY 2003 vs. FY 1980		Cumulative FY 1999–2003 vs. FY 1980	FY 2003 Outlays as Pct. of GDP (FY 1980 = 100)
	Amount	Percent	Amount	Percent		
Education, Training, Employment, Social Services	+$3.8	+7	–$2.7	–4	–$13.1	54
Community and Regional Development	–5.0	–42	–15.1	–69	–65.3	18
Health*	+40.1	+11	+211.1	+117	+960.5	212
Income Assistance	+19.1	+8	+90.6	+54	+430.6	87
International Affairs	–0.4	–3	–10.5	–43	–51.1	33
Total above	+$57.8	+9	+$273.4	+60	+$1,261.5	111
Total, excluding Health and Income Assistance	–$1.5	–2	–$28.3	–26	–$129.6	42
Total, excluding Health, Income Assistance, and Tobacco Legislation	–$3.1	–4	–$29.8	–28	–$136.4	41

Source: OMB 1998. Conversion to constant 1998 dollars was accomplished by using the gross domestic product (GDP) implicit price deflator for all programs except Medicare and Medicaid. For these two programs, the deflator reflects the medical component of the Consumer Price Index.

*Includes health (function 550) and Medicare (570).

settlement). Under the Clinton plan, the share of GDP devoted to federal spending in nonprofit areas, outside of health and income assistance, as of FY 2003 would be around 42 percent of what it was in FY 1980.

IMPLICATIONS FOR NONPROFIT REVENUES

For the nation's private nonprofit organizations, President Clinton's FY 1999 budget would thus provide only modest relief from the fiscal stringency of the past two decades. Excluding health, federal support to nonprofits under this plan would increase by only $0.7 billion, or 4 percent, over FY 1998 levels (see table 3.10). Because FY 1998 levels were well below those that prevailed in FY 1980, however, this means that the budget would still leave federal support to nonprofits (outside of health) 12 percent below its FY 1980 level, or 14 percent without the tobacco settlement. Put somewhat differently, nonprofit organizations outside of the health field will lose a total of $13.1 billion in revenue during FY 1999–2003 compared with what they would have if FY 1980 spending levels were maintained. This is slightly in excess of the total amount of foundation giving in 1996. As a share of GDP and excluding health, federal support of nonprofits in FY 2003 under President Clinton's FY 1999 budget proposal would be only half of what it was in FY 1980.

CONCLUSION

While it has long been clear that the federal government's activities have an important impact on the nation's nonprofit sector, the dimensions of that impact have been difficult for researchers and others to gauge. No ongoing governmental or other tracking system or database follows the flow of funds from government to nonprofit agencies. In order to fill the gap in understanding of the relationship between the federal government and the nonprofit sector, we have attempted to develop better estimates of the effects on nonprofit organizations of federal spending and tax changes.

Our analysis shows that the shift in federal spending priorities that occurred over the period FY 1980–97 had a significant effect on the need for services from nonprofit organizations and on the federal funds available to help nonprofits meet this need.

In particular, these budget shifts generally increased the pressures on nonprofit organizations to expand their services while reducing

Table 3.10 ESTIMATED FEDERAL SUPPORT OF NONPROFITS: PROJECTED FY 2003 SUPPORT UNDER PRESIDENT CLINTON'S FY 1999 BUDGET VS. ESTIMATED FY 1998 AND ACTUAL FY 1980 SUPPORT (In Billions of Constant FY 1998 Dollars)

Budget Function	Proposed FY 2003 vs. FY 1998		Proposed FY 2003 vs. FY 1980		Cumulative, FY 1999–2003 vs. FY 1980	FY 2003 Support as Pct. of GDP (FY 1980 = 100)
	Amount	Percent	Amount	Percent		
Education, Training, Employment, Social Services	+$1.0	+7	–$0.7	–4	–$3.6	54
Community and Regional Development	–0.3	–42	–1.0	–69	–4.5	18
Health*	+15.9	+11	+87.4	+115	+398.9	213
International Affairs	0.0	–3	–0.6	–43	–3.2	33
Total above	+$16.6	+10	+$85.0	+89	+$387.6	164
Total, excluding Health	+$0.7	+4	–$2.4	–12	–$11.3	50
Total, excluding Health and Tobacco Legislation	+$0.3	+2	–$2.8	–14	–$13.1	49

Source: Authors' estimates based on data in OMB (1998). Conversion to constant FY 1998 dollars was accomplished by using the gross domestic product (GDP) implicit price deflator for all programs except Medicare and Medicaid. For these two programs, the deflator reflects the medical component of the Consumer Price Index.
*Includes health (function 550) and Medicare (570).

the resources they had available to do so, at least outside the health field. While private giving provided some relief, moreover, it was generally not sufficient to offset the overall reductions that occurred, although it did manage to offset the direct nonprofit revenue losses by the latter part of the period.

These data highlight the importance of understanding the complex relationships that now link the federal government and the nonprofit sector. While these two sets of institutions are in some sense substitutes for each other, they are also to an important extent partners in responding to public needs. If unintended consequences are to be avoided, both sides of this partnership need to be brought into better view.

APPENDIX A
NOTE ON DATA SOURCES

I. Overall Federal Spending Data

Published sources include the annual volumes containing the president's budget that were released in 1982–98. In addition, unpublished backup material to the published volumes was obtained from the U.S. Office of Management and Budget (OMB) and the executive departments (e.g., Department of Health and Human Services, Department of Labor).

II. Federal Support of Nonprofit Organizations

Authors' estimates of the share of program resources flowing to nonprofit agencies are based on detailed examination of programmatic data, scrutiny of existing program evaluations, and extensive discussions with program managers at the federal, state, and local levels. "Nonprofit share estimates" were calculated in 1981 and 1993. For years between 1981 and 1993, the nonprofit share estimate is calculated as the weighted average of the estimates for the two end years.

III. Deflation Factors

DEFLATORS FOR MEDICARE AND MEDICAID:

Unpublished material from OMB and the U.S. Congressional Budget Office (CBO) on the actual and projected values of the medical services component of the Consumer Price Index (CPI).

DEFLATORS FOR ALL OTHER PROGRAMS:

Published and unpublished material from OMB and CBO on actual and projected values of the gross domestic product (GDP) implicit price deflator.

Notes

This study was supported by funding from the Aspen Institute's Nonprofit Sector Research Fund, Independent Sector, and the Urban Institute. The authors thank Gerald Auten, Virginia Hodgkinson, and Richard Steinberg for comments on earlier drafts of this chapter. They also thank Michael Brotchner, Michelle Chaffee, Kelly Daley, and Brent Dillabaugh for assistance with the research for this chapter.

1. For a more detailed discussion of the estimating procedure, see Salamon and Abramson 1981, pp. 35–80. Our "nonprofit share estimates" were developed for two points in time, 1981 and 1993. For programs for which the nonprofit share estimate changed between 1981 and 1993, we assumed that the change was spread evenly over the 12 years.

2. The guaranteed student loan program, along with other federal credit programs, was excluded from this analysis. Included in research and development outlays is the federal spending on research and development that flows outside the government to public and private, nonprofit colleges and universities and to nonprofit research institutes. Intramural government research spending and support of for-profit businesses for research are not included.

3. In addition to these programmatic changes, reductions have also occurred in the mail subsidy provided to nonprofit, public, religious, and some for-profit organizations. By FY 1997 the value of this subsidy was reduced by $1.4 billion, or 94 percent below FY 1980 levels.

4. Calculations based on effctive tax rate data from Congressional Budget Office Memorandum (1997) and the House Committee on Ways and Means (1993), table 11. The effective federal tax rates by income quintile (lowest to highest) were 8.1, 15.6, 19.8, 22.9, and 27.6 percent in 1980 and 6.2, 14.5, 19.6, 22.4, and 28.8 percent in 1994.

5. Here is a simple example of bracket creep. A tax system taxes the first $10,000 at a zero rate, the next $12,000 at a 10 percent rate, and all other income at a 20 percent rate. A household with $20,000 of income then pays an average 5 percent tax rate and a marginal rate of 10 percent. Now suppose that its income rises to $25,000 because of inflation, a few years of real wage growth, or a second member of the household entering

the labor force. Then the average tax rate rises to 7.2 percent and the marginal rate to 20 percent.

6. Again, one needs to be careful here, as there have also been periods when larger shares of the population have been moved into the estate tax because average individual wealth grew faster then exemption levels in that tax.

7. This exclusion was extended to June 1992, in the Tax Extension Act of 1991.

8. Economists believe that marginal incentives are most influenced by how a tax change affects the "last" rather than the "first" dollar of deductions. For example, suppose that, before the introduction of the phaseout for itemized deductions, a taxpayer had $10,000 in itemized deductions, of which $4,000 was in the form of charitable contributions. Assume that this hypothetical taxpayer earned $33,333 in excess of the base at which itemized deductions were limited, so that the exemption phaseout reduced the amount of itemized deductions that could be taken out by $1,000. Unless noncharitable itemized expenses (in this example, $6,000) were less than that amount, each $1 of charitable giving would still reduce taxable income by $1, and thus the marginal incentive to give on the last $1 would remain at 31 percent.

9. For example, see Lindsay 1987. See also Clotfelter 1987.

10. See Auten, Cilke, and Randolph 1992.

11. See Auten, Clotfelter, and Schmalbeck 1998.

12. As noted in Steuerle and Hodgkinson, this volume, the Smetters model criticizes what he calls "reduced form" equations that don't deal simultaneously with demand and supply of charitable giving. In our examples above, we do not specify precisely what may lead to the demand for giving, allowing even for the possibility that charitable giving may simply be an act of outright generosity, regardless of the benefits derived for the giver. His model formalizes what we have called here (and in an earlier version of this paper presented to ARNOVA in November 1996) a demand for giving into a more elegant model using the economic concept of "externalities"—gains back to the giver for the charitable activity—as the mechanism driving individual giving.

13. The fiscal year figures for private giving reported here are adapted from calendar year data in Hodgkinson et al. 1996. Fiscal year data are used to make the private giving figures comparable to the federal budget figures.

14. Data on private giving are not available for exactly the same program areas as data on federal spending. The crosswalk we developed matched giving for human services with federal spending for social services and employment and training; giving for public benefit and environment with federal spending for community development and environment; giving for education with federal spending for education and research; giving for international affairs with federal spending for international affairs; and giving for arts and culture with federal spending for arts and culture.

15. In contrast to the preceding analysis, which is built on spending data on the hundred or so individual programs of interest to nonprofits, the analysis in this section reflects spending information at the level of the 19 major "budget functions" that make up the federal budget. "Budget functions" are groupings of individual programs that serve a similar purpose, such as community development or health. The six budget functions of concern to nonprofits are: international affairs (function 150); community and regional development (450); education, training, employment, and social services (500); health (550); Medicare (570); and income assistance (600). Receipts from Medicare premiums are excluded from the analysis. These six functions covered in this analysis account for approximately 35 percent of all federal spending and well over 90 percent of all federal assistance to nonprofit organizations.

References

AAFRC Trust for Philanthropy. 1996. *Giving USA 1996*. New York: AAFRC Trust for Philanthropy.

Abramson, Alan J., and Lester M. Salamon. 1986. *The Nonprofit Sector and the New Federal Budget*. Washington, D.C.: Urban Institute Press.

Auten, Gerald E., James M. Cilke, and William C. Randolph. 1992. "The Effects of Tax Reform on Charitable Contributions." *National Tax Journal* 45 (3, Sept.): 267–90.

Auten, Gerald E., Charles T. Clotfelter, and Richard Schmalbeck. 1998. "Taxes and Philanthropy among the Wealthy." University of Michigan Business School Working Paper 98-15.

Clotfelter, Charles T. 1987. "Life after Tax Reform." *Change* (July–Aug.): 12–18.

Hodgkinson, Virginia Ann, Murray S. Weitzman, John A. Abrahams, Eric A. Crutchfield, and David R. Stevenson. 1996. *Nonprofit Almanac, 1996–1997*. San Francisco: Jossey-Bass Publishers.

Lindsay, Lawrence B. 1987. "Gifts of Appreciated Property: More to Consider." *Tax Notes* (5, Jan.): 67–70.

OMB. See U.S. Office of Management and Budget.

Randolph, William. 1995. "Dynamic Income, Progressive Taxes, and the Timing of Charitable Contributions." *Journal of Political Economy* 103 (4): 709–38.

Salamon, Lester M., and Alan J. Abramson. 1981. *The Federal Government and the Nonprofit Sector. Implications of the Reagan Budget Proposals*. Washington, D.C.: Urban Institute Press.

————. 1982. *The Federal Budget and the Nonprofit Sector*. Washington, D.C.: Urban Institute Press.

Smetters, Kent. 1998. "A Free Rider Explanation of the Charitable Giving Puzzles of the 1980s and an Application to Fundamental Tax Reform." Unpublished paper.

Steuerle, Eugene. 1992. *The Tax Decade*. Washington, D.C.: Urban Institute Press.

————. 1998. "The Coming Revolution in the Charitable Sector." *Tax Notes* (17, Aug. 10): 727–28, 859–60.

U.S. Bureau of the Census. 1997. *Statistical Abstract of the United States: 1997*. Washington, D.C.: U.S. Government Printing Office.

U.S. Congress, Congressional Budget Office. 1997. "Summary Federal Tax Information by Income Group and Family Type." Washington, D.C., June 12.

U.S. Congress, House Committee on Ways and Means. 1993. *Green Book*.

U.S. Office of Management and Budget. 1998. *Budget of the United States Government: Fiscal Year 1999, Historical Tables*. Washington, D.C.: U.S. Government Printing Office.

Chapter Four

TAX TREATMENT OF NONPROFIT ORGANIZATIONS: A TWO-EDGED SWORD?

Evelyn Brody and Joseph J. Cordes

INTRODUCTION

Previous chapters have discussed the various roles that nonprofit organizations play in civil society: as independent, private suppliers of goods and services; as agents of the government in delivering services aimed at meeting social needs; and also as contributors to political life and discourse in a democracy. As noted previously, nonprofit organizations have come to rely on a variety of special tax rules to secure an important portion of the resources needed to fulfill these various roles.

Nonprofit organizations have long enjoyed a special relationship with the tax collector. At least since Joseph's proclamation of a land law in Egypt that "Pharaoh should have the fifth part; except the land of priests only, which become not Pharaoh's" (Genesis 47:26), societies have acknowledged the presence of a nontaxable sector. In modern America, the nexus between the government and the nontaxable sector is myriad and complex. Multiple levels of government lay claim to different sources of tax revenue. State and local governments rely primarily on property and sales taxes; the federal government relies primarily on personal and corporate income taxes and payroll taxes. The nonprofit sector embraces a range of mutual, donative, and commercial enterprises, not all of which qualify for exemption under one or more of the foregoing taxes. The government provides supply-side tax subsidies for two specific forms of support for charity, donations and borrowing through bond finance. Both government direct expenditures (Hodgkinson and Steuerle, chapter 2) and demand-side tax expenditures (Smith, chapter 5) provide billions of dollars of additional support to social service charities. Finally, returning to federal-state relations, the state attorneys general enforce the substantive nonprofit laws, but Congress has given the Internal Revenue Service an increasing role in regulating the nonprofit-government border and nonprofit-commercial border (Simon 1987), as well as the financial arrangements between charities and their insiders (Brody 1998a).

A few words on terminology will help focus the following discussion. The public often conflates the terms "nonprofit" and "tax-exempt." Nonprofit entities fall loosely into two categories: charities (including churches, schools, hospitals, and social service organizations) and mutual-benefit organizations (including labor unions, trade associations, and social clubs). While exemption from federal, state, and local taxes is limited generally to corporations and trusts organized under state law as not-for-profit enterprises, so central is the role played by the federal tax law that nonprofits have come to be known by their designation in the Internal Revenue Code. For example, charities are referred to as "section 501(c)(3)" organizations. Most of the special tax treatments discussed in this chapter extend only to charities, while mutual-benefit nonprofits generally enjoy only income-tax exemption. Similarly, "action" organizations, which engage in more than insubstantial lobbying, generally qualify for exemption only as section 501(c)(4) social-welfare organizations— which means that contributions must be made by donors on an after-tax basis. Because of its focus on the tax benefits for charities, this chapter sometimes uses the term "nonprofit" interchangeably with "charity."

Nontaxable status confers financial advantages on nonprofit organizations that are not enjoyed by other providers of goods and services. Tax exemption allows nonprofits to keep much, if not all, of the surplus earned from a range of income-producing activities. In addition, charities receive access to several unique sources of revenue: at the federal level, tax-deductible charitable contributions (also generally deductible at the state level) and the ability to issue tax-exempt bonds; at the state level, property-tax exemption and sales-tax exemption on purchases.

But "what the government giveth" it can also take away—or at least regulate. Tax exemption casts the government in the role not just of benefactor, but also of certifying the "legitimacy" of nonprofit organizations through requirements that organizations must meet in order to qualify for tax-exempt status, and regulating what nonprofits can and cannot do as a condition of retaining their tax-preferred status.

The special tax treatment of nonprofit organizations and the accompanying tax regulations thus comprise a major set of government policies toward the nonprofit sector; and as a result, changes in tax policy can be as important to the nonprofit sector as the ebb and flow of government spending that has been discussed in earlier chapters. Thus, after summarizing the main tax benefits enjoyed by nonprofit organizations, we consider a number of questions raised by the tax treatment of nonprofit organizations:

- What is the economic importance of nontaxable status to nonprofit organizations?
- What policy judgments are reflected in the current tax treatment of nonprofits?
- What strings are attached to receipt of the nonprofit tax exemption?
- How does the existing web of tax provisions and regulations shape the behavior of donors and nonprofit organizations?
- What does the future hold for the tax treatment of nonprofit organizations?

GOVERNMENT POLICY TOWARD NONPROFIT ORGANIZATIONS AS EMBODIED IN THE TAX LAWS

The government acts as a benefactor of the nonprofit sector through the tax laws in two broadly different ways.

First, allowing individuals and corporations to deduct the value of charitable contributions against income and estate taxes provides an important economic incentive for private donors to provide financial support to a wide range of philanthropic enterprises. It is widely recognized that allowing such deductions effectively reduces the out-of-pocket cost of supporting nonprofit organizations by an amount that depends on the donor's tax rate. For example, if the tax rate is 28 percent, allowing a tax deduction for charitable contributions cuts the net cost of contributing from one dollar to seventy-two cents, because the taxpayer "gets back" a tax deduction that saves twenty-eight cents in tax for every dollar contributed. A deduction has the upside-down subsidy effect of having a greater value to those in the highest tax brackets; moreover, only those who itemize their personal deductions may claim income-tax deductions for charitable contributions. The price of giving falls further for gifts of appreciated property—by the capital gains tax that would otherwise have been paid had the donated property instead been sold.[1] The donor may not, however, "zero out" income with charitable gifts.[2]

Second, the federal tax code allows nonprofit *organizations* to devote more financial resources to support their philanthropic missions by exempting them from the obligation of paying corporate or trust income taxes. In addition to the charitable-contribution deduction and entity-level exemption, the federal tax system also subsidizes charities by granting them the ability to issue "section 501(c)(3) bonds," the interest income on which is exempt from tax. Similarly, states typically exempt nonprofits from state income tax, and exempt charities from local property taxes (as well as sales taxes on purchases). Entity-level tax exemption, though quite broad, does not, however, extend to any and all income earned or property owned by the nonprofit organization. In particular, the income must be earned from activities deemed related to the organization's exempt purpose. Since the 1950s, nonprofit organizations have been subject to a federal Unrelated Business Income Tax (UBIT), which is meant to tax nonprofits on the same basis as for-profit corporations on income earned in a "trade or business" that is "regularly carried on" by a nonprofit and not "substantially related" to the nonprofit's exempt purposes (Simon 1987; Hansmann 1989). States that levy corporate income taxes have generally followed the federal government's lead in this area by imposing their own unrelated business income taxes, and most states require that property be used for an exempt purpose in order to qualify for property-tax exemptions.

ECONOMIC VALUE OF THE CHARITABLE DEDUCTION, TAX EXEMPTION, AND TAX-EXEMPT BONDS

What is the economic importance of special tax treatment to charities? The following tables provide data bearing on this question.

Charitable Deduction

Each year the Joint Committee on Taxation estimates the cost to taxpayers, in terms of forgone tax revenue, of providing tax incentives to individuals and corporations to contribute to charitable activities. These estimated "tax expenditures" for fiscal year 1998 are shown in table 4.1.

From the perspective of nonprofit organizations, what matters, however, is not the budgetary cost of tax incentives for charitable deductions, but rather the importance of charitable contributions as a financial resource, and how much additional giving is encouraged by these tax incentives. That is, taking the 1998 numbers in table 4.1, the

Table 4.1 CHARITABLE TAX EXPENDITURES

Estimated Budgetary Cost of Tax Deductions for Charitable Contributions			
Charitable Activity	Corporate Tax Expediture (Billions of $)	Individual Tax Expenditure (Billions of $)	Total
Education	0.9	2.6	3.5
Health	0.7	1.9	2.6
Social Services (i.e., other)	0.9	16.3	17.2

Source: U.S. Congress, Joint Committee on Taxation, 1997a.

Table 4.2 PRIVATE CONTRIBUTIONS BY SUBSECTOR

	Contributions	
Charitable Activity	Amount in Billions of Dollars	Percentage of Annual Funds
Total	$117.9	18.9
Arts and Culture	$4.2	40.0
Education and Research	$15.0	16.7
Health Services	$11.2	4.1
Social and Legal Services	$14.9	30.0
Religious Organizations	$66.3	85.9
Civic, Social, and Fraternal Organizations	$6.3	69.2

Source: Independent Sector, *Nonprofit Almanac, 1996–97*, table 4-2.

charitable-contribution deduction could have increased donations by more or less than the $17 billion in forgone tax, depending on how responsive donors are to the tax incentive. Table 4.2 shows the estimated amount of private contributions received by different types of charities in 1996, and the relative importance of contributions as a source of funding.

Table 4.2 illustrates the varying importance of charitable deductions as a resource for supporting nonprofit activities. On one hand, the figures in the third column, which shows the percentage of annual funds from private contributions, reflect the public-sector budgetary changes that have channeled increasing financial resources through nonprofit organizations. As a result of these government grants and contracts and public and private fees for services, some nonprofits, such as those in health care (most notably hospitals), depend relatively little on charitable gifts. For education and research, and social and legal service organizations, charitable gifts are a major, but not the only, source of revenue. On the other hand, the figures also show that, notwithstanding growth of alternative sources of funding, private contributions remain a significant financial resource for most philanthropic organizations.

Thus, the next question is how much lower private contributions would be if donations to charities were not tax deductible. There is fairly broad empirical consensus among economists who have studied private giving that donors are sensitive to the after-tax cost of giving, although there is a range of estimates of how sensitive. The middle to high end of the range of estimated responses suggests that increasing (decreasing) the cost of giving by 10 percent decreases (increases) contributions by at least 10 percent. The lower end of the range implies considerably more modest responses, with a (permanent) 10 percent increase (decrease) in the cost of giving leading to only a 3 percent decrease (increase in contributions).

Table 4.3 presents some rough estimates of the effect of the charitable tax deduction for the case in which donations are assumed to be fairly responsive to changes in the after-tax cost of giving. Based on a simulation of how contributions would be affected by abolishing the current charitable tax deduction as part of replacing the current income tax with a flat tax, Price Waterhouse found that increasing the cost of giving from current (tax-subsidized) levels to $1.00 would reduce private giving by 32 percent.[3] Applying that factor to the contribution levels shown in table 4.2, one can roughly estimate the drop in contributions that nonprofit organizations would experience if charitable contributions were not tax deductible. These estimates suggest that the total financial resources of nonprofit organizations would

Table 4.3 PRIVATE CONTRIBUTIONS BY SUBSECTOR

Charitable Activity	Current Contributions with Tax Deduction (1)	Estimated Contributions without Tax Deduction (2)	Predicted Change in Contributions (1)−(2)=(3)	Predicted Change as a Percentage of Financial Resources
Total	$117.9	$80.2	$37.7	6.0
Arts and Culture	$4.2	$2.9	$1.3	12.8
Education and Research	$15.0	$10.2	$4.8	5.3
Health Services	$11.2	$7.6	$3.6	1.3
Social and Legal Services	$14.9	$10.1	$4.8	9.6
Religious Organizations	$66.3	$45.1	$21.2	27.5
Civic, Social, and Fraternal Organizations	$6.3	$4.3	$2.0	22.1

Sources: Hodgkinson and Weitzman, Independent Sector, *Nonprofit Almanac, 1996–97*, table 4-2; Price Waterhouse LLP and Caplin and Drysdale, Chartered, "Impact of Restructuring on Tax-Exempt Organizations"; and author's calculations.

be cut by amounts ranging from just over 1 percent to more than 25 percent.

At the same time, as noted in the previous two chapters and as discussed below, charitable giving did not drop as sharply as one might have expected in the 1980s when the price of giving rose, which has led some analysts (e.g., Randolph 1995) to suggest that giving may not be as sensitive to the price of giving as previously believed. If instead donor responses to changes in the cost of giving are at the low end of the estimated range, the same Price Waterhouse simulations indicate that abolishing the tax subsidy would cut donations by a measurable, though much smaller, amount of approximately 14 percent, which would cut the total financial resources of nonprofit organizations by between 0.5 and 12 percent.[4]

Exemption from Corporate Income Taxes

Data tabulated by Pollak and Pettit (Urban Institute 1998, table 3) show that in 1995 charities received almost $35 billion in revenue in excess of their expenses, as shown in table 4.4. No category of nonprofit organizations was found to have expenses in excess of revenue, although of course some individual charities have suffered deficits.

Table 4.4 SURPLUS OF PUBLIC CHARITIES: 1995

Charitable Activity	Amount in Millions of Dollars			Surplus as a Percent of Total Revenue
	Revenue	Expenses	Surplus	Percent
Total	$544,447	$509,756	$34,689	6.5
Total Less Higher Education and Hospitals	$213,914	$199,799	$14,121	11.7
Arts, Culture, Humanities	$13,518	$11,936	$1,582	11.7
Education	$95,834	$86,860	$8,973	9.4
Environment/Animals	$3,819	$3,175	$644	10.2
Health	$336,164	$318,284	$17,888	9.1
Human Services	$65,224	$62,177	$3,046	4.7
International and Foreign Affairs	$4,171	$4,027	$144	3.5
Public and Societal Benefit	$17,232	$15,866	$1,365	7.9
Religion-Related	$3,910	$3,590	$320	8.2
Unknown, Unclassified	$4,576	$3,851	$726	15.9

Source: Thomas H. Pollak and Kathryn L. S. Pettit (1998), *The Finances of Operating Public Charities, 1989–1995,* Urban Institute, tables 3 and 23. These amounts omit churches, which are not required to file IRS Form 990.

The size of the nonprofit surplus is sometimes seen as an indicator of the economic importance of the corporate income-tax exemption (Congressional Budget Office [CBO] 1997a). The reader should bear in mind, however, that the "residual" between income and expense that is measured by the *surplus* of a nonprofit organization is not a measure of *profit*, as accountants and economists would understand the term. For example, donations are appropriately treated as a source of funds to a nonprofit organization for purposes of computing its surplus. But although donations could, in theory, be counted as a taxable receipt for purposes of determining taxable profit, given the stated rationale for organizing as a nonprofit organization, this seems rather unlikely. Similarly, for policy reasons, one might choose not to count "below-market" fees received for providing mission-related services to clients as a taxable receipt.

A more reasonable measure of what might be termed the "potentially taxable income" of nonprofit organizations would be the profit earned on "unrelated" activities undertaken with the specific intent of earning income to support its mission-related activities. This amount is not directly observable from the financial data that is provided by nonprofit organizations, but a crude estimate can be inferred by adding to the amount of investment income received by nonprofit organizations, the revenue that nonprofit organizations reported receiving from activities that are deemed to be "unrelated" to their primary purposes yet nonetheless excluded from taxation. (The gross revenue received from "excluded" activities is assumed to measure the net income garnered by the nonprofit organization, under the assumption that these revenues are produced using labor and capital the nonprofit organization uses to provide its primary goods and services.)

These estimates of "potentially taxable income" of nonprofit organizations are presented in table 4.5. If one assumes that this income would otherwise be taxed at a combined federal and state rate of 40 percent, tax exemption is estimated to increase the resources of nonprofit organizations by roughly $14 billion in the aggregate. Although the details of the calculation are not reported here, that amount is comparable to the aggregate value of the tax deduction for donations to public charities that file IRS Form 990.[5]

Exemption from Property Taxes

Table 4.6 presents data showing the value of the tax exemption from local property taxes. Because of the myriad of local property tax rates, it is extremely difficult to place a precise value on the aggregate value

Table 4.5 POTENTIALLY TAXABLE INCOME OF PUBLIC CHARITIES: 1995

	Amount in Billions of Dollars		
Charitable Activity	Estimated Potentially Taxable Income	Estimated Income Tax Savings	Tax Savings as a Percent of Total Revenue
Total	$34.88	$13.9	2.5
Total Less Education and Hospitals	$5.68	$2.3	1.1
Arts, Culture, Humanities	$1.15	$0.5	3.7
Education	$14.28	$5.7	5.9
Environment/Animals	$0.39	$0.2	4.1
Health	$14.91	$6.0	1.8
Human Services	$1.36	$0.5	0.8
International and Foreign Affairs	$0.21	$0.1	2.3
Public and Societal Benefit	$2.20	$0.9	5.2
Religion-Related	$0.18	$0.1	2.6
Unknown, Unclassified	$0.23	$0.1	2.1

Source: Tabulations provided by Thomas H. Pollak, National Center for Charitable Statistics.

Table 4.6 POTENTIALLY TAXABLE PROPERTY OF PUBLIC CHARITIES: 1995

	Amount in Billions of Dollars		
Charitable Activity	Estimated Potentially Taxable Income	Estimated Property Tax Savings	Tax Savings as a Percent of Total Revenue
Total	$239.17	$6.0	1.1
Total Less Education and Hospitals	$28.48	$0.7	0.4
Arts, Culture, Humanities	$8.62	$0.2	1.5
Education	$68.86	$1.7	1.8
Health	$141.83	$3.5	1.0
Human Services	$42.82	$1.1	1.7
Public and Societal Benefit	$6.69	$0.2	1.2

Source: Based on data in Pollak and Pettit (Urban Institute, 1998, tables 3 and 16).

of the property tax exemption. A recent study by the Minnesota Taxpayer's Association suggests that the midpoint of property tax rates levied in the largest cities of each of the 50 states is approximately 2.5 percent of property value. Using this figure, the value of the property tax exemption is estimated to be roughly $6 billion in the aggregate. This magnitude may understate the aggregate value to the extent that potentially taxable property is valued by nonprofit organizations at book rather than market value.

Ability to Issue Tax-Exempt Bonds

According to data from the Internal Revenue Service Statistics of Income Division (SOI), section 501(c)(3) organizations reported $70 billion in outstanding tax-exempt bonds in 1993 (Hilgert 1997, 126, table 1). Note that after the Tax Reform Act of 1986 and until the Taxpayer Relief Act of 1997, a charity other than a nonprofit hospital could not have outstanding more than $150 million of section 501(c)(3) bonds. A 1996 study (JCT 1996, table 2) reported that in 1992 hospitals issued $13.152 billion in section 501(c)(3) bonds, and nonhospitals issued $9.745 billion. The Joint Committee's revenue estimate for the 1997 Act provision repealing the nonhospital cap totaled $798 million over the 10-year period 1997–2006 (JCT 1997b, appendix). (The Joint Committee's latest tax expenditure budget separately reports the value of the exclusion of interest on state and local private nonprofit educational facilities at $6.2 billion for 1998–2002 and for private nonprofit health facilities at $11.7 billion for 1998–2002 (JCT 1997a).)

Indirect Value of Other Tax Preferences

Of growing importance to charities is the indirect benefit from a host of tax preferences that, deliberately or incidentally, stimulate demand for the services that charities provide (see Smith, chapter 5). The exclusion from workers' income for employer-provided health insurance, for the fifth year in a row, is the largest tax expenditure; while doctors and other proprietary firms benefit, so do the hospitals, dominated by nonprofits.[6] The new HOPE tuition credit, designed to keep college affordable for the middle class, is already the twentieth-ranked tax expenditure; many education experts believe that the credit's value will be captured by colleges and universities through higher tuition charged or lower internal aid granted (Brody 1998a). Nonprofit daycare providers benefit from the dependent-care credit. Nonprofit housing developers benefit from the low-income housing tax credit. While the nonprofits' share of these subsidies cannot be quantified, for 1999 the Joint Committee on Taxation's estimates by "budget function" peg the cost of individuals' tax expenditures (aside from the charitable-contribution deduction) at $10.1 billion for education, at $4.2 billion for social services (ignoring $19.3 billion for the child credit), and at a staggering $85.3 billion for health (totals derived from JCT 1997a, table 1, Individuals).

SUBSIDY OR TAX-BASE DEFINING?
A SOVEREIGNTY PERSPECTIVE

As shown from the estimates in the above tables, the economic values of the special tax treatments for charities increase the resources available to nonprofit organizations for their philanthropic missions.[7] It is tempting to treat these features of the federal and state tax systems as subsidies granted by the government to nonprofit organizations as a quid pro quo in recognition of the philanthropic goods and services they provide. As one of us has argued elsewhere, however, the underlying policy rationale for tax policy toward the nonprofit sector may be better characterized as involving some mix of an explicit intent to subsidize nonprofit organizations and a historic desire to respect the "sovereign" boundaries between the nonprofit and public sectors (Brody 1998c).

Charitable Deduction

While Congress did not grant the deduction for charitable contributions in the 1913 enactment of the income tax, from its 1917 inception the deduction has been designed to provide a government subsidy to charitable activities through the tax code. Concerned that the high marginal tax rates enacted to finance World War I would deter donations, Congress permitted individuals to reduce up to 15 percent of their net taxable income by charitable contributions. From that point on, the scope of the deduction steadily expanded—to broaden the range of charitable activities eligible for the deduction; to extend the deduction to corporate contributions; and to increase the percentage of taxable income (later, adjusted gross income) that could be deducted annually. The legislative history of these changes reflects a clear subsidy motivation. In the 1969 Act, for example, Congress declared that raising the contribution limit from 30 percent of adjusted gross income to 50 percent (for cash contributions to public charities) would "strengthen the incentive effect of the charitable contribution deduction."

That policymakers view the charitable-contribution deduction as a subsidy is suggested through its treatment as a "tax expenditure" by both the Treasury Department and the Joint Committee on Taxation. Tax expenditures—as distinct from provisions that properly measure the tax base—generally include special income tax provisions ". . . analogous to direct outlay programs," in the sense that the tax expenditure and an equivalent direct outlay or subsidy are considered to be "alternative means of accomplishing similar budget policy objectives" (JCT 1997a).

As discussed more fully below, the subsidy conception of the charitable-contribution deduction also appears firmly embedded in debates about fundamental tax reform. For example, some of the recent proposals to replace the income tax with a consumption-based flat tax include, as an express recognition of the desirability of the subsidy, provisions to allow taxpayers to continue to claim deductions for charitable contributions, while those proposals that withhold the deduction do so in a deliberate attempt to properly measure the tax base rather than to provide a subsidy (see generally JCT 1996; Price Waterhouse 1997; Clotfelter and Schmalbeck 1996).

Tax Exemption

Nonprofit organizations clearly have more resources at hand to finance their activities because they generally do not have to pay income taxes, and charities usually can obtain property-tax exemption. In contrast to the charitable-contribution deduction, however, the impetus for the tax exemption appears not to have been to provide an economic subsidy to nonprofits. Rather, tax exemption appears to have emanated from a mix of "tax-base-defining" objectives combined with a historical desire on the part of government (at least in the Anglo-Saxon tradition) to avoid intruding into a sphere of activities believed to "properly" belong to the church and its secular philanthropic successors.

The base-defining rationale is seen most clearly in the treatment of the nonprofit tax exemption in the federal tax-expenditure budget. Notwithstanding its economic value to nonprofit organizations, the federal exemption from corporate income tax is not treated as a tax-expenditure (JCT 1997a [emphasis added]):

> With respect to . . . charities, tax-exempt status is not classified as a tax expenditure because the non-business activities of such organizations generally must predominate and their unrelated business activities are subject to tax. In general, the imputed income derived from nonbusiness activities conducted by individuals or collectively by certain nonprofit organizations is *outside the normal income tax base*.

In other words, tax exemption does not constitute a tax subsidy because the income from the "nonbusiness" activities of nonprofit organizations never rises to the level of taxable in the first place.

That definition, however, begs the question of why income earned by nonprofit enterprises should fall outside of the normal tax base. For example, why should income earned by "commercial charities" such as hospitals be treated differently from income earned by their for-profit counterparts from providing similar goods and services? (See Goddeeris and Weisbrod, chapter 7.) The issue generally applies to any income earned by nonprofits from activities that have a commercial character, even if such activities are deemed to be "related" to the organization's primary tax-exempt purpose. As the proprietary sector makes further incursions into "traditionally" nonprofit industries (such as higher education and social services), and as charities expand their search for "related" sources of revenue, pressures on the definition of a "normal" tax base will increase. (See generally Brody 1996; Ben-Ner and Gui 1993.)

Even if tax exemption for charities represents a subsidy, exemption rather than direct grants makes for a rather inefficient form of subsidy. Consistent with both the history of the tax exemption and its form, perhaps exemption represents an attempt by the government to respect the sovereignty of the nonprofit sector in much the same way that federal tax rules respect the sovereignty of state and local governments. Although no one would argue that the nonprofit sector enjoys true co-sovereignty with the public sector (because the nonprofit sector lacks the compulsory powers that inhere in a sovereign), tax exemption nonetheless carries with it a sense of leaving the nonprofit sector inviolate, and the very concept of sovereignty embodies the independent power of self-governance.

Indeed, parallels between how the federal government treats local governments and the way in which it treats the nonprofit sector are quite striking. (Even JCT 1996 lumped nonprofits together with state and local governments, without commenting on the juxtaposition.) The federal income tax excludes from gross income "income derived from any public utility or the exercise of any essential governmental function and accruing to a State or any political subdivision thereof." States and municipalities that borrow may generally issue bonds whose interest is tax-exempt in the hand of the bondholders. Payments of state and local income and property taxes are deductible from income, but user fees paid to government are treated as nondeductible payments for services.

As already described, each of these intergovernmental tax treatments finds an analogue in the tax treatment of charities. Charities are exempt from the corporate (or trust) income tax, although income from the performance of business activities unrelated to the charity's exempt purpose is taxable. Charities may issue tax-exempt bonds. Contributions made to charities are generally deductible from income. Payments made to a charity for a particular service (such as tuition or for hospital care), however, are not deductible.

Thus, a reasonable case can be made that the underlying purpose of the tax exemption is not to establish a quid pro quo relationship between government and charities in which charities receive the exemption in exchange for doing particular "good things." Instead, as explained below, exemption establishes a relationship of "co-sovereignty" in which government stays out of charities' day-to-day business (by not taxing them), while charities stay out of the business of petitioning government for subvention.

HOW TAX-EXEMPT STATUS AFFECTS THE RANGE AND SCOPE OF CHARITABLE ACTIVITIES

What "strings" go along with being able to receive tax-deductible contributions and with being treated as tax exempt?

The range of organizations that qualify as charities for purposes of receiving tax-deductible contributions is quite broad. That is, despite the subsidy motive that seems to explain the rationale for the charitable-contribution deduction, the government has not, as a matter of policy, tried to target the subsidy to particular uses. (For example, both a nonprofit opposing abortion and a pro-choice nonprofit can qualify for the tax treatment for charities.) Some might argue that open-endedness follows logically from using the tax code to provide the subsidy, because tax subsidies are harder to target than direct subsidies. Yet many tax expenditures do come with "eligibility rules" that try to distinguish between activities that merit subsidy and those that don't. (The tax credit for research and experimentation is a particularly good example.) In the case of the charitable deduction, the only "real" rule is that a nonprofit be recognized as a 501(c)(3) organization.

For charities, the main strings that seem to apply are the restrictions on lobbying and the prohibition on electioneering, again explainable by sovereignty analysis. These limitations can be viewed as an attempt by the "public sovereign" to tell the other that "your boundaries will be respected as long as you stay on your side of the line—don't engage in overtly political activities." Similarly, other rules that determine which commercial activities will be granted tax exemption can be viewed as attempting to police the borders between nonprofit and for-profit organizations (Simon 1987).

Apart from increasing the financial resources of nonprofits, the charitable-contribution deduction and the income-tax exemption affect the range and scope of charitable activities in several ways. The decision to subsidize charitable contributions through a tax deduction, instead of some other means, implicitly favors some philanthropic activities over others.[8] Particular requirements of qualifying for tax exemption also cause nonprofit organizations to act differently than they might otherwise. Lastly, because of its close link to the tax system, the magnitude of the "nonprofit subsidy" will be sensitive to broader changes in tax policy.

CHARITABLE-CONTRIBUTION DEDUCTION

By its terms, the charitable-contribution deduction provides a neutral tax subsidy that is not directly targeted to any particular set of charitable activities. In practice, however, the deduction tends to provide the greatest incentive to give among high-bracket donors (affluent individuals and corporations). One reason is that lower-income taxpayers typically do not itemize deductions and hence do not receive a deduction for charitable contributions. In addition, among itemizers, the subsidy increases with the taxpayer's marginal tax rate.

To describe the government's "share" of donations made, however, does not necessarily describe the additional amount of giving induced by deductibility: Depending on why donors give, the tax subsidy could be more or less efficient. If donors are "inelastic" in their decision to give—that is, if they would give with or without tax deductibility—then the tax subsidy would be wasted. Many theories exist of why people give to charity, and apparently tax considerations are not paramount. A pure altruist cares simply about increasing the charity's output, but a dollar of support from another source (either other private donors or the government) would "crowd out" the altruist's donations once the level of output was satisfactory. Studies have found incomplete crowd-out, however, implying that donors give because of social pressures rather than to support an identifiable need (Jencks 1987, 326–28; Steinberg 1989). James Andreoni (1989, 1990), for example, dubs donors "warm glow altruists," finding that they enjoy contributing to charitable organizations and get greater satisfaction the larger the value of their gift to the charity. The publicity given to many donations suggests a status theory—either signaling to other donors that a certain level of giving to a particular charity is expected of those in the group,[9] or signaling one's wealth or income to the peer group or society at large (Glazer and Konrad 1996). Under these models, giving may even be excessive. (See, e.g., Salamon 1995, 46–8, discussing "philanthropic particularism," "philanthropic paternalism," and "philanthropic amateurism.") William Randolph (1995) recently suggested that even high-bracket taxpayers might really just be time shifting—contributing in years when tax rates are highest, rather than changing their lifetime amount of giving. Proposals to improve the efficiency of the tax subsidy for charity include enacting a floor equal to a low percentage of the taxpayer's adjusted gross income under deductible donations (a floor now exists under the aggregate of all the itemized deductions of high-income taxpayers); and proposals to improve the fairness of the subsidy include substituting a tax credit for the tax deduction.

As a separate matter, if higher-income donors have preferences for giving that broadly reflect those of the population at large, then providing an incentive to contribute that increased with a taxpayer's income would not tend to favor one type of charitable activity over others. Indeed, in the parlance of "optimal tax theory," one might argue that targeting the subsidy in this manner would be a cost-efficient way of encouraging giving, because the subsidy would be aimed at taxpayers who, studies have shown, are more likely to respond to a reduction in the price of giving.

But there is considerable evidence that higher-income donors tend to channel their giving to charities in the arts and education. Thus, providing the subsidy in the form of a deduction, instead of, say, a tax credit available to itemizers and non-itemizers alike, skews the flow of contributions toward charities such as arts and education and away from support of churches (and social service organizations with low-income clienteles).[10]

EXEMPTION AND THE "UNRELATED BUSINESS INCOME TAX" (UBIT)

The attempt to draw boundaries between exempt and commercial activity can lead to suboptimal social policy. Notably, nonprofit hospitals are entitled to section 501(c)(3) tax exemption, but nonprofit physician practices generally are not. The Internal Revenue Service has been struggling with the appropriate limits on "whole hospital joint ventures" and "joint operating agreements" with proprietary partners (*Rev. Rul. 98–15*; Anthony 1997). However, to the extent it makes economic sense for health care to be provided earlier (e.g., prevention rather than treatment), we inefficiently constrain provision of preventive health care by denying charity exemption.

Moreover, the tax exemption can cause nonprofit organizations to become more commercial—but the mechanism through which this happens is a subtle one. If nonprofits act as if a tension exists between earning income to finance their primary mission and undertaking their primary mission, then they will only pursue commercial activities when they can earn a "premium return." Tax exemption, though initially granted to respect the sovereignty of the nonprofit sector, creates opportunities for not-for-profits to earn such returns. Limiting the exemption to "related activities" probably reinforces internal incentives that nonprofits already have to limit their commercial pursuits to areas where excess returns are likely to exist, which involve cost complementarities between the primary mission-related activity and secondary commercial activities (Cordes and Weisbrod 1998).

The requirement that nonprofit organizations pay taxes on income earned from unrelated business activities appears, on its face, to be quite strict; however, the practical operation of the regime can be slippery. First, a particular activity is exempt or taxable depending on the purposes of the entity engaged in it. The Internal Revenue Service thus from time to time issues such odd rulings as the recent declaration that a nonprofit cemetery association may sell caskets for burial in the cemetery and use the proceeds for cemetery maintenance without triggering UBIT (Private Letter Ruling 9814051).

Second, nonprofit organizations have sought out perfectly legal ways of shifting costs from their tax-exempt activities to taxable activities to reduce, if not eliminate, tax liability. Because it is easier to shift costs from tax-exempt activities to taxable activities when these activities are complements in production, nonprofit organizations appear to have been somewhat selective in the types of unrelated business activities they have chosen to undertake (Cordes and Weisbrod 1998; Hines 1998; Sansing 1998). Because many unrelated businesses accordingly make use of assets used in or employees devoted to exempt activities, the allocation of "dual-use" expenses to the taxable activity can minimize net income. Indeed, most UBIT returns report net losses (Riley 1997),[11] and the IRS has had fierce difficulties in reallocating deductions under current law.[12]

In some cases, the combination of tax rules inadvertently solves problems. For example, if a charity has issued tax-exempt bond financing to build the facility, the charity may not use more than 5 percent of the proceeds for a taxable activity; accordingly, in order to preserve the exempt status of its bond financing, the charity will be loath to overallocate the costs of dual-use assets away from the exempt activity.

EXEMPTION FROM PROPERTY AND SALES TAXES

State property-tax exemption does not automatically follow from Internal Revenue Code section 501(c)(3) status, but rather must be independently obtained (although the 501(c)(3) designation is often comparable). Property-tax statutes are often less developed than the federal income-tax regime. In some states, charities can forfeit property-tax exemption by using the property, even in part, for an unrelated business, while in other states, the exemption is apportioned. Similarly, in some but not all states, exemption does not extend to property rented out to commercial tenants. Finally, some states adopt various acreage limits for exempt property held by particular types of organizations.[13] Finally, as described below, in some localities, the statutory exemption has been modified by agreements by exempt owners to make "payments in lieu of taxes." As a separate matter, for some charities, the state sales-tax exemption on purchases is worth more than property-tax exemption.

Recently, tighter state and local definitions for exemption reflect a growing divergence of federal and state policies on tax exemption and a growing acceptance by the states of a quid pro quo rationale, particularly for health care organizations.[14] See "State and Local Initiatives to Limit the Nonprofit Property-Tax Exemption," below.

REMOVING THE CAP ON TAX-EXEMPT BORROWING

The ability of charities to issue tax-exempt debt favors charities that generate a revenue stream sufficiently predictable to support an acceptable bond rating. Moreover, a nonprofit hospital can issue an unlimited amount of 501(c)(3) bonds, and in 1997 Congress removed the prior $150 million cap on nonhospital charities. The ability to issue low-rate debt while earning a market return on investment assets proves irresistible to well-endowed colleges and universities (even some private foundations are bond financing, most often for offices); the arbitrage profits need not be returned to federal government unless the bond is actually secured by the endowment or investment assets (Brody 1997, 890–92).

LOBBYING AND POLITICAL ACTIVITIES

At the political boundaries of charities, it is worth asking whether the tax restrictions on lobbying and the ban on electioneering have really had much effect, or rather have changed the way in which these organizations participate in the political process. Noncharity exempt organizations—such as social welfare organizations, labor unions, and trade associations—operate under looser restrictions. Congress imposes the stricter regime on charities because it does not want tax-deducted charitable contributions to be used for these purposes; however, charities generally view the current lobbying regulations as quite generous. The rules do not limit the production of educational position papers and other publications not involving a "call to action" to contact legislators (IRC 501(h), Treasury Regulations §§ 1.501(h)-1 through -3, 1990). Moreover, in *Regan v. Taxation With Representation* (1983), the U.S. Supreme Court upheld the lobbying limitations against First Amendment challenge out of the recognition that charities can, and often do, establish social-welfare affiliates exempt under section 501(c)(4) to conduct lobbying. In addition, social change can sometimes instead be advanced through litigation. Finally, political campaign activity more often results in settlement and a fine than permanent revocation of exemption.[15]

RELYING ON THE TAX CODE: A NOT SO MIGHTY FORTRESS

Whether intended or not, a consequence of delivering subsidies to nonprofit organizations through the tax code is that nonprofits will suffer the financial effects of major changes made to the tax system for other reasons. The most obvious examples are efforts to reform taxes by broadening the tax base while lowering tax rates, which have the consequence of reducing the subsidy value of the charitable-contribution deduction. The last two decades have provided a preview of these effects. Legislation enacted in the 1980s slashed the top individual tax rate from 70 percent to 50 percent (in 1981) and then to 28 percent (in 1986). (The top rate subsequently increased to 31 percent in 1990 and to 39.6 percent in 1993.) As more taxpayers are captured by the Alternative Minimum Tax (AMT), however, the value of the charitable deduction will fall to 28 percent (or the lower 26 percent AMT rate). In addition, in a move to simplify the tax system for more individuals, the number of itemizers was deliberately reduced by an increase in the standard deduction in 1986. As a result, itemizers fell from 38 percent to 28 percent of filers; given that the charitable-contribution deduction for nonitemizers was allowed to expire in 1986, many taxpayers saw their price of contributing a dollar increase to $1. Surprisingly, however, studies found that expectations of drastic contribution falloffs failed to predict taxpayer response; donations increased overall and at every income level except the highest, where the fall in donations was smaller than predicted (Auten, Cilke, and Randolph, 280, table 7;[16] Clotfelter 1990).

Just as important, however, changes in the effective tax rate on capital income can affect the relative value of the nonprofit income-tax exemption. After all, subsidies to private businesses in the form of tax credits can have unintended effects on nonprofits. In the 1980s, for example, in the first wave of tax reform under President Ronald Reagan, certain sectors of the business community actually enjoyed *negative* income tax rates through the combination of accelerated depreciation and investment tax credits on new equipment (JCT 1982, 35). In this setting the relative advantage resulting from the zero tax rate conferred by the nonprofit exemption was eroded. An implication was that during this period, nonprofits had less incentive than before (or after) to seek out related commercial ventures as a source of income. Some might argue that this was appropriate because it reduced the financial incentive of nonprofits to seek to expand their financial resources by undertaking businesslike activities. Yet, it also may have caused nonprofits to avoid pursuing some "legitimate" opportunities for exploiting cost complementarities between their primary activity and ancillary profit-making activities. Nonprofits should also have found it financially more attractive to engage in nonexempt income-producing activities because these benefited from the investment tax incentives provided to for-profit businesses.

Most recently, nonprofit organizations in the District of Columbia may have unintentionally been put at a disadvantage in the local labor market as a result of well-intentioned efforts to revive Washington,

D.C.'s flagging economy. The recently enacted federal tax credit for hiring new workers by employers in the District will lower the *net* cost of hiring workers to for-profit but not nonprofit organizations. Economic theory predicts that such a subsidy should raise the *gross* cost of labor, as subsidized enterprises expand their hiring. For-profit employers, who are eligible to claim the tax credit, will see their *net* labor costs fall because they will receive a tax credit, but nonprofit employers, who cannot claim the credit, will find it harder and more expensive to hire workers. (The Treasury Department has informally expressed interest in designing a tax program that would benefit nonprofit employers, which employ many difficult-to-hire people.)

Lastly, from colonial times, the states have also granted exemptions to infant business industries (Jensen 1931, 125),[17] a practice enjoying a resurgence as states deliberately choose the tool of property-tax exemption to entice business relocation.[18] Like the case of negative tax rates, such property tax abatement programs have the effect of reducing the relative advantage that nonprofits enjoy from the local property tax exemption. In addition, to the extent that such tax-abatement programs shrink the local property tax base, local governments may look to other sources of revenue, such as limiting the nonprofit property-tax exemption. To some extent, nonprofits might be able to defend the exemption by contending that removing it will encourage mobile nonprofit organizations to move, thereby costing jobs. But the fact that nonprofit organizations do not pay other taxes, while for-profit businesses do, may somewhat weaken that argument.

The remainder of this section describes and discusses several proposals to change some of the tax rules that benefit charities and other nonprofit organizations.

TARGETING THE TAX SUBSIDY

The fact that tax incentives for charitable giving tend to favor certain charities over others has not been lost on policymakers. Thus, recent Republican proposals to grant additional tax credits for contributions to charities that primarily serve the poor can be seen as an attempt by some to better target the tax subsidy that the charitable deduction is intended to provide.[19] The charities, however, closed ranks, asserting that they do not know the income levels of their beneficiaries. As a separate matter, Congress might selectively repeal tax exemption for

particular industries, such as hospitals, continuing the trend to identify overly commercial activities as candidates for taxation.

THE ISTOOK AMENDMENT AND RELATED INITIATIVES

Although the restriction on lobbying has affected how nonprofit organizations participate in the political process, it has not served to
silence them altogether. (A recent example is congressional grousing
about the rather visible role played by Catholic Charities in the welfare
reform debate.) To some, that has been interpreted to mean that restrictions on lobbying appear insufficient to limit the political voice
of nonprofit organizations. As a result, some recent proposals have
been made to define the boundaries between acceptable and unac-
ceptable behavior more tightly. Thus, one version of the Istook amendment would have barred charities accepting federal funding not just
from lobbying (Congress's favorite prohibited activity) but also, in
certain cases, from appealing to the executive branch or the courts
for change (see Reid, chapter 9). In 1998, the House defeated "pay-
check protection," a proposal that would have, among other things,
required exempt organizations to obtain prior written consent from
their members before using any member dues for "political activity."[20]

If, however, in this new age of devolution and privatization, the
nonprofit sector should take on some of the functions previously performed by government—especially in the area of anti-poverty and
social service programs—one can question how much to limit the role
that nonprofit organizations play in public discourse. For example, if
the nonprofit sector is to become more of a partner with government
in delivering social services, how much does one want to limit their
ability to influence the outcome of the political process? (See Reid,
chapter 9.)

EFFECTS OF PROPOSALS FOR FUNDAMENTAL TAX REFORM

The ongoing debate about federal tax reform offers some clear examples of how the "nonprofit subsidy" is at the mercy of broader trends
in tax policy. Superficially, most of the proposals to replace the income
tax with some type of consumption tax appear to exempt charities.
On closer inspection, however, each of the various components of tax-

favored treatment to charity could take a blow, either directly or indirectly.

While the variety of proposals can overwhelm the casual observer, in their details each produces somewhat different threats to nonprofits. Essentially, four models have emerged: (1) the Value-Added Tax ("VAT"), (2) the Flat Tax, (3) the Unlimited Savings Allowance (hence "USA") tax, and (4) the National Retail Sales Tax.[21]

The most visible effect of Congressman Bill Archer's proposal to scrap federal income taxes altogether and replace them with a national consumption-based VAT would be the elimination of the charitable-contribution deduction. Moreover, because all capital income would face a zero federal tax rate, much of the relative advantage conferred by the nonprofit tax exemption would be eroded, as would the advantage associated with being able to issue tax-exempt bonds. (If all interest income is excluded from the tax base, then all bonds are tax-exempt.) The proposals that would apply tax to inputs purchased by charities would remove exemption from all but their "value added" to goods and services—and would require complex accounting and filing obligations to boot. Reform would also eliminate the tax-free treatment of fringe benefits, including health insurance, provided to workers. Finally, the proposals would in general collect a single level of tax on a whole host of "commercial" charitable services, notably health care.

Proposals to replace existing income taxes with a consumption-based "Flat Tax" could have similar ramifications. The Flat Tax is the same as the VAT, except that it gives businesses deductions for wages paid and it taxes workers separately from businesses. This bifurcation permits the tailoring of personal exemptions to household size. Moreover, the charitable-contribution deduction could be retained administratively as part of any flat-tax scheme. Unlike the mortgage interest deduction, which is economically incompatible with the "correct" definition of the tax base under a consumption tax, the charitable deduction could be retained as an explicit means of encouraging a particular type of consumption—charitable contributions.[22] On the other hand, proponents of a "clean" flat tax—one that allows no deductions—have argued against retaining the charitable-contribution deduction, asserting, in part, that it provides a subsidy for certain forms of consumption favored by affluent taxpayers. Clotfelter and Schmalbeck (1996, 230) calculate that the Armey-Shelby Flat Tax, which denies the deduction for charitable contributions, would result in a 10 percent drop in donations by individuals, while the USA Tax, which retains the deduction, would produce an 11 percent increase.

The Price Waterhouse study cited above estimates that, had a 21 percent Flat Tax been in place in 1996, charitable giving by individuals would have been $71 billion instead of $104 billion, and repeal of the estate tax would have cost another $3 billion in lost contributions; by contrast, the USA Tax could have increased individual giving by as much as $34 billion.[23] A Heritage Foundation study, though, estimates that contributions by individuals to charity, particularly religious congregations, would rise by about 3.8 percent under a 17 percent Flat Tax without a charitable-contribution deduction (Barry 1996, 12–13).

Tax reform could also affect the tax treatment of the activities of nonprofits. The staff of the Joint Committee on Taxation describes the main policy issue regarding nonproprietary activity: "One of the most fundamental issues in attempting to measure the value of governmental and nonprofit activities is when should government and nonprofit entities be regarded as producers of goods and services and when should they be treated as consumers?" (JCT 1996, par. 154.) If the goal of the tax system is to tax "the value added with respect to all final goods and services in the economy, then value added by government and nonprofit labor and capital resources should be subject to tax" (par. 165). By contrast, if governments and nonprofits are treated as consumers of self-supplied services, sales to governments and nonprofits would not be inputs in a business activity. The Joint Committee suggests bringing the federal government into the system as well; by not doing so, "the Federal Government would look smaller or more efficient than it otherwise might, and would appear smaller than State and local governments that might undertake some of the same activities" (par. 175).

No country with a transactions tax treats all consumption uniformly. European-style VATs typically tax "necessities" (such as education, health care, food and clothing) at lower rates, either by removing the tax on the value added at the retail stage (but not the tax on the retailer's inputs) or by zero-rating (exempting tax on sales and providing the seller with a refundable credit of the VAT paid on purchases). "Since nonprofit organizations are typically exempt from consumption tax in Europe, they still pay tax on their inputs" (Carroll, Neubig, and Nilles 1995). However, a system that taxes some activities while exempting others will require organizations to allocate inputs between the taxable and the exempt activities. "Aside from the administrative complexities and record keeping costs imposed on nonprofit organizations from the allocation system, the taxing authority also has to bear additional compliance costs because taxpayers have an incentive to allocate expenses to taxable production to offset tax."[24]

The Flat Tax proposal introduced by House Majority Leader Richard Armey and Senator Richard Shelby would exempt governments and nonprofits from the business tax, except for their unrelated business activities. However, the Flat Tax would limit the nonprofit exemption to charities, imposing business taxes on transfers of property or the provision of services by all other nonprofits. The USA Tax would go further and also deny exemption to certain charities, notably child-care centers and educational organizations that undertake policy analysis (e.g., think tanks). Unclear is whether such charities should include gifts and membership dues in their calculation of taxable receipts.

Even if under a VAT Congress exempts governments and nonprofits from their own value added to goods and services, these entities would still pay tax on the value of their purchases from businesses. Moreover, by permitting taxable enterprises to expense invested capital, a consumption tax reduces the relative value of tax exemption, because expensing is the equivalent of exempting the return on the asset from tax. Under a bifurcated VAT such as the Flat Tax, however, the Congressional Budget Office observes: "Because wage payments account for a large portion of the value added attributable to governments and nonprofit organizations, a bifurcated VAT provides generally consistent treatment for those institutions and private businesses" (CBO 1997b, 15). The Flat Tax, though, would tax fringe benefits paid to workers, by denying deductions to businesses and by imposing a tax on nonprofits, thus raising all employers' costs of labor compared with current law. Price Waterhouse (1997) noted that the value of employee health and medical insurance, free parking, spousal travel, and tax-exempt housing comes to an average of about 4 to 5 percent of the expenses of educational organizations.

The proposed National Retail Sales Tax would be levied on business sales to customers of goods and services (other than dues, contributions, and payments to qualified nonprofit organizations). Thus, like a VAT, the National Retail Sales Tax would effectively eliminate the charitable contribution by avoiding collecting a general tax from individuals. In addition, should the federal income tax be replaced by such a retail-level sales tax, uniform administration by the Internal Revenue Service would devolve to 50 potentially different state-level regulatory regimes.

In sum, with the notable exception of the USA Tax, these proposals would, at least in their current form, radically limit the direct and indirect tax subsidies provided to charities. Neither the Flat Tax nor the Retail Sales Tax proposal contemplates using the tax savings for anything other than reducing tax rates across the board.

STATE AND LOCAL INITIATIVES TO LIMIT THE NONPROFIT PROPERTY-TAX EXEMPTION

Within the states, a true sovereignty battle rages. Property-tax exemptions are enacted at the state level, often in the state constitution. However, property ownership by charities tends to cluster in center cities. Because property tax units are local (either municipal, county, or special districts, such as school districts), the burden of exemption is distributed unevenly throughout the state. Worse, the same municipalities that host disproportionately high shares of nonprofit property often suffer a disproportionately high demand for public expenditures.

The local governments are fighting back, using the limited tools at their disposal, such as zoning approval. Revenue-hungry municipalities have been increasing demands that exempt property owners make voluntary "payments in lieu of taxes," or "PILOTs."[25] Some charities have been willing to negotiate PILOTs (usually at a small fraction of the taxes they otherwise would pay) to win local goodwill and zoning waivers. PILOTs measured by the value of the property being taken off the rolls date back to 1928, when Harvard University began making PILOTs to Cambridge, Massachusetts. The PILOT technique recently turned nasty in Pennsylvania: After a state supreme court decision declared that exemption is premised on the charity's providing a substantial degree of gratuitous service, the City of Philadelphia offered to forgo challenges to exemption in return for "voluntary" payments equal to 40 percent of the tax otherwise due (33 percent if the charity acted quickly) (Leland 1996; Gallagher 1997).[26]

In applying PILOTs, the charities that look most attractive to local governments are those (1) that have "income" (excluding, in general, only donations), and (2) whose income comes primarily from patrons outside the taxing jurisdiction. Accordingly, taxing the nonprofit can be viewed as a proxy for taxing the nonresident patrons of the organization. Currently, the practice of challenging exemption or seeking PILOTs focuses on hospitals and institutions of higher education. Under the same theory, municipalities could extend this policy to museums and performing arts organizations—and even to break-even social service nonprofits, thus passing their costs on to government funders, state and federal. (Such a theory might provide a non-constitutional explanation of why municipalities have not sought to tax churches, which rely primarily on donations, and whose benefits are primarily local.)

FUTURE POLICY DIRECTIONS

As noted at the beginning of this essay, tax exemption defines an important nexus between government and nonprofit organizations in the United States. Symbolically, in the public's eye conferral of tax-exempt status is seen as legitimating the activities of individual non-profit organizations. At a more practical level, tax exemption expands the financial resources of nonprofit organizations in a variety of important ways. An important consequence of linking government policy toward nonprofit organizations to the tax code is that the environment in which charities operate can shift in important ways as tax laws change.

Charities are vulnerable to three different types of changes in the tax law. First, change could come head on, if Congress were to deliberately alter the eligibility rules; for example, Congress might repeal the tax exemption of nonprofit hospitals. Second, change could come indirectly as a result of overall changes to the tax structure that affect the value of the charitable-contribution deduction or of the income-tax exemption; for example, Congress might reduce the tax rates on individuals (thus increasing the tax price of giving) or on businesses (thus reducing the relative tax benefit of income-tax exemption). Finally, change could come incidentally through simplifying the tax code of rules that happen to fuel the demand for the types of services charities provide; for example, Congress might strip away the new tuition tax credits or eliminate the exclusion from workers' income for the value of employer-provided health insurance.

The reliance of charities on these types of tax subsidies suggests that nonprofits would not give them up without a fight. Viewing charities as above the political fray was always probably an idealized image, and the growing talk of tax reform is already bringing forth educational efforts by charities. The increasing political visibility of nonprofits will, in turn, likely put increased pressure on the current loose lobbying restrictions. In the process of defending against fundamental threats to their tax subsidies, charities risk appearing like any other special interest—and they could forfeit special claim to subsidies in the process.

Both this chapter and the others in this section suggest that the effects of eliminating all or some of the tax provisions that currently benefit nonprofit organizations would certainly not be uniform. For example, nonprofit organizations that depend on charitable contributions for a large portion of their financial resources have more reason for concern about tax changes that raise the after-tax cost of giving than do nonprofits that depend for their financing on fees-for-service paid out of government spending. Similarly, nonprofit organizations that rely on subsidies for specific social services that are provided through tax credits are more apt to be affected by changes in these provisions than are their counterparts who depend on charitable contributions.

Lastly, any time two different tax regimes could apply to the same activity, the opportunity for "tax arbitrage" exists. There is some evidence that nonprofits have become increasingly aware of these opportunities and sophisticated at exploiting them, by, for example, using unrelated business activities to earn additional revenue, and then "sheltering" such income from tax by overallocating to the taxable activity the expenses of "dual-use" assets. Yet the desire of policymakers to preserve not only the political boundaries between nonprofits and the government but also the economic boundaries between nonprofit organizations and for-profit enterprises may impose limits on this trend. As charities grow more sophisticated in operating both exempt and taxable enterprises, Congress might be unwilling to maintain the existing flexible tax regime. Short of replacing the income tax with a consumption tax, should it prove too hard to define taxable income for nonprofits, Congress could instead simply impose a (probably low-level) tax on investment income, making all nonprofit organizations potentially taxable.

Notes

1. Under the complicated rate structure now in effect, donors have an incentive to donate "collectibles": Tax on the appreciation is saved at the 28 percent capital gains rate instead of the new, lower 20 percent rate.

2. In general, the Internal Revenue Code limits the current deduction to 50 percent of the donor's adjusted gross income (AGI) for cash gifts, and to 30 percent of AGI for gifts of appreciated property; the limitations for gifts to that subset of charities known as

private foundations are 30 percent for cash and 20 percent for appreciated property. Any excess may be carried forward for five years under the same limitations. Moreover, the amount of a gift to a private foundation of property other than publicly traded securities is limited to the donor's basis in the property (I.R.C. § 170).

3. The estimates shown in table 4.3 should be viewed as rather rough "orders of magnitude." The policy simulation undertaken by Price Waterhouse is of the effects of replacing the current income tax with a flat tax that would allow no deductions for charitable contributions. Such a policy change would have effects similar, though not identical to, those resulting from abolishing the current deduction while retaining the income tax.

4. Although the projected decline in giving to religious organizations is striking, one should note that a uniform 32 percent (or 14 percent) reduction in giving would not likely occur across all nonprofit sectors. For example, a significant share of contributions to religious organizations is made by those who do not claim itemized deductions, and whose price of giving is already one dollar (see Clotfelter and Schmalbeck 1996).

5. Churches are not required to file the 990 return. Hence the public charities listed in table 4.5 do not include the churches listed in table 4.2.

6. See Graetz 1991, stating that of total national health expenditures in 1989, 38.5 percent was spent on hospital care; and the one-half of U.S. hospitals that are private, nonprofit institutions account for almost 65 percent of hospital expenses.

7. To use an accounting framework recently sketched out by Steuerle (1998), the charitable deduction increases the amount of charitable contributions of money and assets, and tax exemption allows nonprofits to capture a higher return on their net assets. Tax-exempt bond financing allows nonprofits to earn arbitrage profits on their investments, and property-tax exemption reduces the cost of real-property inputs to charitable activity.

8. The existence of donations uniquely increases the resources of the charitable sector. (The same is true of donations of time.) Henry Hansmann suggests that the income-tax exemption might be designed to compensate nonprofits for their inability to access the capital markets by issuing stock (Hansmann 1981, 72–5.)

9. See Schiff 1990, 9–10 and n. 12 at 16 (describing the "demonstration effects" identified by Feldstein and Clotfelter 1976; Schiff comments: "as the level of giving by others increases, it may take larger donations to 'buy' prestige and the like via giving, and spending on such goods may rise").

10. See Clotfelter and Schmalbeck 1997 and generally the essays in Clotfelter 1992. Because of the different types of charities favored by high-income and low-income taxpayers, though, a tax credit of, say, 25 percent not only would redistribute taxes from taxpayers with higher marginal rates to those with lower marginal rates but also "may result in certain activities, such as education, health care, and the arts, bearing the additional burden nominally imposed on the higher-income contributors. Other activities, such as religion and welfare, might be more likely to benefit from the tax savings given to lower-income contributors" (Bradford 1984, 88).

11. Riley (1997, 75) found: "For each of the Tax Years 1990 through 1993, the percentage of organizations that reported net income on Forms 990-T remained fairly stable, ranging from 44 to 47 percent. The remaining organizations reported zero net income or a deficit. For all four years, the percentage of organizations reporting net income gradually decreased as the size class of gross UBI increased." For 1993, exempt organizations reported a net $1 billion deficit ($4.7 billion in gross unrelated business income; $5.7 billion in total deductions), although 15,067 organizations reported positive net income of $603.6 million and paid UBIT of $180 million. This study covered all exempt organizations, not just section 501 (c)(3) organizations. Trade associations and business leagues (exempt under section 501(c)(6)) reported income from advertising, and social

clubs (exempt under section 501(c)(7)) pay tax on investment income and nonmember sales.

12. In *Rensselaer Polytechnic Institute*, the Service lost an attempt to allow the university deductions only for the marginal costs of renting out a hockey stadium. *Rensselaer Polytechnic Inst. v. Commissioner*, 732 F.2d 1058 (2d Cir. 1984). The Treasury regulations permit an allocation of dual-use expenses on "a reasonable basis." Treas. Reg. 1.512(a)-1(c).

13. See Wisconsin Statutes 70.11 (1995–96) (under (3), up to 80 acres are exempt for colleges and universities; under (4), up to 10 acres for educational, religious, or benevolent associations, but up to 30 acres for churches and religious associations; under (10), up to 40 acres for Y.M.C.A. or Y.W.C.A. training camps or assemblies; under (10m), up to 40 acres for Lions foundation camps for visually handicapped children; and under (11), up to 30 acres for Bible camps).

14. See M. A. Potter and B. B. Longest, "The Divergence of Federal and State Policies on the Charitable Tax Exemption of Nonprofit Hospitals," *Journal of Health Politics, Policy and Law*, Vol. 19, No. 2 (1994): 393–419; Mark Schlesinger and Bradford Gray, *A Broader Vision for Managed Care, Part 1: Measuring the Benefits to Communities*, Vol. 17, No. 3 (May/June 1998): 152–68.

15. See CBN Press Release 1998 (announcing a settlement between the Christian Broadcasting Network and the IRS in which, among other terms, CBN loses its tax exemption in 1986 and 1987 "due to the application of the rules prohibiting intervention in political campaign activities," pays a "significant" amount to the IRS, increases the number of outside directors on its board, and makes "other organizational and operational modifications to ensure ongoing compliance with the tax laws").

16. The price of giving increased even more in 1986 for gifts of appreciated property, when the unrealized appreciation became an item of tax preference under the alternative minimum tax (Auten, Cilke, and Randolph, 271, table 2). This rule was modified in 1990 and repealed in 1993. See also id. at 280, table 7 (showing that between 1979 and 1989, the average contribution (in 1991 dollars) by taxpayers with pre-tax income of $1 million or more dropped from $133,837 to $82,113, and by taxpayers with between $200,000 and $1 million in income dropped from $11,104 to $8,476).

17. Note that early state governments made no sectoral distinctions in bestowing or withholding tax subsidies. New England canal, turnpike, bridge, and manufacturing companies enjoyed the same tax exemption extended to eleemosynary institutions such as Yale College. (Hall 1992, 21.)

18. Hellerstein and Coenen 1996; Enrich 1996 discuss the "New Economic War between the States."

19. See, e.g., Milbank (1996): Republican presidential candidate Bob Dole declared that his proposal for a tax credit of up to $500 for poverty-fighting charities "would present Americans with a stark choice. . . . Give your money to the Department of Housing and Urban Development, or give it to Habitat for Humanity . . .[;] to big government, or to Big Brothers and Big Sisters." But Dole's proposal weakened in the face of budgetary realities. See Wright and Stokeld 1996: Dole's initial plan would have cost up to $120 billion in forgone taxes over the six-year budget period; the revised plan cost just $5.2 billion by permitting taxpayers to claim a credit for only one-half the amount donated, but not more than $50 in 1997 and $100 in 1998 (sunsetting thereafter).

20. Campaign Reform and Election Integrity Act of 1998, H.R. 3581, sec. 101(a) (defining "political activity" as influencing any election for federal office, influencing the consideration of any federal legislation or regulations, and educating individuals about any candidate for federal office or any federal legislation or regulation), 144 *Congressional Record* H. 1764 (Mar. 30, 1998) (recording Roll Call No. 81, 74 yeas and 337 nays).

21. For the Flat Tax, see Robert E. Hall and Alvin Rabushka, *The Flat Tax* (Hoover Institution Press, 2d ed., 1995); H.R. 2060 (July 19, 1995) (Congressman Armey) and S. 1050 (July 19, 1995) (Senator Shelby). For the USA Tax, see the USA Tax Act of 1995, S. 722, introduced by Senator Nunn and Senator Domenici (Apr. 25, 1995). For the National Retail Sales Tax, see the National Retail Sales Act of 1996, H.R. 3039, introduced by Congressmen Shaelfer, Billy Tauzin, and others (Mar. 6, 1996).

22. Deducting interest expense is inconsistent with the proper definition of a true consumption tax base.

23. Price Waterhouse (1997: ¶¶ 13, 14). Because the proposals are designed to be roughly revenue neutral, Price Waterhouse notes, the importance of the income effect is lessened in the aggregate. Id. at ¶ 133. "Giving will decrease 19 percent for each 10 percent increase in the price of giving. This effect swamps increases in giving as a result of increases in income. On average, a family will give about 3 percent more to charity when its income increases by 10 percent and about 3 percent less when its income decreases by 10 percent." Id. at ¶ 12. Price Waterhouse concedes that its estimates of the price elasticity of charitable giving are at the high end of studies and its estimates of the income elasticity for charitable giving are low. Id. at ¶ 182. Using other estimates produces a 24 percent decline rather than a 32 percent decline in giving under the Flat Tax, and a 23 percent increase rather than a 33 percent increase under the USA Tax. Id. at ¶ 187. Because of the lack of data on contributors' basis in donated property, Price Waterhouse could not account for changes in the level of noncash giving, which "may be seriously understating the total price effect of non-cash gifts." Id. at ¶ 157. Finally, the study did not address the difference between permanent and transitory responses to tax restructuring, so their "results may overstate the long-term reactions to tax reform." Id. at ¶ 216.

24. Carroll, Neubig, and Nilles (1995) (comparing the New Zealand model, which imposes the VAT on nonprofit organizations but exempts production of certain goods and services, with the European and Canadian model, which generally exempts nonprofits but taxes certain activities).

25. The term has long been in use to refer to payments made to affected municipalities by the federal government. See Advisory Commission on Intergovernmental Relations 1981. States also pay PILOTs to affected municipalities, but payments often fall short of amounts due. See, e.g., Commonwealth of Massachusetts 1994 (estimating that over the last seven years, cities and towns received about 50 percent of the amount called for in the statutory formula).

26. Leland (1996) found that Philadelphia contacted about 500 nonprofit organizations but entered into only 42 agreements, the rest enjoying "home-free" status; only about $3 million a year was being collected. In 1997 the state strengthened the benefits of voluntary agreements in legislation designed to clarify the constitutional definition of an "institution of purely public charity." Penn. Act No. 55 of 1997, 1997 PA H.B. 55.

References

Advisory Commission on Intergovernmental Relations. 1981. *Payments in Lieu of Taxes on Federal Real Property.* Washington, D.C., September.

Andreoni, James. 1989. "Giving with Impure Altruism: Applications to Charity and Ricardian Equivalence." *Journal of Political Economy* 97 (6): 1447–58.

———. 1990. "Impure Altruism and Donations to Public Goods: A Theory of 'Warm Glow' Giving." *Economic Journal* 100 (401): 464–77.

Anthony, Michael F. 1997. "Tax-Exempt/Proprietary Partnerships: How the Deal Gets Done." *Healthcare Financing Management* (Jan.).

Auten, Gerald E., James M. Cilke, and William C. Randolph. 1992. "The Effects of Tax Reform on Charitable Contributions." *National Tax Journal* (45): 267–90.

Barry, John S. 1996. "How a Flat Tax Would Affect Charitable Contributions." *Heritage Foundation Backgrounder.* Washington, D.C.: Heritage Foundation, Nov. 7.

Ben-Ner, Avner, and Benedetto Gui, eds. 1993. *The Nonprofit Sector in the Mixed Economy.* Ann Arbor: University of Michigan Press.

Bradford, David S., and U.S. Treasury Tax Policy Staff. 1984. *Blueprints for Basic Tax Reform,* 2nd ed. Washington, D.C.: Tax Analysts.

Brody, Evelyn. 1996. "Institutional Dissonance in the Nonprofit Sector." *Villanova Law Review* 41 (2): 433–504.

———. 1997. "Charitable Endowments and the Democratization of Dynasty." *Arizona Law Review* 39 (3): 873–948.

———. 1998a. "The Tax Treatment of Education after the Taxpayer Relief Act of 1997." *Tax Notes* 78 (Mar. 23): 1549–58.

———. 1998b. "The Limits of Charity Fiduciary Law." *Maryland Law Review* 56 (4, Summer): 1400–1501.

———. 1998c. "Of Sovereignty and Subsidy: Conceptualizing the Charity Tax Exemption." *Journal of Corporation Law* 23 (4, Summer, Nonprofit Symposium Issue): 585–629.

Carroll, Robert, Thomas S. Neubig, and Kathleen Nilles. 1995. "Impact of Structural Tax Reform on Nonprofit Organizations." *Tax Notes* 67 (June 26): 1785–94.

"CBN Press Release in Agreement with IRS." Mar. 14, 1998. Available electronically in LEXIS, Fedtax Library, *Tax Notes Today* File, 98 TNT 55-78 (Mar. 23).

Clotfelter, Charles T. 1990. "The Impact of Tax Reform on Charitable Giving: A 1989 Perspective." In *Do Taxes Matter? The Impact of the Tax Reform Act of 1986,* edited by Joel Slemrod (203–35). Cambridge: MIT Press.

———. ed. 1992. *Who Benefits from the Nonprofit Sector?* Chicago: University of Chicago Press.

Clotfelter, Charles T., and Richard L. Schmalbeck. 1996. "The Impact of Fundamental Tax Reform on Nonprofit Organizations." In *Economic Effects of Fundamental Tax Reform,* edited by Henry Aaron and William Gale (211–46). Washington, D.C.: Brookings Institution.

Commonwealth of Massachusetts, Auditor of the Commonwealth, Div. of Local Mandates. 1994. *A Review of the Financial Impact of the C.58 Payments-in-Lieu-of-Taxes (PILOT) Program on Massachusetts Cities and Towns.* Boston, Oct. 27.

Congressional Budget Office. 1997a. "The Potential Effects on Tax Restructuring on Nonprofit Institutions." CBO Papers (Feb.).

———. 1997b. "The Economic Effects of Comprehensive Tax Reform." Available at www.cbo.gov (July).

Cordes, Joseph J., and Burton A. Weisbrod. 1998. "Differential Taxation of Nonprofits and the Commercialization of Nonprofit Revenues." In *To Profit or Not to Profit: The Commercial Transformation of the Nonprofit Sector,* edited by Burton A. Weisbrod (83–105). Cambridge, UK: Cambridge University Press.

Enrich, Peter D. 1996. "Saving the States from Themselves: Commerce Clause Constraints on State Tax Incentives for Business," *Harvard Law Review* 110: 377–468.

Feldstein, Martin, and Charles Clotfelter. 1976. "Tax Incentives and Charitable Contributions in the U.S.: A Microeconomic Analysis." *Journal of Public Economics* 5: 1–26.

Gallagher, Janne G. 1997. "Pennsylvania Charitable Exemption Bill: An End to Litigation?" available in LEXIS, Fedtax Library, *State Tax Today* File, as 97 STN 227-17. (Nov. 25).

Glazer, Amihai, and Kai A. Konrad. 1996. "A Signaling Explanation of Charity." *American Economic Review* 86 (4): 1019–28.

Graetz, Michael J. 1991. "Statement of Michael J. Graetz, Dep. Assistant Secretary (Tax Policy), Dept. of the Treasury, before the Comm. on Ways and Means" (July 10), available in LEXIS, Fedtax Library, TNT File, as 91 TNT 146-10 (July 11), *Treasury Official Testifies on Tax-Exempt Status of Hospitals.*

Hall, Peter Dobkin. 1992. *Inventing the Nonprofit Sector.* Baltimore: Johns Hopkins University Press.

Hansmann, Henry. 1981. "The Rationale for Exempting Nonprofit Organizations from Corporate Income Taxation." *Yale Law Journal* 91: 54–100.

———. 1989. "Unfair Competition and the Unrelated Business Income Tax." *Virginia Law Review* 75: 605–35.

Hellerstein, Walter, and Dan T. Coenen. 1996. "Commerce Clause Restraints on State Business Development Incentives," *Cornell Law Review* 81: 789–878.

Hilgert, Cecilia. 1997. "Charities and Other Tax-Exempt Organizations, 1993." *SOI Bulletin* 16 (4, Spring): 122–34.

Hines, James R., Jr. 1998. "Nonprofit Business Activity and the Unrelated Business Income Tax." Working Paper 6820. National Bureau of Economic Research, Cambridge, Mass.

Hodgkinson, Virginia Ann, Murray S. Weitzman, et al. Independent Sector. 1997. *Nonprofit Almanac 1996–97.* San Francisco: Jossey-Bass Publishers.

JCT. See U.S. Congress, Joint Committtee on Taxation.

Jencks, Christopher. 1987. "Who Gives to What?" In The Nonprofit Sector: A Research Handbook, edited by Walter W. Powell (321–39). New Haven: Yale University Press.

Jensen, Jens Peter. 1931. Property Taxation in the United States. Chicago: University of Chicago Press.

Leland, Pamela J. 1996. "Philadelphia's PILOT Program: A Case Study." Paper presented at 25th annual meeting of Association for Research on Nonprofit Organizations and Voluntary Action ("ARNOVA"), New York City, November.

Milbank, Dana. 1996. "GOP Proposal Would Let Charity Begin at Home with Taxpayers Choosing Their Favorite Causes." Wall Street Journal A20 (June 20).

Pollak, Thomas H., and Kathryn L. S. Pettit. 1998. "The Finances of Operating Public Charities, 1989–1995." Washington, D.C.: Urban Institute.

Potter, M. A., and B. B. Longest. 1994. "The Divergence of Federal and State Policies on the Charitable Tax Exemption of Nonprofit Hospitals. Journal of Health Politics, Policy and Law 19 (2): 393–419.

Price Waterhouse LLP and Caplin and Drysdale, Chartered. 1997. "Impact of Restructuring on Tax-Exempt Organizations" (n.d., released April 28, 1997); available in LEXIS, Fedtax Library, TNT file as 97 TNT 83-21 [April 30, 1997]. Report commissioned by the Council on Foundations and Independent Sector).

Private Letter Ruling 9814051 (Apr. 6, 1998).

Randolph, William C. 1995. "Dynamic Income, Progressive Taxes, and the Timing of Charitable Contributions." Journal of Political Economy 103 (Aug.): 709–38.

Regan v. Taxation With Representation, 461 U.S. 540 (1983).

Rensselaer Polytechnic Institute v. Commissioner, 732 F.2d 1058 (2d Cir. 1984).

Revenue Ruling 98–15. 1998 Internal Revenue Bulletin 12 (Mar. 23): 6–10.

Riley, Margaret. 1997. "Exempt Organization Business Income Tax Returns: Highlight and an Analysis of Exempt and Nonexempt Finances, 1993." SOI Bulletin 16 (4, Spring): 75–98.

Salamon, Lester M. 1995. Partners in Public Service: Government-Nonprofit Relations in the Modern Welfare State. Baltimore: Johns Hopkins University Press.

Sansing, Richard. 1998. "The Unrelated Business Income Tax, Cost Allocation, and Productive Efficiency." National Tax Journal 51 (2): 291–302.

Schiff, Jerald. 1990. Charitable Giving and Government Policy. New York: Greenwood Press.

Schlesinger, Mark, and Bradford Gray. 1998. A Broader Vision for Managed Care, Part 1: Measuring the Benefits to Communities 17 (3, May–June): 152–68.

Simon, John G. 1987. "The Tax Treatment of Nonprofit Organizations: A Review of Federal and State Policies." In *The Nonprofit Sector: A Research Handbook*, edited by Walter W. Powell (67–98). New Haven: Yale University Press.

Steinberg, Richard. 1989. "The Theory of Crowding Out: Donations, Local Government Spending, and the 'New Federalism.'" In *Philanthropic Giving*, edited by Richard Magat. New York: Oxford University Press: 143–56.

Steuerle, C. Eugene. 1998. *Just What Do Nonprofits Provide?* Washington, D.C.: Urban Institute.

U.S. Congress, Joint Committee on Taxation. 1982. *General Explanation of the Revenue Provisions of the Tax Equity and Fiscal Responsibility Act of 1982*, H.R. Rep. No. 97-4961.

———. 1996. *Impact on State and Local Governments and Tax-Exempt Organizations of Replacing the Federal Income Tax*. JCS-4-96, Apr. 30.

———. 1997a. *Estimates of Federal Tax Expenditures by Budget Function, Fiscal Years 1998–2002*. JCS-22-97, Dec. 15.

———. 1997b. *General Explanation of 1997 Tax Legislation* (Dec. 17).

Wright, Carolyn D., and Fred Stokeld. 1996. "Charities Far from Sold on Dole's Proposed Charitable Tax Credit." *Tax Notes* 72 (Aug. 19): 951.

Chapter Five

GOVERNMENT FINANCING OF NONPROFIT ACTIVITY

Steven Rathgeb Smith

INTRODUCTION

Government financing is central to the financing of many nonprofits today. It is also controversial. The ongoing debate about the future of the American welfare state reflects in part a debate on the extent to which nonprofit organizations should be reliant on government funds. Some lawmakers argue that many nonprofit service agencies providing social and health services are too reliant on government funds (Olasky 1996). They recommend scaling back that support and pushing nonprofits to be reliant upon their local community resources, including private donations. Others advocate that greater portions of social services be channeled through nonprofits, including through religious organizations. Many leading nonprofit agencies, including Catholic Charities USA, assert that government funding is essential if these organizations are to provide an adequate level of service; local philanthropy cannot compensate for cutbacks in government funds.

As noted in previous chapters, the ongoing debate on government funding oversimplifies the complex interplay between government and nonprofit organizations, especially the many different routes through which government finances nonprofit activity. The debate also tends to miss a crucial issue: the actual impact of government financing on nonprofits' operations. This paper argues that government financing can have important and enduring effects on both the organizational culture of nonprofits and the nature of the services that they provide.

The paper is organized into five parts. An overview of trends in government financing of nonprofit organizations is followed by a discussion of four key ways through which government finances or encourages nonprofit activity: direct grants and contracts; fees from individuals and third-party organizations; tax credits and deductions; and regulations encouraging nonprofit service delivery. The subsequent section assesses trends in government financing and its effect on nonprofit agencies and the private philanthropic community. The next section analyzes the impact of government financing on nonprofit agencies, focusing on two different policy instruments: government contracts and tax credits. The final section connects the research on the impact of government financing to broader trends in public policy, including devolution and privatization.

PERSPECTIVES ON GOVERNMENT FINANCING OF NONPROFIT ORGANIZATIONS

Government financial support has a long tradition in the United States dating to the colonial period (Salamon 1987; Smith and Lipsky 1993; Hall 1987). Harvard University, the Massachusetts General Hospital, and other leading educational and health institutions received public funding in their formative years. Throughout the nineteenth century and the early twentieth century, government funding of nonprofit service agencies continued, although it tended to be most extensive in the urban areas of the Northeast and Midwest. For example, New York City relied almost completely upon nonprofit sectarian agencies such as Catholic Charities to provide child welfare services. But these arrangements tended to be the exception; most nonprofit agencies relied upon donations and fees and occasional payments from government; this pattern was particularly evident in southern, western, and rural states. Even in states such as New York with substantial government financing of nonprofit organizations, limitations were placed on this public aid due to broad concern that nonprofit agencies were receiving excessive public funding (Fetter 1901).

In the post–World War II period, government financing of nonprofits increased sharply, especially after 1960, fueled by extensive federal spending on a variety of new social and health programs, including community action agencies, community mental health centers, neighborhood health centers, and child protection agencies. In the 1970s, government funding essentially created a national network of mostly nonprofit drug and alcohol treatment programs. Other innovative community agencies receiving federal funds were battered-women shelters, rape crisis programs, and emergency shelters for runaway youth. In the 1980s, the government's principal response to AIDS, homelessness, and hunger was through contracting with nonprofit service agencies.

Government funding of nonprofit agencies increased in the 1980s despite the first major wave of policy devolution from the federal government to the states and local government. In 1981, President Reagan won passage of the Omnibus Reconciliation Act, which reduced federal spending and regulations on many federal social and health programs and devolved responsibility for their administration, at least in part, to the states (Gutowski and Koshel 1984).

A number of factors contributed to the continued escalation in government financing of nonprofit agencies during the 1980s. Many states and localities substituted their own funds for lost federal money. Over time, many states and localities refinanced their contracts with nonprofit agencies to take advantage of federal programs with expanding budgets. The shift was particularly apparent in mental health and some child welfare services where states shifted the cost of service to the Medicaid program. Further, many states continued to privatize services—notably mental health and development disability programs—previously provided by public employees. The result was a marked increase, albeit quite variable depending upon the state, in government funding of nonprofit agencies.

In addition, new federal programs were created to address urgent public problems. The Bush administration inaugurated a sharp rise in federal spending on drug and alcohol treatment and prevention programs and child welfare services. New funding was available for new or expanded child care, preschool, and foster-care programs.

Another big growth area for government funding of nonprofit agencies was low-income housing production. In the last 15 years, the federal government has almost completely withdrawn from the direct subsidization of low-income housing that was built primarily by for-profit developers with funding from the federal Housing and Urban Development (HUD) agency. Filling the void left by these programs, a number of community development corporations (CDCs) and nonprofit housing organizations have been created with seed grants and operational funding from national foundations and government. Typically, CDCs rely upon a mix of public and private funds, including direct grants and contracts, private investors, private donations, and bank loans. Tax credits are particularly important. The shift in housing policy can also be considered a form of devolution—low-income housing policy has shifted from an approach in which HUD administered several new construction and rehabilitation programs with often very detailed regulations and monitoring to a more decentralized approach with a far greater role for state housing agencies, local government, and CDCs and other community housing organizations.

More recently, the devolution of federal policy entered a new stage with the implementation of welfare reform, signed into law in August 1996 by President Clinton. The new legislation replaces the Aid to Families with Dependent Children (AFDC) program enacted in 1935 as a shared federal/state program with wide variations in payment levels to individuals and eligibility standards nationwide. In place of AFDC, new block grant programs to the states have been created and new discretion given to the states in the design of their income-assistance programs, although new federal regulations have been added on several issues, including setting targets for states to meet on the number of people on the welfare rolls, rates of teenage pregnancy, and work participation by welfare recipients. New federal regulations also encourage states to fund faith-based service agencies providing social services.

The impact of welfare reform is still unfolding and will not be known for several years; however, it appears clear already that the effect of welfare reform on nonprofit service agencies will vary greatly between states and even within states (De Vita, this volume). Many nonprofit agencies may actually gain new public funding for services such as child care and welfare-to-work programs. Other nonprofit agencies may lose revenues as state contracts are cut and agency clients lose benefits and eligibility for service. This latter shift is evident in "work-first" programs implemented as part of welfare reform; many clients have lost benefit eligibility as programs have shifted from job training to job placement.

The outlook for government financing of nonprofit agencies in other policy areas is also unclear. The major federal health care programs, Medicaid and Medicare, provide billions of dollars to nonprofit health care institutions, including hospitals, nursing homes, home health care agencies, hospices, and mental health agencies. While some members of Congress would like to fundamentally restructure these programs, it appears more likely that incremental adjustment and reform will occur, leaving them basically intact. Thus, their budgets will continue to grow. Other areas of probable increase in federal funding in the coming years are likely to include child care and preschool programs, child welfare, drug and alcohol treatment, and job training (Abramson, Salamon, and Steuerle, this volume).

In sum, the widely heralded devolution of federal social and health policy is decidedly mixed and incomplete; even welfare reform is a complex blend of states' rights and new federal mandates. The next section examines forms of government financing of nonprofit agencies in more detail.

GOVERNMENT FINANCING OF NONPROFIT ACTIVITY: MANY AND VARIED INSTRUMENTS

Direct government funding of nonprofits often receives most of the attention in the discussion of government financing of nonprofit activity. Government contributes to nonprofit revenues in many different ways, however, in addition to direct grants and contracts, including fees and third-party payments, tax credits and deductions, tax-exempt bonds, and regulations encouraging nonprofit service delivery. Indeed, the contribution of these other forms of government funding to nonprofit revenues is growing in importance to many nonprofits as direct funding and contracts become scarcer and more competitive.

Direct Grants and Contracts

As noted, government funding of nonprofit social and health agencies dates back to the colonial era. In the post–World War II period, an important evolution in the structure of direct public funding of nonprofit agencies has occurred. In the 1950s, government funding of nonprofit agencies was still a niche activity with a predominance in service categories such as child welfare. Typically, public subsidies to nonprofit agencies were provided with relatively minimal accountability requirements; nonprofit agencies were assumed to use the money wisely and in the best interests of their clients. State and local governments—the primary funder of social services in the period— were quite small and underfunded, with little capacity to monitor nonprofit grantees.

Beginning in the 1960s, public funding of nonprofit agencies increased sharply, spurred by large rises in federal funding. Over time, federal, state, and local governments found themselves with sizable and growing amounts of their service activities provided by nonprofit agencies. In some states such as Massachusetts, entire state departments contracted out their services to nonprofit agencies. Initially, many of the new federal and state grants lacked stringent guidelines and regulations. Over time, though, federal, state, and local agencies discovered that they now were in charge of a very large service system, albeit one provided by nonprofit agencies. In order to "rationalize" this system (Brown 1983) and ensure that the government agencies were maintaining accountability for the expenditure of public funds, the regulations governing contracts became increasingly stringent, even to the point of government sometimes specifying the names of the clients to be served by the agency (Smith and Lipsky 1993; Gronbjerg 1993).

In the early years of widespread contracting, most contracts entailed a direct relationship between government and the nonprofit agency. For example, the federal government would directly contract with a local community mental health center to provide mental health services to the local population. Likewise, a state Department of Social Services would directly contract with a local nonprofit child welfare agency. This government–nonprofit agency relationship tended to be the norm until the late 1980s, when a wave of managed care rolled through state and local government.

The advent of managed care has made the relationship between government and nonprofit agencies more complicated and indirect. For instance, in states such as New Jersey and Massachusetts, the state department responsible for child welfare services has replaced its direct contracts for foster care and related services with private, nonprofit agencies with a large contract with a third-party agency that is paid on a capitated basis to manage foster-care services for the state. This third-party agency then subcontracts with private agencies for the provision of services. Managed care is also quite prevalent in mental health services and various health care programs, including state Medicaid programs.

Managed care in the context of government contracting for social and health services presents complicated policy tradeoffs. The new managed-care firm may allow greater opportunity to focus on client and program outcomes and introduce efficiencies into the delivery of contract services. Certainly, managed care helps government avoid an open-ended payment system that seriously threatens the nonhealth parts of its budget. Yet the new managed-care arrangements can introduce great uncertainty about clients and revenues for nonprofit contract agencies because agencies no longer have a guaranteed annual number of clients. By blurring the lines of accountability between state and private agencies, managed-care contracts can create confusion regarding the appropriate agency responsible for ensuring the provision of quality service and the judicious use of public funds. This is a profoundly important policy and management concern because managed care shifts the risk of service delivery outcomes from the state agency (and to an extent the private agency) to the third-party managed-care organization. Usually, however, these managed-care organizations are not very open to outside scrutiny, especially by clients and consumers.

The effect of managed care on government contracting for services with nonprofit agencies varies depending upon the state, with some states embracing managed care extensively and other states and localities hardly adopting it at all. Nonetheless, managed care is likely to continue to rise in prominence in the delivery of government-funded social and health services; thus, its implications for contracting and for nonprofits in particular are potentially profound.

The scope of government contracting with nonprofit service agencies varies greatly across the country, reflecting different political and historical circumstances. States in the Midwest and Northeast tend to do more contracting in part because they had many nonprofit agencies in existence when federal funding arrived in the 1960s and 1970s. Also, many of these states had administrators and elected officials eager to take advantage of federal funding that was earmarked for local nonprofit programs. The Midwest and Northeast also tend to have a longer tradition of local philanthropic support of community organizations, so many nonprofits were able to combine public and private funds to expand services through contracting (especially since some federal programs required matching funds). Southern and western states have tended to do more selective contracting and have relied more heavily upon public-sector service delivery until relatively recently. In these states, enthusiasm among elected officials for privatization and reinventing government is producing greatly expanded contracting even for services long considered in the province of the public sector, such as child protection.

Fees

While direct contracting and grants are the most extensive form of government financing of nonprofit agencies, fees and other less direct financing methods are a growing portion of nonprofit revenues. "Fees" is an umbrella term for an assortment of revenue sources collected from individuals and organizations, including rent payments from homeless shelter residents, reimbursement from public and private health insurance programs, direct payments from clients, and income from technical assistance programs.

On nonprofit agency financial statements, fees are usually on a separate line from direct government grants and contracts, with the implication that fees are not government revenue. In reality, though, fee income for many nonprofit agencies is heavily reliant upon government funds. Some fees are direct government payments such as Medicaid reimbursement for mental health or health care services or Section 8 housing subsidies to low-income housing organizations. The government also subsidizes other fees such as day care fees through tax credits and deductions that increase nonprofit revenues but stimulate demand for nonprofit programs and services to higher levels than they would otherwise be. Government can also contribute to the nonprofits' fee income by agreeing to use their goods and services.

The shift to fee income can provide nonprofits with new sources of revenue, but it can also be highly unpredictable and uncertain, making it difficult for nonprofits to invest in their own programs. Government policymakers may gain greater flexibility over the use of public funds (in contrast to the more fixed and rigid contracting system). Yet government may also sacrifice the advantages of predictability characteristic of many direct contracts.

Tax Credits and Deductions

Like fees, tax credits and deductions are growing as a valuable source of nonprofit revenues either directly or indirectly. Two noteworthy examples of tax credit financing of nonprofits are the child-care and dependent credits and the low-income housing tax credit. The child-care credit can be claimed by individuals and couples on their tax returns. This credit partially offsets the cost of child care and dependent care (such as home health services), making nonprofit (and for-profit) services more affordable. The Low-Income Housing Tax Credit (LIHTC) allows private investors to reduce their tax liability by purchasing tax credits to build low-income housing. This tax credit program is vital to the ability of nonprofit community development and housing organizations to build low-income and affordable housing.

Tax deductions also help finance nonprofit activity by reducing the cost of private donations (Clotfelter 1985). Their value to the individual may be less than it was 20 years ago due to tax reform, which has reduced marginal tax rates (Abramson, Salamon, and Steuerle, this volume). Pending tax proposals such as the flat tax could essentially eliminate the value of the charitable tax deduction and potentially reduce the people's propensity to give (Clotfelter and Schmalbeck 1996). Tax exemptions from corporate income and property taxes also help nonprofit agencies reduce the cost of their programs (see previous chapter by Brady and Cordes).

Tax-Exempt Bonds

Large nonprofit institutions such as hospitals and universities (as well as for-profits) have taken advantage of tax-exempt bonds for decades. These bonds help nonprofit organizations finance the cost of capital improvements such as a new building or the renovation of an older structure. What is new is the growing use of tax-exempt bonds by smaller nonprofit organizations, such as housing development organizations, child welfare agencies, and mental health centers. In part, this new involvement is a ripple effect of federal policy changes. The reduction of federal spending in many areas of social policy—and the concomitant increased competition for remaining public (and private) funds—encourages nonprofits to seek new sources of revenue to finance their operations. In this environment, tax-exempt bonds are an attractive option, especially given that nonprofit agencies can obtain large amounts of financing that are very difficult to find from private donors. Also, debt payments on the bonds can be financed over many years. Many nonprofit and for-profit housing organizations also combine tax credits and bond financing to create a comprehensive package to build and operate low-income housing units. The increasing utilization of tax-exempt bonds, however, raises important concerns about equity and efficiency because the distribution of bond funding can be subject to political influence. The amount of subsidy is proportional to the amount of borrowing (rather than need), and economists have long argued that a portion of the tax subsidy from government bonds is actually garnered by high-income investors and not by the entities issuing the bonds. Furthermore, this form of subsidy may encourage an overinvestment in capital expenditures.

Regulations

Regulations are important to government financing of nonprofit activity. Many government agencies give preference to nonprofit agencies in their contracting for public services. For instance, the state of Massachusetts created a very elaborate network of private social service agencies in the 1970s and 1980s through government contracting; state officials were very reluctant to contract with private, for-profit agencies, so they were essentially excluded from the market for contracts. In Washington state, the state Housing Trust Fund will only provide low-income housing funds to nonprofit organizations.

Many government programs specifically contain set-asides for nonprofit and for-profit agencies. The tax credit program for low-income housing, for instance, has a set-aside for nonprofit housing developers in the IRS regulations. Many states have their own set-asides for nonprofits.

Government regulations on for-profit businesses can even help with nonprofit financing. For instance, the Community Reinvestment Act

(CRA) has been used with varying levels of effectiveness to encourage banks to provide capital for low-income housing projects.

Regulations are obviously different from direct financing, but they nonetheless are important to the overall government financing picture because they "carve out" a role for nonprofit organizations in service delivery and guarantee that nonprofit agencies in specific categories will be assured of government financing.

ASSESSING THE IMPACT OF GOVERNMENT FINANCING OF NONPROFIT ORGANIZATIONS

The actual impact of government financing on nonprofit organizations is the subject of an ongoing debate with origins dating at least to the nineteenth century and the writings of de Tocqueville (1955 ed.). He argued that voluntary associations were critical to democracy because they provided an opportunity for citizen participation and protected liberties from state infringement. Voluntary associations were alternatives to the state and the individual; ideally the boundaries between the state and voluntary associations should be separate and distinct.

In practice, though, the lines between the state and nonprofit service agencies were already blurred in the nineteenth century, given public funding of nonprofit service agencies primarily in the larger, more urban states such as New York, Illinois, and Pennsylvania. Around the turn of the century, an outcry ensued over public funding of nonprofit social welfare agencies. Alexander Fleisher (1914) declared, "Of all the problems in social policy none is more harassing, more complex and perennial than that of determining the proper relation of the state to privately managed charities within its borders. This is the sore thumb of public administrative policy" (p. 110). Many states eventually outlawed or restricted public subsidies and grants to private charities due to concern over mismanagement and the perceived corrupting influence of public money on private agencies (Fleischer 1914; Fetter 1901).

Many private social welfare agencies were opposed to receiving public funds during the early decades of the twenthieth century. They saw their mission as strictly private; public funds would confuse donors and clients and undermine the nonprofit agencies' distinctive niche within the service system. Private agencies were also worried that government funds might interfere with their autonomy (Smith and Lipsky 1993).

In the 1960s and 1970s, the advent of extensive government funding created greater acceptance of government funding by private agencies. Even agencies entirely dependent upon private donations for many decades dropped their reluctance to accept government funds. This support fit with the era's expansive vision that stressed the importance of government support of the needy and disadvantaged. Many private agencies also were losing money due to an inability to meet rising demand through private donations and fees; government funds, at least initially, offered the opportunity to support their services without any major change in mission or service and client mix (Smith and Lipsky 1993).

But opposition developed from many quarters. At a philosophical level, the work of theorists such as Robert A. Nisbet (1969), Robert Nozick (1974), Peter F. Drucker (1969), and Friedrich von Hayek (1960) grew in popularity. Despite great differences in emphasis and focus, these theorists all saw a basic conflict between the state and community, broadly defined. As the state grew, community, including voluntary associations, declined, with deleterious consequences for individual liberty and community life. Peter Berger and Richard John Neuhaus echoed this theme in their influential 1977 monograph, *To Empower People*. In it, they argued that government was a threat to community, including to the church and to voluntary associations. They specifically mentioned the potential risks of government funding to nonprofit service agencies, including the possibility of bureaucratization and higher costs (pp. 38–39). Their very de Tocquevillian message was further expanded by Glazer (1989) and Meyer (1982).

The Berger and Neuhaus perspective on the inevitable clash between the state and voluntary associations was disputed by Kramer (1982; 1987), who suggested that government funding did not necessarily lead to a significant loss of organizational autonomy, partly due to a lack of government oversight and monitoring. Many nonprofit service agencies also believed that the benefits of increased funding made up for any infringement of their autonomy. In a similar vein, Salamon (1987) argued that the government-nonprofit relationship in social services is best conceptualized as a partnership in which both parties benefit: government can take advantage of the flexibility and efficiencies of nonprofit agencies, and nonprofit service organizations receive financial support unavailable in the private philanthropic market.

This chapter presents a different perspective on the government-nonprofit relationship. Government funding of nonprofit agencies does indeed affect the operations of nonprofit agencies, with profound effects on the services and clients of nonprofit service agencies. The specific effects on a nonprofit agency will vary depending upon the type of service, the extent of professionalization, the agency's origins and mission, and the character of the government-nonprofit relationship.

The basic shift within nonprofit organizations due to government funding is rooted in the differing approach to services and clients taken by nonprofits and government. Nonprofits emerge out of a desire of a like-minded "community" of people to address a problem or social need. Examples include battered-women shelters, neighborhood drop-in centers for youth, interfaith homeless shelters, community health centers, and Lutheran Social Services. All such organizations represent a "community" and ideally feel a special obligation to their community of interest. Battered-women shelters may view their obligation as primarily to any abused women in a given locality; community health centers may want to serve anyone in a community regardless of their specific problem; and a drop-in center may serve any adolescent who identifies himself or herself as troubled and in need of help. Responsiveness to a particular community is the guiding norm (Smith and Lipsky 1993; Lipsky and Smith 1989–90).

Government, by contrast, tends to approach services and clients from the standpoint of equity. Government officials charged with distributing funds or services must constantly justify why they provide service to one group rather than another, since government does not have the resources to serve everyone in need. In a democracy, groups can seek redress if they feel they are being unfairly treated; government officials are accountable to these groups and the citizenry in general for their policy choices (Moe 1990). Equity can be interpreted in a variety of ways, but in social and health services, it usually means defining need in order to allocate resources by criteria deemed to be fair—e.g., income, geographic location, and severity of presenting illness.

Initially, government funds provided to nonprofit service agencies through contracts in the 1960s and 1970s were accompanied with relatively minimal accountability requirements. But as the scope of funding expanded, government officials imposed regulations and expectations on nonprofit agencies based upon a norm of equity. For example, nonprofit community mental health centers were required to serve only people with a diagnosis of chronic mental illness; in some cases, centers were awarded special financial bonuses if they met certain performance targets pertaining to their public clients.

Because of their need to be responsive to a particular community rather than to equity as a guiding norm, nonprofit agencies may clash with government over policy matters relating to services, clients, and staff. For instance, a program for troubled youth may prefer to serve any adolescent in the community, but government officials may believe the program should only serve the neediest clients. Indeed government staff may accuse the program of "creaming"—taking only the easiest cases and neglecting the so-called tough cases. Nonprofit agencies often respond to this charge by arguing that they are only providing services within their mission and in any case were never designed to serve very troubled youth. The same disagreement between government and nonprofits can occur when nonprofit agencies favor certain groups such as coreligionists or local neighborhood children.

Accountability for Public Funds

Regulations pertaining to government contracts can be divided into two broad categories: (1) administrative or procedural and (2) programmatic. The former refer to the process governing the contracting relationship: terms of the bidding process; requirements on annual audits; billing requirements; and compliance with relevant federal and state laws such as the Americans for Disabilities Act and the Drug-Free Workplace Act. Programmatic regulations pertain to the substantive content of the service provided by a nonprofit under government contract. Examples include regulations affecting the types of clients, the way in which the service is delivered, the number of professional staff, and space requirements.

The impact of government regulations on nonprofit agencies will tend to vary based upon the type of agency. Nonprofit service agencies can be divided into three basic groups: 1) traditional organizations with a long-standing history in the community such as Lutheran Social Services or the Salvation Army; 2) government-sponsored nonprofit organizations where government provided the initial funding and continues to supply most of the revenue; and 3) service agencies with roots in community initiative. Good examples are youth service agencies, many soup kitchens, and AIDS service agencies.

Many service agencies are started through community initiative, broadly defined; they are often nonprofessional, with a lack of extensive administrative structures. Some originally emerge from an unincorporated group of like-minded people concerned about a social problem. A clear separation between board and staff was often absent; in the beginning, few agencies had full-time executive directors. Government funding requires these agencies to adopt new administrative and accounting procedures, add professionals, institute new financial management practices, and, in some cases, modify existing physical structures.[1]

Administrative and programmatic restructuring in response to government funding is also apparent in the other two groups of agencies but in a slightly different pattern. Traditional agencies may sometimes be required to undertake expensive changes in their programs to comply with government regulations; however, when government funds arrived in significant amounts in the 1960s and 1970s, many of these agencies were already formal organizations with large boards and staff, with professional social workers and psychologists. Over time, new staff regulations are usually added and the client mix changed in a way that forces the agencies to hire more specialized staff; sometimes adaptations to the physical plant may be required. Government-sponsored agencies may demonstrate few changes after the awarding of a contract because they restructured their programs before they responded to a government RFP (request for proposals). As agencies already oriented toward government, they embody the government's expectations on issues such as financial reporting and service delivery.

These organizational changes raise difficult dilemmas and tradeoffs for public policy. One effect is to significantly increase the agencies' overhead costs, requiring them to raise much larger sums of money to fund their basic operations. Due to the scarcity of philanthropic funds, most agencies cannot fund these additional expenses from private donations and thus need government funds for their basic operations in a way that did not exist prior to the receipt of government contracts.

Yet higher overhead expenses are also related to the expansion of services accompanying government funds. Services are more widely available and delivered with more professionalism. Whether services are actually more effective in helping the agencies' clients remains a source of debate (Glazer 1989; Schambra 1997).

ALTERNATIVES TO GOVERNMENT: OPTIONS FOR DIVERSIFICATION

Private Philanthropy

Nonprofit service agencies face many challenges and dilemmas as they seek to raise nonpublic funds, including a lack of capital and stiff

competition. Further, important changes under way in private philanthropy are making the raising of substantial private revenues, especially to support operational expenses—the main focus of government
revenues—quite difficult.

THE UNITED WAY

One possible source of private charitable donations for nonprofit service agencies is the United Way. Ironically though, changes under way
at the United Way may actually increase the dependence of some
nonprofit agencies on government funds.

Historically, the United Way was organized for the benefit of its
member agencies, usually the large agencies in town such as the
American Red Cross, the Boy Scouts and Girl Scouts, Catholic Charities, and family service agencies. These agencies could depend upon
annual allocations that hinged upon the success of the annual campaign. Many UW agencies, such as the Boy Scouts, did not receive
public funds for services, but other UW agencies, such as family service and child welfare organizations, received substantial amounts of
public funds (Smith and Lipsky 1993; Gronbjerg 1993).

In the 1960s and 1970s, the percentage contribution of United Way
funds to a typical agency's budget dropped as government contracting
expanded. Then, in the 1980s, the United Way was pressed to open
membership to a broader array of community agencies, especially the
many service agencies created directly or indirectly by the big buildup
of federal funds in the previous two decades. Gradually, UW chapters
responded, although to varying extents. At present, many UW chapters, including large chapters in Seattle and Washington, D.C., are
shifting to a project-oriented allocation process that essentially re-
peals the traditional concept of membership and entitlement to a
certain allocation every year. Instead, the UW will only fund agencies
offering projects that fit with the overall priorities of the UW chapter.
United Way chapters are more like local community foundations that
give money for short-term purposes, innovation, and start-up costs;
many are even establishing endowments. Many older UW agencies
depended upon regular allocation every year to fund their operational
budget, including administration, and to cross-subsidize money-
losing services such as services to the poor. As government contracting
expanded, UW funding became particularly valuable since government contracts are program or project based and typically do not
provide substantial amounts of money for cross-subsidization. The
changes in UW funding will squeeze these agencies since the effect
will be to limit agencies' ability to cross-subsidize or to invest in

administration. (UW grants for new agencies are typically quite small.) Nonprofits will thus find government funding even more attractive, despite its regulations and guidelines, because UW funding will no longer be a source of unrestricted operating money. Agencies will be tempted to bid on contracts because a new contract may offer more funds and at least a bit more money for administration, and certainly more than UW funding. This also fuels political advocacy by nonprofits to push up their existing contract rates from government.

UW funding is also becoming more like public funding, a sharp departure in orientation. Arguably, 30 years ago, the United Way funded services that had little direct connection to public policy— e.g., the Boy Scouts, the Girl Scouts, the American Red Cross, and the Boys Club. In that sense, it was private philanthropy supporting strictly private programs. But today older programs with no connection to public policy are falling into disfavor for UW funding. Increasingly, the emphasis is on programs with a connection to public priorities such as drug prevention or intervention with high-risk youth. The reasons for this shift are complex. In part, it is the ripple effects of the Reagan cutbacks, which shone a harsh spotlight on the local UW giving patterns. More generally, it may represent the spread of new ideas about social policy and the uses of private philanthropy. UW chapters are even requiring their agencies to be more accountable and to measure the outcomes of their services, which fits with the move to reinvent government by focusing on outcomes.

Private Foundations

The universe of foundations is so diverse that generalizing is hazardous. Many of the large national foundations, such as the Ford Foundation and the Robert Wood Johnson Foundation, have historically played a leading role in funding innovation and social experimentation at the local level. Of late, many of them, such as the Robert Wood Johnson Foundation, the Annie E. Casey Foundation, and the Northwest Area Foundation, are supporting complex action-oriented initiatives to address pressing problems such as substance abuse, crime, at-risk youth, and maternal and child health. Many local foundations give money for high-priority projects such as drug prevention or reducing teen pregnancy.

The national and local foundations tend to give preference to capital projects or to seed money for program innovation. Even the new multi-year projects of the Casey and Robert Wood Johnson Foundations are funded on a declining basis, with the expectation that local sponsors will be found to substitute for foundation funds. The preference for capital and seed projects means that nonprofit agencies interested in obtaining funding to support their ongoing operations are unlikely to receive foundation support; this gives nonprofits an incentive to seek government funds—which will support operational expenses—or to develop alternative means of private funding.

Charitable Giving

Private donations from individuals and corporations are an important source of revenue for some nonprofit service agencies, especially larger ones with name recognition such as the Salvation Army. Yet overall, nonprofit service agencies, especially smaller organizations, have great difficulty generating substantial private donations. Indicative of the problem is the decline in giving to human-service organizations noted by the Independent Sector in its most recent 1996 *Nonprofit Almanac*. Private contributions as a percentage of total revenue of nonprofit social and legal service agencies declined from 32 percent to 20 percent from 1977 to 1992 (Independent Sector 1996, 180). In recent years, giving to nonprofit human service agencies has failed to keep pace with inflation (see chapters two and three, this volume).

The difficulty of generating private donations and keen competition for funds encourage nonprofit agencies to look to government for funding. To be sure, nonprofit agencies may still seek private donations, but the funds will generally be insufficient to compensate for government cutbacks or to greatly expand services. Consequently, nonprofits are very wary of simply relinquishing a contract if government expectations and demands are deemed to be unreasonable or unduly onerous.

Earned Income and For-Profit Ventures

To varying degrees, nonprofit service agencies are more involved in entrepreneurial and for-profit ventures. Those can include an almost dizzying array of initiatives and programs, including cause-related marketing, affinity credit cards, contracts between nonprofit agencies and for-profit companies, and the creation of for-profit subsidiaries or even separate for-profit companies to tap new markets. Nonprofit service agencies are diversifying their revenue base, although we do not really know the extent or success of such diversification.

Nonprofit agencies differ in their ability to tap these revenue sources. Many larger agencies have the capital and financial savvy to undertake certain initiatives, especially cause-related marketing and partnerships with for-profit firms. For example, the Northwest AIDS Foundation in Seattle recently entered into a partnership with Starbucks Coffee in which a percentage of the proceeds from the nationwide sales of a specialty coffee will go to the Foundation. Bridge Housing of San Francisco, a major nonprofit builder of low-income housing, has successfully tapped private investors for funds. Many other smaller community housing organizations have done so as well. Another form of nonprofit/for-profit partnership is a contract between a nonprofit human service agency and a for-profit business where the clients of a nonprofit agency work under contract for a local business. For instance, Pioneer Human Services in Seattle has contracts with Boeing and Starbucks to provide workers for certain production activities and, at Starbucks, maintenance and dishwashing.

Despite the increase in these nonprofit/for-profit combinations, they usually are not a substitute for government funds: they often work in combination with government funds (Bridge Housing or community development organizations are good examples), or they support the activities of a nonprofit agency that eschews government funds, such as Pioneer Human Services.

ORGANIZATIONAL ADAPTATION AND CHANGE: THE IMPACT OF CONTRACTS AND TAX CREDIT FINANCING

The general effects of government financing on nonprofits vary depending upon the agency. Many factors affect the response of nonprofit agencies to government financing, including the history of the organization, the orientation of its leadership, and its service and client mix. The revenue streams of nonprofit service agencies are varied and complex (Smith 1996; Gronbjerg and Smith 1998).

As nonprofit revenues diversify, it is plausible to assume that the response to government financing might change. Diversification might allow nonprofits greater flexibility in their operations and enhance their bargaining position with government, allowing them to even relinquish a contract if they deemed it appropriate. That approach presumes that nonprofit service agencies are one organizational entity that can use various pots of revenues to cross-subsidize different parts of the organization, assuming that the revenues are "fungible"—that they can be moved from one part of the organization to another (Thompson 1967; James 1985).

Paradoxically, the potential of cross-subsidization is diminishing even as revenues diversify. Many reasons account for this change.

First, government funding has declined in real terms for many agencies even if they have been able to keep their contracts. With less "slack" in the budget for a particular program, the agency is less able to move surplus revenue from one contract to another. Second, the emphasis on outcome funding and accountability means that more than ever, agencies are reviewed for their compliance with contract stipulations, including line-item spending. The result is less budgetary flexibility. Third, new regulations prevent agencies from directly subsidizing certain positions, such as fundraisers, with government funds.

The increased difficulty of cross-subsidizing operations with public funds may be positive for public policy in some respects. For example, agencies may be more accountable for their money and less tempted to use it to fund non-program-related expenses. The expenditure of public funds may be more consonant with the purposes of the grant. However, an agency may not have sufficient funds to invest in outcome evaluation, monitoring, and program improvements. Also, nonprofit agencies now have greater incentive to develop sources of earned income and fees and to embark on commercial ventures (Lifset 1989), creating new mixed public, nonprofit, and for-profit hybrid organizations that raise new challenges for nonprofit managers and regulators.

The following sections detail the effects of government financing on nonprofits with two different types of revenues: contracts and tax credits. Many nonprofit organizations, especially community development corporations and nonprofit housing agencies, receive contracts and tax-credits financing. It is useful to examine both types of revenue because contracting involves a direct relationship between government and nonprofits (although managed-care arrangements are changing the relationship), while tax credits are more indirect and involve private investors, for-profit businesses, and different government agencies. Since the policy instruments are different (Salamon 1989; Stone 1996), one might predict that the impact on nonprofits would be different. Yet, as the next sections indicate, these two forms of financing share many similarities in terms of impact on nonprofits, including their relationship with government. These sections contain profiles of different nonprofit organizations chosen to reflect the variety of nonprofit service agencies.

Contracting for Services

CASE ONE

This agency is a large sectarian social service organization in the Pacific Northwest with a $17 million annual budget. The agency fits into the traditional category since it has a long history in the community and provides many different types of services in the Puget Sound region, including home care, a homeless shelter for single men, emergency assistance, adoptions, and a residential facility for teen mothers. About 70 percent of its budget is from government contracts, while another 10 percent is derived from a variety of fees coming from government sources. The agency is much larger than it was in the early 1980s, demonstrating that, despite devolution, many individual agencies, especially large ones, have continued to grow.

This agency, which is central to the overall public service delivery system in the Puget Sound, is sectarian—its services are available to anyone and, indeed, 90 percent of its clients are not affiliated with the agency's denomination. Clients are chosen based upon criteria established in government contracts. For example, its home care program relies entirely upon referrals from the state Department of Social and Health Services (DSHS); clients need to meet the state's criteria for admittance into the program. Many other agency programs are required to use state or city referral criteria. The agency is subject to a variety of state and federal regulations on wage and hour laws, union representation, immigration and citizenship, nondiscrimination, access for the disabled, and Drug-Free Workplace rules. The agency has had to make extensive investments in a financial management system in order to track the agency's many revenue streams. Increasingly, the agency is required to track outcomes for its programs.

The compliance of the agency with many government mandates and regulations, despite an almost bewildering array of government revenue streams, demonstrates the lack of fungibility of its government revenues. In a sense, each government program is almost a self-contained entity with limited ability to cross-subsidize other parts of the operation.

The agency does not simply keep silent about its own goals and priorities. It consistently opposed the welfare reform legislation and continues to subsidize a poverty advocacy organization that uses its facilities. Nonetheless, its legislative priorities focus on obtaining rate increases for its programs threatened with cutbacks. The agency is also an active member of an advocacy coalition of Puget Sound human service providers receiving government funds.

Case Two

Another agency in the Seattle area is a "government-sponsored" agency created about 20 years ago by an entrepreneur interested in the disadvantaged. He was able to obtain city funding for his organization to provide technical assistance and support to nonprofit agencies in Seattle on capital planning and physical plant issues. For instance, if a local nonprofit housing organization needs help with the design of a new housing project, this agency will offer initial help and support. Another example is a social service agency that needs to redesign its physical space in order to accommodate a new program; this nonprofit agency will offer its design services to the social service agency. Essentially, the agency functions as a "technical assistance" outreach activity of the Seattle Department of Housing and Human Services.

From its inception until the early 1990s, the agency depended almost entirely on government grants—primarily federal funds given to the city that were then regranted to the agency. Because government funding was flowing into the agency, the board did little fundraising and tended to defer to the executive director in the management of the organization. The agency received scant earned income, despite the potential of the agency to sell its services to a variety of clients for a fee and still remain within its mission of serving the infrastructure needs of the Seattle nonprofit community.

The requirements of its funding meant that the agency had to be very careful about its choice of clients: they needed to be charitable nonprofit agencies in Seattle. Moreover, its contractual understanding with the city required it to avoid unfairly competing with private, for-profit design firms. Over time, funding has become progressively more restrictive. In the early years, the agency could do community planning and research—i.e., projects that produce information but not necessarily a building with some of the grant funds. Today, it can only do projects that lead to constructed buildings. And next year, in a sign of the increasing narrowness of the funding, the agency will lose all of its city grant funding because that money is being reallocated to the "outcome beneficiaries," meaning the nonprofit agencies currently benefiting from the services of this technical assistance agency.

Like agency #1, public funding for this agency has not declined during the past 15 years, although its major grant will end next year. The continued availability of public funds has created management difficulties for the agency, including board resistance to active fundraising. Absent significant private donations, the agency has sought to increase its fee income. Recently, the agency absorbed a for-profit design firm with a lengthy list of nonprofit clients. The new agency remains nonprofit but with a for-profit subsidiary. The agency now has the potential for substantial earned income.

Despite this new revenue, the agency still faces the same regulations and constraints on its government contracts; earned income has not given it a better bargaining position with the city. Indeed, in some respects, its bargaining position is worse than before. With existing grant funds ending without adequate substitutes, the agency has an incentive to gain favor with government for possible new contracts. The situation is exacerbated by the characteristics of fee income, which tends to be more project-specific and narrower in its coverage than public grant funding.

CASE THREE

This agency has roots in community organizing of Seattle's immigrant community. It provides an array of programs for immigrants, although in recent years it has focused on housing construction and renovation and economic development. Its program mix is similar to many nonprofit community development corporations. Its government funding is diverse; it receives direct contracts for services and money from the city through a special housing fund and state and federal funds for housing and economic development and occasionally participates in the tax credit program for low-income housing.

A persistent dilemma for the agency is its relationship to the city. The agency would like to have the flexibility in the development and implementation of its housing development programs to make its own decisions on a range of important issues—from the determination of a reasonable budget to choosing the architect for its projects to selecting its target client population. Even though the agency is using city funds, the agency believes that the project is "its" project. The city, however, takes the alternative approach—that the nonprofit agency is spending city money, hence the agency is implementing a "city" project, justifying an extensive monitoring role for city officials. City officials believe that they must ensure that money is being spent wisely or they will be held accountable by the city council, the mayor, and the citizenry. Interestingly, most of the money comes from neither the nonprofit nor the city, but from state and national taxpayers.

The city has an extensive prequalification process for grant funds for housing projects. As part of that process, the city works with local nonprofit agencies to develop a proposal that meets the city's budgetary, programmatic, and administrative expectations. The city does not even accept applications from agencies that do not agree to abide by city regulations. This process tends to favor the larger, established agencies that are in a position to meet the city's proposal criteria. As a result, the city tends to award grants to the same handful of agencies every year; it is a competitive bid process, but only a select number of agencies have the management capability to undertake the city projects and are thus eligible.

The criteria employed by the city in the allocation of funds to this agency and other housing organizations fit with the equity norm. These criteria emphasize working families, people with disabilities, the elderly, and families who are victims of domestic violence. In addition, the city strives to target individuals who earn no more than 30 percent of the median income (City of Seattle 1997, 12–13). Although these criteria are perfectly reasonable, many nonprofits, including this one, may want to develop projects for people with higher incomes or single men, for instance; these projects are unlikely to be funded through the use of city funds.

Like the other nonprofits profiled, this agency participates in an advocacy coalition of other nonprofit service providers in their policy area—the coalition of low-income housing developers. The coalition focuses its attention on representing member concerns before the local city and county governments. They lobby for more money and work with government administrators on regulatory policies affecting their organizations.

Tax Credit Financing

As noted, nonprofit organizations benefit from an array of tax credits, including the Low Income Housing Tax Credit (LIHTC) and child care and dependent tax credit. This section focuses on the LIHTC because it has grown substantially as an important source of funds for community-based housing and community development organizations. (The Treasury Department is urging an increase of more than 40 percent in federal appropriations.) These tax credits are also an example of the shift away from direct contract income for community-based agencies to other sources of government funds.

Congress enacted the LIHTC as part of the major overhaul of the tax system in 1986. The LIHTC "may be claimed by owners of residential rental property used for low-income rental housing. The credit is claimed annually, generally for a period of 10 years" (House Ways and Means Committee 1996, 820). The credit amount is based on the qualified basis of the housing units.[2] In order to qualify for the tax credit, a rental unit must meet one of two conditions: 1) 20 percent or more of the aggregate residential rental units are occupied by individuals with 50 percent or less of area median income; or 2) 40 percent or more of the aggregate rental units in the project are occupied by individuals with 60 percent or less of area median income (House Ways and Means Committee 1996, 820). Credit eligibility depends on the existence of a 15-year extended low-income use agreement for the property. If the property ceases to conform to these federal regulations, a portion of the tax credit may be recaptured from the property's owners.

These regulations are part of the federal legislation and are administered by the IRS. The actual allocation of the tax credits, however, is determined by state and local government authorities (usually the statewide Housing Finance agency). The amount of tax credit available to these state agencies is based upon a formula; each state receives an annual credit allocation equal to $1.25 per resident (House Ways and Means 1996, 820). LIHTC budget authority rose from $313 million in 1987 (the first year of the LIHTC) (House Ways and Means 1996, 821) to an estimated $3.2 billion in FY 1998 (Executive Office of the President 1997a, 73).

These regulations provide the rough outline of the program, and the IRS is required to review each project on an annual basis for compliance with federal regulations. The allocation of the tax credits is actually much more complicated, however, and involves a wide variety of public and private actors. A low-income rental housing project using the LIHTC starts with a local nonprofit agency (or for-profit developer). The agency identifies a project that merits funding. It then applies for tax credits to the state housing authority, which in Washington state is the Washington State Housing Finance Commission.

The commission shares the same problem as government agencies responsible for contracting for services: it has far more demand for its money (the tax credits) than it can meet, as the credits are worth a substantial portion of the entire cost of construction. Nonprofit and for-profit developers compete intensely for these tax credits, although most for-profit developers are only interested in projects for the top range of the eligible median income (50 to 60 percent). Nonprofits can serve a lower-income clientele because, in addition to tax credits, nonprofits are eligible for a host of other subsidy programs—from direct cash grants to private donations (not usually a sizable revenue source) to lower interest rates from banks.

Due to the competition for tax credits, the Housing Finance Commission—like its colleagues administering contract funds—tries to employ a fair and equitable process to allocate the credits. The Washington State Commission uses a process similar to other states—the state has an elaborate point system to evaluate a rental housing project proposal. Embedded in the point system are the state's priorities. While all projects must meet federal regulations in order to be even considered for a tax credit, projects receive "extra" points for special provisions such as: 1) the project will involve historic preservation;

2) the residents of the rental housing will have incomes below 30 percent of the median income or have special needs such as mental illness or development disabilities; and 3) the project will serve a geographically underserved area, such as a rural part of the state.

Given this point system, nonprofit and for-profit housing organizations have an incentive to "load up" the project with characteristics that will receive higher points. For instance, an agency may have originally planned to serve families with 50 percent of the median income because that focus fits best with its mission. The point system encourages agencies to serve a lower-income population. That raises a difficult public-policy tradeoff: it may be good public policy to use the tax credits to serve a lower-income population, but it may distort the mission of a nonprofit and in some cases spur it to undertake projects that would be better suited for other organizations. One exaggerated example of the incentives built into the point system is a funded project that was actually sited in two different locations, including one rural location, in order to qualify for extra points. Programmatically, it was not the best project, but it nonetheless received additional points because of its geographic focus. Occasionally, the point system may encourage financially risky projects as well. Recently, a nonprofit housing agency agreed to reduce the required deposit for its renters, at least theoretically allowing a more financially needy resident population; as a result, the agency received additional points. But the agency may not have enough funds to cover the normal rental expenses, potentially causing problems later in the life of the rental project.

Once the tax credits are awarded, the nonprofit agency sells them to investors, who are ultimately the people who benefit from the tax credit. The housing organization will advertise through various outlets that it has been awarded tax credits, inviting investors to "bid" on the credits. In the early years of the LIHTC, the bid process did not generate a lot of interest; typically, nonprofit agencies received less than 40 cents on the dollar. For instance, if a nonprofit housing agency received $1 million in tax credits, it could expect to receive only about $200,000 to $300,000 in actual cash from investors. The remaining funds for the project would come from other public and private subsidies. (Usually, a low-income housing project is structured as a limited partnership where the private investors own 99 percent of the project and the nonprofit agency owns 1 percent but is considered the controlling partner.)

Over time, LIHTC has generated increasing investor participation and interest. A web of different investors now bids on a project, including national equity funds, banks, and large corporations. Currently, agencies can expect to receive 80 cents or more on the dollar. While nonprofit agencies receive "more for their money," few projects are solely tax credit deals. Most low-income housing projects using tax credits contain an array of other subsidies, including tax-exempt bonds, direct cash grants, in-kind help from government (e.g., donations of property and equipment), a below-market interest rate from banks, and in some cases private donations.

The growth of the LIHTC symbolizes both the changes in federal housing policy and the shift from direct grants to other sources of public financing by nonprofit service agencies at the local level. It also illustrates the complex changes in federal policy that make it difficult to generalize about trends such as devolution.

Although federal support for low-income housing dates back to 1937, more than half of all currently outstanding commitments were funded over the past 20 years. Between 1977 and 1996, about 2.8 million net new commitments were funded to aid low-income renters; however, the number of net new rental commitments funded each year steadily declined, from 375,000 to 78,000 (House Ways and Means Committee 1996, 918).

In addition, the federal government moved away from production-oriented (or supply-side) subsidies—such as new construction and rehabilitation and renovation of existing housing—to demand-side subsidies such as vouchers, especially through the Section 8 Existing Housing and Voucher program. Support from HUD for the new construction of low-income housing units dropped from 247,667 units in 1977 to an estimated 17,731 units in 1996 (House Ways and Means Committee 1996, 919). Yet the total number of households receiving assistance increased substantially from 3.2 million at the beginning of fiscal year 1977 to more than 5.7 million at the beginning of fiscal year 1996 (House Ways and Means Committee 1996, 918).

The LIHTC was proposed as part of a complex set of tax subsidies during the tax reform debate of 1984–86. Some believe it was initially suggested as a partial offset to the shift of HUD to demand-side subsidies. However, it is more likely that the origins of LIHTC are due to the politics of the tax reform debate; the tax-writing committees had jurisdiction over subsidies (such as tax credits), not direct expenditures (such as vouchers). Consequently, the LIHTC cannot be viewed as simply a substitute for other government housing finance programs.

In contrast to many of the HUD production-oriented programs, the LIHTC created a long list of supporters and advocates: state and local housing officials, state legislators, governors, Wall Street investors, mayors and city council members, private consultants, nonprofit community-based housing organizations and their supporters, banks, and many large corporations. This extensive, far-flung constituency supports the expansion of the tax credit and helped to defeat efforts by Representative Bill Archer (R-TX), chair of the House of Representatives Ways and Means Committee, to kill the tax credit as part of his efforts to streamline and simplify the federal tax code (Shashaty 1997, 4).

The entirely new political constituency for the LIHTC is similar to the new advocacy groups that emerged in response to government contracting. To be sure, the LIHTC is not the only reason for the proliferation of nonprofit and public organizations supportive of low-income housing. Large national foundations such as the Ford Foundation have subsidized the growth of nonprofit housing organizations and community development corporations directly and indirectly by funding the Local Initiatives Support Corporation (LISC), which has a national office and many local offices throughout the country. The Rouse Company, a major builder of malls and shopping centers, created the Enterprise Foundation, based in Baltimore, to support community-based housing organizations nationwide. (Both LISC and the Enterprise Foundation have their own equity funds to pool private, especially corporate, investors interested in purchasing LIHTCs.) Nonetheless, public policy in the form of the LIHTC is critical: without the LIHTC, which is the major source of funds, the current nonprofit housing infrastructure, including its public and for-profit support, would not exist.

Political support for the LIHTC by nonprofit housing organizations is fundamentally related to internal dynamics of nonprofit, community organizations. Like many community organizations, nonprofit housing organizations are usually undercapitalized and operate on a very thin margin of profitability. They usually have modest contributions, at best, to help with the financing of low-income housing. Since these organizations cannot build low-income housing and charge market rates, they are in the position, not unlike nonprofit social service and health organizations, of always needing to find mechanisms to cross-subsidize the so-called "public goods" aspect of their operations (James 1983). The LIHTC is very attractive to nonprofit organizations because they can build into the project budget a developer's fee, typically 15 percent or less of the total project cost. That money can be used by the organization to support program administration and unexpected costs and to subsidize the core, low-income mission of the organization or be "invested" in the project itself. In essence the tax credit provides the nonprofit with a valuable asset that it can "sell" to private parties.

The developer's fee poses a tricky policy and management dilemma, however, in that many nonprofit organizations cannot stop developing because they need the developer's fee to support their core operations. They have a tremendous incentive to support the continuation of the LIHTC and to compete for tax credits, even if they do not like the criteria established by the state housing finance agencies or even if vouchers would promote a better housing policy, such as greater integration of income and racial groups.

Some nonprofits strive to develop other revenue sources to provide a financial cushion that would allow the agency greater flexibility in choosing projects. However, creating alternative revenue streams is difficult. For example, one potential revenue source is property management. After a project is developed, a nonprofit developer can either manage the facility itself or turn over the management to a nonprofit or for-profit management agency. But it is not easy to "make money" on property management: an agency needs lots of units to gain substantial economies of scale; compliance costs are significant and, perhaps most importantly, many projects are "overleveraged." Public funding agencies such as the state housing commission or city housing departments want to use as little public money as possible to complete a deal, encouraging nonprofit developers to borrow as much as possible. With high borrowing costs, many nonprofit housing agencies engaged in property management are fortunate if they can simply recapture their costs.

Like contracting projects, government funding agencies involved in housing development are trying to shift costs to nonprofit agencies and private-sector funding sources. But the scarcity of private dollars means that many nonprofit housing agencies are financially unable or weak, especially if they do not have a formal affiliation to a private funding source such as a denomination or church.

The popularity of the LIHTC is generating ripple effects on other housing subsidy programs. For example, the move toward expanded use of tax-exempt bonds to develop low-income housing is prompted in part by the scarcity of tax credits. These bonds also do not have the complicated point system of the tax credit system. If states reach their bond cap, however, then a similar dynamic may ensue with the tax-exempt bond program because states would need to develop criteria to allocate the bonds.

LIHTC shares with government contracting for social and health services another important characteristic: the process of awarding the tax credits is fraught with frequently intense political jockeying and maneuvering (Smith and Lipsky 1993). As noted, the state has a point system for awarding the tax credits, but the point system only helps avoid politics to a degree since even the point system is subject to interpretation. Nonprofit housing agencies have an incentive to portray their project in the best possible terms. Some private consultants even help agencies craft a proposal that is likely to be a winner with the state housing commission. The state agency, for its part, is constantly worried that it will be sued, especially by for-profit developers. (Perhaps as one concession to for-profit developers, the state agency has a set-aside program for them.)

Politics intrudes into the allocation process because the proposed projects are so complicated. With multiple funding sources and complex cost projections, the ultimate success of each project hinges on the capacity of the nonprofit developer to successfully bring the project to fruition and sustain the project over a long period. The willingness of the state housing agency to allocate tax credits for a particular project then depends upon the agency's reputation, which is, in turn, related to its political influence.

Reputation is important in the ongoing compliance of the agency with IRS regulations. Once the project is built, the nonprofit housing agency must ensure that its clients remain eligible under IRS guidelines. The IRS conducts a periodic audit of the agency's project to ensure IRS compliance. The IRS does not have nearly enough agents to oversee the countless projects across the country; thus it relies upon the agency for compliance by asking the agency to supply relevant data on client characteristics. Theoretically, the agency could submit erroneous information, but the risks are so high in terms of reputation that the agency has no choice but to strive to provide the requested information as accurately as possible. An added incentive for agency compliance is the involvement of private investors; if the agency serves ineligible clients, the investors are at risk for losing their investments.

A recent example of the responsibility of the nonprofit developer for regulatory compliance is underscored by a new IRS regulation. Concerned about the possible misuse of tax credit funds, the IRS issued a rule barring full-time adult students from living in tax-credit-financed rental units. Nonprofit agencies now have to scramble to investigate the lives of their residents in a way that many agencies find intrusive and uncomfortable. Nonetheless, they need to learn the status of their residents or risk possible complications to their project's success.

Finally, the structure and politics of the LIHTC illustrate the new world of hybrid nonprofit/for-profit/public organizations in three ways. First, Washington state and other states award extra points for a tax credit application from a nonprofit organization. Consequently, some for-profit developers establish so-called "shadow" nonprofits to serve as the applicant organization even though the entity is controlled by the for-profit developer. Second, nonprofits need to sell their tax credits to for-profit investors while retaining the controlling interest in the project. While the IRS and state housing finance agencies have issued regulations defining a controlling interest, it nonetheless remains difficult at times to discern whether or not a for-profit investor is actually running a nonprofit on an ongoing basis (Sheppard 1997). Third, LIHTCs encourage nonprofits to develop linkages with a host of for-profit and public entities in order to put together an acceptable financial package.

From a public-policy perspective, hybrid organizations may have advantages in terms of tapping new forms of financing previously unavailable to nonprofits. In the long run, though, these organizations could raise vexing questions on the proper limits of nonprofit and for-profit accountability and the limits on subsidizing individual investors for the public good.

CONCLUDING THOUGHTS

Government contracting with nonprofit service agencies and the growing LIHTC program suggest three important conclusions about the impact of public policy on nonprofit organizations. First, policy affects nonprofit organizations in many different ways: services, clientele, programmatic orientation, political involvement, and even the extent to which nonprofits have formal and informal relationships with public and for-profit entities.

Second, we may need to rethink how we regard the public and private boundaries within social policy. Comparative research on social policy in advanced industrial countries has often suggested that the smaller public sector and much larger nonprofit sector distinguish the United States from many other countries, especially in Europe (Esping-Anderson 1990; Wilensky and Lebeaux 1957; Flora and Heidenheimer 1982). The emphasis on devolution and decentralization in policy discourse tends to reinforce this perception.

Yet the record of government contracting and the tax credit program suggest that the United States may be distinguished by the way in which it provides social and health services (Rein 1996). Nonprofit organizations, either through direct contracting or the use of tax credit financing, provide an extensive array of social and health services subject to government regulation and oversight. Nonprofit organizations are an integral part of public service delivery and an important political constituency for public programs. The transformed role of nonprofit organizations indicates that devolution—on inspection—may not be as devolutionary as widely believed.

Third, government contracting, tax credits, tax-exempt bonds, and other forms of government financing of nonprofits are complicated and raise difficult tradeoffs and dilemmas for nonprofit organizations, government administrators, and legislators. Contracting can allow nonprofits to expand services and professionalize; but it may divert nonprofits from their original mission and require new means to maintain the accountability for the expenditure of public funds. The LIHTC created a new infrastructure of community housing organizations, but the complexity of the programs undermines the adequacy of existing regulatory structures.

This intricate, intertwined relationship between government and the nonprofit sector defies easy solutions or strategies. Greater accountability over the expenditure of public funds by nonprofits can easily evolve into overregulation and unnecessary intrusion into nonprofits' operations. Trying to disentangle government and nonprofits by deregulation and cutbacks in government funds risks financial destabilization of nonprofit service agencies and compromising the quality of service delivery. Nonprofit agencies without government funding of any sort may possess advantages in terms of flexibility and innovation but are subject to financial and executive instability. In the coming years, policymakers will be challenged to resolve these dilemmas in ways that ensure that the public interest, broadly defined, is served while maintaining a vibrant, healthy nonprofit infrastructure capable of effectively providing services to the citizenry.

Notes

The author wishes to thank Paul Fitzgerald, James McIntire, Kathy Roseth, Chuck Weinstock, and the members of the Urban Institute working group on Nonprofit Organizations and Government for feedback on earlier versions of this paper.

1. The issues faced by nonprofit agencies faced with rising service costs due to government regulations are not unrelated to the problem identified by Bruce Vladeck (1976) in an important, albeit neglected, article on the consequences for nonprofits of the emphasis by wealthy individuals and foundations to give money for capital expendi-

tures. Capital improvements can substantially raise overhead costs, resulting in much higher cash-flow demands. Many nonprofits then suffer financially due to what Vladeck regarded as an overinvestment in capital.

2. The qualified basis refers to the value of the housing for purposes of figuring the amount of tax credit eligibility.

References

Berger, P., and R. N. Neuhaus. 1977. *To Empower People*. Washington, D.C.: American Enterprise Institute.

Bixby, A. K. 1996. "Public Social Welfare Expenditures, Fiscal Year 1993." *Social Security Bulletin* 59 (3, Fall): 67–75.

Brown, L. D. 1983: *New Policies, New Politics*. Washington, D.C.: Brookings Institution.

City of Seattle. 1997. *1995 Housing Levy: Administrative and Financial Plan, Program Years 1996, 1997, 1998*. Seattle: Seattle Department of Housing and Human Services.

Clotfelter, C. T. 1985. *Federal Tax Policy and Charitable Giving*. Chicago: University of Chicago Press.

Clotfelter, C. T., and R. L. Schmalbeck. 1996. "The Impact of Fundamental Tax Reform on Nonprofit Organizations." In *Economic Effects of Fundamental Tax Reform*, edited by H. J. Aaron and W. G. Gale (211–46). Washington, D.C.: Brookings Institution.

de Tocqueville, A. 1955 ed. *Democracy in America*. New York: New American Library.

Drucker, P. F. 1969. *The Age of Discontinuity*. New York: Harper and Row.

Esping-Anderson, G. 1990. *Three Worlds of Welfare Capitalism*. Princeton, N.J.: Princeton University Press.

Executive Office of the President. 1997a. *Budget of U.S. Government, FY 1998*. Washington, D.C.: U.S. Government Printing Office.

Executive Office of the President. 1997b. *Budget of U.S. Government, FY 1998. Analytic Perspectives*. Washington, D.C.: U.S. Government Printing Office.

Fetter, F. A. 1901. "The Subsidizing of Private Charities." *American Journal of Sociology* 7 (3): 359–86.

Fleischer, A. 1914. "State Money and Privately Managed Charities." *The Survey* 33 (31 October): 110–12.

Flora, P., and A. J. Heidenheimer, eds. 1981. *The Development of Welfare States in Europe and America*. New Brunswick, N.J.: Transaction Books.

Glazer, N. 1989. *The Limits of Social Policy*. Cambridge: Harvard University Press.

Gronbjerg, K. 1993. *Understanding Nonprofit Funding*. San Francisco: Jossey-Bass Publishers.

Gronbjerg, K., and S. R. Smith. 1998. "Nonprofit Organizations and Public Policies in the Delivery of Human Services." Paper presented at the 93rd American Assembly conference, "The Future of Philanthropy." Los Angeles, April.

Gutowski, M. F., and J. J. Koshel. 1984. "Social Services." In *The Reagan Experiment*, edited by J. L. Palmer and I. V. Sawhill (307–28). Washington, D.C.: Urban Institute.

Hall. P. D. 1987. "A Historical Overview of the Private Nonprofit Sector." In *The Nonprofit Sector: A Research Handbook*, edited by W. W. Powell (3–26). New Haven: Yale University Press.

Hayek, F. 1960. *Constitution of Liberty*. Chicago: University of Chicago Press.

House of Representatives, Ways and Means Committee. 1996. *The Green Book*. Washington, D.C.: U.S. Government Printing Office.

Independent Sector. 1996. *The Nonprofit Almanac*. Washington, D.C.: The Independent Sector.

James, E. 1983. "How Nonprofits Grow: A Model." *Journal of Policy Analysis and Management* 2 (3, Fall): 350–66.

Kramer, R. M. 1982. *Voluntary Agencies in the Welfare State*. Berkeley, CA: University of California Press.

———. 1987. "Voluntary Agencies and the Personal Social Services." In *The Nonprofit Sector: A Research Handbook*, edited by W. W. Powell (240–57). New Haven: Yale University Press.

Lifset, R. 1989. "Cash Cows or Sacred Cows: The Politics of the Commercialization Movement." In *The Future of the Nonprofit Sector*, edited by V. Hodgkinson et al. (140–66). San Francisco: Jossey-Bass Publishers.

Lipsky, M., and S. R. Smith. 1989–90. "Government, Nonprofit Agencies and the Welfare State." *Political Science Quarterly* 104 (4, Winter): 625–48.

Meyer, J., ed. 1982. *Meeting Human Needs*. Washington, D.C.: American Enterprise Institute.

Moe, T. M. 1990. "The Politics of Structural Choice: Toward a Theory of Public Bureaucracy." In *Organization Theory: From Chester Barnard to the Present and Beyond*, edited by O. E. Williamson (116–33). New York: Oxford University Press.

Nisbet, R. A. 1969. *The Quest for Community*. New York: Oxford University Press.

Nozick, R. 1974. *Anarchy, State and Utopia*. New York: Basic.

Olasky, M. 1996. *Renewing American Compassion*. New York: Free Press.

Salamon, L. M. 1987. "Partners in Public Service: The Scope and Theory of Government-Nonprofit Relations." In *The Nonprofit Sector: A Research Handbook*, edited by W. W. Powell (99–117). New Haven: Yale University Press.

———, ed. 1989. *Beyond Privatization*. Washington, D.C.: Urban Institute.

Schambra, W. A. 1997. "Local Groups Are the Key to America's Civic Renewal." *Brookings Review* 15 (4, Fall): 20–22.

Shashaty, A. R. 1997. "Archer vs. Clinton: The Rematch." *Affordable Housing Finance* 5 (3, May/June): 4.

Sheppard, L. A. 1997. "The Road to Hell Is Paved with Good Intentions." *Tax Notes* 77: 888.

Smith, S. R., and M. Lipsky. 1993. *Nonprofits for Hire: The Welfare State in the Age of Contracting.* Cambridge, MA: Harvard University Press.

Steinmo, S., K. Thelen, and F. Longstreth, eds. 1992. *Structuring Politics.* Cambridge, England: Cambridge University Press.

Stone, D. 1996. *Policy Paradox: The Art of Political Reasoning.* New York: HarperCollins.

Thompson, J. D. 1967. *Organizations in Action.* New York: McGraw-Hill.

Vladeck, B. C. 1976. "Why Nonprofits Go Broke." *The Public Interest* 42 (Winter): 86–101.

Wilensky, H. L., and C. N. Lebeaux. 1957. *Industrial Society and Social Welfare.* New York: The Free Press.

NONPROFITS AND THE DEVELOPMENT OF PUBLIC POLICY

Chapter Six

NONPROFITS AND DEVOLUTION: WHAT DO WE KNOW?

Carol J. De Vita

INTRODUCTION

Devolution has become the policy mantra of the 1990s. Based on the assumption that decisions are best made by people and governmental units closest to the problem, policymakers have embraced the idea of devolution as a way to address local needs. They also have seen devolution as a strategy to cut program costs and to balance the federal budget. As a result, policymaking in the 1990s has been shifting from the federal government to the states and, in some cases, from state governments to local entities. But what do we really mean when we use the term "devolution," and how should we assess its effects on nonprofit organizations?

The concept of devolution certainly is not new to the American political scene. Its roots run deep, going back to the framing of the Constitution with its debate over federal versus state responsibilities. Although the Constitution gives the federal government explicit oversight for a number of policy areas, such as defense, it remains somewhat obscure on how best to address other issues such as economic development or the environment. That ambiguity has fueled a 200-year debate on the proper role of each level of government—national, state, and local—and their respective responsibilities. As a consequence, the policymaking pendulum has swung between periods of more centralized federal leadership to times of dispersed or shared governmental authority. Devolution in the 1990s represents the latest swing of the policy pendulum and calls upon states and local governments to assume a greater role in crafting solutions for the country's social and economic ills.

Although the term "devolution" is widely used, it is not well defined. In current debates, devolution has two popular meanings. It primarily connotes a shift in the locus of responsibility, decisionmaking, or control from the federal government to state or local levels of government. But the term also is used to imply federal budget cuts (or savings) that potentially reduce or limit the role of government in particular policy areas. Although states and local governments generally are not restricted from using their own revenues to compensate for a loss of federal dollars, the willingness or ability of states or local governments to do so is not easily achieved.

The fiscal capacity of states varies widely, and capacities of urban centers are even more varied. Since the mid-1970s, America's cities have faced persistent budget problems (Fuchs 1998). Most cities have seen their tax bases erode as both middle-class residents and businesses move to the suburbs. Left behind are some of the nation's most persistently poor and vulnerable populations. Yet despite fiscal strains, cities must continue to provide basic public services. Faced with stringent budget scenarios, local governments are sometimes left to grapple with the tough administrative decisions that result from devolution. As a result, devolution often evokes fears of a zero-sum game with services as diverse as road repairs, health care, trash disposal, and summer camps for kids pitted against one another in the policymaking process.

Although shifting responsibility for program decisions and administrative policies to lower levels of government is a necessary condition for devolution, budget cuts do not always follow. The ongoing debate over welfare reform, which this chapter will highlight, illustrates the confusion regarding what constitutes "devolution" and how best to measure its effects.

While the concept of devolution is as old as the nation, two factors set the current debates apart from those of earlier times. First, many more actors, including nonprofit organizations, have entered the policymaking arena. These multiple players raise both the complexity of the policymaking process and the stakes in policy outcomes. The debate today is less about which level of government should take the lead in setting policy, but rather how to allocate responsibilities between various public- *and* private-sector players. Second, devolution, with its emphasis on local solutions, is unfolding against a growing trend toward national and global interconnectedness. Today's rapid communication and technological changes not only enhance the sharing of information but also create national and international standards and norms. Devolution, with its emphasis on addressing local differences, raises questions about equity and fairness within a national context. It poses a tension between equity, equality, and uniformity, on the one hand, and diversity and experimentation on the other

(Steuerle et al. 1998). Can local differences and locally based solutions be harnessed to enhance the sum of the parts? Is there a national standard or are there multiple sets of norms?

This chapter will outline the current state of knowledge regarding devolution and its effects on nonprofit organizations. Section I looks at the partnership that already exists between nonprofits and government, and at the tools of devolution that have been used to create program and funding flexibility for local policymakers and service providers. Section II describes the types of nonprofits that are likely to be affected by the devolution of welfare reform policies from the federal government to state and local entities, while Section III presents a closer look at faith-based providers and welfare reform. Section IV provides information on studies under way to assess the effects of welfare reform, and Section V discusses issues that need to be monitored to better assess the effects of devolution on nonprofit organizations and the challenges that the sector is likely to face in the years ahead.

THE GOVERNMENT-NONPROFIT PARTNERSHIP

Passage of the Personal Responsibility and Work Opportunity Reconciliation Act of 1996 (PRWORA)—more commonly known as welfare reform—set in motion a new round of devolution. It is the most visible, and arguably most controversial, effort at devolution in the 1990s and is likely to reshape the existing government-nonprofit partnership, particularly through funding and contracting relationships.

PRWORA fundamentally altered state welfare programs by creating a federal block grant that caps federal aid to the states. In return, states have much more flexibility in running their welfare programs. Under PRWORA, the old Aid to Families with Dependent Children (AFDC) was replaced by a block grant called Temporary Assistance for Needy Families (TANF). States have been given wide latitude for setting program eligibility requirements but, in exchange, must adhere to some specific program parameters. Welfare recipients, for example, are required to find employment within two years of entering the welfare rolls, and there is a five-year lifetime limit for receiving welfare benefits. Failure to enforce these requirements can jeopardize a state's future funding levels under the block grant.

The legislation did not cut federal funding for welfare programs, as some opponents charge. Instead, it sustains funding at levels received under the old AFDC program and increases funding for some critical ancillary services, such as child care and job training programs. Budget "savings," however, were obtained by tightening program eligibility requirements for other welfare-related programs such as Food Stamps and Supplemental Security Income (SSI). Advocates for the poor fear that as individuals become ineligible for government programs, the demand for assistance will overwhelm the services available through private philanthropy.

In this new era of devolution, many policymakers are looking to nongovernmental entities, particularly at the local level, to assume a larger role in building the human, economic, and social capital necessary to bring about change. Nonprofit organizations, especially those that provide services for low-income people, are being challenged to find new ways to alleviate poverty, encourage employment, strengthen families, and reduce long-term dependence on welfare. While public debate generally focuses on the goals and objectives of government policies, the role and capacity of nonprofit organizations in responding to community needs are not well understood. Will nonprofits be able to meet the rising expectations that accompany the goals of welfare reform?

The assumption that nongovernmental organizations present a new or better alternative to government programs for overcoming the problems of poverty and welfare dependence ignores an important fact—namely, that nonprofit organizations are already substantially involved in the delivery of welfare-related services and have been for decades. During the War on Poverty in the 1960s and early 1970s, the federal government used nonprofit organizations as agents for the expansion of the welfare state (James 1987). Many of the services and programs created and funded by federal statute were delivered at the local level by nonprofit organizations, which helped fuel the growth of the nonprofit sector, particularly in service delivery programs. More than 60 percent of the nonprofit human service providers that were operating in the early 1980s were founded after 1960 (Salamon 1985). Rather than displacing nonprofit organizations, the growth in government spending on social welfare programs actually stimulated the expansion of the nonprofit sector—fulfilling the complementary role discussed by Young and by Steuerle and Hodgkinson in this volume.

Government, at every level, provides very few human service programs directly. Instead, government provides funding for an array of services and programs, such as employment and training, health care, child care, foster care, food and nutrition, senior citizen centers, social services, and many more. The actual delivery of services is generally achieved through the use of nonprofit, and sometimes for-profit, service providers. That arrangement has enabled government to control some of its own personnel costs and overhead expenses while maintaining direction and oversight of social welfare programs.

Although cuts in federal spending for many domestic social programs during the 1980s slowed the growth of social welfare programs, nonprofit organizations remained extensively involved in providing social services through contracts with states and local governments (Smith and Lipsky 1993). Indeed, the role of nonprofit organizations has become so prominent in the social service delivery system that they have effectively become "partners" with government in supplying aid to the poor (Salamon 1995).

Several administrative tools and funding mechanisms have been used to establish this partnership and foster more flexibility in program implementation at the local level. Among the most prominent tools are block grants and program waivers. The Johnson administration introduced block grants in 1966 to consolidate several public health grants into a single grant for public health services. The move came in response to state and local government complaints that categorical grants-in-aid were too narrow and rigid to effectively address local needs.

The Nixon administration's "New Federalism" used the block grant mechanism to decentralize many government services away from Washington and toward elected officials in state and local governments. Although nonprofit organizations were not explicitly mentioned as players in this decentralization strategy, they nonetheless became its unintended beneficiaries. The federal government's overall domestic spending rose from 10.3 percent of gross national product in 1969 to 13.7 percent in 1974 (Nathan 1996, 34). The lion's share of that growth went to entitlement programs, such as Social Security, Food Stamps, and Medicaid, but general-purpose funds and broadly based grants-in-aid also saw a steady rise in revenues.

During the 1980s, the Reagan administration also used block grants to consolidate categorical programs, but the intent of the Reagan block grant strategy was to reduce the size of the federal government. Unlike the Nixon era, which saw a steady increase in domestic spending, the Reagan years slowed the rate of growth in domestic spending and in some areas imposed sharp cuts. Excluding Medicare and Medicaid funding, federal spending on social welfare programs declined by roughly 12 percent during the first half of the 1980s and did not return to its 1980 levels until 1991 (Salamon and Abramson 1996, 7). Discretionary programs were hit even harder, falling 25 to 30 percent below

1980 levels between 1980 and 1984. Nonprofit organizations that operated in these service areas often experienced these federal budget cuts as a direct loss of revenues.

Entitlement programs were generally sheltered from federal budget cuts during the 1980s, but states continued to seek greater control and flexibility for implementing social welfare programs. The use of waivers from federal statutes, particularly for AFDC and Medicaid, became the prominent tool for addressing this need. By August 1996, before passage of PRWORA, 43 states had received AFDC waivers (Department of Health and Human Services 1997). Fifteen states had Medicaid waivers to conduct managed-care demonstration projects (Holahan and Liska 1997). The use of waivers opened up new opportunities for nonprofit service providers, particularly those that offer child care, employment and training, and health care services.

While previous attempts at streamlining and downsizing government focused on specific grants-in-aid programs, devolution in the 1990s has sought to rein in entitlement programs, particularly cash assistance programs, such as AFDC and SSI, targeted at low-income families and individuals. In a historic policy shift, the 1996 welfare reform legislation ends the guarantee for AFDC assistance as an entitlement to income-eligible families in need and opens new questions about the structure and viability of America's social safety net.

In part because of waivers that were received well before passage of welfare reform legislation in 1996, some states and localities forged ahead in revamping their welfare systems. Wisconsin and Michigan, for example, are often cited as leaders in welfare reform efforts. Other states have been slower to respond.

Assessing the overall success or failure of welfare reform and devolution will be an extremely difficult task because states are pursuing different policy objectives and implementation strategies, and doing so under different economic conditions (Besharov, Germanis, and Rossi 1997). Although the U.S. economy as a whole has recovered from the recession that hit the country in 1990–91 and is now enjoying considerable growth, the economic health and fiscal capacity of states and local governments vary widely. As a result, current efforts at welfare reform are likely to create 50 state laboratories, each producing a unique model for understanding the dynamics of welfare reform.

The effects of the changes on nonprofit organizations and the strategies that nonprofits use to address them are also likely to vary. The challenges and opportunities facing nonprofits will be determined by their state context. Sharing information among nonprofits within a state and sharing information across states will be a critical part of the adjustment process. Approaches will have to be tailored to address state and local conditions, because a one-size-fits-all strategy is not likely to be effective in the emerging policy environment.

NONPROFITS AND WELFARE REFORM

The realignment of roles and responsibilities under welfare reform and devolution poses new challenges to nonprofit human service providers. Perhaps the most direct challenge will be maintaining their fiscal capacity as the government-nonprofit partnership is redefined. Groundbreaking work by Salamon in the early 1980s showed that government was the single largest source of funding for nonprofit human service agencies (see also chapter 2, this volume) and provided roughly half of all revenues for programs such as employment and training, social services, and mental health (Salamon 1995). Given this heavy reliance on government funding, nonprofits have a vital stake in redefining the new partnerships that are forming as a result of welfare reform and devolution.

Not every type of nonprofit will be affected by such realignments, however. Using Internal Revenue Service data for 1992 and 1994, De Vita and Twombly (1997) examined the number, types, and financial stability of human service organizations most likely to be affected by welfare reform. Based on a national sample of 13 states,[1] the study identified more than 13,500 nonprofit organizations that provided the types of services associated with welfare reform, such as child care, employment and training, emergency food services, and overnight shelters. These organizations represented 70 percent of the nonprofit organizations classified broadly as human service providers in the 13-state sample.

The vast majority of nonprofits in the study (83 percent) offered core human services (such as preschools and child care centers, job training and work readiness programs, multiservice programs, mental health and substance abuse programs, family counseling, and family planning programs) that will, directly or indirectly, help welfare recipients find work and become self-sufficient. Emergency services, such as domestic violence and abuse programs, housing and shelter, emergency food, homeless shelters, and foster care, were offered by fewer than one in five nonprofits in the sample (see figure 6.1). Human service providers are concerned that, as stricter eligibility requirements and lifetime limits for welfare are implemented, the demand

Figure 6.1 DISTRIBUTION OF NONPROFIT HUMAN SERVICE PROVIDERS, 1992

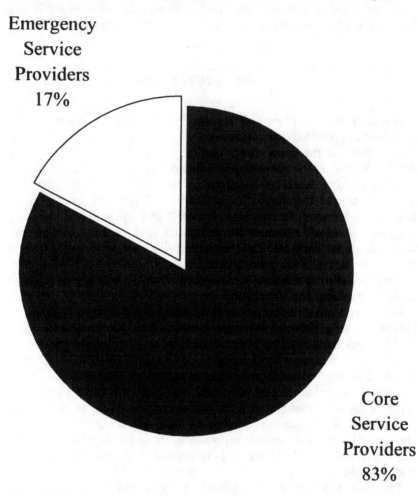

Emergency
Service
Providers
17%

Core
Service
Providers
83%

Source: Author's tabulations of the U.S. Internal Revenue Service Return Transaction File, 1992. Number of Providers = 13,565.

for services, particularly emergency services, will grow. Developing the capacity to meet increased demand will be a challenge for some service providers.

Financially, these human service providers reported growing budgets in the early 1990s, but the organizations are operating with more financial uncertainty and increasingly stringent budgets. Between 1992 and 1994, as the nation was recovering from an economic recession, the budget of the typical nonprofit human service provider was expanding. Median revenues and expenditures increased by roughly 10 percent during this period. But expenditures were rising somewhat faster than revenues, and the cushion between meeting the organization's financial obligations and running an annual deficit narrowed. Only two-fifths (41 percent) of the nonprofits in the study reported positive net balance sheets for both 1992 and 1994 (see table 6.1). Another 39 percent of the organizations had a downward financial trajectory, either reporting net losses for both years or moving from a positive net balance to a negative one. Although the magnitude of these changes was not analyzed, the overall picture of a fluctuating and unstable financial base is a troubling sign and a formidable challenge during this new era of devolution.

CHARITABLE CHOICE AND FAITH-BASED SERVICE PROVIDERS

In addition to the larger and more established nonprofit organizations that file with the IRS, many small grassroots groups and religious congregations are also active in providing community services. Anecdotal evidence abounds of church groups that are working hard to meet the needs of poor and at-risk populations (Demko 1997; Klein 1997). As a result, policymakers have found (or rediscovered) religion as a framework for addressing social problems. Faith-based organizations, particularly local congregations, are being asked to play a more active role in helping welfare recipients and other low-income

Table 6.1 FINANCIAL BALANCE SHEET OF NONPROFIT ORGANIZATIONS IN 1992 AND 1994

End-of-Year Financial Balance	Percent of Organizations		
	All Nonprofits	Core Services	Emergency Services
Positive both years	41%	40%	43%
Gainers*	20	21	19
Decliners**	21	21	21
Negative both years	18	18	17
Total	100%	100%	100%
Number	12,453	10,287	2,166

Source: Author's tabulations from the U.S. Internal Revenue Service Return Transaction Files, 1992 and 1994.
*Negative balance in 1992, positive balance in 1994.
**Positive balance in 1992, negative balance in 1994.

people to become self-sufficient. Although the devolution of the 1990s has created a newfound interest in the social ministries of faith-based organizations, it is less clear what new arrangements or partnerships (if any) will be formed between government and faith-based groups, and how these arrangements will satisfy constitutional guarantees of separation between church and state.

The invisible line separating church and state has always been somewhat permeable. In the late 1800s, for example, New York City gave public monies to faith-based organizations such as the Society of St. Vincent de Paul and the United Hebrew Charities to support their programs for the poor (Bremner 1980). Currently, more than half of the revenues of Lutheran Social Services and Catholic Charities come from government grants and contracts. At least in the field of human services, there is a long-standing although sometimes over-looked alliance between government and large faith-based organizations that provide services to the needy.

To encourage *local* churches and religious congregations to become more active in welfare reform efforts, Senator John Ashcroft (R–Mo.) introduced the Charitable Choice provision into PRWORA (Section 104 of P.L. 104-193). Charitable Choice enables religiously affiliated organizations to compete for government contracts (or accept government vouchers) on an equal basis with secular service providers, without giving up the religious character of the faith-based programs. In the past, religiously affiliated organizations were prohibited from re-ceiving government funds unless they removed religious art, artifacts, scriptures, or other symbols of faith from the service program and the physical site where services were delivered. It was argued that many congregations found such requirements too imposing and that they undercut the spiritual content of the program, which was viewed as necessary for success.

Under Charitable Choice, states cannot discriminate on the basis of the provider's religious character in awarding contracts or establishing voucher systems. Religious artifacts and symbols of faith may be dis-played on the premises and in the program materials. But faith-based providers are prohibited from using money from government contracts to proselytize or conduct religious services or instruction. Like their secular counterparts, faith-based providers are subject to financial audits for the funds received under government grants and contracts.

While the legislative intent of Charitable Choice is to encourage greater participation by locally based religious groups in addressing the needs of welfare recipients and low-income people, there have been no large-scale, systematic studies of what types of community-based programs local congregations actually provide. Moreover, local area studies are just beginning to emerge on the role of faith-based organizations in providing for community needs.

What is striking about this emerging body of literature is the similarity of the findings, even though the research was conducted in different geographic locations and with different types of congregations (Cnaan 1997; Grettenberger and Hovmand 1997; Jackson et al. 1997; and Printz 1997). Nearly all of the congregations in these studies offer some type of community outreach program or social ministry, with the average response ranging from 4 to 13 programs. Emergency services is the focus of most congregational work. In the Washington, D.C., metropolitan area, more than three-quarters of the congregations offered some type of emergency service, such as food, financial assistance, clothing, or overnight shelter (Printz 1997). In a study of faith-based groups serving the black community in Michigan, 75 percent of the faith-based providers offered emergency services (Jackson et al. 1997). In a study of six cities, 60 percent of the congregations offered food pantries and 53 percent had clothing banks (Cnaan 1997). Similar proportions were reported in a study of United Methodist Churches in Michigan (Grettenberger and Hovmand 1997).

Most of these community programs relied on volunteers and operated on very small budgets. Jackson et al. (1997) found that most of the congregations in their study had no paid staff to run the outreach programs and had a median budget of roughly $4,400 per year. Printz (1997) reports a median of one full-time paid staff, with nearly one-third of the congregations having no formal budgets for their social ministries. Of those with budgets, the median was $15,000 per year. In both the Jackson and Printz studies, program revenues came primarily from the congregation's operating budget or from donations. Fewer than 10 percent of the congregations received funding from government sources or foundation grants.

Because religious congregations are an active component of local community life and an important thread in the fabric of civil society, it is not surprising that proponents of devolution have targeted the faith-based community as key players in addressing social issues generally and in providing increased services for families affected by welfare reform. Whether local congregations have the capacity or desire to increase their level of involvement, however, is still largely untested. Grettenberger and Hovmand (1997) found that congregations are selective in the types of services that they are willing to offer or support. Programs for preschool children were most popular, with 51 percent of congregations indicating that they would be receptive to increasing services for children. Youth (43 percent) and elderly (42 percent) programs followed. Much further down the list (ranking eleventh) was services to welfare recipients. Only 12 percent of congregations in the study expressed an interest in expanding this type of outreach program.

If the goal of welfare reform and devolution is to alleviate poverty and foster a more integrated approach to addressing social problems, then a renewed public-private partnership between government and community-based institutions, including faith-based organizations, will be needed. It is unlikely that local congregations, on their own, will be able to do the job (Harvey 1997; Salamon 1995).

ASSESSING WELFARE REFORM

Since PRWORA's enactment in August 1996, there has been keen interest in monitoring changes in state policies and administrative procedures related to welfare reform, particularly as they affect children and families. Far less attention is being paid to the effects of devolution on nonprofit organizations and on the delivery of human services in local communities. The lack of focus on nonprofits may reflect, in part, the fact that many states are still in the early stages of redesigning and implementing their welfare systems. The time limits and sanctions mandated by PRWORA are just beginning to be enacted. As a result, it may simply be too early to tell how welfare reform and devolution will affect nonprofit human service providers or the clients they serve.

Indirect measures of the changing government-nonprofit relationship are likely to come from a number of large-scale, national studies that are already under way. Early findings from these studies are just beginning to appear. The Urban Institute is conducting one of the largest studies of welfare reform and devolution. It is monitoring policy and program changes in income security, health care, social services, and employment and training programs in 13 states over a six-year period. A nationally representative household survey of low-income families is also being conducted as part of the Urban Institute study. The Nelson A. Rockefeller Institute of Government at the State University of New York (SUNY) at Albany is also conducting a multi-year study in 21 states to assess state capacity to implement welfare reform measures. This work focuses on administrative structures and organizational management systems. The Manpower Demonstration

Research Corporation (MDRC) is currently designing a five-year project to investigate how devolution and federal block grants work in America's cities.

Other national studies focus more specifically on the effects of welfare reform on the lives of children and families. The Census Bureau, for example, is mandated under PRWORA to expand its data collection through the ongoing Survey of Income and Program Participation (SIPP). The Bureau will take the 1992 and 1993 SIPP panels and continue to collect data on these individuals through 2001, providing 10 years of longitudinal data on income, work patterns, receipt of welfare, and the condition of children both before and after welfare reform was enacted. This data set is likely to be one of the most significant sources of national data for studying the effects of welfare reform on children and their families. Other longitudinal, but smaller-scale, studies include a study at Princeton University of unwed parents and their children and a multicity study at Johns Hopkins University of the effects of welfare reform on children's socioeconomic and cognitive development.

As intermediaries between government bureaucracies and people who receive public assistance, nonprofit organizations are critical but invisible players in the welfare reform–devolution drama. Attention typically centers either on policy and administrative changes that result from welfare reform or the effects of these changes on low-income women and children. The mechanisms for delivering services are all but lost in the rush to measure and assess the outcomes of welfare reform on government programs and welfare recipients. Getting an accurate picture of the government-nonprofit partnership at the state and local levels will be an important component of understanding the strengths and weaknesses of policy devolution, however. A large-scale, systematic research agenda that focuses on the evolving government-nonprofit relationship in the post–welfare reform devolution era has yet to be developed.

ISSUES TO BE MONITORED

While welfare reform policies provide a context for assessing devolution, a broader issue that devolution poses is how nonprofits and government will redefine their current partnership. At least three factors are likely to shape the dynamics: the financial capacity and accountability of nonprofit organizations, competition with for-profit providers, and the role of nonprofit organizations as advocates in the policymaking process.

Financial Capacity and Accountability

A key factor in the nonprofit-government relationship is the financial capacity of nonprofit organizations. Although nonprofits' reliance on government funding varies by the type of service provided, it is a key source of funding for many nonprofits, particularly those that provide human service programs. Can nonprofit organizations diversify their funding bases and decrease their reliance on government funds? Can they expand their service programs if demand increases beyond current funding levels?

As policymakers respond to changing social, economic, and political demands, some nonprofits are likely to see increases in government funding (child care, for example), while others (such as emergency services) could see government funding levels stagnate or possibly decline. A likely scenario is that nonprofits will try to change their funding mix through commercial income or private giving.

Since the 1980s, nonprofits have moved toward greater reliance on commercial income, that is, charging fees for their services. This trend can be seen in many parts of the nonprofit sector, such as health care, child care, and arts and cultural programs. But for nonprofits that primarily serve the poor, this strategy simply is not viable. Fee income, alone, is unlikely to cover program costs, and subsidies would still be required. Increased reliance on commercial income also raises many questions about the role and mission of the nonprofit sector and its competition with for-profit firms.

Nonprofits may also try to diversify their funding mixes by seeking more support from private foundations and individual donations. The stock market's exceptional performance in recent years has spurred foundation giving. Foundations contributed an estimated $11.8 billion to nonprofit organizations in 1996—an increase of roughly 12 percent over the previous year (Kaplan 1997, 37). More than two of every five dollars was given to educational and health organizations, with human service organizations receiving 17 percent of foundation grant dollars, and arts and humanities groups getting 12 percent. Nonprofit organizations concerned with environmental issues, science and technology, or international affairs received no more than 5 percent (each) of foundation grant dollars in 1996.

The allocation of foundation grants has become a source of some debate. The National Commission on Philanthropy and Civic Renewal has argued in its report *Giving Better, Giving Smarter* that private foundations could be more effective in addressing community needs if they allocated more of their grants to local and religious charities that help poor people to become self-sufficient. This recommendation has set off a debate on the distribution of foundation support, the grantmaking criteria used by foundations in awarding grants, and how to determine which organizations are most suitable or effective in helping people in need.

But the heart of private philanthropy is not foundation grantmaking but contributions from individuals. Individual donations represented 80 percent of all private giving in 1996 and accounted for nearly $120 billion—a sum more than 10 times greater than foundation giving (Kaplan 1997). If nonprofits are seeking new sources of revenue, donations from individuals form the largest pool of nongovernmental resources.

The bulk of private giving, however, goes to religious organizations. Close to half (46 percent) of all private giving went to religious groups in 1996, according to *Giving USA*. These gifts include funds for sacramental programs, building campaigns, and social ministries. Secular education and health programs received 22 percent of private giving, while human services received 8 percent, and arts, culture, and humanities programs, 7 percent. All other programs and services accounted for less than 20 percent of private, nongovernmental donations in 1996.

Proposed changes in tax policies, such as allowing non-itemizers to deduct charitable contributions from their federal income taxes, could provide incentives for individuals to give more. Although econometric models suggest that the capacity for private donations is immense, the propensity to give, based on past behavior, is much smaller, especially for social welfare spending. One study estimates that private giving would offset, at most, 10 cents of every dollar of government revenues for social service programs (Steinberg 1996). Given these constraints, the government-nonprofit partnership is likely to remain the most viable source of revenue with which nonprofit human service providers sustain their program operations.

Despite long-range concerns about levels and sources of funding, a more immediate problem is the mechanisms for obtaining and using funds. The hope that devolution would bring greater autonomy and flexibility to local nonprofits has not become a reality (De Vita and Capitani 1998; Pindus et al. 1998). For example, local authorities may determine funding needs, but in many cases the state makes the final determination before releasing funds. Nonprofits also note that funds often remain categorical and lack the flexibility that local providers desire for addressing local needs. Accounting requirements have become more complicated and burdensome under devolution. Providers must certify that funds are not used for lobbying, and they must file separate accounts for each funding agency. From the nonprofit provider's perspective, devolution has brought more bureaucratic red tape, not less.

Monitoring funding levels and sources, as well as the flexibility and accountability of funding, will be a critical gauge of the nonprofit sector's ability to address community needs and local concerns. Because government plays a vital role in subsidizing many nonprofit organizations, attempts to weaken this relationship could pose serious challenges, especially to nonprofits that serve the poor. Although nonprofits may seek to diversify their funding bases, the expectation that private funds can fully replace government monies is unrealistic (see Steuerle and Hodgkinson, this volume). The gap is simply too great, given current patterns of resource allocation.

Competition

Devolution has brought increased competition to the nonprofit sector. As the government-nonprofit partnership is redefined and government contracts out for more services, greater emphasis is being placed on the efficient and effective use of resources. Anecdotal evidence suggests that, rather than competing with one another, nonprofits are forming partnerships and seeking ways to collaborate in order to stretch resources and maximize their effectiveness in the community. But the extent to which these arrangements are being made (or their success) is largely unknown. One study of religious congregations found that nearly half of the church leaders said that they would consider collaborating with other groups, but just over 10 percent had actually done so in the past (Printz 1997). At this time, it is unclear if calls for collaboration among nonprofit providers are just a politically correct response for the 1990s or are a real trend.

Nonprofit providers, however, perceive competition with for-profit service providers as a significant threat. Competition with for-profits is most apparent in the health care field, but some nonprofit leaders believe that it will soon emerge in child welfare services as well. The extent of competition between nonprofits and for-profits is likely to vary by industry and by state. But the entrance of for-profit firms into areas regarded by many as the domain of the nonprofit sector has shaken the business-as-usual complacency of many nonprofits and, in some cases, has instilled a fear that nonprofits are losing their place in the community.

Three issues generally surround the debate over competition between for-profit and nonprofit providers. First, nonprofits are frequently challenged to show that they are delivering services in the most efficient manner possible. Management issues, such as staffing patterns, resource utilization, and costs, are scrutinized to measure efficiency. Second, quality-of-care issues are raised for both nonprofit and for-profit providers. Are corners being cut and quality sacrificed to obtain a competitive advantage in the marketplace? And third, are indigent populations being served? Nonprofit providers are skeptical that for-profits will provide adequate services for low-income and indigent population groups. For-profit providers counter that the amount of charity care that some nonprofits provide does not warrant their tax-exempt status. While not every nonprofit organization will be directly or adversely affected by these challenges, competition with for-profit providers will stimulate the debate on what constitutes a nonprofit and charitable enterprise.

Advocacy

Nonprofit organizations play a variety of roles in civil society, but their role as advocates—for specific causes, for specific population groups, or for specific programs—has, at best, been overlooked or misunderstood and, at worst, misrepresented or maligned. The nonprofit sector has traditionally served as a voice for articulating public needs and preferences. While only a small share of nonprofit organizations make advocacy and legislative activity their primary concern, almost all are affected by changes in public policies. The right to monitor and respond to policy debates is, therefore, an essential part of a participatory democracy.

The political climate of the 1990s and the devolution of policymaking and program authority to states and local government have raised potential barriers for nonprofits to exercise their voice in public debates. On the national level, some conservative legislators, led by Representative Ernest Istook, Jr. (R–Okla.), have come to view some nonprofit organizations as self-interested players in the welfare system, or at least as confusing their advocacy and service positions when federal funds are provided for the latter. In this context, Representative Istook has repeatedly introduced legislation that would limit the ability of nonprofit organizations to participate in legislative advocacy if they receive more than a certain percentage of their funding from government sources. Although the bill has not passed to date, it represents a serious attempt to curtail the political participation of the nonprofit sector in the legislative process.

At the state and local levels, nonprofit groups' primary concern is their perceived inability to gain access to or legitimacy in policymaking arenas. Poor communication between state officials and nonprofit providers is also cited as a serious problem. In Michigan, some leaders in the nonprofit community express concern that their state's welfare reform plan was passed quickly with little input from the nonprofit sector. Others believe that only the larger nonprofits were invited to public hearings and, even then, their views were not taken seriously (De Vita and Capitani 1998). In Texas, nonprofit leaders say that they are not regularly informed by the state of welfare reform changes, and local providers often hear conflicting information from their clients (Pindus et al. 1998, 60).

If a key tenet of devolution is to decentralize decisionmaking, then monitoring who participates in the political process and how voices are heard will be an important part of assessing policymaking under devolution. Access to the political process and effective communication between the nonprofit sector and various levels of government will be essential components in assessing how effectively welfare reform is implemented.

Whether one judges current efforts at welfare reform and devolution to be a success or failure will depend in no small part on the criteria used for assessing the outcome. In the case of welfare reform, many proponents point to the reduction in welfare rolls as evidence that the new policies are working. Critics stress that there is almost no information at this time to judge if people are truly being lifted out of poverty and becoming self-sufficient or if they are falling through the holes of the social safety net.

Time will be a key factor in determining the long-term implications of welfare reform and devolution. Nearly everyone agrees that robust economic conditions have favored the creation of jobs and the reduction in welfare rolls. The real test will come during an economic downturn. Will the federal government stay the course or will political pressures swing the policy pendulum once again to return program responsibilities to the federal level? Will the government-nonprofit partnership grow stronger or will competitive forces weaken the relationship?

At the moment, there are more questions than answers, but the questions should serve as a blueprint for assessing the strengths of the nonprofit sector, as well as its weaknesses. Devolution poses a critical test of the character, structure, contributions, and cohesiveness of the nonprofit sector. This new era of governance also presents nonprofit organizations with an important opportunity to reaffirm their place in civil society.

Note

1. The 13 states correspond to the states under study by the Urban Institute's *Assessing the New Federalism* project. They include Alabama, California, Colorado, Florida, Massachusetts, Michigan, Minnesota, Mississippi, New Jersey, New York, Texas, Washington, and Wisconsin. Together, these states contain 50 percent of the U.S. population and 49 percent of the nonprofit human service providers as defined in this analysis.

References

Besharov, Douglas J., Peter Germanis, and Peter H. Rossi. 1997. *Evaluating Welfare Reform: A Guide for Scholars and Practitioners.* College Park, MD: School of Public Affairs, University of Maryland.

Bremner, Robert H. 1980. *The Public Good: Philanthropy and Welfare in the Civil War Era.* New York: Alfred A. Knopf.

Cnaan, Ram A. 1997. "Social and Community Involvement of Religious Congregations Housed in Historic Religious Properties: Findings from a Six-City Study." Final Report to Partners for Sacred Places, December 2. Philadelphia: University of Pennsylvania.

Demko, Paul. 1997. "Faith-Based Charities to the Rescue?" *The Chronicle of Philanthropy* 10 (5, Dec. 11): 1.

Department of Health and Human Services, Office of the Assistant Secretary of Planning and Evaluation. 1997. *Setting the Baseline: A Report on State Welfare Waivers.* Washington, D.C.: U.S. Government Printing Office, June.

De Vita, Carol J., and Jill Capitani. 1998. "Michigan Nonprofits and Devolution: What Do We Know?" Working paper prepared for the Nonprofit Sector Research Fund. Washington, D.C.: Aspen Institute.

De Vita, Carol J., and Eric Twombly. 1997. "Nonprofit Organizations in an Era of Welfare Reform." Paper presented at the annual meeting of ARNOVA, Indianapolis, December 4–6.

Fuchs, Ester R. 1998. "The Permanent Urban Fiscal Crisis." In *Big Cities in the Welfare Transition,* edited by Alfred J. Kahn and Sheila B.

Kamerman (43–73). New York: Cross-National Studies Research Program, Columbia University School of Social Work.

Giving Better, Giving Smarter. 1997. Washington, D.C.: The National Commission on Philanthropy and Civic Renewal.

Grettenberger, Susan, and Peter Hovmand. 1997. "The Role of Churches in Human Services: United Methodist Churches in Michigan." Paper presented at the annual meeting of ARNOVA, Indianapolis, December 4–6.

Harvey, Thomas J. 1997. "Solutions to Poverty Must Be Based on More Than Faith." *The Chronicle of Philanthropy* 10 (5, Dec. 11): 50.

Holahan, John, and David Liska. 1997. "Reassessing the Outlook for Medicaid Spending Growth." In series *Assessing the New Federalism: Issues and Options for States*, A-6 (March). Washington, D.C.: The Urban Institute.

Jackson, Maxie C., Jr., John H. Schwitzer, Marvin T. Cato, and Reynard N. Blake. 1997. "Faith-Based Institutions' Community and Economic Development Programs Serving Black Communities in Michigan." Paper presented at the annual meeting of ARNOVA, Indianapolis, December 4–6.

James, Estelle. 1987. "The Nonprofit Sector in Comparative Perspective." In *The Nonprofit Sector: A Research Handbook*, edited by Walter H. Powell (397–415). New Haven: Yale University Press.

Kaplan, Anne E., ed. 1997. *Giving USA.* New York: The AAFRC Trust for Philanthropy, Inc.

Klein, Joe. 1997. "In God They Trust." *The New Yorker*, June 16.

Nathan, Richard P. 1996. "The 'Nonprofitization Movement' as a Form of Devolution." In *Capacity for Change? The Nonprofit World in the Age of Devolution*, edited by Dwight F. Burlingame et al. (23–55). Indianapolis: Indiana University Center on Philanthropy.

Pindus, Nancy, Randy Capps, Jerome Gallagher, Linda Giannarelli, Milda Saunders, and Robin Smith. 1998. *Income Support and Social Services for Low-Income People in Texas.* Washington, D.C.: The Urban Institute Press.

Printz, Tobi J. 1997. "Services and Capacity of Religious Congregations in the Washington, D.C., Metropolitan Area." Paper presented at the annual meeting of ARNOVA, Indianapolis, December 4–6.

Salamon, Lester M. 1985. "Government and the Voluntary Sector in an Era of Retrenchment: The American Experience." *Journal of Public Policy* 6: 1–20.

———. 1995. *Partners in Public Service: Government-Nonprofit Relations in the Modern Welfare State.* Baltimore: Johns Hopkins University Press.

Salamon, Lester M., and Alan J. Abramson. 1996. "The Federal Budget and the Nonprofit Sector: Implications of the *Contract with America*." In

Capacity for Change? The Nonprofit World in the Age of Devolution, edited by Dwight F. Burlingame et al. (1–22). Indianapolis: Indiana University Center on Philanthropy.

Smith, Steven Rathgeb, and Michael Lipsky. 1993. *Nonprofits for Hire: The Welfare State in the Age of Contracting.* Cambridge: Harvard University Press.

Steinberg, Richard. 1996. "Can Individual Donations Replace Cutbacks in Federal Social-Welfare Spending?" In *Capacity for Change? The Nonprofit World in the Age of Devolution,* edited by Dwight F. Burlingame et al. (57–79). Indianapolis: Indiana University Center on Philanthropy.

Steuerle, C. Eugene, Edward Gramlich, Hugh Heclo, and Demetra Smith Nightingale. 1998. *The Government We Deserve.* Washington, D.C.: The Urban Institute Press.

Chapter Seven

WHY NOT FOR-PROFIT? CONVERSIONS AND PUBLIC POLICY

John H. Goddeeris and Burton A. Weisbrod

INTRODUCTION

In 1991, the managers and directors of Health Net, a nonprofit California health maintenance organization, proposed to purchase it and convert it to a for-profit firm. Though nonprofits initially dominated the HMO industry, the market share of for-profits was increasing, and a number of nonprofit HMOs, as well as hospitals, had already converted in California and elsewhere. In the evolving market for health insurance and health care, lack of access to equity capital is believed to put nonprofits at a decided competitive disadvantage.[1]

Insiders offered $108 million in cash and promissory notes for all of Health Net's assets—to be given to a nonprofit charitable trust. The deal was nearly approved, until consumer groups and others protested that the price was too low. A bidding war for the HMO ensued. When the California Department of Corporations approved the conversion in early 1992, the insiders paid $300 million—nearly three times the original offer—but for only 20 percent of Health Net stock; the money and the remaining 80 percent of the stock in the converted HMO went to the new foundation (Hamburger, Finberg, and Alcantar 1995). Assuming that the $300 million was a fair price for 20 percent ownership—and it may have understated what the buyers were willing to pay—then the entire HMO was worth at least $1.5 billion. Had the original offer been accepted, the new owners would have received assets worth $1.5 billion or more at a cost of $108 million (only a small part of which was in cash). The conversion would have transferred $1.4 billion to the insider group. A massive appropriation of public assets—accumulated with the help of governmental subsidies and tax exemptions—nearly occurred.

Since 1994, when the national Blue Cross and Blue Shield Association agreed to consider affiliations with for-profit firms, Blue Cross plans in California, Georgia, Indiana, Virginia, and Wisconsin have converted. In addition, plans in Colorado, Connecticut, Maine, Missouri, North Dakota, and New York have made formal proposals to become for-profits (Tauhert 1997). In a number of those cases, the value of assets to be transferred to a public or charitable purpose at the time of conversion has been a subject of dispute. In Georgia, for example, legislators approved a law in 1995 that permitted Blue Cross and Blue Shield of Georgia to convert to for-profit status without paying anything to a surviving foundation. Some two years later, however, nine charities sued BCBS of Georgia (now a for-profit) to collect a sum on the order of $400 million, claiming that the 1995 law was unconstitutional and that the public was being deprived of money owed to it because of the public subsidies the insurer had received (Marchetti 1997). Blue Cross and Blue Shield of Missouri has now agreed to transfer to a nonprofit foundation all of its shares in the for-profit RightChoice Managed Care, Inc., currently worth about $156 million. In 1994 Blue Cross Missouri had transferred "hundreds of millions" of its assets to RightChoice and then took the wholly-owned firm public by selling 20 percent of the stock. After first approving, the state of Missouri later demanded that the public be compensated since the for-profit's assets had benefited from various tax-related subsidies (Miller 1998b).

In the hospital industry, even more nonprofits have shifted to for-profit. While the share of beds controlled by for-profit firms remains relatively small and rather stable—about 10 percent in both 1984 and 1994 (Claxton, Feder, Shactman, and Altman 1997)—the number of conversions has been unusually large in the last several years. Nationwide, following a decade in which the average was about nine per year, 34 hospital conversions from nonprofit to for-profit took place in 1994, 58 in 1995, and 63 in 1996 (Langley and Sharpe 1996). The pace slowed a bit in 1997, in the wake of federal investigations of Columbia/HCA—the nation's largest and most aggressive for-profit hospital chain—and the ensuing resignation of its CEO. State attorneys general and other regulatory bodies have increased their scrutiny of hospital conversions. Still, 50 conversions were completed or pending in 1997 (Japsen 1998).

Conversions are not limited to the health care sector. In another recent case, the nonprofit Minnesota Public Radio (MPR) sold a for-profit subsidiary to a private firm, with multimillion dollar payments being made to officials of the subsidiary through a type of phantom stock option (Abelson 1998a, 1998b). While not so clearly a conversion—because the subsidiary was already for-profit—the large gains in the transaction by individuals closely linked to the nonprofit MPR have made it controversial.

The dividing line between the nonprofit and for-profit sectors, both in revenue sources and in the way that organizations behave, is increasingly blurred (Weisbrod 1997). Symptomatic of that blurring is the growing prominence of conversions from one organizational form to another. While changes in organizational form occur in all directions, conversions from nonprofit to for-profit have recently drawn much public attention, especially in health care. The examples above highlight the public policy issues raised generally by nonprofit conversions.

We begin this chapter by considering the concept of conversion itself and suggest that it is fundamentally a matter of transfer of control over assets between parties that face different incentives and constraints on their behavior. As such, conversion is not an all-or-nothing proposition; the concept encompasses a variety of more or less complete forms of transfer of control. Next we discuss what might motivate a nonprofit to convert, because understanding the motivation is useful in formulating public policy responses. We pay special attention to events in health care, where most of the current activity is occurring. We then turn to the important policy questions: (1) When is a conversion socially desirable? That is, when is it likely to be economically efficient and distributionally equitable? (2) How can public policy promote desirable conversions and discourage undesirable ones?

One might wish that a minimal policy role were appropriate—that an "invisible hand" mechanism applies to nonprofit conversions, so that they would naturally take place when, and only when, they enhance economic efficiency, harming no one in the process. Alas, we are not so optimistic. A transfer of assets from nonprofit to for-profit control could sometimes increase social value, but that is by no means assured. Conversions might be motivated by private gain, as the Health Net example suggests.

The fundamental point is that conversion of assets controlled by a nonprofit to an independent for-profit firm constitutes transfer of the assets from an organization legally prohibited from distributing its profits or surplus to managers into an organization that faces no such constraint. Thus, some mechanism is needed to prevent assets from being accumulated through the aid of public subsidies to a nonprofit and then being transferred to a private firm that distributes ownership of the assets without restriction. Fostering an environment that allows for and even facilitates efficient conversions without also encouraging inappropriate transfers of wealth is a significant challenge.

Under existing law, conversions of nonprofits normally require regulatory approval. In some cases, as with complete conversions to for-profit status, formal approval is required in advance. In other, more partial transfers of control, such as may occur in a joint venture with a for-profit firm or a contracting-out of the management of a nonprofit, prior approval is not required, but the regulator may subsequently penalize the nonprofit or require that it cancel the arrangement.[2] For conversion to occur, therefore, more than a desire to convert must be present. The regulatory agencies must also consent, at least tacitly—an important matter that has received little previous attention.

Although this volume focuses on relationships between government and nonprofits, discussion of conversions from nonprofit to for-profit is not out of place. Government is no disinterested bystander with respect to conversions. It is often a major purchaser in markets where nonprofit and for-profit firms compete; hospitals, nursing homes, and health insurers come quickly to mind. Government subsidies and tax abatements also facilitate the accumulation of assets in nonprofit organizations, assets that could be transferred to private firms through conversion. Government regulators rule on conversion proposals. Finally, very similar issues to those surrounding nonprofit conversions are also present when government privatizes—sells assets or contracts out functions to the private sector.

WHAT IS A CONVERSION?

Conversion is fundamentally about changes in control over an organization's assets and responsibility for its liabilities. After a change in control, assets may be deployed in different ways and for the benefit of different individuals or groups. Public policy concerns revolve around efficiency—whether or not a change enhances the social value the assets will produce—and around fairness—whether some parties benefit improperly at others' expense.

WHAT IS SPECIAL ABOUT CONVERSIONS BY NONPROFITS TO FOR-PROFITS?

While this chapter primarily focuses on changes from nonprofit to for-profit control, we do well to keep in mind that many different forms of organizations provide goods and services (Hansmann 1996). Government organizations directly provide services, such as education and hospital care, often in competition with nonprofits and for-profits. In addition to the investor-owned firms that we normally think of as for-profits, there are also various other privately owned organizational forms, including, for example, worker-owned or customer-owned cooperatives and mutual organizations.

Conversions occur across and within all of those organization types. The market for corporate control is often lauded as an important mechanism for disciplining management to seek maximum value for shareholders, thereby enhancing the efficiency of the economic system. Yet even mergers and buyouts within the corporate sector often raise concerns about improper private gain by insiders, since it is by no means always clear that corporate executives' financial incentives coincide with stockholders' interests.[3] Prudential, the nation's largest life insurer and currently a "mutual" organization owned by its policyholders, recently made news with plans to convert to a shareholder-owned company, and other mutual insurers may follow. The reports have a familiar ring to those who have followed discussions of nonprofit conversions. Management claims a need for access to equity capital, while consumer groups express concern that managers are motivated by private gain, even at policyholders' expense (Scism 1998).

So what, if anything, is special about *nonprofit* conversions to for-profit status that merits particular public policy concern? We see three points that make nonprofit conversions different and of greater importance to public policymaking than other types of conversions.

Lack of Private Ownership

In a private firm, with clearly defined private owners, the current owners can be expected to resist any transfer of control that undervalues their ownership shares. The more diffuse the ownership and the less transparent the value of shares, however, the less effective the check on self-dealing by management insiders is likely to be. The essence of a nonprofit organization is that no individuals have a legal claim to the organization's assets or net income, both of which may be hard to measure but, in some cases, have tremendous value. In the sense that the owners are the public at large, incentives of owners to exercise oversight are extremely diffuse in a nonprofit. Managers and directors have both the control needed to arrange conversions and some potential incentive to do so, as the Health Net case suggests, although board members' moral and legal fiduciary responsibilities are surely important countervailing influences.

Different Legal Constraints

When organizations operate under different legal constraints, transactions between them may exploit the differences for private gain without a corresponding social benefit.[4] While this problem can exist for transactions between various forms of private for-profit organizations, it is a particular concern for conversions of nonprofits (Cordes and Weisbrod 1998). Many nonprofits benefit from preferred tax treatment, including the tax deductibility of donations, exemptions from sales and property taxation, and other subsidies not available to for-profits. The largest benefits go to nonprofits that are tax-exempt under Section 501(c)(3) of the Internal Revenue Code. Others typically receive an exemption from corporate profits taxation. Public policies that give any advantage to nonprofits thereby provide a "wedge" that disadvantages for-profit competitors and creates opportunities for nonprofit managers to accumulate assets which, if conversion were arranged, could lead to private benefit.

Different Objectives

Although problems of managerial incentives exist in all complex organizations, those that are privately owned may generally be expected to seek maximum value for their owners. Conversion from one type of privately owned organization to another may then have only modest effects on how the organization behaves. Whether an insurance company is a mutual owned by its policyholders or a corporation owned by its stockholders may not matter greatly for the products it offers or its responsiveness to customers, despite the formal difference in ownership. In a reasonably competitive insurance market, owners' interests are strongly linked to satisfying policyholders. Thus, the public policy case for limiting conversions is weaker when both the selling and acquiring organizations have the goal of pursuing the private interests of their owners rather than when the selling organization has broader social goals than the acquirer, as is generally the case with nonprofit conversions. If in fact nonprofits behave differently than for-profits—an issue about which we will have more to say—conversion from nonprofit to any form of privately owned firm could change the organization's objectives in ways relevant to policy. For that reason, the privatization of governmental assets through sale to for-profit ownership—or even contracting for management services—presents problems similar to the conversion of nonprofits to for-profits.

COMPLETE AND PARTIAL CONVERSIONS

The extreme case of nonprofit conversion occurs when an entire organization changes its legal form from nonprofit to for-profit, or is sold to a for-profit. Even such a seemingly clear change of organizational form, however, is complicated by the fact that the nonprofit's assets do not belong to individuals. If the nonprofit sells its assets and ceases to exist in its previous form, where do the proceeds of the sale go? Normally that value is passed to another nonprofit organization, frequently a newly created charitable foundation. Valuing the assets to be transferred, however, is often a most contentious issue, as exemplified by the Health Net case and a number of Blue Cross conversions.

Transfers of control can occur in other ways and to varying degrees. For example, joint ventures between nonprofit and for-profit firms are increasingly common. In arrangements between the for-profit Columbia/HCA and various nonprofit hospitals, the formerly nonprofit hospital became a for-profit venture, jointly owned by Columbia and the original nonprofit (or a new foundation) but managed by Columbia, which exercised substantial control over the use of the hospital assets. Attorneys general in at least two states, California and Michigan, have recognized the transfer of control over nonprofit assets in this type of joint venture and have successfully opposed such a transfer in well-publicized cases (Whitehead, Johnson, and Moore 1997). The IRS has also been reviewing the question of whether joint ventures between nonprofits and for-profits should retain tax-exempt status and has concluded that control is the key determinant (Burns and Lagnado 1998). Similarly, the formation by a nonprofit of a for-profit subsidiary can lead to a transfer of control, since a major motivation for creating such a subsidiary may be to gain access to equity capital by selling part ownership to the public. When that happens, the assets held by the subsidiary shift at least partially to for-profit control.

Yet another form of partial conversion occurs when a nonprofit contracts with a for-profit firm for management services. Whether such a contract involves significant public policy issues depends on how much control is transferred—that is, the degree to which the for-profit firm is effectively constrained—and on the reward structure for the for-profit management firm, which affects its incentives to use its discretionary authority in various ways. While such transfers of managerial control have been happening with increased frequency in the nonprofit hospital industry, similar conversions-by-delegation are occurring in the public sector. Public schools in Minneapolis, Hartford, and elsewhere have been put under private sector management by firms such as The Edison Project and Apollo Group, Inc., and prisons have been increasingly privatized through management contracts with firms like Corrections Corporation of America and Behavioral Systems Southwest. In all of those cases, the nonprofit (or public) organization was neither sold nor formally converted; instead, control was transferred to a private firm for a finite period of time, and with a variety of contractual constraints.

One might argue that contracting with a for-profit does not necessarily imply a transfer of control, if the contract is well specified. Theoretically, the for-profit contractor could be provided with incentives to pursue the nonprofit's social goals, however complex and subtle those goals might be. But if a nonprofit institution's most valuable and most common social dimensions of performance are very difficult to define in a contract and to monitor (Weisbrod 1988), then any transfer of managerial authority to a for-profit can be expected to alter performance away from those hard-to-monitor dimensions. That would be the case as long as the difficulty of writing a complete contract allows the for-profit contractor discretion in ways that affect the degree to which the nonprofit's goals are realized.

Because transfers of control to for-profits can take many forms and be of varying degrees, the complete conversions or sales of nonprofits now drawing attention in health care are likely the tip of a much larger "iceberg" of shifts toward for-profit control over nonprofit assets and activities. Moreover, such shifts may be occurring in other industries but less visibly than in health care. That possibility carries a major implication for public policy: If an increasingly strong "searchlight" of public attention is focused on particular forms of conversion, then the goals that motivate transfers of control over assets (examined below) are likely to be pursued through other, more subtle, means. There will be more joint ventures, partial buyouts, and complex interorganization contracts that preserve the apparent and legal independence of each nonprofit organization but actually shift control and financial benefits to for-profits.

State Regulation of Health Care Conversions

While the federal IRS exercises some regulatory oversight on nonprofit conversions, state regulators play a particularly central role. Their authority to oversee health care conversions has traditionally derived from state nonprofit corporation law and common law that applies to charitable trusts, as well as law specific to particular types of health care institutions. The extent of this authority and how it applies to complex transactions between nonprofits and for-profits have, however, often been unclear. In the words of one legal expert speaking at a 1996 conference (Schriber 1997), "Regulators have too many authorities and too little guidance."

In the wake of the heightened interest in health care conversions, at least 16 states have recently passed legislation that deals specifically with conversions of hospitals. (In several cases, the laws also apply to health insurers and health maintenance organizations.) While the legislation generally casts a broad net in requiring prior regulatory approval of conversions, usually by a state's attorney general, the extent and form of oversight vary across states in important ways. Some differences are indicated below.

Precisely what transactions should be deemed to be "conversions"? The National Association of Attorneys General (NAAG), in its 1997 Resolution on "Conversion of Nonprofit Health Care Entities to For-Profit Status," called for written notice "before a nonprofit health care entity sells, leases, conveys, exchanges, transfers or otherwise disposes of all or substantially all of its assets" (Volunteer Trustees Foundation for Research and Education 1998, 8). We note that this formulation appears to permit disposition of assets that are less than "substantially all," which could permit a series of partial dispositions that, over time, would constitute a virtually total transfer.

Most state legislation has included a broad list of the types of transactions that trigger regulatory review, similar to the NAAG Resolution. There is variation in definitions of the extent of control that may be transferred before approval is required. For example, regulatory approval is required in California, Connecticut, and Oregon, if a "material" or "significant" amount of control is involved; in Arizona, for any disposition of assets of $1 million or more; in Wisconsin, Nebraska, and Ohio, for any change of at least 20 percent of "ownership or control"; in Louisiana and South Dakota, for any change of ownership or control of at least 30 percent of voting rights or assets; in Colorado and Georgia, if a transfer of 50 percent or more of assets over a five-year period is involved; and in Virginia, if a disposition of "all or substantially all of the assets" is involved.

With respect to the valuation of assets involved in a conversion, state requirements are more alike, focusing on payment of fair prices for the nonprofit's assets. There is, however, some variation in language. In Arizona, evidence is required demonstrating "due diligence" in negotiating terms and disclosing private benefit by a director, officer, or employee. In California and Connecticut, the Attorney General must determine that "fair market value" is being received. In Ohio, the Attorney General must determine that "full and fair market value" is received for the assets. In Rhode Island, the Attorney General must determine not only that fair market value is received for the assets but also that management contracts are "fair" and that "assets have not been manipulated . . . so as to decrease their value . . ."

For more information on recent state legislation see:

Butler, Patricia. 1997. "State Policy Issues in Nonprofit Conversions." *Health Affairs* 16 (2): 69–84.
Shriber, Donald. 1997. "State Experience in Regulating a Changing Health Care System." *Health Affairs* 16 (2): 48–68.
U.S. General Accounting Office. 1997. *Not-For-Profit Hospitals: Conversion Issues Prompt Increased State Oversight.* December.
Volunteer Trustees Foundation for Research and Education. 1998. "The Sale and Conversion of Not-For-Profit Hospitals: A State-By-State Analysis of New Legislation," Washington, D.C.: Volunteer Trustees Foundation for Research and Education.

WHAT MOTIVATES CONVERSIONS?

Choice of Organization Form

Economists usually view individuals as maximizing their well being or utility subject to the constraints imposed by their environment, including the legal system. It is useful to model organization behavior in the same way—as the pursuit of some objective or set of objectives subject to constraints. From that perspective, the choice of organizational form, nonprofit or for-profit, is a choice of constraints under which an organization will operate, because these constraints differ between the nonprofit and for-profit forms. A particular form is presumably chosen because it is the most conducive to the attainment of the founders' goals.

Constraints are imposed by both the legal system and the market. As we have noted, nonprofits generally receive certain tax advantages relative to for-profit firms. They also face a legal "nondistribution constraint" not imposed on private firms—a restriction against distributing any profits or surplus to managers or others connected with the organization (Hansmann 1980). Nonprofits are restricted, in effect, from access to equity capital because they may not grant private ownership shares in the organization, although they may have greater access to tax-exempt bond financing than do for-profit firms.

Market conditions also constrain behavior. Both for-profit and nonprofit firms are constrained by demand conditions—buyers' willingness to pay—when they sell output, though not necessarily identically. In some cases, buyers prefer to purchase from nonprofits, perhaps because they regard them as more trustworthy. Trust is particularly important for goods with essential attributes that are difficult to monitor directly—e.g., the "tender loving care" provided in a nursing home or day care center—leaving buyers concerned that sellers will exploit their informational advantage for personal gain. If at least some buyers regard nonprofit status as a signal of trustworthiness, demand will differ between the two types of organizations, even if all the easily observable characteristics of their services are identical.

Suppliers of resource inputs may also treat nonprofits differently from for-profits. As previously noted, volunteer time appears more readily supplied to nonprofit firms, and paid employees sometimes offer to work for nonprofits at a lower wage, according to several empirical studies (Preston 1989; Roomkin and Weisbrod 1999; Weisbrod 1988; but cf. Goddeeris 1988). Some employees appear willing to sacrifice monetary compensation to work for a nonprofit organization, perhaps because they identify with its goals and derive satisfaction from working to achieve them.

In light of their numerous differences in constraints, some providing advantages to nonprofits, others to for-profits, the optimal choice of organization form depends on the organization's objectives as defined by the founder, top management, and directors, subject to IRS approval. Suppose, for example, that the founding managers of a new medical clinic care about two things—their own monetary compensation and the provision of some collective service, such as subsidized health care for the poor.[5] In either the nonprofit or for-profit sector some tradeoff is likely between the two goals of managerial compensation and the level of collective goods provision that can be supported. But maximum monetary rewards to the founders may be higher in the for-profit sector, since the nondistribution constraint does not limit compensation. Larger collective good output may be possible in the nonprofit sector, however, due to tax advantages and the ability to attract donations and volunteer labor. Managers who place relatively little value on the collective goods would then organize as for-profits, but those with a strong enough preference for providing such services would choose the nonprofit form. The two forms may thus coexist; even when they compete head-to-head in the same markets, the differential constraints permit nonprofit and for-profit managers to pursue somewhat different goals.

Potential Conflict of Interest for Nonprofits with For-Profit Subsidiaries:
The Case of Minnesota Public Radio

A recent case involving Minnesota Public Radio (MPR) illustrates the complex relationships that can exist between nonprofits and for-profits (Abelson 1998a, 1998b; Miller 1998a). The nonprofit Minnesota Communications Group owns both MPR, also a nonprofit, and a for-profit subsidiary called Greenspring. William H. Kling is president of both MPR and Greenspring, and his compensation at Greenspring included "Value Performance Units" (VPUs), similar to stock options often provided to private-sector executives. Greenspring has now agreed to sell its Rivertown catalogue business—originally launched to market products related to MPR's "Prairie Home Companion" program—to the Dayton Hudson Corporation for $120 million, of which about $90 million will be added to MPR's endowment. Mr. Kling is personally receiving $2.6 million in the deal through the sale of his VPUs, and about two dozen other Greenspring executives are similarly receiving a total of $4.7 million. It appears that the VPUs could only be "cashed out" for the officers when the subsidiary was sold. MPR "fought the release of the salary and bonuses of its top executives, saying that it hurt the ability of the for-profit operation to recruit talent," but the state of Minnesota passed a financial disclosure law requiring their release (Levy 1998). The VPUs, referred to as "phantom stock options," were regarded by the board of trustees as essential for attracting outstanding managerial leadership in competition with for-profit firms (Rothschild 1998).

The Minnesota Communication Group's decision to permit the sale may be a sensible one for MPR. It is certainly possible that the Rivertown business will be more valuable as a part of Dayton Hudson, so that the income generated by the increase in endowment could exceed the expected income the business would produce if the sale did not take place. MPR may also prefer the more stable endowment income stream. The compensation package for the executives, with its contingent valuation, depending on sales prices, may have been an important motivator for the creation of value in Rivertown, which now provides a substantial revenue source for MPR. Nonetheless, the sale, and previous to it the close relationship between the nonprofit MPR and the for-profit subsidiary, Greenspring, raises questions. When top executives of a nonprofit also have a significant financial interest in a closely related for-profit, is there a potential for conflict of interest in the management of the nonprofit?

Why Would a Nonprofit Want to Convert?

Why would an organization that has chosen to form in one way later want to convert? A conversion decision is in some ways like the original decision about organization form. If either the objectives of an agency's decisionmakers or the constraints it faces have changed, the agency may wish to reconsider its original choice. Most nonprofit organizations are exempt from property taxes that private firms must pay; if property tax rates were cut, the advantage of the nonprofit tax exemption would be reduced. Thus a government decision to reduce property taxation could induce an organization with a sufficiently weak preference for the nonprofit form to switch status (Cordes and Weisbrod 1998; Hansmann 1987).

Given that conversion activity has accelerated in one particular sector—health care—rather than throughout the economy, it seems more likely that the cause involves changes in constraints—the legal, regulatory, and market environment—rather than changes in organizational objectives. It is not clear why organizational objectives would shift systematically, but only in this one field. Below, we will discuss briefly how changes in the healthcare marketplace may have contributed to interest in conversions, and whether such changes can be expected in other industries.

The distinction between objectives and constraints is not entirely tidy. In the absence of operational measures of "success" analogous to profit or share prices, a nonprofit organization's goals are determined significantly by its key decisionmakers. Those goals often change over time, however, and sometimes in response to changes in constraints imposed on the organization. Goals may change as a nonprofit, in pursuing its original mission, encounters budgetary constraints and takes on board members who represent sources of actual or potential finance. As an example, in the early 1980s, a nonprofit food bank in Phoenix that had local volunteers as directors witnessed a struggle in which food manufacturers, such as Beatrice Foods and Kraft, and food marketers, including the Grocery Manufacturers of America and the Food Marketing Institute, rather than the volunteers, came to exert control (Birnbaum 1982). If financial constraints become more stringent, it is plausible that in the course of time an organization's goals might change considerably, as managers and directors with greater concern about, and skills with, fundraising and finance replace those whose visions were of public service outputs. Such a change could contribute to a decision to convert, as the altered goals become less compatible with the constraints under which the nonprofit operates.

There are also important differences between a decision to convert and the initial choice of organizational form. A desire to convert may evolve naturally over an organization's life cycle, for example, even if its external environment and its goals do not change. For a newly established nonprofit organization with few assets, the nondistribution constraint may be of little consequence, as the nonprofit has little or nothing to distribute.[6] If the organization is successful, however, and the market value of its assets grows, its managers and board face an increasing opportunity and temptation to distribute some of that market value to themselves. At the same time, the success of the organization may increase the opportunities for it to exploit the equity capital market as a for-profit firm.[7] If public policy permits conversions to occur in a manner that effectively subverts or even weakens the nondistribution constraint, a conversion may occur at that point. Within such a policy regime, some organizations may even pursue a long-range strategy of forming as nonprofits and, if successful, converting to for-profit status.

On the other hand, if the nondistribution constraint is effectively enforced even during the conversion process, as state and federal laws intend, the assets accumulated by the firm while a nonprofit would not be available to be siphoned off for private gain. That diminishes the private gain motivation for converting. At the same time, if the conversion does occur and the for-profit firm's behavior shifts toward maximization of market value and away from collective goods provision, it does not *necessarily* imply that collective goods are lost in the process. The income from the accumulated assets could be redirected toward the continued provision of collective goods (as could revenue from the increased taxes, if any, that the firm now pays as a for-profit entity, although the disposition of the taxes is outside the control of the firm's decisionmakers).

CONVERSIONS IN HEALTH CARE

The incentive to convert exists for any nonprofit organization that has accumulated valuable assets, assuming that its leaders could then capture even part of the nonprofit's value for their own financial gain. Why, then, has health care been such a focus of conversion activity but not other industries in which nonprofits play a prominent role (for example, higher education, museums, and day care)? Why within the health care sector have there been so few conversions of nonprofit nursing homes and home health care agencies? And why have conversions among hospitals and health insurers accelerated *recently*?

A full analysis of those issues is beyond the scope of this chapter.[8] It is plausible, however, that conversions of nonprofit hospitals, HMOs, and Blue Cross plans have been influenced heavily by changes in the legal and regulatory environment, as well as in the nature of market competition, that have made it more difficult for nonprofit health insurers, and some nonprofit hospitals, to survive competition with for-profits. In other words, changes in constraints may be leading to reconsideration of which organizational form is optimal for many health care nonprofits, and they are opting for conversion.

One can point to a number of policy changes that have reduced advantages for hospital and HMO nonprofits, making it more difficult for them to finance collective goods while surviving in the market.[9] For HMOs, the end in 1983 of federal grants and loans for HMO development appears to coincide with, and perhaps stimulated, the shift toward for-profit status. For the Blues, tax advantages have been withdrawn over time. Exemption from the federal corporate income tax was ended in the Tax Reform Act of 1986; many states have also limited special tax treatment of Blue Cross plans. Changes in tax policy in the 1980s also reduced the advantages of nonprofit hospitals over for-profits with regard to the issuance of tax exempt bonds (Sloan 1988).

At the same time that those changes in tax policy have been legislated, the nature of competition in the health care marketplace has also been changing. An era in which third-party payors passively reimbursed hospitals for their self-reported costs or charges has given way to one of standardized payment rates and even active price competition for patients. The public and private health care financing system and government policies of most of the post–WW II era (including the Hill-Burton Act of 1946, which subsidized construction of hospital beds) encouraged an enormous buildup of hospital capacity. As the total number of hospital admissions began to fall in the early 1980s (as a result of technological changes but also economic pressures to rein in hospital spending), occupancy levels fell and have remained at quite low levels.

The occurrence of hospital and HMO conversions is coincident with and surely related to a drive toward consolidation in parts of the health care sector. Some analysts have stressed a link between excess capacity, particularly in hospitals, and both consolidation and conversions. As the market for hospital services has become more price competitive and the level of overcapacity more apparent, hospitals have come to view affiliation with larger organizations as necessary for survival. The most attractive suitors have often, though not always, been for-profits (Coye 1997; Hollis 1997), and a large number of hospital conversions have been sales to or joint ventures with for-profit chains, such as Columbia/HCA and Tenet Healthcare Corporation.

Similarly, as government and employers have sought to become more prudent purchasers of health care, health insurers have also found an increasing need to compete for enrollees on the basis of price and to embrace managed-care principles. In turn, pressure has been generated to expand and to achieve economies of scale and market power. Increased emphasis on cost containment has decreased the degree to which market competition tolerates differences in behavior between nonprofit and for-profit insurers, including HMOs. In addition, the perceived need to grow has elevated the importance of access to capital as increasingly critical to survival for health insurers, and as favoring for-profit firms over nonprofits, which cannot sell equity interests.[10]

Access to equity capital, one advantage that investor-owned for-profits clearly enjoy over nonprofits, appears consistently in arguments for conversions—including, for example, Prudential's plan to convert from a mutual to a stockholder-owned firm, and MPR's decision to sell its for-profit Rivertown subsidiary. While more research is needed, we remain somewhat skeptical of the importance of this advantage, including its application to health insurers. Nonprofits do have access to the debt market and often even to tax-exempt bonds. The importance of debt finance, in both sectors, is illustrated by the recent decision of the for-profit HMO, Oxford Health Plans, to sell $350 million of debt over the next few months (Abelson 1998c). While Oxford will also sell a similar amount of stock to a private investment firm, (an option not available to a nonprofit), the fact remains that the equity market is not the only source of capital available to finance expansion. There has been little discussion and analysis of why access to capital in general and equity capital in particular is of such great—and increased—importance for health insurers. The health insurance industry appears to be going through a transitional period of high capital investment in information technology and network building associated with the adoption of more aggressive managed-care techniques. It also appears that part of the interest in access to equity capital is for financing acquisitions, as the health insurance industry consolidates. Interestingly, either of those motives suggests that if for-profits have an advantage in that regard, its importance is temporary. A "mature" insurer that is not expanding rapidly and for which capital investment is a fairly constant share of revenues ought to be able to finance itself largely with internal funds.

It is difficult indeed to determine the extent to which conversions in health care are socially efficient responses to changes in the external economic environment in which hospitals and HMOs operate, and the extent to which conversions reflect opportunistic behavior by insiders. Both have been made possible by dramatic changes in those markets, changes not matched in other markets where nonprofits are significant players. The social gain is an important matter that remains unresolved. It is clear that personal financial enrichment of key nonprofit officials has often been present in conversions, particularly of nonprofit HMOs (witness the original Health Net proposal), and in at least some proposed conversions of Blue Cross plans. It is widely alleged that in many of the HMO conversions, insiders were able to purchase ownership shares at low prices before the converted organizations were valued in the stock market and then profited enormously when the organizations "went public" and something closer to a true market value was established for the assets of the former nonprofit (Fox and Isenberg 1996; Hamburger, Finberg, and Alcantar 1995). That private financial gain, through subversion of the nondistribution constraint, motivates at least some HMO conversions not only cannot be ruled out, but according to one knowledgeable observer, has generally been the case. Leonard Shaeffer, the CEO of WellPoint Health Systems, formerly California Blue Cross, which itself converted to for-profit in a highly controversial deal, stated:

> Before the conversion of WellPoint, the value of every single company that converted to for-profit status was significantly underestimated. What was granted to charity turned out to be much less than was realized a week, a month, or a year later, when Wall Street placed a true market value on the for-profit HMO that resulted from the conversion. Almost all of the value created went to the management and boards of these companies . . . FHP International, Foundation Health, Pacificare, TakeCare, you name it. These are companies that today are led by multimillionaires who achieved that status by virtue of receiving stock that was dramatically undervalued at the time of conversion (Iglehart 1995, 142).

When Is Conversion Socially Desirable?

It is clear that conversion of a nonprofit can be financially advantageous to the buyers and the managers representing the sellers. Less clear are the conditions under which a conversion is socially beneficial. From the point of view of conventional benefit-cost analysis, a conversion is desirable if it leads to a higher social value of production. Social value is ordinarily conceived as the aggregate of what members of society are willing to pay for what the organization produces (Haveman and Weisbrod 1975). Such an analysis attempts to set aside issues of equitable distribution, that is, of whether the distribution of gains and losses from a change are distributed fairly. This division between efficiency issues—or maximizing social value—and equity or fairness issues, while often not fully tenable, has proven highly useful in organizing thought about the consequences of economic changes.

Clearly, conversions can have consequences for both efficiency and equity, affecting resource allocation and output distribution, and whether concerned citizens and policymakers will regard a particular conversion as desirable depends on both types of effects. Efficiency issues are easier to analyze. We are generally less comfortable about making strong value judgments about "equity," because there is no widely shared definition of what the term implies. We offer the following principle, however, which encompasses both efficiency and equity considerations: *A conversion is desirable if it is "Pareto-improving."*

In other words, to warrant regulatory approval, a conversion should make all parties—not simply the transacting parties—better off, or at least none worse off, as compared with what would happen if the conversion did not occur. Pareto improvements are hard to come by anywhere in the economy, as nearly any real-world change that affects large numbers of people will produce some losers, but conversions ought to be arranged to come "close" to meeting the requirements, even if side agreements for compensation of potential losers—e.g., the medically indigent in the case of health care conversions—are required. That principle is in keeping with the common law doctrine of *cy pres*, which requires that the assets of a converting charitable nonprofit be dedicated to purposes as close as possible to those for which the nonprofit was originally set up.

Notice that the Pareto improvement principle does not preclude private gain for those who organize the conversion; in a free enterprise economy, the pursuit of private gain is an essential driving force motivating growth and efficient change. A Pareto improvement requires only that other groups also gain in the process. Indeed, it is desirable that those who control a nonprofit's assets have an incentive to seek out Pareto-improving conversions and to respond favorably when such opportunities exist. A useful, though not necessarily essential mechanism is one in which officers of nonprofits share in the greater price that they negotiate for the sale of the organization— thereby encouraging an efficient principal-agent relationship. MPR, for example, apparently provided its executives an incentive to build up the profitability and hence the sales value of the for-profit subsidiary, and then to maximize the sale price. While such incentives always have the potential to go too far, their total absence would lead to lost opportunities for social gains.

The Pareto improvement concept should be interpreted in a forward-looking way. The relevant consideration is not, for example, the charity care a nonprofit clinic has provided in the past, but what it would be able to give in the future should it remain in the nonprofit form. External forces, such as decreased government grants, could cause such prospects to change.

Turning to the efficiency question, can a conversion of a nonprofit firm to for-profit ever increase social value? A "no" answer is difficult to defend. Because of the stronger incentives for minimizing costs and responding to consumer demands that come with private ownership and control of assets, and perhaps greater flexibility associated with access to equity capital, it is certainly plausible that the same resources could produce greater value in the for-profit than the nonprofit sector. Were it not so, we must question why the for-profit is the primary form of organization in most industries. The evidence, however, is surprisingly thin.

The root issue involves one of the central questions confronting researchers who study the nonprofit sector: Do nonprofits and for-profits operating in the same industry behave differently, and if they do, in what ways? If the answer is no, then conversions should have few efficiency consequences, and the key issues are all distributional. But if organizational form does influence behavior, then a change of form may lead the organization to act differently, which could influence efficiency in either direction. It might enhance efficiency, as we already noted, through the stronger incentives for efficient production coming from private ownership and the flexibility associated with access to equity financing. Alternatively, it would reduce social value insofar as the increased emphasis on what is privately profitable led to neglect of services that are valued collectively but difficult to sell profitably—for example, hospital provision of indigent care, university provision of basic research, and museums' and zoos' provision of cultural and species preservation activities.

As an empirical matter, we submit that because of measurement difficulties, the extent of differences between nonprofits and for-profits remains an open question. Direct measurement of outputs and their differences across institutional forums is difficult. In part that reflects the general problems of measuring outputs in the service sector, where most nonprofit organizations operate. In part it also reflects the complexity and subtlety of the outputs society expects from non-profits. As with governmentally provided outputs, nonprofit organizations are typically utilized precisely in those markets where private enterprise is least promising—where "tender loving care" in nursing homes and day care centers is difficult to monitor and consumers are often asymmetrically underinformed; where aid to the "poor" is similarly hard to monitor and, hence, to reward; and where the collective-type outputs provided by government are supplemented.

Even in the case of hospitals, where the question has been most extensively studied and the differences in legal and regulatory constraints now seem relatively small, we do not think the evidence is sufficient to reject the possibility of subtle but important differences between nonprofit and for-profit behavior (see, however, Sloan 1998 for a survey that emphasizes evidence of similarity between for-profit and nonprofit hospitals in the provision of services to the poor). Indirect indicators of comparative institutional behavior in various industries have sometimes shown substantial differences. Among nursing homes, nonprofits have been found to have lower prices, higher staff-patient levels, higher patient satisfaction, and longer waiting lists (Weisbrod 1998). Among hospitals, CEOs in for-profits receive a substantially greater share of their compensation as performance-based bonuses and receive substantially greater overall compensation (Roomkin and Weisbrod 1999). Among day care centers, nonprofits have been found to have higher ratios of staff to children and better-educated staff (Mauser 1993).

APPROPRIATE PUBLIC POLICY: GUIDING THE INVISIBLE HAND

Competitive Bidding

If a nonprofit is to be sold to a for-profit buyer, how should the price be determined? An obvious approach is to open the process for bids and then sell to the highest bidder (presuming it is appropriate to sell at all, a key issue to which we return below), but it is not without problems. The process can be costly and time-consuming (Schaeffer 1996) and is in any case less straightforward than it may appear. Consider the ambiguity of precisely what is to be transferred from the nonprofit to the for-profit purchaser. A sale would naturally include the items that appear on the organization's balance sheet, its assets and financial liabilities. But what of the organization's "obligations," which may be more or less formal, to provide collective goods—those that we value as a community but which cannot be profitably sold in the market? Suppose a nonprofit hospital has been providing some charity care for poor and uninsured patients, scientific research, medical training, or community health education. Suppose also that this hospital is considering sale to a private for-profit hospital chain. Would a sale require the new owner to provide those services at the same level? Clearly, the value of the nonprofit to a for-profit buyer would be greater if such unprofitable obligations could be avoided, so it would not be appropriate to compare offers solely on price, if they differ in the dimension of commitment to charity care or other public service outputs. Conversion agreements now frequently specify that the for-profit buyer will provide the same level of charity care as a former nonprofit hospital (Claxton, Feder, Shactman, and Altman 1997). A central problem with such a contract, however, is the difficulty of defining, monitoring, and enforcing the agreement, especially over time. The precise measure of "charity care," for example, is by no means clear, nor is the measure of "research" or "community education."

If competitive bidding is to be used, it is thus very important to define terms carefully and operationally, to make sure that offers being compared are truly comparable. This is one argument for preferring "complete" to partial conversions. Different suitors will undoubtedly prefer different terms for a joint venture deal, making offers difficult to compare. Columbia/HCA has participated in joint ventures in which it receives, in addition to ownership share, a fee for managing the new organization. Clearly, a higher management fee increases the price it would willingly pay for its share of the joint venture. Such issues exist whether the selling price is determined by a bidding process or by an investment banking firm that attempts, on the basis of its knowledge and experience, to estimate what a competitive bidding process would generate.

The nonprofit's decisionmakers—formally and legally the board of trustees—should have some flexibility to choose among bids and not necessarily accept the highest. Even in the context of a complete conversion or outright sale, difficulties of specifying all the relevant terms of the contract are great. Another reason that the highest bid may not be the best is the social interest in maintaining competitive pricing in product markets. In a community with just two hospitals, hospital A may be in a position to offer the highest bid for hospital B, because the combined hospitals would be able to engage in monopoly pricing, an advantage that other potential buyers of hospital B would not have. A's advantage does not come from an ability to use resources more efficiently, but from being better positioned to extract payment from consumers. In that case, antitrust considerations might rule out hospital A as a potential buyer, but the issue can exist in less extreme circumstances.

Comparing Value as Nonprofit and For-profit

From an efficiency perspective, an organization should convert if the net present value of the services it could produce is higher as a for-profit than as a nonprofit. By *net* present value we mean net of the opportunity costs of other resources (labor, new capital, and other productive inputs) that the organization will have to obtain to produce output. Ideally the organization should choose the sector in which

$$\text{(Value of services produced)} \tag{1}$$
$$\text{minus (Costs of resources used)}$$

is maximized. (In the expression above and what follows, all flows are to be interpreted as present values.) Conversions for which expression (1) is higher in the for-profit sector are at least potentially Pareto-improving, because in principle the extra "surplus" value could be used to compensate groups that would otherwise lose and thus make everyone better off. How close are the decisionmakers in a nonprofit likely to come to applying this rule naturally in their own considerations about conversion?

A nonprofit that is considering conversion, if it is motivated by service to its constituents rather than the private gain of its decisionmakers—clearly a key assumption, the validity of which depends in part on the regulatory environment surrounding conversions—would compare the surplus it generates *for its "constituents"* if it continues to operate as nonprofit with what it would generate if it converted (sold to a for-profit). By constituents we mean anyone who benefits from the services the organization provides, including paying customers and anyone benefiting indirectly from collective goods.[11] Organizational survival, while perhaps very important for the management and employees of the nonprofit, is not, in itself, a social goal. The surplus for constituents from continuing to operate as a nonprofit is:

$$\text{(Value of services produced)} \qquad \text{(2a)}$$
$$\text{minus (Revenue from sales)}$$

The difference between expression (2a) and the socially relevant expression (1) is that we have assumed that the nonprofit counts only the costs borne by its constituents, which we have equated with its revenue from sales.

If the nonprofit sells to a for-profit, the surplus that can serve its constituents is

$$\text{(Sale price) plus (Value of services produced)} \qquad \text{(2b)}$$
$$\text{minus (Revenue from sales)}$$

This expression captures the idea that the proceeds of the sale can also be used to serve the constituents of the old nonprofit. Because the converted firm may behave differently than if it had not converted, the final two terms will likely take different values in expression (2b) than they do in expression (2a). However, if the for-profit agrees to subsidize the provision of certain services, it may continue to provide some surplus value to constituents of the nonprofit.

If we make some additional assumptions, we can arrive at expressions more directly comparable to the efficiency criterion of expression (1). In the long run, a nonprofit must generate sufficient revenue—through sales, government subsidies, and donations—to cover the payments it makes to obtain resources. If we assume that the payments it makes for resources equal their opportunity costs, then (2a) can be rewritten as

(Value of services produced)

minus (Costs of resources used)   (3a)

plus (Subsidies and donations)

Our treatment of donations in this analysis warrants some comment. Clearly nonprofits use donations—as they do government subsidies—to support the provision of services, substituting for other sources of revenue, as implied by expression (3a). From a social perspective, donations to a specific organization are not free, as they displace either donations elsewhere or some other form of spending of value to the donor. Our analysis assumes that the nonprofit does not consider the opportunity costs of donations in making its decisions.

For a for-profit, profit = revenue from sales − costs of resources − taxes, where profit is defined in the economic sense, and costs of resources include a normal return on invested capital. In a competitive bidding process, the sale price offered for the nonprofit should approach the expected value of profit for the bidder. Making the simplifying assumption that sale price and profit are equal, we may rewrite (2b) as

(Value of services produced) minus   (3b)
(Costs of resources used) minus (Taxes)

Comparing (1), (3a), and (3b), we see that if the nonprofit's decisionmakers value services in the same way that society does (aggregate willingness-to-pay), but do not treat subsidies and donations as part of their costs or value the taxes that a for-profit pays, there would be some bias against efficient conversions. That is, the prospect of lost subsidies and donations and increased taxes could deter an organization from converting even when doing so could increase social value. It follows that the smaller the difference in tax treatment between the two sectors and the less important donations are to the nonprofit, the closer its incentives are to unbiased with regard to conversions.

Can a regulator scrutinize a proposed conversion to determine whether it is efficient? The regulator may be able to arrive at a reasonable approximation to the surplus generated in the for-profit sector by taking the offered sale price and adding expected taxes and any losses (marginal revenue minus marginal cost) the for-profit is expected to generate on any community collective goods obligations it has agreed to take on. The last element assumes that the social value of those community obligations is equal to their cost of production. That assumption is reasonable if society's best alternative is to purchase those services at cost from that vendor or another whose full costs would be similar.[12] The more difficult problem for the regulator is to estimate the social surplus generated if the firm continues to operate as nonprofit. Valuing the collective good outputs a nonprofit produces is particularly difficult. Market values are not directly relevant, though in some cases inferences can be drawn from them.[13] Decisionmakers at the nonprofit are likely to be better informed about the organization's future possibilities as a nonprofit than a regulator would be. While they may better understand their organization's collective good outputs, they may not have special expertise as to how the rest of society values them. Thus, it seems more likely that they will overestimate that value than underestimate it, creating another bias against conversions, even when they are efficient.

The analysis in this section relied on an assumption that nonprofit decisionmakers are not motivated by private gain. However, we highlighted earlier the bias of nonprofits toward conversions even when they are not efficient, because of the potential for private gain. We still see considerable danger of inefficient conversions that produce private gains but social losses (and unfairly redistribute wealth) if there is not careful regulatory scrutiny. The social policy challenge is how best to provide an incentive for managers to seek efficient conversions by allowing them some share in the gains, while guarding against inefficient and inequitable transfers of wealth. This is an important question that merits further attention.

CONCLUSION: WHICH INDUSTRY IS NEXT?

A nonprofit conversion will only occur if two conditions are met: the decisionmakers (board of trustees) in a nonprofit request it, *and* the public regulators approve it. The relatively intense burst of conversion activity in HMOs, Blue Cross plans, and hospitals could, therefore, have arisen from an increase in the desire to convert by the nonprofits, or in the willingness of the regulators to approve conversions, or in some combination of the two. We identified above two main types of motivation for a nonprofit to convert: (1) a perception of *social* bene-fit—a decision that its nonprofit mission would be better served by reorganizing as a for-profit and passing the value of its assets to a new charitable organization—or (2) *private* benefit to executives and board members without commensurate social gains. The first could arise at about the same time for many similarly situated organizations when external circumstances change, as they have in major segments of the health care market. The second could arise at any time in any industry in which nonprofits have amassed sizeable wealth.

The private gain motive is clearly stronger for a wealthy organiza-tion than it is for, say, a small neighborhood day care center struggling to stay afloat. Consider a major art museum that, through donations, has amassed collections worth hundreds of millions of dollars. If its managers could arrange to purchase it at a price well below its true value and begin selling paintings, they could benefit enormously at public expense. Arguably, something like that happened in the early HMO conversions. So why did the HMO Health Net convert but not the Art Institute of Chicago?

We hypothesize, first, that other things being equal, a conversion is more likely to be *proposed* by a nonprofit when the potential for private gain is greater, and this depends on the organization's wealth. Second, we hypothesize that the probability of regulatory *approval* depends on how effectively the nonprofit can make the case that a conversion would be socially efficient. The case is easier to make the greater the extent to which the industry is one in which nonprofits already compete with for-profits, and the stronger the evidence that because of changing circumstances the for-profits are enjoying in-creasing success. Resistance to the idea of a shift to for-profit owner-ship is then likely to be weaker, and the organization may be able to credibly claim that conversion is necessary for its very survival. The greater the informational advantage the nonprofit insiders have over the regulators in assessing the viability of the nonprofit, the greater their opportunity for arranging a conversion in a way that benefits them privately. Such an advantage will be greater in a fast-changing industry, in which the value of an organization is changing rapidly as are the relative advantages of the nonprofit and for-profit forms. That scenario much better describes the HMO industry in the 1980s and early 1990s than it does the world of art museums or higher education, where massive wealth also provides fertile ground for private gain.

Regulators, of course, should learn to be wary of insiders' claims. It may be that regulators were "asleep" during some early HMO and hospital conversions, but increasing public attention to the issue will make it much more difficult for nonprofit insiders (or savvy for-profit buyers) to appropriate public assets through conversion. By underscoring the watchdog role of regulators we do not mean to imply that top managers and trustees of nonprofits are generally self-serving, unconcerned with the public interest. Nonetheless, it is important to understand the incentives confronting those leaders to balance public and private interests.

Aside from pure attempts to subvert the nondistribution constraint, upon which regulators can be expected to cast an increasingly wary eye, we expect more interest from nonprofits in conversions in industries where changes have occurred that reduce advantages that nonprofits formerly held while increasing the apparent advantages of the for-profit form—access to equity capital being the most obvious one. Growth in for-profit market share in an industry—through new entrants and the growth of existing for-profits—should be a signal that some nonprofits may begin to think about conversion. In this regard, higher education is an industry worth watching.

Although still a small segment of the entire industry, for-profit higher education appears to be growing rapidly. Echoing arguments heard in the healthcare industry for some time, for-profit higher education firms claim that their access to equity capital allows them to respond more quickly to changing demand (Strosnider 1998).

The for-profit University of Phoenix is establishing new campuses around the country and advertising low tuition made possible by disdaining provision of the collective good, research, and promising only the private good, coursework for paying consumers. A plausible speculation is that colleges will find, as many nonprofit hospitals have already found, that competition from for-profit firms will force prices—in this case, tuition—down to levels that will not permit colleges to finance research or student financial aid that displaces full-pay students. Nonprofit colleges that are not among the elite schools could be placed in the competitive position of either converting to for-profit, in order to obtain access to capital to finance expansion and take advantage of scale economies in advertising and, perhaps, production, or see their student clientele wither away. That scenario, while highly speculative, provides food for thought as we peer ahead to consider whether another industry will join hospitals and HMOs in the conversion "derby."

Notes

1. This chapter draws in some places on our paper "Conversion from Nonprofit to For-Profit Legal Status: Why Does It Happen and Should Anyone Care?" in *To Profit or Not to Profit: The Commercial Transformation of the Nonprofit Sector*, edited by Burton Weisbrod, New York: Cambridge University Press, 1998.

2. In fact, the IRS in 1998 revoked the tax exemption of a Florida charity, the Anclote Psychiatric Center, on the ground that it sold its hospital, 15 years earlier, to a company owned by its board members, for an amount that the IRS claimed was almost $1.2 million less than the hospital was worth (Moore and Williams 1998).

3. A recent example of conflict is a controversy involving the "repricing" of stock options, lowering the price at which executives can buy shares when a company's stock price falls. Management in some companies have repriced options without seeking shareholder approval (Bryant 1998).

4. A case in point involved the nonprofit Bennington College (Galper and Toder 1983), which sold its buildings to a private firm and then leased the buildings back. This changed nothing in the way the buildings were used, but because of differences in liability for taxes the sale was advantageous to both parties. Congress later prohibited such sham transactions.

5. Such a set of objectives has been hypothesized and termed "bonoficing" (Weisbrod 1988).

6. The nondistribution constraint could be a crucial one even for a new firm if it is important that the firm be able to attract investment capital, and if equity capital is more easily obtained than alternative sources of funds such as loans or donations.

7. Its ability to borrow in the bond market might also improve even if it remained a nonprofit. The key issue is the changing *relationship* between the costs of borrowing and of selling equity.

8. The March/April 1997 issue of *Health Affairs*, devoted to hospital and health plan conversions, is a good source of additional discussion. See also Cutler and Horwitz 1997, and Wilkins and Jacobson 1998.

9. Changes are not uniform, however, across the spectrum of nonprofit healthcare providers. There is little evidence, for example, of systematic conversions of nonprofit nursing homes.

10. A few illustrative examples, of many that could be cited, of the emphasis placed on access to equity capital: Leonard Schaeffer, then of Group Health of Minnesota, "In order to [protect our traditional markets and expand to new markets], we must have large amounts of capital. Capital markets are only interested in for-profit entities" (Iglehart 1984); Norwood Davis of Virginia Blue Cross and Blue Shield, "We want the same access to the capital market as the other players" (Freudenheim 1994); Michael Stocker of Empire Blue Cross of New York, "We have to have the potential to raise capital. . . . We can't raise it as a not-for-profit" (Freudenheim 1996).

11. One element of value that may exist only as long as the firm remains a nonprofit is any special contribution of nonprofits to civil society, emphasized elsewhere in this volume.

12. A case in point is a for-profit hospital that agrees to support some level of indigent care for which marginal cost exceeds revenue. If the relevant alternative is for government to purchase that care at cost from the same hospital, the social value of taking on the obligation is the same as the present value of the government spending that it replaces.

13. For example, as noted with regard to community obligations taken on by for-profits, if a service, such as indigent care, is one that can be purchased from another vendor, the purchase price provides at least an upper bound on its value.

References

Abelson, Reed. 1998a. "At Minnesota Public Radio, a Deal Way above Average." *New York Times*, March 27.
————. 1998b. "Nonprofit Work Gets Profitable." *New York Times*, March 29.
————. 1998c. "Oxford Health Plan's Turnaround Strategy Emerging." *New York Times*, April 25.
Birnbaum, Jeffrey H. 1982. "Charity That Delivers Surplus Food to Needy Is Split by Accusation." *Wall Street Journal*, October 25.
Bryant, Adam. 1998. "Stock Options That Raise Investors' Ire." *New York Times*, March 27.
Burns, Judith, and Lucette Lagnado. 1998. "IRS Rules Threaten Alliances Made by For-Profit and Nonprofit Hospitals." *Wall Street Journal*, March 5.
Claxton, Gary, Judith Feder, David Shactman, and Stuart Altman. 1997. "Public Policy Issues in Nonprofit Conversions: An Overview." *Health Affairs* 16 (2): 9–28.
Cordes, Joseph J., and Burton A. Weisbrod. 1998. "Differential Taxation of Nonprofits and the Commercializtion of Nonprofit Revenues." In *To Profit or Not to Profit: The Commercial Transformation of the Nonprofit Sector*, edited by Burton A. Weisbrod (83–104). New York: Cambridge University Press.
Coye, Molly Joel. 1997. "The Sale of Good Samaritan: A View from the Trenches." *Health Affairs* 16 (2): 102–7.
Cutler, David, and Jill R. Horwitz. 1997. "Converting Hospitals from Not-for-Profit to For-Profit Status: Why and What Effects." Unpublished working paper, National Bureau of Economic Research, Cambridge, Mass.
Ferris, James M., and Elizabeth A. Graddy. 1996. "Structural Changes in the Hospital Industry and the Nonprofit Role in Health Care." In *Nonprofit Organizations as Public Actors*, edited by Astrid Merget, Ed Weaver, and Virginia Hodgkinson. San Francisco: Jossey-Bass Publishers.
Fox, Daniel M., and Phillip Isenberg. 1996. "Anticipating the Magic Moment: The Public Interest in Health Plan Conversions in California." *Health Affairs* 15 (1): 202–9.
Freudenheim, Milt. 1994. "Blue Cross Lets Plans Sell Stock." *New York Times*, June 30.

————. 1996. "As Blue Cross Plans Seek Profit, States Ask for a Share of the Riches." *New York Times*, March 25.

Galper, Harvey, and Eric Toder. 1983. "Owning or Leasing: Bennington College and the U.S. Tax System." *National Tax Journal* 36: 257–61.

Goddeeris, John H. 1988. "Compensating Differentials and Self-Selection: An Application to Lawyers." *Journal of Political Economy* 96: 411–28.

Hamburger, Eleanor, Jeanne Finberg, and Leticia Alcantar. 1995. "The Pot of Gold: Monitoring Health Care Conversions Can Yield Billions of Dollars for Health Care." *Clearinghouse Review*: 473–504.

Haveman, Robert H., and Burton A. Weisbrod. 1975. "Defining Benefits of Public Programs: Some Guidance for Policy Analysts." *Policy Analysis* 2: 169–96.

Hansmann, Henry. 1980. "The Role of Nonprofit Enterprise." *Yale Law Journal* 89 (5): 835–901.

————. 1987. "The Effect of Tax Exemption and Other Factors on the Market Share of Nonprofit Versus For-Profit Firms." *National Tax Journal* 40: 71–82.

————. 1996. *The Ownership of Enterprise.* Cambridge, Mass.: Belknap.

Hollis, Stephen R. 1997. "Strategic and Economic Factors in the Hospital Conversion Process." *Health Affairs* 16 (2): 131–43.

Iglehart, John K. 1984. "HMOs (For-Profit and Not-for-Profit) on the Move." *New England Journal of Medicine* 310: 1203–08.

————. 1995. "Inside California's HMO Market: A Conversation with Leonard D. Schaeffer." *Health Affairs* 14 (4): 131–42.

Japsen, Bruce. 1998. "An Off Year for Consolidation." *Modern Healthcare* 40 (2): 40.

Langley, Monica, and Anita Sharpe. 1996. "As Big Hospital Chains Take Over Nonprofits, a Backlash Is Growing." *Wall Street Journal*, October 18.

Levy, Mellissa. 1998. "Dayton Hudson to Acquire Rivertown Trading Co. Catalogs." *Minneapolis Star Tribune*, March 24.

Marchetti, Domenica. 1997. "Georgia Charities Sue to Recover Millions in Blue Cross Deal." *Chronicle of Philanthropy*, September 18.

Mauser, Elizabeth. 1993. "Comparative Institutional Behavior: The Case of Day Care." Ph.D. diss., University of Wisconsin, Madison, Wis.

Miller, James P. 1998a. "Public Radio Outlet in Minnesota Reaps $120 Million in Sale of Direct Marketer." *Wall Street Journal*, March 24.

————. 1998b. "Blue Cross Missouri Agrees to Settle Legal Fight on Creating For-Profit Unit." *Wall Street Journal*, April 23.

Moore, Jennifer, and Grant Williams. 1998. "Court Backs Decision to Revoke Charity's Status." *Chronicle of Philanthropy*, August 27.

Preston, Anne E. 1989. "The Nonprofit Worker in a For-Profit World." *Journal of Labor Economics* 7: 438–63.

Roomkin, Myron, and Burton A. Weisbrod. 1999. "Managerial Compensation in For-Profit and Nonprofit Hospitals: Levels, Composition, and Implications for Organization Behavior." Unpublished working paper, Department of Economics, Northwestern University, Evanston, Ill.

Rothschild, Steven M. 1998. Personal communication.

Scism, Leslie. 1998. "Prudential to Go Public in Effort to Stay Competitive." *Wall Street Journal*, February 2.

Schaeffer, Leonard D. 1996. "Health Plan Conversions: The View from Blue Cross of California." *Health Affairs* 15 (4): 183–7.

Sloan, Frank A. 1998. "Commercialism in Nonprofit Hospitals." In *To Profit or Not to Profit: The Commercial Transformation of the Nonprofit Sector*, edited by Burton A. Weisbrod (151–68). New York: Cambridge University Press.

Strosnider, Kim. 1998. "For-Profit Higher Education Sees Booming Enrollments and Revenues." *The Chronicle of Higher Education*, January 23.

Tauhert, Christy. 1997. "Collaborative Reengineering." *Insurance and Technology* 22 (12): 28–32.

Weisbrod, Burton A. 1988. *The Nonprofit Economy*. Cambridge, Mass.: Harvard University Press.

———. 1997. "The Future of the Nonprofit Sector: Its Entwining with Private Enterprise and Government." *Journal of Policy Analysis and Management* 16 (4): 541–55.

———. 1998. "Institutional Form and Organization Behavior." In *Private Action and the Public Good*, edited by Walter W. Powell and Elisabeth Clemens (69–84). New Haven, Conn.: Yale University Press.

Whitehead, Roy, Clint Johnson, and Michael Moore. 1997. "Avoiding State Intervention in Not-for-Profit/For-Profit Affiliations." *Health Care Financial Management* (Dec.): 56–62.

Wilkins, Aaron S., and Peter D. Jacobson. 1998. "Fiduciary Responsibilities in Nonprofit Health Care Conversions." *Health Care Management Review* 23 (Winter): 77–90.

Chapter Eight

CLASH OF VALUES: THE STATE, RELIGION, AND THE ARTS

Robert Wuthnow

INTRODUCTION

Nonprofit organizations have long been recognized as important for maintaining America's basic values. In addition to nurturing such ideals as compassion, cooperation, and civic participation, nonprofits sometimes provide the central locations in which specific values are proclaimed and enacted. Religious organizations, comprising a large share of the overall nonprofit sector (see Introduction, this volume), are the most notable example. The arts is another area in which non-profit organizations and values often intersect. As faith-based and arts organizations have moved from primarily private support to greater government funding and regulation, however, those nonprofits have become arenas for debate over the appropriate role of government in influencing and promoting values.

This chapter examines the controversies that have arisen in recent years over government funding for religious and arts activities, focusing especially on the so-called "Charitable Choice" provision of the 1996 welfare reform legislation and the debate about funding for the National Endowment for the Arts (NEA). I argue that the "clash of values" that is evident in each of those controversies is indeed serious, but that it is not primarily (or simply) a "culture war" that reflects fundamental differences in world views, as some have suggested. Nor is it explicable, as others have suggested, strictly as a clash perpetuated by well-organized special interest groups. It is, rather, a clash over the character of civil society—specifically, between two long-standing visions of how America should be governed: one, a national vision of close or centralized coordination between government and civil society; the other, an associational vision of loose or decentralized relationships between government and civil society.

CONTESTED TERRAIN

The welfare reform bill, signed into law on August 22, 1996, by President Clinton, included the controversial "Charitable Choice" provision sponsored by Senator John Ashcroft (R–Mo.) (Denny 1996; Goode 1997). As noted in chapter 6, this provision permits churches and other religious or faith-based nonprofit organizations to receive federal funds for use in providing social services to their communities. Supporters argued that faith-based organizations were such a valuable resource for distributing help to the needy that they should not be excluded from receiving such funds, while critics charged that the measure represented a serious breach of the constitutional wall separating church and state.

During the same period that interest in welfare reform was developing, a campaign emerged to cut federal spending on the arts by drastically reducing the budget of the National Endowment for the Arts or by terminating the agency entirely. The debate focused on whether public funds should be channeled to local and regional nonprofit arts associations by the NEA, especially when some of those funds were used for artistic projects that dealt with controversial subjects. NEA supporters retorted that the arts are not only intrinsically worthwhile but also contribute to the general good in a way that merits support from society as a whole. Pointing to artistic works that portrayed such controversial themes as sexuality and profanity, the NEA's critics argued that taxpayers were being asked to support projects that violated their standards of decency and morality (Bolton 1992; Adler 1993; Balfe 1993).

Although the Charitable Choice and NEA scenarios seem quite different, they exemplify a common concern about the ways in which public funding for nonprofit activity influences—and is influenced by—the religious, moral, and aesthetic values the public at large holds most deeply. By the early 1990s, the social and legal services subsector of the nonprofit sector had grown to approximately $56 billion in annual revenue, half of which came from government, while the health services subsector had annual receipts of $261 billion, of which 41 percent came from government. If tax subsidies are considered, this proportion would be higher (Abramson, Salamon, and Steuerle, this volume; Hodgkinson 1996; Salamon 1995; Smith and Lipsky 1993; Wolch 1990). Approximately 6,700 religion-related organizations had come into existence, receiving a total of $1.7 billion in public support, while more than 340,000 congregations that were not eligible for public support took in approximately $58 billion in annual revenue from private sources.

The Ashcroft provision reflected tensions about the relative advantages and disadvantages of social service provision by religious organizations, compared with secular nonprofits and government agencies, in being able to express their implicit and explicit values (Watt 1991). To some, the growth of secular nonprofits and their increasing levels of support from government put religious organizations at a competitive disadvantage. For others, the autonomy of religious congregations with respect to government funding was a privilege that needed to be protected vigilantly.

In the same period, overall annual revenue for arts and cultural organizations had risen to approximately $8 billion, of which only 15 percent came from public sources of all kinds and only slightly more than one percent came from the NEA. For many, however, NEA support was critical because it symbolized public commitment to the arts and helped to support innovative projects that might not draw the interest of private donors. With overall support of the arts having grown more slowly in the 1980s than it had during the 1970s, NEA's continuing involvement was also considered by many arts organizations to be more important than ever before (Scheff and Kotler 1996). In addition to jeopardizing that support, the debate about NEA funding raised fundamental questions about artists' autonomy and whether they should be held accountable to the tastes and interests of the wider public.

In neither case, however, was it immediately apparent *what* values were being debated. In their haste to support or oppose the Ashcroft proposal and the NEA, spokespersons for various parties generated a plethora of arguments that mixed questions about basic values with a wide range of more expedient considerations, such as political advantage and questions of efficiency. Nor was it obvious *why* those and similar cases were generating as much interest as they did or *how* they may have been influenced by broader social currents. These questions deserve close scrutiny if we are to understand how the public funding of nonprofit organizations is likely to be shaped by discussions of basic social values in the future.

ANATOMY OF THE ASHCROFT AND NEA DEBATES

The Ashcroft proposal emerged in a climate of antigovernment sentiment that had been prominent during the Reagan administration and then became more pronounced during the 1994 congressional election (Dionne 1992; Robinson, Colliau, and Robinson 1995). Republican candidates called for sweeping reforms of the welfare system on grounds that it was inefficient, costly, and ineffective. Government funding for social services should be smaller, they argued, and thus must be administered more efficiently, a task that was widely considered to be done best by nonprofit organizations. Those organizations were also expected to help accomplish the legislation's aim of promoting self-sufficiency among welfare recipients and incorporating them into the workforce. The idea that churches and other faith-based nonprofits could shoulder more of the burden of providing social services gradually gained support in both parties. Lawmakers expressed hope that churches would provide a wide range of services, from temporary food and shelter, to voluntary day care and transportation, to job training, counseling, tutoring, and low-income housing. In speeches following the bill's signing, President Clinton suggested that congregations consider creating jobs for unemployed members of the community. House Speaker Newt Gingrich made similar pleas (Rodrigue 1996). The Charitable Choice legislation reflected the premise that churches and faith-based nonprofits could help not only through their own contributions and volunteering but by receiving public funding as well.

Lawmakers recognized the potential for the Ashcroft proposal to result in religious discrimination or to promote the establishment of religion by giving some faith-based organizations an advantage. They were also concerned that existing arrangements sometimes made it difficult for faith-based providers to engage in service delivery without altering their basic mission and administrative structure. The wording of "Charitable Choice" in Section 104 of the Personal Responsibility and Work Opportunity Reconciliation Act of 1996 (PRWORA) offered detailed rules about the conditions under which faith-based organizations could receive federal funding. States were given the option of excluding all nongovernmental entities from the use of funds they received through federal block grants for assisting the needy. But, as discussed in chapter 6, if states dispensed any of those funds through nonprofit organizations, then faith-based nonprofits could not be excluded. Faith-based nonprofits included congregations, nonprofit service providers affiliated with religious organizations, and nonprofit service organizations that may have been founded on the basis of religious beliefs and teachings. The legislation distinguished between two ways in which federal funds might be received by such organizations: "Direct" funds consisted of support received by the organization in the form of a contract with the government to provide services; "indirect" funds consisted of remuneration received from the government in return for vouchers that clients might submit to a nonprofit organization in return for a service rendered. Because indirect funds came from situations in which clients presumably were able to choose between faith-based and other providers, somewhat looser conditions were imposed than in cases where faith-based nonprofits contracted directly with government. In both cases, however, an attempt was made to balance and protect the rights of providers and those of clients.

Under the Charitable Choice provision, providers were permitted to apply religious tests (such as being a member of a particular denomination or vowing to abstain from alcohol) in hiring personnel but were prohibited from discriminating on other grounds, such as race, gender, disability, or national origin. They were permitted to maintain the "religious environment" of their organization, rather than having to remove religious icons, art, or publications in order to be eligible. They were not required to alter their administrative structure in order to comply with government standards, because that structure was sometimes derived from theological and ecclesiological considerations, and they could isolate the portion of funds received from government for reporting purposes rather than having to disclose all sources and distributions of funds. Clients were given the right to choose among religious and nonreligious providers and could not be refused services on the basis of their religion, religious beliefs, or religious practices. Clients who felt they had been discriminated against could bring civil suits against providers.

The NEA controversy occurred amidst rising public concern about government expenditures as well, but funding itself was less the issue than the controversial uses of the funds. In 1981, budget director David Stockman proposed cutting the NEA's budget by 50 percent, and during the remainder of the Reagan administration, NEA funding (like that of the National Endowment for the Humanities and some educational programs) was reduced moderately. In 1989, following a widely publicized event involving a controversial photograph by Andres Serrano (of a plastic crucifix immersed in urine), which was part of an NEA-sponsored exhibit, conservative groups called for abolishing the NEA (McGee 1995). During the summer of 1989, members of Congress frequently referred to Serrano's work and to Robert Mapplethorpe's homoerotic photographs in debating budget allocations for the NEA. In 1990, Congress passed a law that required the NEA to take account not only of artistic excellence in making grants but also considerations of decency and respect for public values. Although the law appears to have had relatively little impact on NEA activities in the years immediately following its approval, it was challenged in 1992 by performance artist Karen Finley and in 1996 was overturned by the Ninth U.S. Circuit Court of Appeals and then appealed to the U.S. Supreme Court (Van Camp 1997).

Having already cut appropriations by 40 percent in 1995, NEA's congressional opponents renewed their efforts to cut all funding for the agency. On July 11, 1997, the House of Representatives passed by a one-vote margin a bill to replace the NEA with block grants to state arts councils and local school boards. In the Senate, Senators Ashcroft and Jesse Helms sponsored a similar bill, arguing that the NEA was, among other things, helping elitist organizations rather than supporting country musicians or artists who might appeal to "people driving pickup trucks" (Trescott 1997). The Senate defeated the Ashcroft-Helms proposal and several others, however, thus averting elimination of the NEA but leaving its long-term future the subject of continuing conflict.

Both issues have occasionally been interpreted as controversies simply about ways to reduce government spending. Critics of the NEA sometimes argued, for example, that its elimination would be a major boon to taxpayers who were already struggling to make ends meet, while NEA supporters claimed the agency's budget amounted to only 37 cents per taxpayer per year. Yet the two debates were also about the values represented when public support was channeled to nonprofit organizations. In the case of Charitable Choice, interest groups that perceived religion to be under siege by secular social institutions quickly rose to support the proposal on grounds that congregations should not be discriminated against in receiving federal funds. Efforts to abolish the NEA alarmed museums and local artists' associations that had been recipients of NEA funding, partly because of its financial implications but also because the very value of artistic expression appeared to be in question. As writer Madeleine L'Engle remarked, "I don't often write letters, but I wrote one to Mr. Gingrich. 'Dear Mr. Gingrich. A great country has always been noted by the attention it pays to the arts. Does your present point of view indicate that you no longer think we are a great country? Sincerely yours'" (personal interview).

As each debate developed, broad questions were raised about the ways in which deeply held values in the public at large were being reinforced or undermined by government's support of nonprofit organizations. But the values under consideration were not primarily about whether or not to help the needy or how much to support the arts. Nor could these values be understood in terms of how religious or nonreligious various sectors of the public might be, or whether people valued the arts or did not. The debates were more fundamentally about how best to structure American democracy so that other values could be preserved.

Charitable Choice sparked debate about the rights of religious communities to express their beliefs and teachings. Proponents of the legislation argued that religious communities were inhibited in what would otherwise be a natural inclination to serve the needy because their leaders feared government regulation would follow from federal funds. Opponents expressed a similar concern about government intrusion but perceived the Ashcroft proposal as an invitation for greater intrusion rather than less.

The Ashcroft bill was contested on grounds that it would infringe on individuals' religious freedom as well. Whereas the concerns expressed about religious communities emphasized the likelihood that government regulation would impose uniform standards on otherwise diverse traditions, the concerns about individual religious freedom stressed the likelihood that government funding would inevitably favor some traditions more than others and thus make it harder for individuals to pick and choose on the basis of conscience alone.

Apart from the issues it raised about religion, the debate over Charitable Choice included more general concerns about the character of local communities. On the one hand, both its supporters and opponents saw merit in strengthening the capacity of local community organizations to dispense services in ways consistent with their diverse traditions, needs, and lifestyles. On the other hand, both sides also recognized the need for federal involvement if services were to receive adequate funding and if potential inequities were to be avoided.

The NEA case revolved around a similar set of issues. Although Serrano's *Piss Christ* offended the religious sensibilities of many of the NEA's opponents (just as Robert Mapplethorpe's homoerotic art did), the controversy took on broader importance because it introduced questions about the relationship between government funding and the uses of tax dollars for the activities of artists and arts organizations. Although the works of Serrano, Mapplethorpe, Karen Finley, and others were denounced from pulpits and in newspapers, members of Congress would have had little opportunity to censor such works had it not been for the 1990 amendment requiring the NEA to pay attention to decency and public values. In response to several congressional investigations of individual artists and widespread publicity, NEA's director wrote that works depicting lesbian, gay male, and other explicit sexual activities would no longer be funded.

Finley's suit—filed along with three other plaintiffs—against the NEA charged that their First Amendment rights to freedom of speech had been violated by the NEA's denial of their grant applications. The plaintiffs' lawyers argued that the NEA had treated their applications unfairly by taking into consideration political pressures and that parts of Finley's application had been released to the media without her permission. The case, however, included the more general argument that "public subsidization of art, like public funding of the press and university activities, demands government neutrality."

The neutrality argument asserts the value of artistic expression, like that of scientific or other scholarly activity, and thus calls on government to provide support for artists. Yet the argument recognizes that professional expertise is required to make judgments about art and asks government to allow the allocation of public funding to be made by representatives of the artistic community itself. In its ruling on the Finley case, the appellate court determined that Congress's requirement that the NEA take into account considerations of decency and public morality opened the door for potential violations of neutrality, because ideas about decency and other values were too varied to be defined objectively. The court explicitly sought to exclude any possibility that government procedures would infringe on artists' freedom to express their own values, however unpopular they might be with the general public.

In his dissenting opinion, Judge Andrew J. Kleinfeld drew a distinction between government censorship and government's right to influence the content of activities it subsidizes, and he argued that the latter consideration should prevail. Ironically, although that distinction failed to persuade the other justices, Kleinfeld's arguments against censorship provided strong support for the idea that government should not interfere in artists' activities. Noting that a cross immersed in urine is likely to offend the religious beliefs of most Americans, Kleinfeld cited numerous other similar examples, ranging from Lenny Bruce's monologues to Allen Ginsberg's poetry to Modigliani's nudes, and argued that none should be subjected to censorship.

The court's decision that Congress could not impose standards of decency and morality on the NEA left its critics with no apparent recourse other than reducing or eliminating its funding or providing block grants to states for use by regional arts councils and local school boards. The last option was a way to devolve responsibility to other jurisdictions where other legal precedents and concerns about community norms might prevail. Like the Charitable Choice legislation, the NEA decision made it possible for nonprofit organizations to receive federal funding but also demonstrated that controversies would continue about which organizations would be eligible and which would not.

PUTTING THE CONTROVERSIES IN A WIDER CONTEXT

The degree to which contested values are evident in these debates suggests that there may indeed be a "clash of values" that constitutes what has sometimes been called a "culture war." Popularized by Patrick Buchanan's 1992 speech to the Republican National Convention, the idea of a "religious and cultural war" has been used repeatedly in reference to recent discussions of the arts, multiculturalism, education, and social welfare, not to mention abortion and homosexuality (Nolan 1996; Horton 1994; Sine 1996). In scholarly analyses, observers have argued that many of these discussions are arising because of a deeper division in the fundamental values of the American people. This division has been described as a conflict between "orthodox" and "progressive" world views, with each view presented as a somewhat simple stereotype: Orthodoxy is characterized by belief in strict, unalterable moral and religious principles; progressivism is said to be morally relativistic and less certain about the existence of God or of any absolute standards of truth (Hunter 1991).

Orthodoxy vs. Progressivism

According to this interpretation, adherents of orthodoxy are predisposed to resist artistic works that violate traditional definitions of morality rooted in sacred principles, while progressives are less likely to find those works offensive because they do not believe in such principles. As James Davison Hunter (1991, 249) concludes, "The idea that the battle over the arts is related to the tensions between two different conceptions of the sacred is not far-fetched. How else can one explain the passion and intensity on both sides of the cultural divide were it not that each side, by its very being and expression, profanes what the other holds most sublime?" By the same token, the idea of Charitable Choice should be attractive to orthodox believers because of their commitment to religion and their fear that secular government is a source of moral relativism, while progressives would be more likely to see Charitable Choice as a dangerous step in the direction of government-supported religious absolutism.

If the culture wars argument is correct, nonprofit organizations may find themselves increasingly embroiled in conflicts over fundamental values whether they receive government funding or not. Indeed, the culture wars argument suggests that it is not so much the public funding of nonprofits but broader shifts in values themselves that may be at the root of controversies such as those concerning Charitable Choice and the NEA. Depending on how seriously these contested values are taken, the most advisable strategy for nonprofit administrators may be to engage fully in the present culture war or to seek some way of avoiding it altogether. Nonprofit organizations dealing with inevitably controversial issues, such as abortion or gay and lesbian issues, for example, may be compelled to fight hard for the rights of their constituencies, while many nonprofit service organizations that provide help for needy members of the community may be able to avoid such conflicts (Hunter 1994).

But the culture wars explanation provides only a partial, and indeed misleading, interpretation of the ways in which government support of nonprofit organizations is linked to current debates about values. It is true that the American public is divided in many of the ways that the culture wars argument suggests: Surveys show that public opinion is split on such specific issues as abortion and school prayer, and that people also vary in terms of identifying themselves as, say, religious and political conservatives or religious and political liberals (Wuthnow 1996a). Studies also show that underlying differences in religious identities and in world views are related to the ways in which people think about social welfare and their preferences in music and the arts (Bryson 1996). But the culture wars interpretation exaggerates the extent to which the public is polarized on such issues. Many Americans define themselves as religious and political moderates and their views on particular issues do not align themselves consistently as adherents of orthodoxy or progressivism (Wuthnow 1996b). Other research shows that opinions on most social issues (abortion being the exception) have not become more polarized in recent decades (DiMaggio, Evans, and Bryson 1996).

The most plausible aspect of the culture wars interpretation concerns the role played by evangelical and fundamentalist Christians in the Ashcroft and NEA debates. Charitable Choice was widely favored in evangelical and fundamentalist publications because it symbolized a remedy for the antireligion bias that many in those quarters believed had become increasingly predominant over the previous three decades as a result of Supreme Court decisions against school prayer and favoring abortion. Much of the concern about "objectionable" art that led to the NEA debates was consistent with evangelical views of morality as well. Research showed that evangelicals tended to have somewhat different tastes in art and music than nonevangelicals and that the two held different views about morality in general and on such specific issues as sexuality (Bryson 1996; Hunter 1994). Nevertheless, studies cast doubt on the validity of the culture wars interpretation by showing that evangelicals and nonevangelicals differed little on many social attitudes and that rank-and-file evangelicals were often less concerned or strident about these issues than their leaders (Wuthnow 1991; Wuthnow 1994; Smith 1998).

Special Interest Groups

The culture wars interpretation serves more usefully when it directs attention toward the many special interest groups that have arisen to articulate positions on social issues and to exert pressure on policymakers (Evans 1996). The number of such special interest groups has grown dramatically as a proportion of the nonprofit sector during the last 30 years, and their role in national policy debates, as well as coverage in the media, has expanded accordingly (Wuthnow 1989; Berry 1997). Opponents of Charitable Choice included such prominent interest groups as Americans United for Separation of Church and State, the American Civil Liberties Union (ACLU), and People for the American Way, while supporters included the Center for Law and Religious Freedom and the Center for Public Justice. The ACLU, having helped defend John Scopes in 1925 against charges of violating Tennessee law by teaching evolution, and having been a vocal opponent of the Religious Right in the 1980s, was regarded by conservative religious leaders as being opposed to the expression of religion more than simply being concerned about civil liberties. The ACLU was active in the Finley lawsuit as well, while such organizations as the Eagle Forum, the American Family Association, and the Christian Coalition encouraged citizens to write letters to Congress opposing the NEA.

Those various interest groups were able to attract sympathetic hearings on Capitol Hill. Among the new Republicans elected to the Senate and House of Representatives in 1994, more than half (including Senator Ashcroft) identified themselves as evangelical Protestants. Ashcroft received help in drafting the Charitable Choice legislation and in publicizing it through the Center for Law and Religious Freedom and the Center for Public Justice. Additional support for the legislation came from such religiously conservative interest groups as Charles Colson's Prison Ministries and James Dobson's Focus on the Family, both of which stood to gain from being able to solicit government funding for their service programs, as well as from large independent evangelical churches that operated their own closely controlled service activities rather than encouraging adherents to participate in the work of secular nonprofits.

The special interest interpretation, like that of the culture wars argument, provides a portrait of American society as being driven largely by acrimonious and contentious organizations that care more about promoting their own interests and agendas than promoting tolerance, reconciliation, or commitment to common values. It is for that reason that many observers argue that American democracy itself is in jeopardy. As Jean Bethke Elshtain (1995) notes, these interest groups seem most intent on spewing forth "a cascading series of manifestos that tell us we cannot live together; we cannot work together; we are not in this together; we are not Americans who have something in common, but racial, ethnic, gender, or sexually identified clans who demand to be 'recognized' only or exclusively as 'different.'" Such differences, she believes, have brought us to the point that we "are in danger of losing democratic civil society" (p. xii).

The implication of this view is that the growth of nonprofit organizations in recent decades has contributed to the erosion of American democracy rather than strengthened it. Whereas an earlier view, such as that expressed by Alexis de Tocqueville in the 1830s, would have regarded nonprofits as "associations" helping citizens to govern themselves and to participate peacefully in the democratic process, the current interpretation suggests that nonprofits have become the instruments of social division and decay. Thus, it is possible for a widely heralded examination of contemporary civic life such as Robert Putnam's (1995) "Bowling Alone" to lament the decline of civic associations and to decry the rise of special interest groups while dismissing nonprofits as having no positive contribution to make to the promotion of social cohesion. Similarly, it is possible in conversations with nonprofit administrators to hear the wish expressed that religious and other organizations concerned with contested values would somehow disappear.

But that view of the relationship between nonprofit organizations and the basic values on which American democracy rests is seriously flawed. Although special interest nonprofit organizations played a role in the Charitable Choice and NEA discussions, they were remarkably quiet on those issues compared with controversies surrounding abortion and funding for church-related schools. Moreover, spokespersons for several of the leading lobbying organizations, such as the Southern Baptists' Christian Life Commission, took positions in opposition to groups with whom they had collaborated on other issues. More important, the special-interest interpretation provides a misleading view of the relationship between nonprofits and controversies about basic values because it fails to take account of another dynamic in contemporary life—the tension in American civil society between social forces that promote centralization and standardization, on the one hand, and those that favor decentralization and diversity, on the other hand (Cohen and Arato 1992).

Centralization vs. Decentralization

Discussions of American democracy have highlighted this tension in a number of ways. Centralization and standardization have been emphasized in debates over national integration and nationalism; over the role of centralized government at the national level; and about the growing importance of administrative bureaucracy, coordination, and rationality in public life (Bendix 1977; Meyer 1980). Decentralization, diversity, and autonomous associations have been stressed in discussions that privilege the roles of state and local government, that express concerns about totalitarianism and see strong community-level organizations as a countervailing force, and that favor the autonomy and pluralism of regional, racial, and ethnic subcultures (Nisbet 1962).

Although political theorists have often sided with one or the other of these polarities, the need for both—and for maintaining balance between them—has been recognized throughout American history. This is evident in the *Federalist* papers and in the nation's Constitution, both of which express concerns about protecting states' rights and individual freedoms while also ensuring sufficient coordination at the federal level. Alexander Hamilton's emphasis on the need for a strong national union has generally been balanced by James Madison's emphasis on separate interests and the need for a system of checks on majoritarian rule. In de Tocqueville's writing, strong local and regional associations are seen as a way of mediating between the insular values and interests of local communities and the standardizing tendencies he associated with democratic governing institutions and the mass media. Yet de Tocqueville's emphasis on associations came at a time when Jacksonian reforms were helping to create a stronger sense of national unity, while the Bonapartist reforms in de Tocqueville's native France were undermining some of the provincial distinctions that had always helped to reinforce associationalism. By the end of the nineteenth century, national integration of the United States was facilitated through railroads and industry, and pensions for Civil War veterans, military hospitals, and a system of state-run insane asylums and prisons were adding to the standardization of social life. But thousands of local associations, ranging from women's clubs to fraternal orders, had arisen as a countervailing force, while the nation's churches still reflected local and ethnic traditions to a great extent (Skocpol 1992). In the early decades of the twentieth century, ideas about government's role in planning social programs became increasingly prominent, but associationalism also prevailed (Graham 1976). As European social theory came to be more widely known in the United States, Max Weber's concerns about the growing bureaucratization of modern societies found their counterpart in Emile Durkheim's efforts to find strength in religious communities, professional associations, and other forms of corporatism (Weber 1978; Durkheim 1992). Following in that tradition, a more recent interpretation is offered by Jurgen Habermas (1981), who emphasizes the rationalization of social life that comes with growing needs for coordination by bureaucratic governing and economic institutions, on the one hand, and the more traditional, intuitive, value-laden experience of the "life world," on the other hand.

The tension between what might be called the national view of American civil society and the associationalist view runs through the debates surrounding the Ashcroft provision and the NEA. Social welfare has generally been deemed an issue that requires active involvement by the federal government. Funds are raised through a national system of taxes, regulations ensure that standard definitions of eligibility prevail, and national involvement is desired in order to monitor recipients who might attempt to exploit the system by moving from state to state. Even with the local emphasis in the recent welfare reform bill, a principle of national involvement has been retained.

At the same time, many of the criticisms of the welfare system have focused on its impersonality and the large government bureaucracy that has arisen to administer it. Public opinion surveys generally show more support for individual or private efforts to help the needy than for government welfare programs, and the surveys also show more support for small, local nonprofit organizations than for large, national or bureaucratic forms of association (Wuthnow 1991). In contrast to the national emphasis, those with associationalist leanings have focused on the need for local communities to administer services and to promote self-sufficiency among recipients, and they have found support for their arguments in the American tradition of volunteerism and church-related charities. In making it possible for faith-based organizations to receive federal funding, Charitable Choice recognized both the necessity and the dangers of government standards being applied to religious organizations. But it was also an attempt to use the local, diverse, and presumably more personal forms of caring available in congregations to provide services. The NEA debate centered around similar issues. A national system of funding for artists was deemed desirable by many lawmakers, yet there was also concern for protecting the autonomy of diverse artistic groups and interests.

In the debates over Charitable Choice, both sides attempted to show that theirs was the best way to achieve an appropriate balance between national coordination of social services and the role of local associations. Supporters of the measure argued that government was already so actively involved in the funding of nonprofit service organizations that faith-based nonprofits should not be excluded. The restrictions that the legislation would place on government were, in their view, sufficient to protect the autonomy of diverse religious congregations that might decide to apply for public funding. Opponents focused on what the courts had termed the "pervasive sectarianism" of religious organizations. Apart from its legal meaning, this phrase was a convenient rhetorical device for highlighting the centrifugal forces that might be unleashed by strengthening religious groups. Sectarianism connotes religious warfare, proselytization, heated theological disputes, and efforts by particular religious groups to seize political power. The danger of providing public funding to sectarian groups, critics charged, was that some groups would inevitably use their existing power to acquire more than their fair share of those funds and that the same groups might be tempted to use the funds to gain even greater power in their communities.

The debate about public funding for nonprofit arts organizations included similar arguments. When it established the NEA in 1965, Congress explicitly recognized the need for diversity by asserting that "conformity for its own sake is not to be encouraged" and that "no undue preference should be given to any particular style or school of thought or expression" (U.S. Congress 1965). The 1990 amendment that required the NEA to take into account "general standards of decency and respect for the diverse beliefs and values of the American public" proved to be a statement that could be interpreted both in support of and against diversity. While it explicitly mentioned diverse beliefs and values, the amendment's language meant that artistic works such as Serrano's or Finley's could be subjected to standards of morality held by the wider public rather than being judged strictly in terms of their artistic merit. The amendment in effect threatened to extend the government's capacity to impose uniformity on the artistic community.

The tension between national and local or associational emphases runs through many of the other debates that have arisen in recent years about American democracy. On the one hand, the growth of government funding in many areas of civic life, as well as greatly expanded government regulations, has extended the role of national government well beyond its traditional functions. Indeed, the past half-century has witnessed greater supervision of civil society by central government along a wide variety of dimensions, including regulation of equality in hiring practices, the establishment of national standards in education, and federal requirements in housing policies and the conduct of business. Although many of those developments have been debated, they are generally supported because of the growing need for standardization and uniform laws in an otherwise complex society. From airline safety standards to greater coordination of research and technology, such developments have enabled Americans to live together in an anonymous and interdependent society. On the other hand, the nation has also become increasingly diverse in recent years. Racial and ethnic diversity have increased as a result of new immigration and in response to greater awareness of the importance of group identities. Telecommunications, travel, and computing have made it possible for local communities to interact more easily with one another without necessarily adopting common values. As standard definitions of individual rights have been promulgated, new calls have been voiced for people to exercise their responsibilities as members of communities. And concerns about the standardizing effects of litigation, consumerism, and self-interest have been met with stronger pleas for participation in civic organizations, churches, and other local associations.

IMPLICATIONS FOR PUBLIC POLICY AND THE NONPROFIT SECTOR

The specific impacts of Charitable Choice and the debate about NEA projects have thus far been less significant than many had either hoped or feared. Contrary to the view that churches would generally prefer to administer service programs directly rather than set up separate nonprofits to do so, the latter option has become so well institution-alized that it seems likely to remain the preferred option. Indeed, many clergy in local congregations appear unaware of the Charitable Choice legislation or, if aware, are relatively uninterested, thus reinforcing the concern expressed by some public officials that Charitable Choice may ultimately benefit large national faith-based providers. Local churches and synagogues have a long history of establishing specialized organizations, ranging from cemetery and mutual insurance associations in the nineteenth century to interfaith food distribution programs and homeless shelters in the twentieth century. Forming separate nonprofit organizations permits churches to cooperate more easily with other congregations, restricts the churches' financial and legal liabilities, and permits overburdened clergy to attend to their own work while nonprofit professionals operate the service programs. Many faith-based nonprofits were initiated by clergy councils or interested individuals three decades ago during the initial expansion of the Great Society programs and now have strong expertise in delivering services that few individual congregations could match. Many have also developed close working relationships with secular nonprofits, hospitals, welfare agencies, and community foundations. Perhaps because of their accumulated expertise, these nonprofits, rather than churches themselves, have been the most active participants in new government-nonprofit partnerships in Texas, Mississippi, Michigan, and Maryland, where early efforts to experiment with Charitable Choice programs were initiated.

The impact of the NEA debates has also been less dramatic than sometimes suggested. Although many nonprofit arts organizations have had to tighten budgets, individual artists generally deny that they have modified their work in order to avoid controversy or to make themselves more acceptable candidates for public funding. In their view, NEA support has been relatively minor compared with other sources of funding, and it has in any case been funneled more toward established organizations than toward individual artists. As one artist who had served on NEA review panels observed, the NEA has "had very little impact in the past [because] it has never really come to terms with the intractable problem of supporting individual artists" (personal interview).

Much of the debate about religion and the arts in the nonprofit sector has, of course, been restricted to questions of efficiency and effectiveness. The nonprofit sector is intensely competitive, with local and national organizations competing for scarce government and private funding. Public officials and nonprofit managers alike make claims and counterclaims about the effectiveness of different organizations. Thus far, however, research does not clearly establish that faith-based nonprofits are necessarily more (or less) effective in providing social services or that nonprofit arts organizations are necessarily more efficient than for-profit organizations. Indeed, the nonprofit management literature is often remiss in focusing too much attention on those issues and thus missing the importance of the larger questions of values that are being debated. Local clergy, just like artists and administrators of other community organizations, are often the first to admit that they simply do not know what impact more—or less—government funding (and regulation) may have on their activities.

The lack of a more sweeping impact from the Ashcroft and NEA debates does not mean that the issues they have raised are unimportant or that they will cease to be of concern to policymakers and nonprofit professionals. Advocates of complete separation of church and state are likely to take little solace in the fact that most public funding for faith-based service organizations is channeled through specialized nonprofits rather than through churches. Fears that clients may be exposed to prayers or religious teachings in these organizations are not unfounded. Individual professionals whose salaries or programs are partially supported by public funding often pray with clients or tell them where they can find a welcoming house of worship. For those who believe that spirituality is an interest of virtually everyone, however, such prayers and personal advice seem only natural. Similarly, arts organizations and churches continue to be engaged in controversies about the values expressed in artistic works. As most Protestant denominations have struggled to clarify official positions concerning their stance toward homosexuality and the ordination of women, gay and lesbian and feminist artistic works have sparked heated reactions among church members. In their growing efforts to engage more actively with the artistic community, church leaders have found themselves faced with unexpected occasions for reflection on the deeper meanings of their own traditions.

At a more general level, the tensions concerning centralization and local diversity are likely to continue because both aspects of social life are deeply cherished, and neither can be preserved simply by favoring one form of legislation or another. Most Americans watch television programs that depend on nationally administered laws regulating broadcasting, and a growing share of the public pays attention to national news or reads national newspapers, rather than focusing only on local issues. Most Americans favor the continuation of nationally sponsored Social Security and Medicare programs, and they benefit from laws regulating food and drugs and from efforts to protect the environment. The highly controlled national conformity that may be required during war, or that was a fact of American life during the Cold War, is nevertheless balanced by strong traditions of local autonomy and self-determination. As centralized bureaucracies have proven inefficient in many areas of public life, Americans have been able to experience greater freedom to pursue their own diverse lifestyles and to devote their energies to more local and fluid forms of civic participation, such as neighborhood task forces, family charities, and informal volunteering. Indeed, the literature decrying the decline of American democracy in the early 1990s can partly be understood as a realignment in public thinking necessitated by the conclusion of the Cold War. Sensing that strong central government was perhaps no longer as urgently needed to protect national security or to compete militarily and economically with other nations, Americans have found themselves increasingly attracted to arguments about the importance of reviving their associationalist expressions of democracy.

Nonprofit organizations lie at the intersection of the opposing forces of centralization and decentralization and the social conditions in which they are rooted. The growth of the nonprofit sector during the past four decades could not have come about without strong government support, as well as a legal framework in which to define nonprofit activity. In conforming to national standards regarding tax reporting and tax exemption and in following government regulations on receiving and dispensing funds, nonprofits have been instrumental in bringing the effects of central government to local communities. But they have also taken the place of some local and regional voluntary associations, helping to stimulate citizens' participation in their local communities. The tensions evident through the Charitable Choice and NEA debates are for those reasons likely to surface for nonprofit organizations not directly involved as well. Indeed, spokespersons in those debates have alluded frequently to the possibility of setting precedents for other actions, such as providing public funding for private nonprofit schools through a voucher system or making it possible for faith-based lobbying organizations to operate with fewer restrictions.

An important implication of the present tensions between national and associational views of American democracy, therefore, is that the controversies in which nonprofit organizations are currently involved are not restricted to organizations that deal directly with religious or artistic values. In a larger sense, all nonprofits are part of controversies about fundamental values because nonprofits are inevitably faced with making decisions that respond to the centralizing forces, on the one hand, and the decentralizing forces, on the other hand, that characterize contemporary social life. If they respond too strongly to centralizing forces, either in seeking to comply with government regulations or in attempting to compete more effectively with one another by focusing on efficiency and rationality, nonprofits run the risk of compromising values like compassion and standards of highest-quality service tailored to the needs of individual clients. They may inadvertently abandon the faith traditions or the visions of their founders, moving instead toward therapeutic, bureaucratic, or instrumental modes of operation. Still, nonprofit organizations that fail to adapt to some of the broader cultural changes that have come about as a result of greater government involvement in service delivery may find themselves at a serious competitive disadvantage with other nonprofits.

For their part, the administrators of nonprofit organizations can initiate activities that mitigate the tensions created by these opposing forces within their own programs. One strategy is to create specialized organizations that are able to respond to government funding in different ways. As already discussed, many religious congregations prefer to establish separate faith-based nonprofit service organizations so that the congregations themselves do not run the risk of invoking government regulations. Within faith-based nonprofits, small and more fluid structures help to maintain a more personal atmosphere, while large organizations (such as community development corporations) create committees to safeguard the interests of religious investors or neighborhood groups against alternative pressures from banks and government agencies. Artists who emphasize the value of peer review in judging projects or grant applications are in this way maintaining the internal autonomy of the artistic community while facilitating the mechanism by which government funding for the arts can be dispensed.

The nonprofit sector as a whole can continue to serve as a vehicle for mediating opposing social forces. The presence of a large and vibrant nonprofit sector means that government initiatives can be channeled through those organizations, rather than through new agencies that must be established. The internal diversity of the nonprofit sector is particularly important in that respect. Large, national nonprofits can deal directly with federal agencies, while smaller, local nonprofits can work in partnership with religious congregations, families, and informal groups.

The mere presence of an apparent clash of values does not in itself indicate that American democracy is in danger. The strength of democracy lies partly in its system of administrative checks and balances, which inevitably generate different interests. Religious conservatives are likely to continue lobbying to make their interests heard, and so are their opponents. These voices will be part of public deliberations because nonprofits have been organized to solicit funds and to pay professionals to make themselves heard. As society becomes more diverse, interest groups will continue to bring conflicting values into the public arena.

For their members, clients, and other constituents, nonprofit organizations' most important contribution to the strengthening of civil society may be encouraging greater levels of trust and cooperation in local communities and in the wider public. Simply participating in voluntary associations does not in many cases generate such trust, yet nonprofit and other community organizations typically depend on the goodwill of participants and thus often devote effort to repairing mistrust and bringing diverse groups together (Wuthnow 1998). Trust does not in principle require agreement, but it does appear harder to sustain when people do not share common backgrounds or values. Nonprofit organizations can generate trust by bringing people from diverse backgrounds together around common purposes. Trusting one another enough to express divergent opinions may be the most vital feature of American democracy and must be preserved in the years ahead.

References

Adler, Amy M. 1993. "Why Art Is on Trial." *Journal of Arts Management, Law, and Society* 22: 322–34.

Balfe, Judith Huggins. 1993. *Paying the Piper: Causes and Consequences of Art Patronage.* Urbana, Ill.: University of Illinois Press.

Bendix, Reinhard. 1977. *Nation-Building and Citizenship*, rev. ed. Berkeley and Los Angeles: University of California Press.

Berry, Jeff. 1997. "Citizen Groups in American Politics." Unpublished paper presented at the Conference on Civic Engagement in American Democracy, Portland, Maine.

Bolton, Richard, ed. 1992. *Culture Wars: Documents from the Recent Controversies in the Arts.* New York: New Press.

Bryson, Bethany. 1996. "'Anything but Heavy Metal': Symbolic Exclusion and Musical Dislikes." *American Sociological Review* 61: 884–99.

Cohen, Jean L., and Andrew Arato. 1992. *Civil Society and Political Theory.* Cambridge, Mass.: MIT Press.

Denny, Doreen. 1996. "Landmark Welfare Law Reforms." *Congressional Press Releases,* October 23.

DiMaggio, Paul, John Evans, and Bethany Bryson. 1996. "Have Americans' Social Attitudes Become More Polarized?" *American Journal of Sociology* 102: 690–755.

Dionne, E. J., Jr. 1992. *Why Americans Hate Politics.* New York: Touchstone Books.

Durkheim, Emile. 1992. *Professional Ethics and Civic Morals.* London: Routledge.

Elshtain, Jean Bethke. 1995. *Democracy on Trial.* New York: Basic Books.

Evans, John. 1996. "'Culture Wars' or Status Group Ideology as the Basis of U.S. Moral Politics." *International Journal of Sociology and Social Policy* 16: 15–34.

Goode, Stephen. 1997. "Secular Faith Fails: God Is King of the Hill." *Washington Times,* March 31.

Graham, Otis L., Jr. 1976. *Toward a Planned Society: From Roosevelt to Nixon.* New York: Oxford University Press.

Habermas, Jurgen. 1981. *The Theory of Communicative Action,* 2 vols. Boston: Beacon.

Hodgkinson, Virginia A., and Murray S. Weitzman. 1996. *Nonprofit Almanac, 1996–1997: Dimensions of the Independent Sector.* San Francisco: Jossey-Bass Publishers.

Horton, Michael S. 1994. *Beyond Culture Wars.* Chicago: Moody Press.

Hunter, James Davison. 1991. *Culture Wars: The Struggle to Define America.* New York: Basic Books.

————. 1994. *Before the Shooting Begins: Searching for Democracy in America's Culture Wars.* New York: Free Press.

McGee, Celia. 1995. "A Personal Vision of the Sacred and Profane." *New York Times,* January 22.

Meyer, John W. 1980. "The World Polity and the Authority of the Nation-State." In *Studies of the Modern World-System,* edited by Albert Bergesen (109–38). New York: Academic Press.

Nisbet, Robert A. 1962. *Community and Power.* New York: Oxford University Press.

Nolan, James L., Jr., ed. 1996. *The American Culture Wars: Current Contests and Future Prospects.* Charlottesville, Va.: University of Virginia Press.

Putnam, Robert. 1995. "Bowling Alone: America's Declining Social Capital." *Journal of Democracy* (Jan.): 65–78.

Robinson, James W., Russ Colliau, and Jim Robinson. 1995. *After the Revolution: A Citizen's Guide to the First Republican Congress in Forty Years.* Washington, D.C.: Prima.

Rodrigue, George. 1996. "Gingrich Aims for Kinder Image." *Dallas Morning News*, August 14.

Salamon, Lester M. 1995. *Partners in Public Service: Government-Nonprofit Relations in the Modern Welfare State*. Baltimore, Md.: Johns Hopkins University Press.

Scheff, Joanne, and Philip Kotler. 1996. "Crisis in the Arts: The Marketing Response." *California Management Review* 39 (Sept.): 28–59.

Sine, Tom. 1996. *Cease Fire: Searching for Sanity in America's Culture Wars*. Grand Rapids, Mich.: Eerdmans.

Skocpol, Theda. 1992. *Protecting Soldiers and Mothers: The Political Origins of Social Policy in the United States*. Cambridge, Mass.: Harvard University Press.

Smith, Christian. 1998. *American Evangelicals: Embattled and Thriving*. Chicago: University of Chicago Press.

Smith, Steven Rathgeb, and Michael Lipsky. 1993. *Nonprofits for Hire: The Welfare State in the Age of Contracting*. Cambridge, Mass.: Harvard University Press.

Trescott, Jacqueline. 1997. "Senate Spares NEA: Bids to Eliminate Agency's Funding Are Defeated." *Washington Post*, September 18.

U.S. Congress. 1965. *111 Congressional Record* 13: 108.

Van Camp, Julie C. 1997. *Freedom of Expression at the National Endowment for the Arts: An Interdisciplinary Curriculum Project Funded by the American Bar Association, Commission on College and University Legal Studies, through the ABA Fund for Justice and Education*. Long Beach, Calif.: California State University, Department of Philosophy.

Watt, David Harrington. 1991. "United States: Cultural Challenges to the Voluntary Sector." In *Between States and Markets: The Voluntary Sector in Comparative Perspective*, edited by Robert Wuthnow (243–87). Princeton, N.J.: Princeton University Press, 1991.

Weber, Max. 1978. *Economy and Society*, trans. by Guenther Roth and Claus Wittich. Berkeley and Los Angeles: University of California Press.

Wolch, Jennifer R. 1990. *The Shadow State: Government and Voluntary Sector in Transition*. New York: Foundation Center.

Wuthnow, Robert. 1989. *The Restructuring of American Religion: Society and Faith since World War II*. Princeton, N.J.: Princeton University Press.

———. 1991. *Acts of Compassion*. Princeton, N.J.: Princeton University Press.

———. 1994. *God and Mammon in America*. New York: Free Press.

———. 1996a. "Restructuring of American Religion: Further Evidence." *Sociological Inquiry* 66 (Aug.): 303–29.

———. 1996b. *Christianity and Civil Society: The Contemporary Debate*. Philadelphia: Trinity Press International.

———. 1998. *Loose Connections: Joining Together in America's Fragmented Communities*. Cambridge, Mass.: Harvard University Press.

Chapter Nine

NONPROFIT ADVOCACY AND POLITICAL PARTICIPATION

Elizabeth J. Reid

INTRODUCTION

Nonprofits strengthen democracy by giving citizens a variety of opportunities to meet and talk, build civic skills, and assemble their resources for joint action. They also help bring the norms and values of society to public decisionmaking. Nonprofits "engage people outside either the marketplace or the state; their entities are independently organized and self-governing; they give voice to social demands and diverse viewpoints; they deliver services to varied constituencies; and they serve as monitors and watchdogs of the other sectors, and, at times, of their own performance" (Boris 1998, 6).

When necessary, nonprofits ask government to address their concerns or initiate action. Sometimes they muster broad support for comprehensive political reform, but generally they are part of incremental changes in current laws. Through advocacy, nonprofits may instill their group's perceptions of the common good into wider notions of the public good or public interest. Policy advocacy is broadly defined as "any attempt to influence the decisions of any institutional elite on behalf of a collective interest" (Jenkins 1987, 297). While nonprofit advocacy can influence corporate and nonprofit decisionmakers as well as legislators and government officials, this chapter focuses on attempts by nonprofits to influence government decisions.[1]

When like-minded people discuss politics and issues, they often reinforce their affiliations and views. Civic activities in formal (incorporated) and informal organizations are not always directly political but can influence the interest, efficacy, information, and partisan affiliation of citizens in political affairs (Berry, Portney, and Thomson 1993, 256). For example, Nine to Five, a national working women's organization, grew out of the informal discussions of several women who then organized Boston clerical workers for workplace improvements and legislative action. Likewise, when congregations have strong views on issues, members are more likely to choose candidates or parties to match their concerns.

Small nonprofits, informal associations, and the local chapters and networks of larger groups are the backbone of political voice in communities around the country. In one study of political participation, 92 percent of political activity had a state and local connection. Of the participants who were politically active beyond voting (volunteering, contacting, donating), 8 percent did so exclusively in national politics, 51 percent exclusively in state or local politics, and 41 percent in activity that combined the state or local level with national participation (Verba, Schlozman, and Brady 1995, 66).

People learn grassroots skills and build relationships in community, religious, and workplace associations in ways that are transferable to politics. Nonpolitical activity may increase public confidence about what can be accomplished through collective activity. A community self-help activity, like cleaning vacant lots, can instill pride and a sense of accomplishment. It may also enlighten the participants about what the community can do and what needs addressing through legislation or partnership with government or business.

Large groups active in national politics are often the focus of attention in publicized political contests. These organizations, like other politically active groups, have come under public scrutiny as lawmakers, organizations, and concerned citizens have wrestled with the role of interest groups in the policy process and in electoral campaigns. Some national and state political initiatives aimed at reforming the conduct of politics in legislatures and in elections target the political advocacy activities of nonprofits. Reform proposals attempt to manage campaign costs, lessen the influence of money in elections and policymaking, avoid the misuse of nonprofit organizations in partisan activity, and reverse declines in voting and public trust in government.

This chapter focuses on the activities of charitable and social welfare nonprofits and the influence of laws and regulations on citizen participation and nonprofit advocacy.[2] Proposals to reform nonprofit advocacy and political practices are difficult to evaluate because they reflect different priorities. Some aim to reduce taxpayer subsidization of nonprofit advocacy and to direct charitable contributions toward charitable activity.[3] Others aim to dampen the role of "interested money" in elections. Whatever the motivation and intentions, changes in the regulation of nonprofit political advocacy are likely to affect civic representation and citizen participation in policymaking and elections.

NONPROFIT POLITICAL ADVOCACY

Politically active nonprofits contribute to democratic governance by *representing* civic concerns in policymaking, by enlarging opportunities for citizen *participation* in public decisions, and by creating *accountability* between government and citizens.

Some nonprofits, especially large ones, are consciously political. They employ advocacy and group action regularly to accomplish their organizational goals. They prepare for political activity through organizational planning and outreach to the public and to elected officials. They commit resources to advocacy activities, public policy research and information, and collaborative strategies for political action. Many small groups, on the other hand, "back into" political action out of occasional necessity to solve a problem. They may become more active after experiencing the necessity for, or the benefits of, political advocacy, or they may withdraw from advocacy if tensions arise from funding sources, organizational leaders and members, rules and regulations governing advocacy, or lack of progress pursuing political goals.

REPRESENTATION

Through lobbying and communication about broad social objectives and issues that directly affect their constituencies, nonprofits provide representation for collective interests and values in civil society. They advocate positions and views as part of nonprofit program work, lobby government officials on specific legislation, communicate with their members and the public on policy issues, speak on behalf of those who are connected with the group, evaluate candidates for public office at election time, and employ legal advocacy to move collective concerns past logjams in the political system.

Nonprofit representation can open the political system to new voices through group competition. No one group is likely to dominate political life when a wide variety of organized interests is expressed. Group representation gives many people a chance to have their issues heard, but income and education inequalities affect nonprofit representation and hinder participation of low-income people in politics.

Only 2 percent of welfare recipients report belonging to an organization concerned about their program, compared to 34 percent of people receiving veterans benefits and 24 percent of Social Security recipients (Verba, Schlozman, and Brady 1997, 79–80). Data collected in 1967 indicated that the richest people were three times as likely to be active members of organizations as were the poorest. The ratio was the same in 1990.

Nonprofit representation has been criticized for many reasons. The pejorative "special interests" label is sometimes attached to groups that exert a powerful influence on political decisions through large expenditures of organizational funds for advocacy. Many of these groups, however, have broad public involvement in their organizations and wide public support for their objectives (Hrebenar 1997).

Interest groups have also been criticized for being better at interest articulation (raising and defining interests and issues and bringing new information and constituencies to policymaking) than interest aggregation (assembling interests and working out priorities and compromises for programs). This assessment may be overly critical. Fashioning a compromise is not always possible, once the political process is under way. Polarized elected leadership, interested groups, and disengaged citizens are all part of the bottleneck when a political solution cannot be found. Some nonprofits use public education and collaborative strategies for consensus building to overcome political divisiveness and polarization. They share information across partisan lines and build relationships across organizations and interests to establish common policy frameworks.

Citizen Participation

Nonprofits encourage political action among their members and other citizens, and they offer opportunities for individuals to use their skills for civic and political purposes. Nonprofits also organize group action, such as group lobby days, letter-writing campaigns, boycotts, public meetings, demonstrations, candidate forums, and voter registration.

The personal networks that people develop in nonprofits often motivate them to action. A study by the American Association of Retired Persons (AARP) found that citizens feel more effective when they work as a group on policy issues than when they act alone. People are also more likely to participate in activities when they are asked by someone they know.

Engagement builds personal efficacy, and this sense that one is capable and influential appears to lead to action. People with more education and income are more likely to participate because they tend to have accumulated useful participatory skills early in life—in active, affluent families and in good schools. These skills are reinforced at work, in social networks, and in nonprofit organizations. A Philadelphia study showed that older, affluent, well-educated residents approached government more often and felt more empowered. Furthermore, government listens. "Philadelphians who feel empowered, live in quality neighborhoods, and are older have the most success in getting local government to act" (Pew Research Center 1997, 53).

Voting is the most common and accessible form of individual citizen participation. Turnout for the last 30 years, however, has been slowly declining for the overall population. The statistics paint a picture of a public disengaged from politics, especially when coupled with measures of high distrust of government.[4] The figures are even more dismal for low-income people, but the participation gap closes somewhat when people are involved with a politically active nonprofit or are part of a social movement that encourages voting and face-to-face contacts, as well as opportunities to build and use political skills.

American electoral politics discourages participation by many citizens. Campaign costs have skyrocketed over the last 15 years, and the heavy emphasis on money has led people to conclude that they cannot compete with the "big bucks." The wealthiest 10 percent of the population (with incomes of over $75,000 per year) donates more than half of the campaign dollars. The bottom 19 percent (less than $15,000 per year) donates only 2 percent of the campaign dollars (Verba, Schlozman, and Brady 1997, 79). These differences heavily affect participation. Candidates value money over other forms of citizen participation and encourage donations over other forms of electoral participation, such as volunteerism. Organizations that mobilize voters and organize regular communication with government officials on policy issues offer an influential alternative to money in politics.

POLITICAL ACCOUNTABILITY

Groups with constituencies that engage in political action affect what public officials hear, and what public officials hear contributes to what political business gets accomplished.

One study found that politicians hear messages differently when they are delivered face to face, a fact that makes low-income grassroots advocacy organizations important to decisionmaking (Verba, Schlozman and Brady 1997, 79). Direct voice and votes are often poor people's only political resources. Last year, for example, the Dade County Human Services Coalition brought low-income mothers to a public meeting of agencies and officials to speak about their difficulties in securing work, child care, and health care. The Board agreed not only to investigate the systemic problems contributing to the mothers' difficulties but also to help remedy their personal grievances with unscrupulous businesses and training agencies. Thus nonprofits offer ways beyond voting to express political satisfaction or dissatisfaction with government performance.

TYPES OF NONPROFIT ADVOCACY ACTIVITIES

No one activity or group is likely to determine a political outcome, so nonprofits engage in a wide range of advocacy activities. Some activities take place in civil society (such as grassroots advocacy or social movement advocacy) and some in the formal institutions of government (such as lobbying and testifying), but they reinforce each other in the political process. For example, after Mothers Against Drunk Driving (MADD) built community networks across the country, it was able to take on the more difficult task of promoting federal standards for illegal blood alcohol levels.

Nonprofit advocacy at the state and local levels is different from advocacy at the national level. At the local level, it often involves face-to-face contact between local politicians and nonprofit leaders. Groups frequently pursue strategies of cooperation and partnership, though conflict with government decisionmakers may occur when government fails to act on what groups want (Berry, Portney, and Thomson 1993). Nonprofit advocacy in state and national politics is regularly conducted by lobbyists and organizational representatives, often through congressional staff. There is often intense competition among larger organizations attempting to promote their causes.

Nonprofit communication networks among local citizens, local offices, national offices, coalitions, and representatives are important sources of information and guidance for citizens who want to influence broader national policy and program development. These networks serve as pipelines through which local concerns reach national decisionmakers and through which national issues reach communities for discussion and action.

Organization Building, Program Work, and Advocacy

Nonprofits build organizational resources—organizational knowledge, skills, leadership, and financial resources—to increase their capacity for effective political action,[5] but advocacy may also occur as part of the routine tasks of organization building and program work, sometimes referred to as programmatic advocacy (Hopkins 1992, 35).

There is no distinct line between the activities necessary for building strong organizations and advocacy, or between public education and advocacy, or between promoting a service mission and advocacy. The difficulty of distinguishing among these functions can cause problems for regulators and lawmakers wishing to limit the amount of advocacy permissible by groups or to allow the charitable tax deduction for educational activities but not for advocacy. For nonprofits, however, the greater the integration of service, advocacy, and public education, the greater the opportunities to use organizational resources effectively for raising their agenda and concerns in the development of public policy.

Organization-building activities that contribute to effective advocacy include:

BUILDING POLITICAL RESOURCES: VOLUNTEERS, MONEY, FACILITIES

Most nonprofits ask people to join, donate, or volunteer, and they raise money from a variety of private individuals and foundations (Zald and McCarthy 1987). In the 1980s, many groups amassed new resources to hire staff and enhance facilities via direct mail campaigns. Smaller organizations often do very successful fundraising and organizing by having staff or community volunteers visit homes, distribute research materials, ask for contributions, and build contact lists for future action.

ORGANIZATIONAL POLICYMAKING

Meetings and conventions prepare leaders and members for grassroots action on policy issues. Organizational policy established at meetings guides future advocacy; training sessions build skills and knowledge of public policy issues; and social events build personal relationships and state and local networks for political action.

INTERNAL EDUCATIONAL ACTIVITIES

Some nonprofits provide training to build expertise, interest, and motivation among members and leaders of local groups. Independent training centers have provided grassroots leadership development for community leaders since the 1930s. Newsletters are another common form of nonprofit political education, keeping members and the public informed on public policy and offering a source of alternative views and specialized information not readily available through commercial media. When used for advocacy, they are likely to present analyses interpreted for their readers' interests.

RESEARCH AND MONITORING ACTIVITIES

Some nonprofits conduct research, monitor the performance of government agencies and elected officials, or track specific policy issues. They often share their findings with others in forums and conferences.

"Action" Advocacy

In addition to institution building, nonprofits decide where, when, and how to "weigh in" politically. Due to financial or other organizational constraints, most groups decide which activities will create the most impact and when. They aim their efforts at various decisionmakers in the institutional settings described below.

LEGISLATIVE ADVOCACY

Nonprofits lobby, testify, and build contacts with legislators and their staffs. Lobbying and other face-to-face contact with decisionmakers is often called direct advocacy or direct lobbying.

Nonprofits use research to persuade legislators and garner public support. Organizations with high credibility as advocates generally provide well-supported information.

Nonprofits also provide valuable feedback for public policy evaluation. Through their close association with communities and citizens, many nonprofits offer an assessment of the social impact of policy from their civic vantage point. For example, nonprofits and government have collaborated to implement the new rules, meet job requirements, provide social services, and evaluate impacts of the welfare reforms in the Personal Responsibility and Work Opportunity Reconciliation Act (PRWORA) of 1996 (see chapter 6, this volume).

GRASSROOTS ADVOCACY

Grassroots advocacy, sometimes referred to as indirect advocacy, is an attempt to influence public decisions, including legislation, by shaping public opinion and mobilizing individual and collective action (McCarthy and Castelli 1998). Groups mobilize individuals to call, write, boycott, or demonstrate. Grassroots political action builds common skills, experiences, and social solidarity among participants. Sometimes, this action expands into social movements, such as the civil rights or temperance movement.

PUBLIC EDUCATION AND PUBLIC OPINION SHAPING AS ADVOCACY

The boundary between information as education and information as influence is not clear. Proponents of stricter advocacy laws call for clearer distinctions between education and advocacy, while others resist restrictions as an impingement on free speech and a disincentive to participation.

Nonprofit organizations may spend considerable time and money on research, public education, and consensus building before they develop a policy proposal or ballot issue. These activities often generate ideas for policy solutions and develop public awareness.

ELECTORAL ADVOCACY

All nonprofits may engage in *nonpartisan* election activities, such as voter registration and get-out-the-vote campaigns, and, except for 501(c)(3) organizations, may engage in certain partisan activities as well. Nonprofits often appeal to strong group identities, such as religious or cultural values, gender, and national allegiance, in ways that lead to voter participation at election time.

Some nonprofit organizations successfully blend educational activities, legislative advocacy, grassroots advocacy, and electoral advocacy to create pressure for political change. They may set up separate organizational structures—one for charitable or educational functions, one for legislative advocacy, and one for election activity—to extend the range of resources and political activities available to them to accomplish their political goals. The complex administrative and legal requirements of a full-fledged political operation require substantial resources, so usually only large groups have one.

LEGAL ADVOCACY

A rich tradition of advocacy through the courts has developed in this country to defend groups of disabled, minorities, children, women, and others. Ralph Nader founded public interest advocacy, another strand of popular legal advocacy. More recently, individual rights advocates have used legal advocacy to challenge affirmative action and environmental regulation.

Administrative or Agency Advocacy

Nonprofit groups often shape and use government agency rules, administrative design, and program development processes to influence how programs will be implemented once they are legislated.[6]

Workplace Advocacy

Workplace advocacy is not merely the concern of unionists, though labor organizations often provide substantial resources for joint advocacy action. Health and safety issues, trade and wage issues, and workplace concerns draw together a wide range of groups on occupational hazards, jobs, and benefits.

Corporate Advocacy

In an era of deregulation and government devolution, many nonprofits have turned toward businesses in order to influence corporate policy decisions. Nonprofits use consumer and public opinion pressure and sometimes engage stockholders to increase corporate responsiveness and accountability to social concerns.

Media Advocacy

Even small organizations now have press strategies, such as placing op eds, issuing press releases, meeting with community editorial boards, and appearing on radio and TV talk shows. Some groups stage catchy local media events to dramatize their concerns. Other groups have well-organized communications and regular contact with journalists and opinion makers in the press to keep open channels of public information. One of the hottest sources for nonprofit policy information and action is the World Wide Web.

International Advocacy

Increasingly, nonprofits are political actors in the global economy, especially those with international networks on cross-border issues such as human rights, environmental standards, and labor standards. They often influence decisions in international institutions, such as the United Nations or the World Trade Organization, urging those organizations to pass resolutions, develop standards, and build programs on a wide range of issues.

TYPES OF POLITICALLY ACTIVE NONPROFIT ORGANIZATIONS

There are many different types of organizations in the nonprofit sector, with distinct organizational traditions of political advocacy (Wilson, 1973). Nonprofits generally engage in a mix of constituent services, public education, and advocacy that fluctuates in response both to external political, social, and legal conditions and to internal factors such as organizational mission, practices, and leadership (Minkoff 1998). Some groups are more politically active than others, however, because the law permits them to engage in a wider range of activity and because they have a tradition of doing so. Unions, professional organizations, and social welfare organizations are examples.

Social service organizations and other charitable groups primarily concerned with the delivery of services occasionally use advocacy to meet their program goals, but studies have indicated that these groups seldom participate in the policy process. The Center for Community Change reports that many of these 501(c)(3) groups shy away from advocacy because of constraints on time, fears that they may drive away potential funding sources, and misconceptions about the legality of lobbying (Center for Community Change 1996, 9). Some data indicate that few resources of these organizations are committed to direct or grassroots advocacy regulated by the Internal Revenue Service (IRS). One study found that among 3,400 501(c)(3) organizations across the country, only 16 percent show expenditures on advocacy activity. For half of these, the expenditures were 10 percent or less of total spending (Salamon 1995). Certain types of 501(c)(3) organizations engage in more advocacy than others. Legal service groups and multiservice organizations (nonprofits with a variety of services) are more likely to engage in policy advocacy, while arts and culture organizations are less likely (Salamon 1995).

NEIGHBORHOOD ASSOCIATIONS AND COMMUNITY ORGANIZATIONS

Local organizations are often informal civic gatherings or small formally established nonprofits.[7] Community and neighborhood associations weave neighbors together socially around local policy issues, such as safety, streets, and recreation. Neighborhood economic development groups, for example, work in low-income communities to secure funding for projects, build housing, and create jobs. Local schools bring parents together in parent-teacher organizations to volunteer and to communicate with decisionmakers. Community support networks for fire and police link citizens to local elected and administrative officials and involve citizens in solutions to community problems (Katz 1997).

Some organizations emphasize public action and advocacy to solve community problems and acquire needed services. The Center for Community Change and similar groups help local organizations understand how to be effective advocates in their communities, use the policy process to raise issues and gain improvements, and link with national groups to get the technical advice and political training they need to be effective locally. Community building—an approach to developing resident-led institutions—stresses ways in which leaders in distressed neighborhoods can help bring about needed change (Kingsley, McNeely, and Olsen 1997).

At the same time, some groups fear losing valuable financial support from government or private donors when they take a political stand. A spokeswoman for United Way of North Carolina clearly describes the tension: "Our organization lives and breathes on whether locals want to pay dues to us. . . . We like to pride ourselves on being nonpartisan and on being able to bring our more conservative business communities and more liberal service providers together" (*Philanthropy Journal Online* 1996).

Religious Organizations

Churches and religious institutions make up the single largest category of associations to which Americans belong, and many of them are politically active. Eighty-five percent of the population maintain some identification with a religious tradition: 25 percent go to church only for special observances, and 60 percent attend regularly or fairly regularly (Leege and Kellstedt 1993, 3).

Religious organizations build strong social networks that reinforce volunteerism and political expression. An Independent Sector study found that the frequency of attendance at religious services has a major influence on the proportion of respondents who give and volunteer. In the same study, 26 percent of those who donated said they were asked to do so by someone at church. Of those who volunteered, 55 percent said they learned about their volunteer activities at a religious institution (Independent Sector 1994, 8). Religious affiliation also reinforces voting. People who attend church every week are 15 percent more likely to vote in presidential elections (Rosenstone and Hansen 1993, 158). Religious groups are particularly important associations to low-income people and help them gain tools for civic action and political advocacy.

Some religious organizations have particularly strong political traditions. African Americans are substantially more likely than any other group to report exposure to political stimuli at church, where they get more requests for political participation and messages from the pulpit about political matters (Verba, Schlozman, and Brady 1995, 383–4). Additionally, church-based social networks provide opportunities for informal political information sharing and connections. Evangelical groups transfer their networks and experiences to politics. The Christian Coalition generates voting records on a collection of conservative Christian policy issues that help voters with strong religious preferences make decisions at election time. Some religious groups also have a tradition of social justice and social action that brings religious values to the policy process. The Friends Committee on National Legislation, for example, is a nationwide grassroots network of Quakers that brings their values to bear on public policy.

Many churches provide space and resources to nonprofits. The Industrial Areas Foundation, for example, works adeptly within the framework of churches to build its congregation-based community organizations and tap church members' well-honed organizational skills for community action. Moreover, a study about the Campaign for Human Development, the U.S. Catholic bishops' program that funds antipoverty community organizations, found that advocacy was one of the primary ways that "poor empowerment" groups achieved their organizational goals (McCarthy and Castelli 1994).

PHILANTHROPIC ORGANIZATIONS

Foundations, while not permitted to engage directly in political advocacy, have great impact on advocacy and political expression in the nonprofit sector as well as on public opinion. They fund deliberative forums where nonprofit practitioners consider ideas, policy options, and grassroots strategies. They fund public education campaigns and programs for groups that may use direct advocacy to solve common problems. For example, the Neighborhood Funders Group, with its 136 member foundations, links funders with low- and middle-income neighborhood groups. One of the Group's goals is to educate grantmakers about public policy issues affecting community development. The Neighborhood Funders Group also facilitates coalition building and last year enhanced communication between labor and community groups on economic issues and also among policymakers, activists, and funders on participation by low-income people in welfare-to-work efforts.[8]

Foundations are credited with a major role in the conservative ascendancy to national political prominence (Covington 1997). The Bradley Foundation, for example, has funded cable television station National Empowerment Television (NET), which provides programming for such groups as the Christian Coalition, the Eagle Forum, and the National Rifle Association. The Foundation also works to shape values and research in academic institutions, such as the University of Chicago and George Mason University. In addition, it has worked with think tanks, such as the Heritage Foundation, to expand a Town Hall computer network.

Some policy forums subsidized by foundations bring together local nonprofit leaders and activists to consider organizational options. The Minnesota Council of Nonprofits and the Union Institute recently sponsored a conference in conjunction with the Robert Wood Johnson Foundation. Nonprofits from community-oriented arts, social services, neighborhood, and research organizations sent staff and leaders to grapple with how to build civic and political participation in their organizations.

POLICY RESEARCH ORGANIZATIONS

Policy research organizations are a mainstay of Washington, D.C., where they can strongly influence national policy development and decisions.[9] They generate data and reports, sponsor forums on policy issues, and disseminate information through regular publications. They span the political spectrum from avowedly nonpartisan to clearly ideological.

State-based policy think tanks, important in universities and in state capitals, also generate their own data, apply national data to state policymaking, and provide state data and research for national policymaking purposes. In Maine, for example, policy research organizations teamed up with community groups to propose a state-funded education program in the wake of educational benefits cuts from recent changes in the welfare laws.

ISSUE- AND VALUE-BASED ORGANIZATIONS

Common issues and values bring citizens together to form nonprofit groups that pursue organizational goals through political advocacy. A diverse array of 501(c)(4) organizations, sometimes called social welfare organizations or interest groups, engage in advocacy on environmental, taxpayer, arts, legal, health, and many other issues. Some action organizations with large networks and political action committees (PACs) have become prominent and popular political actors. Interest groups may form strong networks on single issues, such as abortion, or on a variety of issues in broader movements, such as the environment. Some have strong, well-organized, and politically active constituencies, such as the elderly.

Many action organizations have been highly successful in articulating interests, framing issues, and bringing new information into the political debate. Their influence stems in part from their ability to attract public support and resources for popular issues otherwise not addressed politically. Some causes have attracted the vast financial resources of the business sector. Taxpayer campaigns, for example, often pursue measures that benefit the bottom line for businesses. Popular causes can be at a severe financial disadvantage if business opposition to their policy proposals or initiatives mounts.

IDENTITY-BASED ORGANIZATIONS

People with common identities often construct organizations and engage in politics for their mutual benefit. Veterans' organizations are a good example of such groups. They are organized as strong vertical networks capable of political advocacy from the community to the national level. At the local level, these groups sponsor parades, services for veterans, and youth clubs, and they connect with community networks of social clubs, service organizations, and mutual benefits associations.

Race, ethnicity, gender, and sexual preferences find common expression in nonprofits, coloring the development of American society and politics. Common identity groups build communities of interest, engage in grassroots activity, register and mobilize voters, pursue legislative and legal reform, and gradually wind their way into the mainstream of American life through social and political activism. Religious and ethnic groups, for example, may have nonprofits that affect policymaking, such as organizations of American Jews and Arabs that contend for favorable U.S. policies in the Middle East.

EDUCATIONAL INSTITUTIONS

Colleges and universities lobby on education issues and funding, but they may also provide forums for exploring research and ideas that shape public policy. Student activism has been at the center of many national debates, including the civil rights movement and the movement against the war in Vietnam.

WORKPLACE ORGANIZATIONS

Workplaces are also important sites for association, organization, and political action. Unions now operate much like interest groups, with the capacity to provide services to members and be an effective political presence for working people on broad economic and social policy issues. The union public policy agenda includes minimum wages, child labor laws, workplace health and safety issues, and trade and family issues such as health care and child care.

Professional associations are strong advocates for their professions and sometimes for public interests. They help to establish professional standards and conduct public and member education on the profession's requirements. Professional associations lobby on issues of concern to their members, which may or may not run counter to public opinion. For example, lawyers lobbied against the popular consumer measure of no-fault insurance, which could reduce both lawyers' fees and individuals' ability to sue. There is a growing trend among working women to shift their activism to professional associations and unions rather than traditional neighborhood and civic groups.[10]

BUSINESS AND TRADE ASSOCIATIONS

From Main Street to Wall Street, trade and business organizations promote an antitax, antiregulatory legislative agenda and are active in electoral politics. Like unions and issue advocacy groups, business and trade nonprofits have substantial funding for their agendas. Approximately 70 percent of all organizations with a presence in Washington, D.C., represent business (Schlozman and Tierney 1986, 67–9). The Chamber of Commerce, the National Association of Manufacturers, and other business councils are well integrated into community affairs and local politics and often face off against labor organizations and advocacy groups on trade and environmental policy and other public issues. Business and trade groups may also confront nonprofits that represent civic concerns about product use.

SPECIALLY REGULATED POLITICAL ORGANIZATIONS

Political parties and PACs occupy a unique position as tax-exempt nonprofits regulated by the Federal Election Commission (FEC). They are organized as nonprofits but are so closely associated with the electoral process that they are popularly viewed as quasi-governmental organizations. In the mid-1970s, party conservatives disillusioned with past Republican practices pulled together disparate forces from interest groups such as veterans, evangelists, pro-life advocates, small business, and tax reformers. They influenced state and local races as well as the nomination of Ronald Reagan and eventually articulated a new conservatism for the Republican Party and the country.

POLITICAL COALITIONS AND NETWORKS

Groups align to strengthen their effectiveness at different levels of local, state, and national decisionmaking. They combine resources (volunteers, money, expertise), share knowledge, and extend their channels of communication to new groups and constituencies. Groups may align on issues, values, interests, or by party affiliation or ideology. Some nonprofits build short-term alliances to accomplish an immediate political objective. Other coalitions, such as the National Council of Churches, last for generations, shaping voter preferences and policy outcomes. Networks and coalitions are particularly important to small groups because they connect their mission to a larger vision, their members to other people, and their resources to additional resources for political influence.

Policy networks and coalitions align groups around specific issues and work on many types of legislation in a policy area, such as taxes or children. In broad networks, one or more dominant groups are often central to the coalition's success. The Children's Defense Fund, for example, influences children's policy through state chapters and local networks of participating organizations and influential individuals.

Some networks and coalitions offer a way for nonprofits to work together with groups that may have otherwise differing goals, such as cross-sector coalitions that include nonprofits, businesses, and individuals. Others serve specific sectors. The National Governors' Association is an example of a nonprofit alliance of government interests; business has its Chamber of Commerce; and the nonprofit sector has its broad coalitions and networks, such as the Alliance for Justice, Independent Sector, and the Let America Speak Coalition, to keep abreast of policy affecting all nonprofits.

Social movements are coalitions and networks on a grander scale and are part of the rich history of activism in the United States. Large twentieth-century movements include the temperance movement, the civil rights movement, the women's movement, the labor movement, and more recently the environmental movement. There are also smaller movements of farmers, students, evangelicals, Native Americans, Latinos, disabled people, elderly people, and gay and lesbian people.

POLITICAL STRATEGIES AND NONPROFIT ADVOCACY

Political engagement produces social change by altering the way public concerns are addressed. Different views about the process of change produce different strategies for the conduct of nonprofits in politics.

In one view, change comes through *power*, or the exercise of influence over competing interests and resources in the political process. Nonprofits are competitive groups in a competitive political process. The stronger the nonprofit's resources, access, and networks of influence in the political process, the more likely it is to be heard and to influence policy outcomes. National policymaking politics are often power politics involving conflicts, with polarized group positions giving way to compromise at various stages of policymaking. Elections are also power politics with winner-take-all rules. Financial resources buy media access and give groups and individuals a chance at public opinion making. "Interested" information is used strategically to promote a particular view, and knowledge is the power to persuade.

In another view, change is evolutionary and learning is a primary route to change. The more information, deliberation, and participation on issues, the better equipped individuals, groups, and governments are to balance self-interest and common interests and thus move toward a policy settlement. In this view, nonprofits provide the "civic space" and information for group deliberation, idea sharing, and self-discovery and awareness.

A variant is that change results from pragmatic, collaborative action. Pragmatic politics creates change through doing. Nonprofits are often partners with government and business in mutual endeavors that stress pragmatic politics. This view emphasizes the identification of mutual goals, strategies to accomplish goals, negotiated program work between interested but sometimes distant parties, learning through doing, and empowerment through cooperation. Groups use combinations of political strategies to move forward organizational goals. In practice, all three processes shape policy and the relationship between government and nonprofits (Callahan et al. 1998).

CURRENT AND PROPOSED REGULATORY POLICY FOR ADVOCACY BY NONPROFITS

Some nonprofit legislative and electoral advocacy is subject to a set of rules and reporting requirements. These rules and guidelines for political action are continually refined as organizations undertake new political practices. Government is particularly interested in controlling and directing the activities of groups that receive tax-deductible gifts and those that receive government funds to ensure that public funds are not used for partisan political purposes and are limited in their use for policy advocacy. This section examines current and proposed advocacy regulations for their impact or potential impact on political advocacy by charitable organizations [501(c)(3)] and social welfare organizations [501(c)(4)].

The rules for participation in the political system are overly complex for many organizations, especially small nonprofits. Nonprofits must decide what is education and what is advocacy, account for advocacy in different ways, and stay abreast of interpretations of the rules, which can be time-consuming and complicated. Indeed, some nonprofits exist primarily to help other nonprofits understand what they can and cannot do when they engage in political action. A recent round of political reform proposals has created additional uncertainty about what is permissible political activity.

Rules alone do not cause or prevent nonprofit advocacy or citizen participation, but they influence most advocacy activities. These rules and regulations can:

- Shape nonprofit access to decisionmakers.
- Spell out the authority and autonomy of nonprofit groups to engage in certain policy decisionmaking activities and in raising and using organizational resources for advocacy.
- Enforce a system of accountability and penalties for certain types of advocacy and for advocacy reporting violations.[11]

In theory, formal rules about the relationship of government and nonprofits in politics should not inhibit citizen association, citizen voice, and nonprofit resource building for political participation. Whether government should restrict advocacy at all is part of a larger public dialogue about balancing the need for democratic participation, democratic rights, and the rationales for regulating political activity of participating nonprofits.

The IRS, the Office of Management and Budget (OMB), and Congress have the authority to regulate nonprofit legislative and electoral advocacy. Other rules promulgated by administrative agencies further define nonprofit access, authority, autonomy, and accountability in government programs, but they are too numerous to review here. Nonprofits may also be regulated at the state level, though those laws are also too extensive to review here. In general, though, state regulation of nonprofit political activity is less stringent.

Ideally, political regulation of nonprofits should strike a balance between the broad protections of speech in the First Amendment and the rationale for regulation. Courts have generally construed limitations on nonprofit advocacy narrowly so as not to interfere with political speech. Restrictions can generate many interpretations, however, and for public benefit or charitable organizations subject to the strictest advocacy limitations, the devil is in the details. One foundation manager recommends that nonprofits get legal advice on tax law and political law before embarking on a highly visible political advocacy campaign. Nonprofits must choose among different types of advice: "There are three ways to ask about [how the law may affect nonprofit action on] potential policy initiatives: (1) We want to be totally protected, so tell us what we can do to achieve that. That will elicit the most conservative opinion. (2) Tell us what is possible but would not put us out there on the end of the limb. That will get a middle-of-the-road opinion. (3) How far can we push the envelope? That will result in the most liberal opinion" (Yates 1997).

IRS Regulations on Advocacy

The IRS regulates some aspects of legislative and electoral advocacy for all tax-exempt, nonprofit organizations. The most complex rules for legislative advocacy apply to charitable organizations, but all tax-exempt groups have stringent restrictions on electoral advocacy (Hopkins 1992). Chart 9.1 summarizes the regulations on 501(c)(3) and 501(c)(4) organizations.

ADVOCACY BY 501(c)(3) ORGANIZATIONS

The IRS limits advocacy for 501(c)(3) charitable, religious, scientific, educational, and literary organizations, also called "public benefit organizations" or "public charities." In practice, 501(c)(3) organizations cannot spend more than about 20 percent of tax-exempt contributions for advocacy activities.[12] The limitation is designed to prevent them from carrying on propaganda or influencing legislation as a *substantial* part of their activities.[13] Most 501(c)(3) organizations are small, with few resources for political action. According to the National Center for Charitable Statistics, there were approximately 654,000 501(c)(3) groups in 1996; more than half (400,000) had gross receipts of less than $25,000 (IRS 1996).

Some view the deductibility of donations as a tax subsidy to 501(c)(3) nonprofits, arguing that the government forgoes substantial revenues that it would otherwise have collected as tax on personal income.[14] Under that reasoning, the Supreme Court has ruled that free speech does not mean subsidized speech and upheld the advocacy limits for 501(c)(3) organizations (*Regan v. Taxation with Representation of Washington*, 462 US 540 (1983)). Some tax advocacy groups

Chart 9.1 RESTRICTIONS GOVERNING LOBBYING AND POLITICAL ACTIVITIES

Description	501(c)(3) Charitable Organizations	501(c)(4) Social Welfare Organizations
Key tax rules	May receive deductible contributions. No federal gift tax on contributions.	Tax-exempt but contributors do not receive deduction. Donor may owe federal gift tax on contributions over $10,000. Organizations taxed on investment income to the extent of electioneering expenditures.
General permitted activities	Charitable and educational activities, including public education, lobbying (for public charities).	May engage in any activity permitted a 501(c)(3) organization, plus any activity that serves public purposes, such as lobbying and advocacy in the public interest.
Is lobbying allowed?	Public charities: Yes, to a limited extent—subject either to 501(h) limits or to requirement that it not be "substantial." Private foundations: No lobbying allowed.	Yes, lobbying may even be the organization's exclusive activity.
Is an affiliated PAC allowed?	No (but affiliated 501(c)(4) may have PAC).	Yes.
What campaign-related activities are allowed?	Nonpartisan voter registration, voter education, and get-out-the-vote efforts. Campaign intervention is strictly prohibited.	May engage in nonpartisan activities permitted 501(c)(3)s. May engage in electioneering as long as it is not the organization's primary activity and is not (except "MCFL") express advocacy.*
Is express advocacy allowed?	No.	Election laws prohibit express advocacy unless organization qualifies as an MCFL corporation.
What issue advocacy activities are allowed?	A wide range of "issue advocacy" activities, including educational and lobbying activities. Tax laws limit issue advocacy that promotes or criticizes particular candidates, and they prohibit electioneering.	Neither election laws nor tax laws limit issue advocacy.
What disclosure is required?	No requirement to disclose their donors to the public.	Most are not required to disclose their donors to the public. MCFL corporations making express advocacy independent expenditures must register and file regular, publicly available reports with the FEC.

Source: Adapted from Elizabeth Sellers and Janne Gallagher, Caplin & Drysdale Chartered, Washington, D.C.

*A special exemption for partisan or express advocacy by a 501(c)(4) group was established in *FEC v. Massachusetts Citizens for Life, Inc.*, 479 US 238 (1986) (MCFL), allowing nonprofits promoting political ideas to engage in independent expenditures for or against a candidate.

have asked whether granting a tax exemption to all nonprofits also subsidizes political speech. Some groups would prefer to tax a broader number of activities in all types of nonprofits and further restrain permissible political activity.

Beyond the desirability for unfettered speech, there are several other rationales for allowing 501(c)(3)s to engage fully in political affairs as an exempt activity. "The deductibility of charitable gifts can also be rationalized as a recognition that money that is given away for charitable purposes should not be considered part of a taxpayer's income base because that money is not available to be spent for his or her private benefit. This rationale has the added benefit of validating charities' independence from government, while the subsidy theory makes these institutions ultimately subordinate as recipients of government largesse" (Rees 1998, 10).

Another rationale derives from American democratic pluralistic traditions that promote the engagement of many political groups in the policy process. In this framework, the tax deduction provides an incentive for individuals to distribute their resources without government interference to groups that can publicly air social concerns.

ADVOCACY FOR OTHER NONPROFIT ORGANIZATIONS

All other categories of tax-exempt groups can lobby without IRS restriction. Social welfare organizations (consumer, taxpayer, environmental, senior, civic, and other issue lobbies), veterans' organizations, labor organizations, business and professional groups, social clubs, and fraternal organizations can all engage in unrestricted legislative advocacy. They may also engage in limited partisan political activity with the public as long as it is not a substantial part of their group's activity. Communication with members on partisan concerns, such as candidate ratings and endorsements, is permissible. They may form and to some extent administer the activities of an affiliated PAC through which they may engage in a wide range of partisan action.

Charitable and social welfare organizations may formally affiliate, or they may work in loose networks and coalitions. A 501(c)(3) organization can establish an affiliate 501(c)(4) organization to engage in substantial lobbying and political activities that are not partisan. The IRS is concerned about the potential for commingling of lobbying and nonlobbying funds and thus requires strict accounting for funds and transfers between organizations.

OMB Regulations on Advocacy

Circulars issued by the OMB are binding restrictions on federal executive agencies. Agencies, in turn, regulate grant and contract arrangements. Circular A-122, "Cost Principles for Nonprofit Organizations—Lobbying Rules," last revised in 1984, strictly prohibits the use of federal funds for lobbying.

The primary purpose of the rules is to establish governmentwide principles so that nonprofit grantees do not use appropriated federal funds for lobbying. The OMB restrictions prohibit federal, state, or local electioneering with federal funds. Direct lobbying at the federal level of government, executive branch lobbying, grassroots lobbying, and legislative liaison activities in support of unallowable lobbying activities are also prohibited. Current OMB restrictions do not include lobbying at the local level of government, technical presentations upon the request of government for information, contacts with executive branch other than lobbying, or lobbying on regulatory actions.

Congressional Legislation on Advocacy

Administrative Procedure Act (APA)

This 1946 act is the basic congressional framework for rule making, though more recent statutes have altered some of its processes. Congress directs agency decisionmaking through administrative procedures and program legislation, and it can monitor agency performance. Congress can also use the appropriations process for rule making. Moreover, it has the authority to approve presidential appointees to agencies, to investigate, to provide oversight, and to use the legislative veto. It is through this authority that Representative Ernest Istook (R–Okla.) and other representatives have sought to establish additional separate guidelines for legislative and electoral advocacy, some of them inconsistent with guidelines by the IRS and the Federal Election Commission (FEC).

Lobbying Disclosure Act

Congress passed a lobbying disclosure law in 1995 to correct previously ineffectual reporting standards that resulted in few lobbyists actually registering. Now groups with more than $20,000 in lobbying expenditures in six months and a staff member spending 20 percent of his or her time on lobbying must register with the Secretary of the Senate and the Clerk of the House. Groups must register if they are making lobbying contacts or efforts in support of lobbying activities, such as research and policy preparation. Grassroots lobbying, such as volunteer contacts with legislators on specific legislation, is not reportable, an omission that some groups consider to be a loophole in the law.

Nonprofits must file detailed semiannual reports on specific issues, bills, agencies contacted, names of employees of the organization who made contacts, and an estimate of total expenses. The Simpson-Craig amendment to this legislation barred 501(c)(4) organizations that lobby from receiving federal grants, but these organizations may form an affiliate 501(c)(3) organization to carry on their charitable activities.

FEC RULES

Congress passed the current federal election laws in the 1971 and 1974 Federal Election Campaign Act (FECA). The intent was to cover all money spent for campaigns and for the influence of federal elections, though in practice this has been very difficult to achieve. An early Supreme Court ruling, *Buckley v. Valeo*, in 1976 gave Congress broad scope to regulate partisan contributions to prevent corruption, but the Court narrowly and clearly defined campaign activity to avoid discouraging political speech. This case established the standard for express advocacy as support for or against a candidate. It also established that individuals and political committees could spend unlimited amounts of their own money on an independent basis (that is, not coordinated with a campaign). This limited the FEC's regulatory reach and opened the way for many other forms of political spending beyond the campaign laws, including the practice of independent expenditures and issue advocacy.

Issue Advocacy and Voting Records

Two areas of political activity, issue advocacy and voting records, often fall into gray areas of regulatory action. The IRS and the FEC may differ on whether issue advocacy is public education, legislative advocacy, or express advocacy, and when and how it is regulated. Some issue advocacy refers to political speech or political messages that do not expressly advocate the election or defeat of a federal candidate, and is most often funded through soft money expenditures.[15] It is political education with persuasive voter information. Television advertising aired near election time is the most controversial issue advocacy. A public education advertisement can mention a candidate in conjunction with a vote or some other action, but it cannot urge the election or defeat of the candidate.

Other issue advocacy simply urges the support or defeat of a legislative proposal or policy on a ballot initiative and is thus legislative advocacy. Issue advocacy is considered educational activity when it is designed to provide information to voters and the public about issues; in that case it is not subject to regulation. Messages delivered in conjunction with an election or that mention a candidate's name, though constructed to fall outside the scope of regulation, attract the attention of the IRS and the FEC as potential violations.

Issue advocacy has raised concerns about political practices by nonprofits. A report by the Annenberg Public Policy Center estimates that organizations and political parties spent between $135 million and $150 million on issue ads during the 1995–1996 election cycle (*Responsive Philanthropy* 1998). Party committees transferred funds to 501(c)(4) organizations in 1996, which then used the funds for issue advocacy in the 1996 elections. Americans for Tax Reform came under fire for its $4.6 million donation from the Republican National Committee for Medicare issue advocacy by mail. President Clinton created a firestorm of protest when he credited soft money contributions with influencing the 1996 vote.

The IRS regulations include advocacy activities that "suggest" how people should vote. The IRS standard comes into play most frequently when evaluating nonprofit descriptions of legislative voting records for potential partisanship. If a description of how a legislator voted on key abortion legislation, for example, then stated the organization's views and directed the reader to vote pro-life, it would probably not be permitted by the IRS. To the FEC, this example would be issue advocacy rather than express advocacy or electioneering, and thus fall outside the scope of FEC regulation.

PROPOSED REFORMS OF LEGISLATIVE AND ELECTORAL ADVOCACY

The pace of advocacy reform proposals increased after 1994, when conservatives built new majorities in Congress, and they have subsequently materialized at all levels of government. Some fear what they consider the substantial potential impact of these reforms on political participation in democratic governance. Others view the rules as necessary to deter the "buying" of elections or simply to ensure that federal tax dollars go to purposes for which they were intended. Charitable organizations, politically active public interest groups, and labor organizations have been most directly affected by and the most active opponents of proposed reforms.

Some reforms are part of a broader call to end tax subsidization of political activity and aim to limit how nonprofits can use privately raised funds. The most prominent legislation, known as "the Istook amendment," was first introduced in December 1995. This amendment sought wider restrictions on advocacy by charitable groups that receive federal grant monies. The thrust of the bill has entered the legislative mainstream and has been attached in varying forms to many different pieces of legislation but has not been passed.

Nonprofits have strengthened existing alliances and formed new ones in networks such as the Alliance for Justice, OMB Watch, and the Let America Speak Coalition to communicate and coalesce on regulatory issues. As a result, nonprofits have become better informed and better able to respond to regulatory changes affecting advocacy. State councils of nonprofit organizations have been important coalitions for tracking state-level regulatory change.

Most 501(c)(3) organizations are politically active only when their organizational mission requires them to be. Social service groups, for example, were an organized voice on national welfare reform and are now active at the state and local levels in new programs. Since they are heavily dependent on government contracts, however, their visibility on political issues may negatively affect future funding in a political environment where service provisioning, but not political action, is acceptable. Even if Istook-type amendments continue to languish, their language sends a strong message to service providers.

Other areas where reforms are being considered include issue advocacy or the practice of running strongly worded television ads or promoting legislative positions in conjunction with an election; voter registration and other grassroots activities through political party expenditures; the use of nonprofits by candidates and elected officials for political purposes; and taxation of nonprofits and political activities.

The Istook Approach: Increased Advocacy Limits on Federal Grantees

Legislation sponsored by Congressmen Istook, David McIntosh (R–Ind.), and Robert Ehrlich (R–Md.) has sought to curtail advocacy by nonprofit groups receiving federal grants. Nonprofits were only about 6 percent of federal grantees in 1995 when these legislative reforms first appeared. The reforms created new definitions for advocacy, different from the current IRS definition on direct advocacy and grassroots lobbying (described in the previous section), and required separate nonprofit reporting to comply with additional regulations.

The original Istook amendment to the Labor, Health and Human Services Appropriations Bill for fiscal year 1996 was titled "Limitations on Taxpayer Subsidized Political Activity." The sponsor claimed to be ending welfare for lobbyists. Supporters of the bill argued that groups receiving federal grants are able to devise ways to devote money to advocacy that would otherwise be used for services. These advocacy reformers harken back to legal services organizations and their use of federal funding to build the institutional infrastructure for legal advocacy claims (West 1981).

The amendment cast a wide regulatory net across the range of political advocacy activities, prompting opponents to label it a "gag rule."[16] The amendment has resurfaced frequently with various modifications and has also generated interest in similar reforms at the state level. The 1998 session of the Georgia legislature considered a provision that would have barred nonprofits that receive any state funds from lobbying, even with private funds.

What do these bills have in common? Each would limit the amount of privately raised funds that can be used by federal grantees for advocacy purposes, each expanded the definition of advocacy so as to regulate more activities, and each set forth new reporting and paperwork requirements for charities. A picture emerges of regulatory action that is designed to virtually end all nonprofit advocacy practiced by organizations that receive federal funds. The proposals would do this by extending the scope of regulated activities, extending regulation across government institutions from the national to the local level, limiting communication and cooperation among groups, increasing administrative requirements by tightening disclosure and reporting, and disallowing grants to groups that lobby.

Overall, the measures try to separate nonprofit service delivery from nonprofit political representation. The legislation assumes that a nonprofit service organization devoid of an independent capacity to influence policy development would best use a grant for the intended purposes. Should such legislation be passed at the national or state level, it would alter the long-standing relationship of government and nonprofits in the development of public policy.

The many examples of nonprofit advocacy in this chapter demonstrate that civic and political life are interwoven at the local level, where there is often no clear distinction between executive and legislative authority. Partnership with local officials is necessary to the success of government programs. Opponents of Istook-type changes claim that such regulation could impede communication, especially if groups withdraw from contact with government for fear of violating the law. Advocacy at the local level is very difficult to isolate and prohibit; for that reason it is not regulated under the existing OMB regulations.

Proposed restrictions on coalitions could hurt citizens and groups—particularly small nonprofits—that are interested in information sharing and joint political action. One of the most important aspects of nonprofit political engagement is that it can monitor and present findings to government and the public. Some observers contend that public policy is likely to be less effective if it is not rooted in the practical knowledge and experience of nonprofits in local programs. Nonprofits, close to people in their communities and work, offer a way for citizens to become connected. Government should not create the perception that political participation may jeopardize an organization's tax status, nor should government restrict legitimate nonprofit activity to volunteerism or service.

Prior Permission Proposals

Proposals that would require various nonprofit members or donors to approve dues or contributions used for political activity are being considered at the national and state levels of government. Nonprofits currently direct their financial resources toward organizational goals determined by officers or representatives. These proposals would shift the responsibility for such decisions from the nonprofit to the individual donors or members.

Recasting the relationship between members or contributors and nonprofits may offer individuals more choice, but it could potentially fragment political consensus in organizations, limit scarce political resources, and weaken common political action. Supporters of prior permission proposals are concerned that dues and donations to groups are too often dispersed without members' regular consent and knowledge of the extent of the organization's political activity. These legislators are particularly concerned that union contracts with payroll deductions grant too much authority to unions and too little to individual discretion.[17]

The 1998 campaign finance reform legislation, H.R. 3485, included a provision that required nonprofits to receive members' permission annually before engaging in political activity.[18] Nonprofits would have been required to send members an annual notice indicating what political activities they were planning and estimating spending on political activities in the forthcoming year. Members could then voice their approval or disapproval for using their dues or contributions for such activity. All tax-exempt groups were to be covered, and the FEC, not the IRS, was to enforce the new regulation.

Opponents of the measure believe the law could weaken nonprofits' ability to speak out collectively on public policy matters and could reduce organizational resources if the contribution process is made more complex. They note that politically active organizations already make their activities public through reporting and through visible public action. In addition, donors and union members already have the right to withdraw their support from organizations, and for 10 years unions have offered members the option of separating and suspending the portion of their dues used for political purposes. Opponents fear the changes may also make organizations more averse to political risk-taking and tame the voices of citizens active in those organizations most affected by the change.

California voters defeated a reform proposition, California 226, on a June 2, 1998, ballot initiative that would have required employees' express permission for payroll deductions for political purposes.[19] Labor organizations were the primary target of Proposition 226, but other nonprofits would have been affected because the initiative would have affected such payroll deductions as charitable contributions.[20] The practical impact of the measure would have been to limit or stop nonprofit involvement in policy debates over ballot initiatives, which is permitted by the IRS.

Campaign Finance Reforms

The 1970s campaign finance reforms were intended to reduce the role of money in politics, but the practice of politics has overwhelmed the original objective of the law.[21] There may be a public consensus to reform campaign practices, but there is no clear political consensus on how to do it.[22] Questions under consideration by the FEC, the IRS, nonprofits, and the public include: Is a group's activity public education or electioneering? When does a group's advocacy activity constitute a tax subsidy for political speech, if ever? What is the extent of the subsidy for 501(c)(3)s and 501(c)(4)s doing advocacy, lobbying, and electoral activity, if any? When is it appropriate, if ever, for party committees to use soft money to fund 501(c)(3)s for voter registration? Can guidelines be established to prevent politicians from steering campaign support money to nonprofits? Can business PACs steer money to nonprofits as a circuitous route to accomplish their political goals? There is no nonprofit consensus about the best policy option for campaign reform. Groups are divided among proposals that seek to reform a particular problem or package of problems and those aimed at changing the whole system of campaign financing.

SUMMARY

Finding ways to protect and enhance nonprofit advocacy and citizens' participation is a necessary nonprofit activity and is central to an open, participatory democracy. Government, though concerned with the need to ensure that nonprofit tax policy is properly structured, must not inhibit society's democratic, participatory institutions. Disincentives embedded in the rules and regulations that govern nonprofit political action may deprive people of opportunities to work in common through nonprofits to influence basic public decisions about their communities.

Current regulations present conflicting terms and guidelines for action. Large nonprofits have found effective ways to use their resources for political action and to cope with the organizational rigors of engaging in advocacy, but small nonprofits are likely to be overwhelmed by the complexity of current regulations and thus not participate. Rationalization and restructuring of the nonprofit sector are occurring as tax law, campaign law, and nonprofit practice are slowly sorted out, managed, and revised. What will form the basis of future decisions about political advocacy practices, taxation, and citizen participation in nonprofits? How will those decisions affect democratic practice? How will changes in laws regulating nonprofit advocacy affect political expression and nonprofit capacity to act politically to accomplish organizational goals?

Craig Jenkins (1987) concluded an article on nonprofit policy advocacy 10 years ago with a forecast: "The best hope for political advocacy would appear to be a broad popular upsurge in political participation." He and others believe that nonprofit influence on public policy results from the popular support nonprofits mobilize and the alliances they make with each other and with political decision-makers. He reasoned that the best "public interest" bargain nonprofits can make in a political system where groups compete for political influence is one where a broad range of interests from civil society are represented through political participation and policy advocacy.

Some political analysts today diagnosing the "crisis in democracy" point to the decline of associational activity within civil society and question the health of civil society itself. They call for a campaign of civic renewal led by nonprofits to restore voter participation and volunteerism in the associations of civic life. Robert Putnam (1995, 65–8) elevated the discussion when he suggested that the norms and networks of trust and reciprocity derived from the "art of association" are necessary to the development of an engaged civic community and are perhaps declining. Other analysts, such as Sidney Verba, point to the high levels of association in the United States and the fact that people who associate with one another in many kinds of nonprofits are more likely to have the skills, resources, and motivations for political engagement.

Nonprofit organizations are central to the success of civic and political participation and renewal. Few public policy choices are more crucial to a vibrant democracy than those that enable nonprofits to engage in advocacy, sustain citizens' interest and participation in public life, and provide opportunities for citizens to shape government and society.

Notes

Thanks to Dan Oran, Rachel Mosher-Williams, Elizabeth Boris, and Eugene Steuerle for their editorial help. Thanks also to Janne Gallagher and Tom Harvey for their public comments on the working draft at the June 1998 Conference on Nonprofits and Government.

1. Advocacy in practice spans a wide range of organizational activities, only some of which are subject to regulation. See Elizabeth Boris and Rachel Mosher-Williams, "Nonprofit Advocacy Organizations: Assessing the Definitions, Classifications, and Data," a paper presented to ARNOVA 26th Annual Conference, Dec. 4–6, 1997, about advocacy in 501(c)(3) and (4) groups.

2. This chapter is based on a more extensive working paper on politically active organizations in the nonprofit sector. "Nonprofit Advocacy and Political Participation," November 1998, by Elizabeth Reid, is available through the Urban Institute, Center on Nonprofits and Philanthropy, 2100 M Street, N.W., Washington, D.C. 20037.

3. *Taxpayer subsidization* of nonprofits is often politically charged terminology. But the idea behind the popular slogan has gained some currency among economists and tax lawyers who question the tax deduction and tax exemption for nonprofits that engage in political activity. See Evelyn Brody and Joseph Cordes, "The Tax Treatment of Nonprofit Organizations," in this volume for a fuller discussion of the issue.

4. For some causes of that distrust, see Eugene Steuerle, Edward Gramlich, Hugh Heclo, and Demetra Smith Nightingale, 1998, *The Government We Deserve*, Washington, D.C.: The Urban Institute Press.

5. See Rees (1998) for a full discussion of characteristics of nonprofits that the U.S. Congress identified as effective advocates on six different policy issues.

6. Nonprofit "program advocacy" is terminology used in two ways. As used here, it can describe attempts to influence government programs or administrative agencies. A second common usage refers to ways nonprofits carry out their organizational missions by promoting the importance of their programs to the public. Both are influential activities, but not regulated. The first is considered essential to the working partnership

of government and nonprofits in delivery of government services, particularly at the local level of government. The second is ongoing nonprofit public education activity.

7. Most neighborhood groups are 501(c)(3) or 501(c)(4) organizations. However, many community organizations are informal organizations or formally organized groups with under $25,000 in gross receipts and are not required to file with the IRS.

8. For an analysis of how philanthropy became a social force in the United States from 1953 to 1990, see Jenkins, Craig J., and Abigail Halcli, 1996, draft paper presented to NYU Conference on Philanthropic Foundations in History, November. See also Covington, Sally, 1997, *Moving a Public Policy Agenda: The Strategic Philanthropy of Conservative Foundations*. National Committee for Responsive Philanthropy, Washington, D.C.

9. For a comparison of different kinds of research organizations in Washington, D.C., see Rich, Andrew, and R. Kent Weaver, 1998, "Advocates and Analysts: Think Tanks and the Politicization of Expertise" in *Interest Group Politics*, 1998, Fifth Edition, Allan J. Cigler and Burdett A. Loomis, editors. Washington, D.C.: Congressional Quarterly, pp. 235–53.

10. For more on this topic, see Skocpol, Theda, 1997, "Building Community Top Down or Bottom Up." *Brookings Review*, Fall; and Waldman, Amy, 1997, "Labor's New Face: Women Renegotiate Their Role," *Nation* 265 (8):11–16.

11. No group seems to be immune from investigation about political activity, now that the exposure of campaign violations has become a political battleground. Twenty-six nonprofit advocacy groups were subpoenaed in 1997 for their role in political influence and election violations, though the investigating committee dissolved without action. House Speaker Newt Gingrich was investigated for his political activities in conjunction with a charitable, educational organization. Issue advertising in the 1996 elections erupted into an organizational war between conservative and progressive nonprofits.

12. According to the 1990 IRS rules, groups can "elect" to use a simplified accounting method (501(h)) that allows expenditures of 20 percent on lobbying if the nonprofit's budget is under $500,000, 15 percent of the next $500,000, 10 percent of the third $500,000, and 5 percent of the remainder. Or, groups may use an alternate method based on the old law that says lobbying cannot be a substantial part of the organization's work, though this accounting method is most advantageous to very large groups. This option is not available to religious organizations. They follow a slightly different set of alternative accounting guidelines known as the "insubstantial" test. The organization Charity Lobbying in the Public Interest, 2040 S Street, N.W., Washington, DC 20009, provides more information on the 1976 501(h) reforms and the groups that elect 501(h).

13. The term "substantial" is used to qualify many activities associated with nonprofit advocacy, and it varies by usage and context. Substantial public support qualifies a definition of charity; substantial advocacy qualifies the amount of advocacy permissible for a charitable organization to retain its charitable tax status; substantial partisanship qualifies the amount of partisan activity permissible for groups to retain their tax exemption; and substantial revenues refers to the amount of revenue lost by the government by extending a subsidy.

14. For more information on levels of charitable giving and who is taking the tax deduction, see "Profiles of Individual Charitable Contributions by State," 1998, Center on Nonprofits and Philanthropy, Urban Institute, Washington, D.C.

15. *Soft money* refers to unregulated expenditures by political parties and organizations in conjunction with elections.

16. For a full accounting of the provisions of each version of Istook and the impact on nonprofits, see "Handcuffing America's Charities," Let America Speak Coalition, November 1995.

17. *CWA v. Beck*, 487 US 735 (1988), established limits on political use of dues from non-union employees and gave dues-paying union employees the right to request and receive a refund for the portion of their dues spent on political activities.

18. Political activity is defined as activities to influence elections, federal legislation, federal regulations, or education of individuals about candidates for federal office or about federal legislation, law, or regulations. Membership is not defined.

19. "Political purposes" are defined as attempting to influence voters in support of or opposition to a candidate or ballot initiative at the state or local level.

20. See Gallagher, Janne, and Robert Boisture memorandum "Impact of California Proposition 226 on Payroll Deductions for Charitable Purposes." Caplin and Drysdale, Washington, D.C.

21. Current federal election campaign provisions can be found in The Federal Election Campaign Act of 1971 and the Federal Election Campaign Act Amendments of 1974, 1976, and 1979.

22. See Corrado, Anthony, Thomas E. Mann, Daniel R. Ortiz, Trevor Potter, and Frank J. Sorauf, 1997, *Campaign Finance Reform: A Sourcebook*, Washington D.C.: The Brookings Institution for a thorough discussion of issues in campaign finance reform.

References

Berry, Jeffery, Kent Portney, and Ken Thomson. 1993. *The Rebirth of Urban Democracy*. Washington, D.C.: Brookings Institution.

Boris, Elizabeth. 1998. "Trust, Service, and the Common Purpose: Philanthropy and the Nonprofit Sector in a Changing America." In *Final Report of the 93rd American Assembly*, April 23–26.

Boris, Elizabeth, and Rachel Mosher-Williams. 1997. "Nonprofit Advocacy Organizations: Assessing the Definitions, Classifications, and Data." A paper presented to ARNOVA 26th Annual Conference, Dec. 4–6.

Callahan, Steve, Neil Mayer, Kris Palmer, and Larry Ferlazzo. 1998. "Rowing the Boat with Two Oars." *NFG Reports*, Fall.

Center for Community Change. 1996. "How and Why to Influence Public Policy." Issue 17, Winter.

Corrado, Anthony, Thomas E. Mann, Daniel R. Ortiz, Trevor Potter, and Frank J. Sorauf. 1997. *Campaign Finance Reform: A Sourcebook*. Washington, D.C.: The Brookings Institution.

Covington, Sally. 1997. *Moving a Public Policy Agenda: The Strategic Philanthropy of Conservative Foundations*. Washington, D.C.: National Committee for Responsive Philanthropy.

Gallagher, Janne, and Robert Boisture. "Impact of California Proposition 226 on Payroll Deductions for Charitable Purposes." Memorandum. Washington, D.C.: Caplin and Drysdale, Chartered.

Hopkins, Bruce. 1992. *Charity, Advocacy and the Law*. New York: John Wiley and Sons, Inc.

Hrebenar, Ronald J. 1997. *Interest Group Politics in America*, 3rd Edition. New York: ME Sharpe.

Independent Sector. 1994. *Giving and Volunteering in the United States*, Volume I. Washington, D.C.: Independent Sector.

Internal Revenue Service. 1996. Return Transaction File.

Jenkins, Craig. 1987. "Nonprofit Organizations and Policy Advocacy." In *The Nonprofit Sector: A Research Handbook*, edited by Walter W. Powell. New Haven: Yale University Press.

Jenkins, Craig J., and Abigail Halcli. 1996. "Grassrooting the System? The Development of Social Movement Philanthropy, 1953–1990." Draft paper presented to NYU Conference on Philanthropic Foundations in History, November 1996.

Katz, Bruce. 1997. "Give Community Institutions a Fighting Chance." *Brookings Review*, Fall.

Kingsley, Tom, Joseph McNeely, and James Olsen. 1997. *Community Building, Coming of Age*. Washington, D.C.: Development Training Institute and Urban Institute.

Leege, David C., and Lyman A. Kellstedt. 1993. *Rediscovering the Religious Factor in American Politics*. New York: ME Sharpe, Inc.

Let America Speak Coalition. 1995. "Handcuffing America's Charities." Washington, D.C., November.

McCarthy, John D., and Jim Castelli. 1994. *Working for Justice: The Campaign for Human Development and Poor Empowerment Groups*. Washington, D.C.: Life Cycle Institute, The Catholic University of America.

———. 1998. "The Necessity of Studying Organizational Advocacy Comparatively." Paper presented at the Institute for the Study of Government and the Nonprofit Sector Symposium on Nonprofits and Government. Indianapolis, Ind., May 30.

Minkoff, Deborah. 1998. "Organizational Barriers to Advocacy." Paper for Aspen Institute Nonprofit Strategy Group on Advocacy, November.

Philanthropy Journal Online. 1996. "State Nonprofits Intensify Political Lobbying Activity." September 1.

Putnam, Robert. 1995. "Bowling Alone: America's Declining Social Capital." *Journal of Democracy* 6, January.

Rees, Susan. 1998. "Effective Nonprofit Advocacy." Washington, D.C.: Aspen Institute.

Responsive Philanthropy. 1998. "Will Closing a Campaign Finance Loophole Strangle Nonprofit Issue Advocacy?" Winter/Spring.

Rich, Andrew, and R. Kent Weaver. 1998. "Advocates and Analysts: Think Tanks and the Politicization of Expertise." In *Interest Group Politics*, Fifth Edition, edited by Allan J. Cigler and Burdett A. Loomis. Washington D.C.: Congressional Quarterly.

Rosenstone, Steven J., and John Mark Hansen. 1993. *Mobilization, Participation and Democracy in America*. New York: Macmillan.

Salamon, Lester M. 1995. "Explaining Nonprofit Advocacy: An Exploratory Analysis." Draft paper prepared for delivery at the Independent Sector Spring Research Forum.

Schlozman, Kay Lehman, and John Tierney. 1986. *Organized Interests and American Democracy*. New York: Harper and Row.

Skocpol, Theda. 1997. "Building Community Top Down or Bottom Up." *Brookings Review*, Fall.

Steuerle, Eugene, Edward Gramlich, Hugh Heclo, and Demetra Smith Nightingale. 1998. *The Government We Deserve*. Washington, D.C.: The Urban Institute Press.

The Pew Research Center for the People and the Press. 1997. "Trust and Citizen Engagement in Metropolitan Philadelphia: A Case Study."

Verba, Sidney, Kay Lehman Schlozman, and Henry Brady. 1995. *Voice and Equality: Civic Voluntarism in American Politics*. Cambridge, Mass.: Harvard University Press.

———. 1997. "The Big Tilt: Participatory Inequality in America." *The American Prospect*, May–June.

Waldman, Amy. 1997. "Labor's New Face: Women Renegotiate Their Role." *Nation*. 265 (8): 11–16.

West, Giuda. 1981. *The National Welfare Rights Movement*. New York: Praeger.

Wilson, James Q. 1973. *Political Organizations*. New York: Basic Books.

Yates, Gary. 1997. "Public Policy: Activities of a Health Foundation." *Grantscene*, Spring.

Zald, Mayer, and John D. McCarthy. 1987. *Social Movements in an Organizational Society*. New Brunswick, N.J.: Transaction Books.

INTERNATIONAL DIMENSIONS

Chapter Ten

GOVERNMENT-NONPROFIT RELATIONS IN INTERNATIONAL PERSPECTIVE

Lester M. Salamon

INTRODUCTION

The recent debate in the United States over the appropriate roles of government and private, voluntary institutions in coping with public problems is hardly taking place in a vacuum. To the contrary, similar issues are also being debated in other parts of the world as questions have arisen about the capability of government on its own to cope with the social welfare, developmental, and other challenges of our time.

Unfortunately, solid information about the actual role that nonprofit organizations play, and about the relationships that exist between those organizations and the state, has been even more limited abroad than it has been in the United States. This has given rise to a variety of misconceptions—some of them ideologically inspired—about the real relationships that exist abroad and about their implications for the American scene. Under these circumstances, a careful examination of experience in other countries can usefully inform the American debate, clarifying options that may have been prematurely closed and deepening understanding about the best way to structure our own government-nonprofit ties.

It is the purpose of this chapter to provide such an examination. To do so, the discussion falls into five major parts. First, we take up the basic concepts that seem to frame American understanding of the relationship between government and the nonprofit sector, both in our own country and abroad, and the expectations this creates about overseas experience. Against this backdrop, we next examine the actual realities of overseas experience, focusing particularly on the overall scale of nonprofit activity abroad and the extent of government financial support for it. Third, we turn our attention to the causes of what turns out to be a widespread, and growing, pattern of government-nonprofit cooperation abroad and the varying forms that this cooperation takes. Fourth, we explore the risks posed by this pattern of cooperation and the factors that determine the extent to which these risks have actually been borne out. Finally, a concluding section outlines some of the implications that the chapter's findings hold for government-nonprofit relations in the United States.

Clearly, it is impossible in a single chapter to cover such a broad topic comprehensively. Even if space considerations alone did not impose serious constraints, the general lack of knowledge in the area would restrict the discussion anyway. Solid empirical data on the scope of the nonprofit sector and the extent of public support for it has become available only very recently and is still available only for a limited number of countries, most of them in the more developed north (Salamon and Anheier 1996; Salamon and Anheier 1998b).[1] While some information is available on the developing countries, it is more uneven and impressionistic (Anheier and Salamon 1998; Civicus 1994; Fisher 1993). More limited still is empirical data on the extent of government support to nonprofit organizations and on the *consequences* of such support. While anecdotes and horror stories abound, few systematic objective analyses have been done, making it difficult to reach verifiable conclusions (Kramer et al. 1993, 179). The great diversity of international experience in this field makes it even more difficult to support general observations across countries and fields. Furthermore, patterns change over time, so that what may be true in one country in one field at a point in time may change dramatically in a later period. Even when we focus, as we do here, on the fiscal dimensions of the interaction between nonprofit organizations and the state, therefore, serious analytical and interpretive problems remain.

Despite these difficulties, some tentative conclusions do seem possible. First, it seems clear from the available evidence that the nonprofit sector is a far more substantial presence abroad than most Americans seem to recognize and than prevailing theories would lead us to expect. Second, far from inhibiting the growth of the nonprofit sector, the expansion of the state seems more likely to encourage it. At the very least, government-nonprofit cooperation turns out to be widespread internationally and to be a major factor explaining the sector's scale and growth. Finally, despite the risks it poses, government-nonprofit cooperation appears to offer a variety of advantages as well, and the benefits seem generally to outweigh the costs. Let us examine the evidence that leads to these tentative conclusions.

THE PARADIGM OF CONFLICT: THE AMERICAN
CONCEPTION OF GOVERNMENT-NONPROFIT RELATIONS

A useful starting point is the conception of government-nonprofit interaction that seems to dominate American thinking on this topic. That conception took shape through more than a century of political conflict over the relative roles of government and nonprofit institutions in responding to social and economic needs in the latter nineteenth and early twentieth centuries. One of the principal arguments advanced by those opposed to expanded government involvement in social welfare activity during this period was that such involvement would undermine a long-standing American pattern of relying on private, nonprofit institutions instead. Reflecting a deep-seated national aversion to government bureaucracy, this line of argument gave rise to a powerful "paradigm of conflict," a conviction that an inherent conflict exists between nonprofit institutions and the state. According to this argument, the growth of government weakens private, nonprofit institutions, displacing nonprofit functions and "crowding out" private charitable contributions. Societies therefore have to choose between pinning their faith on government and relying instead on private voluntary responses.

This line of thinking provided a strong rationale for resisting the New Deal's social policies. More recently, it resurfaced as a central tenet of the new conservative movement of the 1970s and 1980s. "The real conflict in modern political history," sociologist Robert Nisbet thus wrote in his influential The Quest for Community, "has not been, as is so often stated, between State and individual, but between State and social group" (1990 [1953], 98). The inherent goal of the state, Nisbet argued, is to eliminate all intermediary institutions that lie between it and the individual. Only two basic models of social welfare provision are therefore contemplated by this theory: a Third Sector Dominant Model featuring limited government action and extensive reliance on the "third sector" (nonprofits) instead to both finance and deliver basic services; and a Government Dominant Model featuring extensive government action and a limited third sector.[2] What distinguishes the American experience from its overseas counterparts, according to this view, is that Americans, at least until the New Deal or the Great Society, followed the first model, whereas European countries pursued the second. The great challenge of American policy during the current period, according to this theory, is to undo the deviation from the historic pattern that the expansion of government during the New Deal and the Great Society represented and to return America to the Third Sector Dominant Model that is its rightful course. As Ronald Reagan put it in explaining the budget cuts and program reforms that became the hallmark of his administration: "We have let the state take away the things that were once ours to do voluntarily." The best way to strengthen the nonprofit sector, therefore, was to get the state out of its way.[3]

Given this paradigm of conflict, it follows that countries such as those in Europe, with significantly higher levels of government social welfare spending than in America, should have largely nonexistent nonprofit sectors. Furthermore, this conceptualization would lead us to predict relatively little interaction, or at least little supportive interaction, between government and the nonprofit sphere. Indeed, the more extensive the level of government social welfare spending, the less extensive we might expect such interaction and support to be. Finally, to the extent government provides support to the nonprofit sector, the paradigm of conflict would lead us to expect such support to be, at best, corrosive of nonprofit independence and destructive of nonprofit advocacy.

To what extent does reality conform to what this paradigm suggests?

PREVAILING REALITIES

The Scale of Nonprofit Activity Abroad

The answer, it appears, is not very well. In the first place, the nonprofit sector is actually a far more significant presence in countries throughout the world, including many where government social welfare provision is quite extensive, than the paradigm of conflict would lead us to expect. Research that this author has conducted as part of the Johns Hopkins Comparative Nonprofit Sector Project shows, in fact, that nonprofit organizations constitute a massive social and economic force well beyond the borders of the United States. Nonprofit organizations thus account for:

- Forty percent of all hospital patient days in Germany;
- Fifty-five percent of all residents in residential care facilities in France;
- Three-fourths of all students in higher-education institutions in Japan; and

- Much of the social service provision in Italy (Salamon and Anheier 1996, 24).

While the scale of the American nonprofit sector—at nearly 8 percent of full-time equivalent employment (see also Steuerle and Hodgkinson, this volume)—is quite large, it is by no means the largest in the world, at least when measured as a share of employment. To the contrary, in at least four of the 22 countries examined as part of the Johns Hopkins Comparative Nonprofit Sector Project (the Netherlands, Ireland, Belgium, and Israel), nonprofit employment as a share of total employment actually exceeds that in the United States, and by a substantial margin. More generally, the nonprofit sector averages 5 percent of total employment in the 22 countries studied, making it one of the largest economic sectors.[4] Indeed, nonprofit employment in these countries exceeds the combined employment in the largest private company in each of these countries by a factor of six to one.

Illustrative of the surprising nonprofit presence abroad is the situation in Germany.[5] Government is clearly a larger presence in the German welfare state than in the American, accounting for 35 percent of gross domestic product, compared with just over 20 percent in the United States (OECD 1997; Bixby 1997). Reflecting this, a far more elaborate network of public social protections is available in Germany, guaranteeing universal pensions for the elderly, children's allowances, basic income support, and health insurance.

To conclude from the significant level and range of government social welfare activity that Germany is a case of the Government Dominant Model, however, is to misread significantly the character of the German welfare state. To the contrary, side by side with government is a massive network of private, nonprofit organizations that share important social welfare functions.

At the center of this network are six large conglomerates, the so-called "free welfare associations" (freie Wohlfahrtsverbände). Included here are the Catholic and Protestant social welfare agencies—Caritas and Diakonisches Werk, respectively, which are massive federations of local welfare agencies spread throughout the country. The former is rooted in Catholic social ethics and is integrated into the religious hierarchy. The latter began in 1848–49 as a welfare-oriented evangelical movement, often in conflict with the secular political world.

These two massive, religiously oriented social welfare networks have in turn helped inspire the creation of four others: the Arbeiterwohlfahrt (Workers' Welfare Association), founded in 1919 as a vehicle for reconciling workers with the capitalist state and historically linked to the Social Democratic Party (Bauer 1978); the *Zentralwohl-fahrtsstelle der Juden in Deutschland* (The Central Welfare Association for Jews in Germany), created in 1917 to coordinate the numerous Jewish local welfare committees and activities and reestablished after World War II to provide assistance to concentration camp victims; the *Deutscher Paritätischer Wohlfahrtsverband*, a consortium of nondenominational, nonpartisan private welfare organizations founded in 1920; and the *Deutsches Rotes Kreuz* (German Red Cross), which functions as both a relief organization and a social service organization.

These free welfare associations represent a major presence on the German social welfare scene, with an estimated 650,000 full-time equivalent employees and 1.5 million volunteers (Spiegelhalter 1990; Anheier 1991). Taken together, they run 68,466 institutions in the areas of health care, youth, and family services, as well as services for the handicapped, elderly, and the poor (Bundesarbeitsgemeinschaft 1990). As reflected in table 10.1 below, these organizations account for more than 60 percent of the employment in such fields as family services, services for the elderly, services for the handicapped, nursing home care, and child day care, though they are less prominent in such fields as vocational training, clinic and hospital care, education, libraries, and culture and the arts (see table 10.1).

Nonprofit institutions are even more powerfully present in the Netherlands. Seventy percent of all elementary and secondary school pupils in the Netherlands attend private, nonprofit institutions, and nonprofits dominate the provision of health care and welfare services

Table 10.1 NONPROFIT, FOR-PROFIT, AND PUBLIC SHARES OF SOCIAL SERVICE EMPLOYMENT IN GERMANY, BY FIELD

	Share of Employment in			
Industry	For-Profit Sector %	Nonprofit Sector %	Public Sector %	Total Employment in Industry
Family services	9.4	73.1	17.5	28,566
Services for the elderly	17.7	67.6	14.7	67,140
Services for the handicapped	9.5	83.7	6.9	96,518
Nursing homes	20.2	63.0	16.8	128,510
Child day care	1.0	62.3	36.7	155,874
Vocational training	17.6	21.5	60.9	202,898
Clinics and hospitals	14.2	34.2	51.0	722,734
Other health institutions	47.6	36.2	16.2	91,586

Source: Anheier 1991.

as well. As shown in figure 10.1, recent estimates put employment in
the Netherlands' nonprofit institutions at more than 12 percent of
national employment, or nearly one in every eight workers, propor-
tionally 50 percent larger than in the United States (Salamon and
Anheier 1998b; Burger et al. 1997, 3, 22).

Even in Sweden, perhaps the classic "welfare state," nonprofit institutions exist in profusion, though they take a slightly different form,
functioning less as service providers than as vehicles for social advo-

Figure 10.1 NONPROFIT SHARE OF TOTAL EMPLOYMENT, BY COUNTRY, 1995

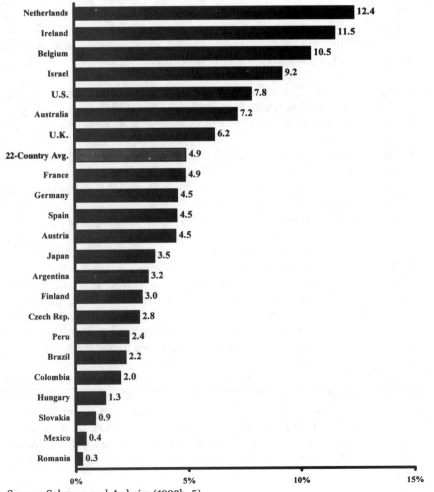

Source: Salamon and Anheier (1998b, 5).

cacy and social integration. An official 1987 report identified close to 200,000 membership associations in Sweden, and the country's 9 million people account for 30 million separate "memberships" in various voluntary organizations. Beyond that, nearly half of the Swedish population are active volunteers in such organizations, roughly comparable to proportions in the United States (Lundström and Wijkström 1997, 222).

Nonprofit organizations are somewhat less prominent in the developing world but are very much in evidence there as well. Indeed, a "global associational revolution" seems to be under way in many of these countries as well, a massive upsurge of organized private, voluntary activity that is significantly boosting the scale and diversity of nonprofit institutions virtually everywhere (Salamon 1994; Civicus 1994). Evidence of this phenomenon takes a wide variety of forms and is apparent in widely disparate areas, such as:

- The more than 1 million registered nonprofit organizations that recent research has uncovered in India (Sen 1998);
- The more than 210,000 nonprofit organizations operating in Brazil (Landim 1998);
- The more than 3 percent of the workforce employed by nonprofits in Argentina (Salamon and Anheier 1998b);
- The large nonprofit conglomerates such as BRAC and the Grameen Bank in Bangladesh; and
- The Rural Reconstruction Movement in the Philippines.

In short, a sizable and vibrant nonprofit sector does not appear to be a particular monopoly of the United States. To the contrary, nonprofit organizations are present in substantial numbers in other countries as well. What is more, though their numbers have expanded considerably in recent years, their presence is hardly new. Rather, the tradition of nonprofit activity elsewhere stretches back at least as far as the American experience, and in many cases much farther. Finally, the prevalence of nonprofit organizations does not seem to vary inversely with the size of government social welfare spending, as the paradigm of conflict would suggest. Instead, sizable nonprofit sectors seem to be highly consistent with large-scale government social welfare activity. Indeed, of the countries for which reliable data are available, the ones with the largest government social welfare spending—e.g., France and the Netherlands—have the largest nonprofit sectors.

PARTNERS IN PUBLIC SERVICE:
GOVERNMENT-NONPROFIT COOPERATION

The nonprofit sector exists to a surprising degree in settings where the "paradigm of conflict" would predict its absence; a major reason for this appears to be that government and the nonprofit sector cooperate in these settings to an extent that this paradigm fails to acknowledge. In short, the coexistence of sizable nonprofit sectors and large-scale government social welfare activity is no accident. Rather, one helps cause the other. Governments in many different settings have come to rely extensively on nonprofit organizations to assist them in the solution of public problems. The result is an often elaborate pattern of government-nonprofit cooperation and support. Indeed, one of the single most important determinants of the size of the nonprofit sector around the world turns out to be the extent of government support for it (Kramer et al. 1993, 2).

This point finds strong support in the results of the Johns Hopkins Comparative Nonprofit Sector Project, perhaps the most comprehensive recent analysis of the scope and revenue structure of the nonprofit sector internationally. According to this study, as of 1995, an average of 42 percent of the income of the nonprofit sector in the 22 countries examined came from government. That is four times larger than the share provided by private philanthropy (11 percent) and is exceeded only by the support generated by fees and charges (47 percent) (Salamon and Anheier 1998b). This situation does not apply to just a handful of countries, moreover. Rather, government support was the first or second most important source of nonprofit income for all the countries examined in the study. And in some countries, including particularly all four that exceed the United States in the relative size of their nonprofit sectors, government is the *major* source of nonprofit support, accounting for well over half of total nonprofit income (see figure 10.2). Finally, government support is not restricted to a narrow range of fields. Rather, of 10 major service fields examined in depth in the 22 countries, government support turned out to be the major source of revenue in four and the second largest source of revenue in five (Salamon and Anheier 1998b, 12) (see table 10.2).

Other studies reveal a similar pattern in other countries. An examination of nonprofit agencies serving the handicapped in four Western European countries revealed that government support averaged 87 percent of agency income in Italy, 50 percent of the income of large

Figure 10.2 SOURCES OF NONPROFIT REVENUE, BY COUNTRY, 1995 (19
        COUNTRIES)

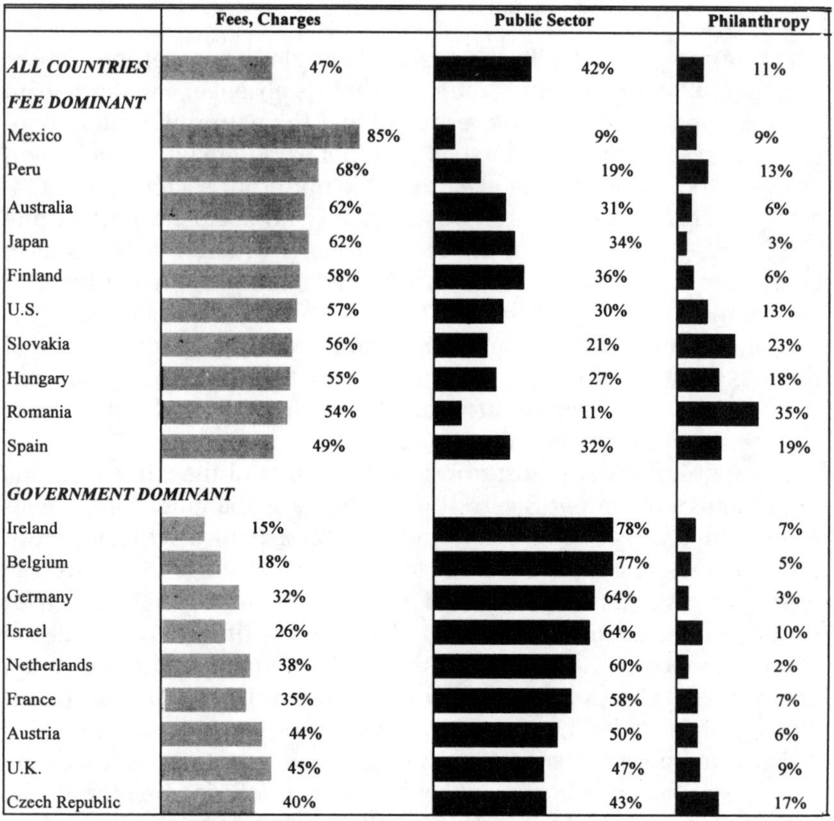

	Fees, Charges	Public Sector	Philanthropy
ALL COUNTRIES	47%	42%	11%
FEE DOMINANT			
Mexico	85%	9%	9%
Peru	68%	19%	13%
Australia	62%	31%	6%
Japan	62%	34%	3%
Finland	58%	36%	6%
U.S.	57%	30%	13%
Slovakia	56%	21%	23%
Hungary	55%	27%	18%
Romania	54%	11%	35%
Spain	49%	32%	19%
GOVERNMENT DOMINANT			
Ireland	15%	78%	7%
Belgium	18%	77%	5%
Germany	32%	64%	3%
Israel	26%	64%	10%
Netherlands	38%	60%	2%
France	35%	58%	7%
Austria	44%	50%	6%
U.K.	45%	47%	9%
Czech Republic	40%	43%	17%

Source: Salamon and Anheier (1998b, 11).

agencies in the United Kingdom, more than 90 percent of nonprofit
income in the Netherlands, and more than 40 percent of nonprofit
income in Norway (Kramer et al. 1993, 64, 26, 68, 93). Even in Sweden, the nonprofit sector has close, cooperative ties with the state.
Although the state delivers more of the health, social welfare, and
educational services directly in Sweden than it does in Germany, the
Netherlands, or Italy, it nevertheless supports the nonprofit sector in
other spheres—e.g., culture, adult education, and sports. What is
more, extensive cooperation exists between nonprofit organizations
and government in the traditional social service fields at the local level
(Lundström and Wijkström 1997, 239–40).

Table 10.2. SOURCES OF NONPROFIT REVENUE, 1995, BY FIELD (19 COUNTRIES)

	Percent of Income From			
	Public Sector	Fees, Charges	Philanthropy	Total
Health	59%	28%	13%	100%
Education	50	42	8	100
Social services	42	40	18	100
Civic, advocacy	39	37	24	100
Environment	35	41	24	100
Development, housing	34	51	15	100
International	33	25	41	100
Culture, recreation	22	63	15	100
Philanthropic	16	49	35	100
Professional	7	86	7	100
Average	42%	47%	12%	100%

Source: Salamon and Anheier (1998b, 12)

Government support has also proved to be a highly dynamic source of income in many of these settings, easily exceeding the growth rate of other sources of support. In England, for example, statutory fees and grants rose from one-third to two-thirds of agency income between 1975 and 1987. Government support to nonprofit organizations in Italy increased by 40 percent between the mid-1970s and the mid-1980s (Kramer et al. 1993, 113). And in France, a veritable revolution occurred in the early 1980s, as the Socialist government of François Mitterand turned decisively to nonprofit organizations to revitalize an increasingly bureaucratized welfare state (Ullman 1998).

In the developing world, government support for nonprofit organizations appears to be more limited but far from absent. As a general rule, developing country governments have been somewhat more suspicious of nonprofit organizations, at least those committed to fundamental social and political change. Authoritarian regimes in Argentina, Brazil, Chile, Egypt, and Ghana have thus severely restricted the right to associate at various points in the recent past, provoking antagonisms on the part of nongovernmental organizations that have often been difficult to diffuse.

Even in these settings, however, cooperative ties are on the rise. This reflects the "new policy agenda" that has recently gained credence among northern development agencies, emphasizing private markets and private initiative as the most effective vehicles for promoting growth and stressing the importance of democratization and "civil society" as mechanisms for keeping private initiative alive.

Reflecting this, a much larger share of development assistance is finding its way to both northern and southern nongovernmental organizations (Hulme and Edwards 1997a, 7). Although indigenous governments in the developing world have been less inclined to share resources with local nonprofit institutions, such partnerships have a long history in numerous places, such as India and Pakistan (Sen 1998, 215–16; Salamon 1995, 254), and have begun to develop elsewhere as well, most prominently in Latin America (Robinson 1997, 75). Thus, for example, Chile's FOSIS program channels significant assistance to grassroots development organizations for innovative development projects, and Argentina's CENOC agency within the Ministry of Welfare provides technical assistance and access to government decisionmaking to grassroots nonprofit agencies in that country.

In short, in addition to the Third Sector Dominant and Government Dominant models depicted in the "paradigm of conflict," a "third route" seems to be available for coping with public problems (Salamon 1995; Salamon and Anheier 1993, 1998a). This third route features extensive cooperation between government and the nonprofit sector, with government providing the financing and nonprofit organizations helping to deliver the services or perform the functions that government finance is supporting. This pattern appears to be widespread in most Western European welfare states and to be gaining ground as well in significant parts of the developing world. Indeed, this Collaborative Model may well be on its way to becoming the global norm.[6]

THE RATIONALE AND "SOCIAL ORIGINS" OF THE COLLABORATIVE MODEL

How can we explain the apparently widespread and growing pattern of government-nonprofit collaboration? One answer undoubtedly lies in the programmatic advantages that government-nonprofit collaboration seems to enjoy. In a word, this pattern makes it possible to combine the relative strengths of government and the nonprofit sector while avoiding, or minimizing, their respective weaknesses (Salamon 1987, 1995).

Government, especially democratic government, has a clear advantage, for example, in setting broad societal priorities through a democratic political process, generating revenues, and etablishing "rights" to certain basic benefits rather than treating them as mere privileges. But because of its size and cumbersomeness, government also has inherent disadvantages as a deliverer of basic services and promoter of development. Indeed, a veritable "crisis of confidence" in the capabilities of the state appears to be under way throughout the world—in the advanced welfare states of the West, throughout the former Soviet bloc, and in the developing regions of Africa, Asia, and Latin America (Salamon 1994; World Bank 1997).

For a wide range of social functions, the disadvantages of the state are nicely matched by the advantages of the nonprofit sector, and vice versa (Salamon 1987). Nonprofit organizations have great difficulties in raising resources and establishing "rights" to benefits, but they bring to the equation smaller scale and resulting *flexibility*; greater *responsiveness* to popular demands and grassroots inputs; an *ability to tap underutilized resources*, including voluntary contributions of time and money; the *capacity to empower* individuals and communities, not just service their needs; and *credibility and trust* resulting from the fact that they are not engaged primarily in the pursuit of profit (Johns Hopkins Institute for Policy Studies 1997). By combining the two sets of institutions in efforts to solve public problems, therefore, it is possible to reap the respective strengths of each while avoiding their respective limitations.

While programmatic factors provide part of the explanation for the widespread, and growing, reliance on the Collaborative Model throughout the world, they hardly provide the full explanation. More is involved in the choice of social and political arrangements than programmatic effectiveness, after all. Questions of power and influence are also at work. What is more, for all its advantages, government-nonprofit cooperation also carries significant risks, as we will see more fully below, and different social and political groupings weigh those risks differently. To understand the pattern of social provision that prevails in a society, a "social origins" approach is therefore needed (Salamon and Anheier 1998c). What such an approach suggests is that the Collaborative Model can be reached through a variety of different "routes."

The Corporatist Route

Illustrative of the complex sets of social factors that can give rise to government-nonprofit collaboration are the situations in the Netherlands and Germany, both of which have rich histories of such collaboration stretching back for decades.

THE NETHERLANDS

The prominent position that nonprofit organizations hold in the Netherlands is a byproduct of that country's origins in an uprising against the centralized power of the Habsburg monarchy. The result was a deep-seated hostility to centralized power that was further reinforced by an internal division between Catholics and Protestants. When an intense conflict erupted between the country's Catholic and Protestant citizens over control of public education in the late nineteenth and early twentieth centuries, therefore, it was natural for the Netherlands to react by seeking a compromise that relied heavily on a partnership between government and private, nonprofit institutions. The heart of the resulting "Dutch solution" was to retain governmental funding for elementary and secondary education but to turn the operation of the publicly supported schools over to private, sectarian groups. This pattern was then extended to other spheres—health care, social welfare, and even international aid—each of which came to be characterized by an intimate partnership between public authority and private, nonprofit groups, with the public sector assigned the task of generating the revenue and the private, nonprofit groups assigned the task of delivering the actual services.

The result of this system was a widespread *pillarization* of Dutch society, the division of society into separate religious and ideological groups, or "pillars," each served by its own network of nonprofit organizations but each heavily subsidized by the state. Thus, there are Catholic hospitals, Protestant hospitals, union hospitals, and unaffiliated hospitals; Catholic schools, Protestant schools, worker-affiliated schools, and unaffiliated schools; and so forth—all heavily supported by public funds. In a sense, public authority and resources were expropriated for the use of private, nonprofit groups, creating an immense nonprofit sector and a pervasive pattern of government-nonprofit support (Burger et al. 1997, 4–5; Kramer 1981).

GERMANY

A similar complex set of social and political factors explains the emergence of a strong collaborative pattern in Germany. They include a long history of federalism among relatively autonomous German "states;" the conservative pattern of modernization that Germany pursued and the resulting survival of such "premodern" social institutions as the Catholic Church and its theory of "subsidiarity," which called for leaving social functions to the unit closest to the problem;

and the disruptive influence of National Socialism, which created a backlash against excessive centralization of social functions. Coupled with the influence of the postwar occupation regime, which sought explicitly to build up Germany's network of voluntary organizations, the result was to set a course toward close working partnerships between the state and nonprofit groups (Anheier 1992; Salamon and Anheier 1998a).

These partnerships are not simply left to administrative discretion, moreover, but are firmly implanted in public law. Between 1950 and 1975, three separate laws were passed implementing the principle of government support to nonprofit institutions as a cornerstone of German social policy (Anheier 1992; Salamon and Anheier 1993). The Social Assistance Act of 1961, Germany's basic social welfare law, thus obliges the "public bodies responsible for social assistance" to "collaborate with the public law churches and religious communities and with the free welfare associations" and to do so in a way that acknowledges "their independence in the targeting and execution of their functions." What is more, in Section 3 the act requires the public bodies to "support the free welfare associations appropriately in the field of social assistance." Finally, the act virtually guarantees a local monopoly to the nonprofit providers by forbidding public agencies from establishing their own offices at the local level "if suitable establishments of the free welfare associations . . . are available, or can be extended or provided" (Deutscher Verein 1986).

Subsequent legislation then spelled out the implications of these basic relationships in particular policy fields. Thus, the Youth Welfare Act stipulates particular nonprofit roles in the provision of youth services, and other acts assign additional responsibilities in such fields as health finance and employment and training. Finally, the Social Code, enacted in 1976 to codify and systematize the various bodies of social legislation that were enacted between the late nineteenth century and the 1970s, restates in Article 2 the primacy of individual help and care over any form of private or public social assistance, and then establishes in Article 3 the obligation for the public sector and the nonprofit sector to work together to "effectively complement one another for the benefit of those receiving assistance" (Deutscher Verein 1986). In a sense, the code thus formalizes the basic framework for government-nonprofit interaction in the operation of the German welfare state. Given these legal provisions, it should come as no surprise that the state is a massive benefactor of the nonprofit sector in modern Germany and that a sizable nonprofit sector exists.

The Privatization Route

A slightly different set of pressures led to the expansion of government-nonprofit cooperation in the United Kingdom. There a conservative government saw the promotion of the voluntary sector and the establishment of contract relationships between the voluntary sector and local governments as a way to reduce social welfare spending and relieve a fiscally overburdened "welfare state" (Hartley and Huby 1986). Where formerly nonprofit organizations had received small amounts of general support from state agencies, the Thatcher government, through its National Health Service and Community Care Act of 1993, divested itself of much of the responsibility for health care and social services, turning these functions over to local governments and empowering the authorities to enter into competitive contracts with nonprofit and for-profit groups. The hope was that, by contracting out the provision of human services and requiring nonprofit organizations to compete for the resulting contracts, the system's efficiency would be increased, with resulting savings in the provision of services. What is more, by forcing decisions about the appropriate level of human services out of the hands of centralized government bureaucracies down to levels of government closer to the taxpayers, conservative politicians hoped to reduce the overall level of public spending on social welfare purposes (Wistow et al. 1996, 9–10). Government contracting with nonprofit providers was thus part of a broader strategy to reduce the level of government social welfare activity.

The Reform Route

Fiscal considerations are not the only ones that have prompted greater reliance on the Collaborative Model to carry out important governmental functions, however. Also important has been dissatisfaction with the performance, as opposed to the cost, of prevailing public or private systems. That concern doubtless also played a role in the shift toward a market-oriented approach to social welfare provision in the United Kingdom in the 1980s and 1990s (Wistow et al. 1996, 5–8), but it is even more clearly apparent in France and other Western welfare states and seems increasingly important in the developing world.

DEVELOPED COUNTRIES

The recent history of social policy in France demonstrates the role that increased cooperation between government and the nonprofit sector can play, not in dismantling the welfare state but in strengthening it in important ways. As Claire Ullman (1998) has shown, the Socialist government led by François Mitterand turned to government support of nonprofit organizations in France in the early 1980s to overcome a pervasive "crisis of state capacity," a widespread loss of faith in the ability of the state to accomplish its social welfare goals using prevailing statist approaches. Under Socialist Premier Mauroy, the French government inaugurated a bold decentralization plan in the early 1980s that delegated major new social welfare responsibilities to local governments and encouraged them to turn to private, nonprofit associations for help. The result was to stimulate a rapid growth of local nonprofit organizations in a country where such institutions had long been viewed as inconsistent with a revolutionary tradition that viewed the democratic state as the preferred vehicle for expressing the general will of the people (Archambault 1997; Ullman 1998). As Ullman (1998, 164) notes:

> In the course of the 1980s, the relationship between nonprofit social service providers and the French welfare state changed dramatically. The Socialist government offered nonprofits unprecedented roles in the administration of welfare state programs, delegating to them significant new responsibility for the implementation of public programs and providing them with substantial public funding. Indeed, every major poverty policy initiative of the 1980s in France relied on nonprofits for its implementation, including a campaign against hunger and homelessness, a law implementing a national right to housing, and, more important, major legislation creating a guaranteed minimum income.

Similar developments were evident in Italy and other Western European welfare states as well (Barbetta 1997; Kramer et al. 1993, 91).

DEVELOPING WORLD

The same set of dynamics now also seems to be at work in parts of the developing world. During the 1960s and 1970s, a host of nongovernmental organizations (NGOs) took shape in these countries as a result of expanded communications capabilities, growing numbers of educated middle-class elements frustrated by the lack of economic and political opportunities, and outside support from foreign foundations and religious institutions (Salamon 1994). Confronting regimes that resisted their calls for greater grassroots empowerment and freedom of political expression, such organizations naturally developed a generally hostile posture toward the powers that be and the governmental apparatus they controlled. Indeed, these NGOs were often the breeding ground of resistance movements that challenged existing political and economic elites.

As these resistance movements gained influence during the 1980s, however, either by assuming power themselves, as in South Africa, or by stimulating democratic reforms that allowed other liberal elements to gain control, as in Argentina, Brazil, Chile, and the Philippines, they found themselves simultaneously cut off from overseas financial support and better positioned politically to push for state policies that would enlist them actively in the development process. Such pro-NGO policies also received a boost from the major multilateral development agencies, which were becoming increasingly concerned about the limits of a purely state-centered approach to development and have consequently urged indigenous governments to adopt policies supportive of both nonprofit and for-profit involvement. The upshot has been growing experimentation with assistance programs enlisting nonprofit agencies as partners in development (Ritchey-Vance 1991; Clark 1992).

THE CONSEQUENCES OF GOVERNMENT-
NONPROFIT COOPERATION

From the discussion above, it should be clear that government-nonprofit cooperation takes a variety of forms and serves a variety of purposes. Not surprisingly, the consequences of such cooperation also vary considerably. On the one hand, such cooperation offers considerable programmatic advantages to the extent that it effectively blends the public sector's strength as a generator of revenues and the nonprofit sector's strength as a flexible mechanism for meeting human needs. But those advantages bring with them certain risks to both the nonprofit sector and the state.

The Risks

So far as the nonprofit sector is concerned, excessive dependence on state support can rob it of its most cherished qualities—its independence and its ability to represent the powerless and advocate on their behalf. Over time, therefore, the Collaborative Model can potentially distort the mission of nonprofit organizations and transform them into mere agents of the state. Particularly vulnerable is the advocacy function of nonprofit groups, its role in pushing for changes in government policy. In addition, nonprofits can lose their flexibility, as the demands of state contracting induce them to become administratively more cumbersome and bureaucratic.

But the Collaborative Model also poses risks for the state. With state-financed services increasingly delivered by private, nonprofit groups, citizens can easily forget the real source of the benefits they receive. In the process, public support for government can atrophy. Government may also create nonprofit constituencies that then lobby against policy changes that might decrease their own funding. In addition, where suitable private providers are not available, government can find itself in the unhappy position of having to purchase what the prevailing system of private agencies can provide, rather than the mix of services it considers most needed (Salamon 1995; LeGrand and Bartlett 1993; Starr 1992). Finally, government can find itself without the capability even to monitor, let alone deliver, the services it finances, creating even more enormous possibilities for misuse of funds and inefficiencies than direct action often entails.

Regrettably, there is little solid empirical data with which to evaluate the extent to which these risks actually materialize. What is more, the extent to which they do is likely to vary in response both to a variety of external factors and to the particular form that the government-nonprofit cooperation takes. It is therefore necessary to review how these external and internal factors are likely to affect the result before reaching any general judgments about what the consequences of government-nonprofit cooperation have actually been.

Evaluating the Risks: The Impact of External Factors

Among the external factors affecting the impact of government-nonprofit cooperation on both the nonprofit sector and the state, three seem most important.

ALTERNATIVE SOURCES OF SUPPORT

The first of these outside factors is the presence or absence of *alternative sources of nonprofit support*. Where such support is available, even if in modest amounts, the prospects that nonprofits can enter cooperative arrangements with government without losing their independence and character increases considerably. Such support can take the form of private charitable giving from individuals, corporations, or foundations; or of fees and service charges from those who use the services that nonprofits provide. As we have seen, the latter has been far more important as a source of support, averaging 47 percent of total income in the 22 countries examined in the Johns Hopkins Comparative Nonprofit Sector Project. Since such fee income is far less plentiful in the developing world, we would expect that local nonprofits might face more serious obstacles in retaining their independence from the state in such settings, unless foreign assistance is made available to them instead.

While private philanthropy and fee income are the principal sources of funding diversity, multiple sources of government support can also have the same effect. Governments are not monoliths, after all, and nonprofit agencies can often achieve a degree of autonomy by playing one level of government against another, or balancing support from one ministry or agency against that of others.

ATTITUDES TOWARD THE STATE

Also important are *cultural traditions concerning the state*. Where habits of deference to state authority are strong, nonprofit organizations are at greater risk in their dealings with the government. Where such habits are less evident and nonprofit organizations enjoy the moral advantage, the same level of government support can yield much less government control.

This factor may help explain the significant difference that exists between the treatment of nonprofit organizations in Germany and Japan. In Germany, a strong tradition of decentralization has long existed, reinforced by a long history of church resistance to government control. The upshot has been a fairly solid base for protecting the integrity of the free welfare associations that deliver most of the state-financed services. Indeed, German public authorities are required by law to consult the free welfare associations in matters of social policy, and an elaborate consultative apparatus has been established to implement that requirement. Nonprofit advocacy is thus not only officially sanctioned, but also legally required. What is more, government must secure the associations' endorsement for the establishment of public sector organizations in the social welfare field. In a sense, therefore, nonprofit organizations are not only guaranteed a share of public resources, but also a share of the authority for making public policy.

A wholly different relationship between government and the nonprofit sector has evolved in Japan. Here, as well, a far more sizable nonprofit sector exists than traditional accounts tend to acknowledge. Nonprofit institutions deliver much of the higher education, social services, residential care, and medical services in Japan (Salamon and Anheier 1996). They do so, moreover, with extensive governmental support. In the fields of health and social services, for example, Japanese nonprofits receive 95 percent and 65 percent of their income, respectively, from government sources (Salamon, Anheier, and Sokolowski 1996, 51). In addition, formal laws stipulate the roles that nonprofit institutions can play in these different fields.

Unlike in Germany and the Netherlands, however, where the laws operate to constrain the state and empower the nonprofit providers, in Japan the opposite comes closer to the truth. Nonprofit organizations require the explicit approval of the government ministries in their respective fields in order to be incorporated, and those that accept government support must also accept extremely close governmental supervision and control. Indeed, a provision of the Japanese Constitution of 1949, originally inserted by the allied victors in World War II to establish a clear division between government and the nonprofit sector by prohibiting public authorities from financing religious and charitable institutions, has come to be interpreted as permitting such financing only when the recipient organizations function essentially as quasi-public institutions (Amenomori 1997, 198–99).

INFORMATION ASYMMETRIES

A third important factor affecting the impact that government funding has on the nonprofit sector is the information asymmetries that contracting relationships inevitably entail. As emphasized in what has come to be known as "principal-agent theory," the principal in any contractual relationship faces a difficult dilemma in ensuring that its "agent" is truly adhering to the terms of the contract (Moe 1984; Pratt and Zeckhauser 1985; Kettl 1993). This is so because the agent—in this case the nonprofit agency—is always in possession of more information about how the contract is being implemented than the principal—in this case the government. The agent is therefore able to "shirk" some contractual obligations and interpret others to its liking. For the principal to prevent this, money must be invested in information gathering and processing and then suitable sanctions applied, all of which can be costly and time-consuming. What is more, the more complex and ambiguous the task, the more difficult it is for the principal to control the activities of the agent, and the more leeway the agent has to exercise its own discretion. Contrary to the simplistic assumption embodied in the popular notion that "who pays the piper calls the tune," in complex principal-agent relationships the agent often ends up in more effective control of the outcome than the principal. And since the relationships in which governments turn to the nonprofit sector are most often complex, involving efforts to solve difficult social problems, the likelihood that governments could exercise close supervision and control, even if they wanted to, is remote.

Evaluating the Risks: The Impact of Internal Factors

In addition to these external factors, the impact of government funding of nonprofits depends on a variety of factors internal to the relationship.

DIFFERENT TOOLS

In the first place, funding arrangements between government and the nonprofit sector can differ in terms of the specific *"tool" of government action* that is used (Salamon 1989). Such tools vary widely, from general support grants through specific purchase-of-service contracts to voucher payments that governments provide to clients. In Germany, for example, government uses four different tools to subsidize nonprofit activities (Anheier 1992):

Direct subsidies and block allocations to support the basic operations of nonprofit service providers in certain key fields. These subsidies can originate from either the national or the state governments and show up as specific budget line items indicating "subsidy to [nonprofit organization] in accordance with the [Social Assistance Act or Youth Welfare Act, etc.]." Such subsidies are also provided for capital expenditures associated with the construction of schools, day-care centers, and hospitals.

Grants for particular projects that fall within the public interest as stipulated in relevant sections of the Budget Structure Act. These flows support activities other than the basic operations and investments supported by the statutory funds. For example, a special program aimed at the transition of handicapped youth to work would be supported with a public grant rather than a statutory subsidy.

Reimbursements of nonprofit organizations for services provided to individuals or families on behalf of the state as a result of statutory transfers of particular responsibilities to voluntary organizations.

Fee-for-service contracts made with nonprofit organizations on behalf of public or private insurance schemes or the social security system, under which nonprofit organizations deliver particular services to specified clients on behalf of the insurance agencies. These tend to be "civil law" transactions in the German system, i.e., private contracts for the delivery of particular services.

These different tools have different implications for the nature of the relationship that is created between government and the nonprofit sector, determining to a marked extent whether a "partnership" or "vendor" type arrangement is formed (Gidron, Kramer, and Salamon 1992). Specific purchase-of-service contracts, for example, leave the least room for discretion to the vendor, whereas general support grants typically leave the most. In between are various voucher and reimbursement systems, which shift more of the control to the purchaser (Salamon 1981). All of these forms operate, however, within the general constraints defined by "principal-agent theory," as described above. What is more, they are affected by the degree of complexity of the task. Within these constraints, however, the type of tool can affect the outcome to a significant degree.

DURATION

Partnership systems also differ with respect to the *duration* of the partnership relationships they establish. In the United States, for example, purchase-of-service contracts are typically formally rebid every year or two, although it has become common in practice for agencies that win contracts in one year to retain them subsequently (Gronbjerg 1991, 5–24). In Germany and the Netherlands, by contrast, government relationships with nonprofit agencies last for decades and often take on the character of permanent, institutionalized ties (Anheier 1991; Burger et al. 1997). Not surprisingly, government agencies can exercise more influence over relationships that have to be reestablished every year or two than over those that become semi-permanent and institutionalized. As one recent study has put it: "The longer the history of funding, the less likely is it to be terminated and the greater the autonomy enjoyed by the recipient agency. . . . [T]he closer the links between funder and recipient, the more dependent the funder becomes on the work of the recipient organization" (Kramer et al. 1993, 65–6).

DEGREE OF FORMALITY

Finally, government-nonprofit relationships vary in the *degree of formality* they exhibit.

At one extreme is the situation in Italy, where few formal policies govern relationships between local governments and the nonprofit agencies with which they contract for services, and where the general posture local governments take toward their nonprofit contractors has been summarized as: "I do my duty and you do yours" (Kramer et al. 1993, 65). Under these circumstances, nonprofit agencies have considerable leeway with regard to program objectives and their own responsibilities.

At the other extreme is the situation in Germany, where a highly structured set of policies governs the relationships between government and the nonprofit sector. Indeed, the policy is formalized in an explicit doctrine, the doctrine of "subsidiarity," which in turn is embodied in a variety of formal legal provisions (Anheier 1991, 1992). Inspired by nineteenth-century Jesuit thinking and Catholic moral philosophy, this doctrine came to real prominence in Pope Pius XI's encyclical *Quadragesimo anno* of 1931. Because of the great strength of the church in Germany and the link between the church and the Christian Democratic Party that came to power in the postwar world, the doctrine of subsidiarity became a central pillar of the postwar German state. It defined a working compromise between the state and the church under which the church agreed to endorse state action in the social welfare field, but only if the state agreed to let the church, and its affiliated social welfare agencies, deliver the services thus created. The system won the early support of the Allied victors in the Second World War, who sought to avoid the reemergence of a highly centralized German state and therefore endorsed a system that kept as many matters as possible in local and private hands. The doctrine of subsidiarity essentially holds that the responsibility for caring for individuals' needs should always be vested in the unit of social life closest to the individual—the family, the parish, the community, the voluntary association—and that larger or higher-level units, such as the local government or the national state, should only be enlisted when a problem clearly exceeds the capabilities of the primary units. Thus, individuals should turn first to their families, then to their local community, then to their voluntary association, then to their unit of local government, and only then, if no relief is forthcoming, should the national government be involved. What is more, the doctrine holds that the higher units have an obligation not only to avoid usurping the position of the lower units but also to help the lower units perform their role.

Rather than take any chances, the advocates of subsidiarity in the German context pushed to enshrine the principle in formal law. The consequence is the dense network of legal and financial relationships between the state and the nonprofit sector described earlier, and a formal set of institutional links between the German state and the free welfare associations in the development of German social welfare policy. These arrangements include a formal consultative committee that gives the free welfare associations regular access to state decisionmaking on social welfare policy, state distribution of "church tax" revenues to the major religious denominations, and formal legal obligations for local governments to enlist the free welfare associations in the implementation of public social policy (Salamon and Anheier 1998a). In a sense, the free welfare associations enjoy in the social welfare area a position similar to that of the various business and labor groups in the relevant areas of economic policy: They not only have a seat at the table; they enjoy a virtual veto over policy initiatives that the state might propose.

Not surprisingly, the degree of formalization affects the impact that government funding has on both the nonprofit sector and the state. As a general rule, the more formalized the relationship, the more influence the nonprofit providers are able to exert, particularly through legal claims against the state. By contrast, in the more ad hoc systems, nonprofits are far more vulnerable to shifts in state policy and practice. As a result, the establishment of formal state obligations to rely on nonprofit organizations and share power with them is often a goal of nonprofit advocacy.

While it strengthens the hand of the nonprofit providers, however, such formalization also often causes these providers to take on more of the characteristics of their counterpart agencies in government. The formalization of government-nonprofit ties, in other words, can be a two-edged sword, enhancing nonprofit power but at the cost of causing them to surrender some of their flexibility and nonbureaucratic character.

Evaluating the Risks: Effects on Nonprofit Agencies

Given these diverse forces, what can be said about the effect that extensive government support to nonprofit organizations has on these organizations? In particular, to what extent have fears about nonprofit loss of independence, autonomy, flexibility, direction, and advocacy commitment as a consequence of public support proved accurate?

Agency Autonomy

From the discussion above, it should be clear that no single answer to this question is possible. At the same time, it seems reasonable to conclude from the evidence at hand that the risks of government-nonprofit cooperation for nonprofit providers have probably been exaggerated.

In their study of contracting relationships in four Western European countries (Italy, the Netherlands, Norway, and the United Kingdom), Ralph Kramer and his colleagues found little support for the thesis that government contracting distorts the mission of nonprofit agencies or robs the agencies of their autonomy (Kramer et al. 1993, 166–69). "An important finding of this study," the authors report, "is that financial dependence does not mean organizational dependence, even in those cases where public funding accounts for a high proportion of the total income" (Kramer et al. 1993, 65). The one exception appears to be the Netherlands, where government reliance on nonprofits is perhaps the most extensive, but the complaints that nonprofits have recently voiced there about undue governmental interference must be viewed against a context of past governmental willingness to finance nonprofit providers without asking much of anything in return.

More recent studies in the United Kingdom reach a similar conclusion. A summary of this research concludes that fears about nonprofit loss of independence with the growth of the "contract culture" have so far proved "unduly pessimistic" (Taylor 1997, 11). While problems certainly exist in some quarters, the growth of local authority contracting with nonprofit providers has apparently been far more positive than many nonprofit agencies expected; it has clarified objectives, strengthened management systems, evened the playing field, and improved the quality of information available to users. The major difficulty appears to be calibrating reimbursement rates so that they cover the core administrative costs of the agencies in addition to the direct service costs related to the contracts (Taylor 1997, 12–14).

Advocacy

Interestingly, this finding even carries over to the advocacy function of nonprofit agencies. As Kramer and his colleagues note: "Reliance on public funding . . . did not seem to inhibit either [voluntary nonprofit organization] advocacy and political lobbying efforts, or their self-perception as being autonomous from the state. . . ." (Kramer et al. 1993, 167). Indeed, Ullman's study of the French case shows that government support of nonprofit organizations, far from inhibiting nonprofit advocacy, can actually stimulate it. As Ullman (1998, 170) notes:

> Once nonprofits became involved in implementing the government-funded poverty plans, they were politicized. They began to question the government's definition of the problems of the new poor and *les exclus* and to develop their own policy demands. . . . Through their lobbying, nonprofits extended their involvement in the welfare state from the social service programs at its periphery to the social insurance role at its core.

Research in the United Kingdom has shown a similar connection. Summarizing this research, Taylor (1997, 14) notes that "fears that advocacy and campaigning would suffer are offset by the fact that a market in care has encouraged investment in information and advice, and studies elsewhere have found little evidence that advocacy is squeezed out by contracts."

The ability to preserve a significant nonprofit advocacy role in the face of growing government support may reflect the privileged position that nonprofit advocacy enjoys in much of the world. In many respects, advocacy has been viewed as the fundamental function of nonprofit organizations, even in countries where nonprofits play little role in service delivery. Typical in this regard is the historic role of the *folkrörelse*, or popular mass movements, in Sweden. More than 40 percent of the numerous associations that exist in Sweden identify themselves as such mass movements (Lundström and Wijkström 1997, 224). These movements developed in the late nineteenth and early twentieth centuries in the form of a powerful labor movement, an equally strong temperance movement, and a movement in support of the free churches. This tradition has persisted in more recent years, as evidenced by the growth of an environmental movement, a women's movement, consumer cooperatives, the sports movement, and adult education institutes. The powerful antiwar movement that made Sweden well known in America for its hostility to the war in Vietnam is just one manifestation of this much broader phenomenon. Far from abjuring a policy role, in other words, nonprofit organizations in Sweden have specialized in creating a distinctive definition of their role in society as "schools for democracy" rather than direct providers of welfare services.

The same perspective on the role of the nonprofit sector has emerged more recently in the developing world. By providing vehicles for citizen action, nonprofit organizations are seen as guarantors of a "new kind of governance" that not only makes the state more responsive and accountable but also creates greater space for citizen "self-organization" (Morales and Serrano 1997, 99). In the process, the new governance helps guarantee an open arena for private initiative (Hulme and Edwards 1997a, 7). Democratization and freedom for the market to operate are thus seen as mutually reinforcing byproducts of nonprofit expansion.

Reflecting this, nonprofit advocacy is generally well protected in law in most developed, and many developing, countries—much more so, in fact, than it is in the United States. Thus, while American nonprofits eligible to benefit from the charitable tax deduction subsidy are prohibited from engaging in political campaign activity and cannot devote more than 20 percent of their expenditures to lobbying (i.e., attempting to influence actual legislation) (Hopkins 1992, 327–52), few such restrictions are placed on the political and policy activities of nonprofit organizations in most other advanced industrial democracies (Salamon 1997). In Sweden, for example, no legal restrictions on the political or policy activities of nonprofits exist. In France as well, nonprofit organizations are permitted to lobby, actively participate in political campaign activities, and even raise money for political campaigns, with the only limitation being that such political activities be identified in the organization's bylaws as part of its general aims (Salamon 1997). The provisions of German law are somewhat more restrictive, but only partially so. German nonprofit organizations cannot engage directly in political campaign activities. They are permitted without limitation to lobby for legislation furthering their missions, however (Salamon 1997). Only in the United Kingdom, in fact, do restrictions on nonprofit political activity even approach American ones in level of severity, but the British restrictions appear more loosely drawn. Thus, charitable status is not available in the United Kingdom to organizations whose *principal* purpose is to promote a political party or seek changes in government policy. Organizations can still secure charitable status if they use political means for pursuing another principal purpose, however.

That nonprofit advocacy has survived the growth of government support to nonprofit organizations is also a product of deliberate policy. Many of the government programs affording nonprofit organizations access to government funding also afford them access to government policymaking. Perhaps the classic example of this, as we have seen, is Germany, where the expansion of government support to nonprofit agencies was accompanied by the creation of a formal consultative arrangement for nonprofit input into state decisionmaking. The expansion of government funding of nonprofit organizations in France was similarly accompanied by political reforms that opened a seat on the prestigious Economic and Social Council to the nonprofit sector (Ullman 1998, 169). Although early moves toward greater contracting with nonprofits in the United Kingdom included fewer explicit provisions for nonprofit input into policy, the new Labor government has made clear its intention to broaden such channels in the future by establishing a "compact" with the nonprofit sector for the design of health and community care and generally moving " 'from a contract culture to a partnership culture' " (Taylor 1997, 21).

In short, the risk of sacrificing nonprofit advocacy activity as a consequence of increasing government support of nonprofit agencies seems not to have materialized in many places. To the contrary, involvement in government programs may have both motivated non-profit agencies to increase their advocacy activity and stimulated states to open new avenues for nonprofit input into the making of policies they will implement.

BUREAUCRATIZATION

While there is little evidence that government support robs the non-profit sector of its independence or undercuts its advocacy function, there is some evidence that such support contributes to the sector's bureaucratization. Government grants and contracts tend to be large in scale, precipitating expansion of recipient organizations and, in some cases, favoring organizations that are large to begin with (Taylor 1997, 15). What is more, government grants and contracts typically contain formal stipulations and monitoring requirements that neces-sitate professionalization of agency management structures. These are not, of course, wholly, or even mostly, negative developments, but they do contribute to a certain loss of flexibility on the part of nonprofit providers. The more formal the collaborative arrangement with gov-ernment, the more likely are these bureaucratization effects. Thus, in Germany, where collaboration is both highly developed and extremely formal, the free welfare associations have become highly bureaucra-tized institutions with complex management structures and staffing systems. These developments have, in fact, prompted serious concerns about the responsiveness of nonprofit organizations in a number of European countries, where elaborate partnerships with the state have in the past led nonprofit organizations to de-emphasize their links to their citizen base and to take on much of the character of public agencies. In response, however, significant efforts at organizational renewal are under way in many of these countries, often with state encouragement and support (Kramer et al. 1993, 142–44, 180).

DEVELOPING COUNTRIES

The extent to which the findings summarized above apply to the developing world is difficult to determine with precision. For one thing, experience with government support to nonprofit organizations is much shorter there. For another, serious research on nonprofit-government interaction is even more limited in developing countries than it is in the more developed ones. Finally, the factors that might lead us to expect greater governmental control of nonprofit organiza-tions in these countries are counterbalanced by other elements that would lead us to expect less effective control. Greater government control might be expected to result from the less formalized contracting procedures, more authoritarian political regimes, fewer opportunities for outside scrutiny of government decisionmaking, and fewer alternative sources of funding for nonprofits in these countries. Counterbalancing these factors, however, are growing international pressures to involve nonprofit organizations in the implementation of government policy, the international linkages that nonprofit agencies in many countries now enjoy, and the inability of government bureaucracies to monitor nonprofit activity effectively.

Perhaps reflecting this balance of forces, nonprofit agencies are finding it increasingly possible to work with governments in a wide assortment of developing settings, from Chile, Colombia, Argentina, and Brazil in Latin America to South Africa and Ghana in Africa and Pakistan and Bangladesh in South Asia. Even the advocacy function of the nonprofit sector seems to be surviving these relationshhips and growing in legitimacy. The Colombian constitution of 1991, for example, obliges the state not only to accommodate, but actually to promote, greater grassroots involvement in policy decisionmaking. Brazilian associations, which once stood outside the political process during the dictatorship period of the 1960s and 1970s, are increasingly taking an active role in it, significantly stretching the boundaries of political acceptability (Landim 1998, 331). The experiences of citizen movements in South Africa and in the Philippines have also motivated greater political engagement on the part of nonprofit organizations. Indeed, the Asia-Pacific region has been credited with having "some of the most potent citizens' movements this century," particularly in Thailand, India, Nepal, and the Philippines (Morales and Serrano 1997, 98–9), not to mention Indonesia more recently.

Evaluating the Risks: Effects on the State

The implications for the state of this emerging partnership with nonprofit organizations are somewhat more difficult to assess. For one thing, the state is no more a single entity than the nonprofit sector. Different departments have different relationships with nonprofit providers, and much of the contracting activity takes place at the local level, so that impacts are diffused.

For a variety of reasons, however, there may be more reason to be concerned about the effect that contracting has on government than about the effect it has on the nonprofit sector. These concerns arise from a number of quarters.

LACK OF A COMPETITIVE MARKET

Much of the recent enthusiasm for contracting with nonprofit and for-profit providers springs from a faith in the market—or multiple and competitive suppliers—as a mechanism to improve effectiveness and reduce costs. By contracting out services that would otherwise be provided by government agencies, efficiency is supposed to be improved as competition is injected into the service system.

Underlying this argument, however, is the assumption that functioning, competitive markets exist in the fields in which government contracting with nonprofits occurs. In practice, however, such markets have been found to be lacking in many cases (LeGrand and Bartlett 1993; Wistow et al. 1996, 164–5; Ullman 1998, 173). In such circumstances, government agencies find themselves obliged to purchase the range of services the existing array of agencies can provide rather than the set they would ideally prefer. Far from controlling the nonprofit sector, government consequently finds its policies controlled by nonprofits instead.

LACK OF MONITORING CAPABILITY

Also limiting the ability of governments to control their nonprofit agents are the costs and difficulties of monitoring nonprofit performance in a complex contracting regime. As noted earlier, monitoring is hardly automatic. To the contrary, it involves often costly procedures that few governments are prepared to finance. Moreover, the move to contracting often robs governments of the internal capabilities for judging the performance of their contractors. As governments "thin out," they not only share functions with outside agents, they paradoxically also lose the capability to hold the agents accountable.

LOSS OF PUBLIC SUPPORT

Over the long run, the real danger to governments is that contracting out the delivery of important services may dilute the public support that governments need to govern. For all its programmatic advantages, contracting has the unfortunate political disadvantage of breaking the link between the taxes citizens pay and the services they receive. When services reach citizens through nonprofit agencies that are partly financed by the state, partly financed by charitable contributions, and partly financed by user fees, significant confusion can easily arise about what taxpayers are getting for their money. Over time, this can reduce support for government programs and undermine citizen attachment to the state that taxes them but delivers few direct services in return. The long-term consequence of government-nonprofit cooperation can thus be to undermine the political support on which this cooperation ultimately depends. To avoid this, serious efforts must be devoted to educating the public about the partnership arrangements that exist.

CONCLUSIONS AND IMPLICATIONS

Contrary to the paradigm of conflict that has long dominated American thinking, sizable nonprofit sectors thus exist in many countries outside the United States. Indeed, in some countries this sector plays a role that is even more extensive than in the American context. What is more, the nonprofit sector operates to an important extent not as an alternative to the state, as the paradigm of conflict and its Third Sector Dominant Model would suggest, but as a partner with the state, and often a significant partner at that.[7] Government plays a major role in financing nonprofit activity in virtually every country where a sizable nonprofit sector exists. Such state support easily outdistances the support these organizations receive from private charity and often surpasses the support they receive from fees and charges. In a sense, the nonprofit sector in many parts of the world has enlisted the state as its chief fund-raiser, particularly for programs focused on the poor. In the process, the Collaborative Model, rather than the Third Sector Dominant Model or the Government Dominant Model, is fast becoming the international norm.

From the evidence at hand, moreover, nonprofit organizations appear to be able to enjoy these relationships with the state with far less sacrifice of their autonomy and independence than is often assumed. While Japanese nonprofit organizations have been held closely in check, this situation clearly predated the expansion of governmental support and seems rooted far more deeply in national traditions. Elsewhere, nonprofit organizations have been able to retain considerable autonomy vis-à-vis public authorities even while relying heavily on public resources. Indeed, in Germany and the Netherlands, public authorities are under a political and legal *obligation* to support nonprofit institutions, giving these institutions a distinct bargaining advantage. Government dependence on nonprofit organizations is far less pronounced elsewhere but still exists. As nonprofits are drawn more heavily into the government program orbit, moreover, their policy activism paradoxically increases rather than declines, contrary to widespread expectations.

This is not to say, of course, that all facets of the relationship between nonprofit organizations and the state are positive. Immense uncertainties attend the expansion of government contracting with nonprofit providers, and enormous risks confront the nonprofit organizations. Paradoxically, the most serious of these risks appears to be not the weakening of the nonprofit sector as a result of state subsidies, but its excessive strengthening. By making nonprofit organizations large and strong, state subsidies can also make them overly bureaucratic and unresponsive. What is more, this arrangement can leave government with insufficient in-house capability to monitor the resulting ties and can weaken citizen attachment to even the most democratic regime. While the evidence at hand strongly suggests that these risks, while real, are far from certain and that the balance of benefits and costs clearly favors the extension of these collaborative ties, the risks must nevertheless be borne in mind.

The implications of these findings for the development of public policy toward the nonprofit sector in the United States are serious. As the preceding chapters show, partnership between government and the nonprofit sector is widespread in the United States. This partnership is far less coherent and structured in the United States, however, than it appears to be in most other developed, and many developing, nations, except perhaps for Italy (Salamon 1995). No overarching principle governs the relationships between nonprofit organizations and government in the United States; many of these relationships are worked out at the local level on a program-by-program basis. In addition, the role played by the different partners varies from program to program. So loose is this structure, in fact, that most Americans are hardly aware of its existence, even though most government human service spending is managed through it. Under these circumstances, the risks of popular misunderstanding are immense, and the strains on nonprofit providers far greater than seem sensible.

Under these circumstances, American policymakers could usefully take a page from the book being written by their foreign counterparts about how to make the new model of government-nonprofit cooperation succeed. At a minimum, what is needed is a more explicit acknowledgment of the partnership pattern that exists and a disavowal of the "paradigm of conflict" that has dominated much of our political rhetoric in recent years, impeding progress toward making these complex relationships function more effectively. Beyond that, more explicit channels of communication must be opened between government agencies at all levels and nonprofit providers at the design stage of public policy, as the Labor government in the United Kingdom has done with its commitment to forge a "compact" with the nonprofit sector. Finally, more concrete steps should be taken to improve current contracting and reimbursement arrangements—by improving the training of personnel on both sides, by simplifying procedures, and by facilitating coordinated approaches to complex social problems.

By enshrining the ideal of the pristine nonprofit sector in its national iconography, Americans are in danger of turning their back on a central development that is strengthening the nonprofit sector on the world scene: the growing partnership between the nonprofit sector and the state. Ironically, therefore, a better understanding of international experience may hold the key to preserving and enhancing the set of institutions that Americans have long considered their unique contribution to the world.

Notes

1. The most comprehensive and systematic study available to date on the scope, structure, and financing of the nonprofit sector internationally is the Johns Hopkins Comparative Nonprofit Sector Project, which the author directs. The initial phase of this project developed systematic empirical data on the scale of the nonprofit sector in eight countries (France, Germany, Hungary, Italy, Japan, Sweden, the United Kingdom, and the United States). In addition, the project developed somewhat less detailed information on five developing countries (Brazil, Egypt, Ghana, India, and Thailand). More recently, the project has extended its coverage to 22 countries, including nine Western European countries (Austria, Belgium, Finland, France, Germany, Ireland, the Netherlands, Spain, and the U.K.), four Central European countries (the Czech Republic, Hungary, Romania, and Slovakia), four non-European developed countries (Australia, Israel, Japan, and the U.S.), and five Latin American countries (Argentina, Brazil, Colombia, Mexico, and Peru). For a summary of project results, see Salamon and Anheier 1996; Salamon and Anheier 1997b; and Salamon and Anheier 1998b. For a discussion of the developing country results, see Anheier and Salamon 1998.

2. For further description of these models, see Gidron, Kramer, and Salamon 1992.

3. The "paradigm of conflict" also finds support in some of the recent economic theories of the nonprofit sector, which explain the existence of a nonprofit sector in terms of inherent limitations of the market and the state. Thus, nonprofit organizations exist, even in a democracy, according to this line of theory, because democratic governments can only respond to those demands for collective goods that enjoy majority support. Where great diversity exists in a society, making it difficult to reach agreement on the range of collective goods to supply publicly, nonprofit organizations are more likely to exist in order to fill the gaps (Weisbrod 1977). What this could suggest, however, is that the size of the nonprofit sector in a country is likely to be inversely related to the size of the government sector: Where government is large, the nonprofit sector is likely to

be small. Where the government sector is small, the nonprofit sector is likely to be large.

4. For purposes of this research, the nonprofit sector was defined as the set of entities that share five crucial features: (i) they are *organizations*; (ii) they are *private*, i.e., not part of the governmental apparatus; (iii) they do *not distribute profits* to their owners; (iv) they are *self-governing*; and (v) they have some meaningful *voluntary* involvement (Salamon and Anheier 1998b). This definition embraces a slightly larger set of institutions than are commonly covered in treatments of the nonprofit sector in the United States. In particular, it includes social clubs and professional and business associations in addition to the more narrow 501(c)(3) and 501(c)(4) organizations.

5. The discussion here draws heavily on Salamon and Anheier (1993)

6. Gidron, Kramer, and Salamon (1992) suggest that this "third route" may really comprise two different variants—a Dual Model, which features joint government-nonprofit activity, but each in its respective sphere; and a Collaborative Model, which features actual joint action in the same sphere. Most of the examples offered here suggest that the Collaborative Model is the more common.

7. This fits most closely the complementary, rather than adversarial, pattern outlined by Young (this volume).

References

Amenomori, Takayoshi. 1997. "Japan." In *Defining the Nonprofit Sector: A Cross-National Analysis*, edited by Lester M. Salamon and Helmut K. Anheier (188–214). Manchester, U.K.: Manchester University Press.

Anheier, Helmut K. 1991. "Employment and Earnings in the German Nonprofit Sector: Structure and Trends." *Annals of Public and Cooperative Economics* 62 (4): 673–94.

————. 1992. "An Elaborate Network: Profiling the Third Sector in Germany." In *Government and the Third Sector: Emerging Relationships in Welfare States*, edited by Benjamin Gidron, Ralph M. Kramer, and Lester M. Salamon (31–56). San Francisco: Jossey-Bass Publishers.

Anheier, Helmut K., and Lester M. Salamon, eds. 1998. *The Nonprofit Sector in the Developing World*. Vol. 5 of the Johns Hopkins Nonprofit Sector Series, edited by Lester M. Salamon and Helmut K. Anheier. Manchester, U.K.: Manchester University Press.

Archambault, Edith. 1997. *The Nonprofit Sector in France*. Vol. 3 of the Johns Hopkins Nonprofit Sector Series, edited by Lester M. Salamon and Helmut K. Anheier. Manchester, U.K.: Manchester University Press.

Barbetta, Gian Paolo, ed. 1997. *The Nonprofit Sector in Italy*. Vol. 6 of the Johns Hopkins Nonprofit Sector Series, edited by Lester M. Salamon and Helmut K. Anheier, Manchester, U.K.: Manchester University Press.

Bauer, Rudolph. 1978. *Wohlfahrtsverbände in der Bundesrepublik, Materialien und Analysen zu Organisation, Programmatik und Praxis, Ein Handbuch.* Weinheim, Germany: Basel.

Bixby, Ann Kallman. 1997. "Public Social Welfare Expenditures, Fiscal Year 1994." *Social Security Bulletin* 60 (3): 40–45.

Bundesarbeitsgemeinschaft der Freien Wohlfahrtspflege (BFW). 1990. *Gesamtstatistik 1990.* Bonn: BFW.

Burger, Ary, Paul Dekker, Tymen van der Ploeg, and Wino van Ween. 1997. "Defining the Nonprofit Sector: The Netherlands." *Working Papers of the Johns Hopkins Comparative Nonprofit Sector Project 23,* edited by Lester M. Salamon and Helmut K. Anheier. Baltimore: Johns Hopkins Institute for Policy Studies.

Civicus. 1994. *Citizens: Strengthening Global Civil Society.* Coordinated by Miguel Darcy de Oliveira and Rajesh Tandon. Washington, D.C.: Civicus.

Clark, John. 1992. *Democratizing Development: The Role of Voluntary Organizations.* West Hartford, Conn.: Kumarian Press.

Commission on Private Philanthropy and Public Needs. 1975. *Giving in America.* Washington, D.C.: U.S. Department of the Treasury.

Deutscher Verein für öffentliche und private Fürsorge. 1986. *Voluntary Welfare Services.* Frankfurt am Main: Deutscher Verein (in-house publication).

Fisher, Julie. 1993. *The Road from Rio: Sustainable Development and the Nongovernmental Movement in the Third World.* Westport, Conn.: Praeger.

Gidron, Benjamin, Ralph M. Kramer, and Lester M. Salamon. 1992. "Government and the Third Sector in Comparative Perspective: Allies or Adversaries?" In *Government and the Third Sector: Emerging Relationships in Welfare States,* edited by Benjamin Gidron, Ralph M. Kramer, and Lester M. Salamon. San Francisco: Jossey-Bass Publishers.

Gronbjerg, Kirsten. 1991. "Managing Grants and Contracts." *Nonprofit and Voluntary Sector Quarterly* 20 (1, Spring): 5–21.

Hartley, Keith, and Meg Huby. 1986. "Contracting-Out Policy: Theory and Evidence." In *Privatisation and Regulation: The UK Experience,* edited by John Kay, Colin Mayer, and David Thompson (284–96). Oxford, U.K.: Oxford University Press.

Hopkins, Bruce R. 1992. *The Law of Tax-Exempt Organizations,* 6th ed. New York: John Wiley and Sons, Inc.

Hulme, David, and Michael Edwards. 1997a. "NGOs, States, and Donors: An Overview." In *NGOs, States, and Donors: Too Close for Comfort?* edited by David Hulme and Michael Edwards (3–22). London: Macmillan.

Hulme, David, and Michael Edwards, eds. 1997b. *NGOs, States, and Donors: Too Close for Comfort?* London: Macmillan.

Johns Hopkins Institute for Policy Studies. 1997. "The Nonprofit Sector and the Transformation of the Modern Welfare State." Statement prepared by participants in the Ninth Annual Johns Hopkins International Fellows in Philanthropy Conference, Rome, July.

Kandil, Amani. 1998. "The Nonprofit Sector in Egypt." In The Nonprofit Sector in the Developing World, edited by Helmut K. Anheier and Lester M. Salamon (122–57). Manchester, U.K.: Manchester University Press.

Kendall, Jeremy, and Martin Knapp. 1997. The Nonprofit Sector in the U.K. Vol. 8 of the Johns Hopkins Nonprofit Sector Series, edited by Lester M. Salamon and Helmut K. Anheier. Manchester, U.K.: Manchester University Press.

Kettl, Donald. 1993. Sharing Power: Public Governance and Private Markets. Washington, D.C.: Brookings Institution.

Kramer, Ralph. 1981. Voluntary Agencies in the Welfare State. Berkeley, Calif.: University of California Press.

Kramer, Ralph M., Håkon Lorentzen, Willem B. Melief, and Sergio Pasquinelli. 1993. Privatization in Four European Countries: Comparative Studies in Government–Third Sector Relationships. Armonk, N.Y.: M.E. Sharpe.

Landim, Leilah. 1998. "The Nonprofit Sector in Brazil." In The Nonprofit Sector in the Developing World, edited by Helmut K. Anheier and Lester M. Salamon (53–121). Manchester, U.K.: Manchester University Press.

LeGrand, Julian, and Will Bartlett. 1993. Quasi-Markets and Social Policy. London: Macmillan.

Lundström, Tommy, and Filip Wijkström. 1997. "Sweden." In Defining the Nonprofit Sector, edited by Lester M. Salamon and Helmut K. Anheier (215–48). Manchester, U.K.: Manchester University Press.

Morales, Horatio, and Isagani Serrano. 1997. "Finding Common Ground in Asia-Pacific Development." In NGOs, States, and Donors: Too Close for Comfort? edited by David Hulme and Michael Edwards (93–103). London: MacMillan.

Moe, Terry. 1984. "The New Economics of Organization." American Journal of Political Science 28 (Nov.): 739–77.

Nisbet, Robert. 1990. The Quest for Community: A Study in the Ethics of Order and Freedom. Oxford, U.K.: Oxford University Press, 1953. Reprint, San Francisco: Institute for Contemporary Studies Press.

OECD (Organization for Economic Cooperation and Development). 1997. National Accounts. Paris: OECD.

Ponsgsapich, Amara. 1998. "The Nonprofit Sector in Thailand." In The Nonprofit Sector in the Developing World, edited by Helmut K. Anheier and Lester M. Salamon (294–347). Manchester, U.K.: Manchester University Press.

Pratt, John W., and Richard J. Zeckhauser, eds. 1985. *Principals and Agents: The Structure of Business.* Cambridge, Mass.: Harvard Business School Press.

Ritchey-Vance, Marion. 1991. *The Art of Association: NGOs and Civil Society in Colombia.* Vol. 2 of the Country Focus Series, edited by Diane B. Bendahmane. Washington, D.C.: Inter-American Foundation.

Robinson, Mark. 1997. "Privatising the Voluntary Sector: NGOs as Public Service Contractors?" In *NGOs, States, and Donors: Too Close for Comfort?* edited by David Hulme and Michael Edwards (59–78). London: MacMillan.

Salamon, Lester M. 1981. "Rethinking Public Managment: Third-Party Government and the Tools of Government Action." *Public Policy* 29 (Summer): 255–75.

————. 1987. "Of Market Failure, Voluntary Failure, and Third-Party Government: Toward a Theory of Government-Nonprofit Relations in the Modern Welfare State." *Journal of Voluntary Action Research* 16 (1–2, Jan.–June): 29–49.

————. 1989. *Beyond Privatization: The Tools of Government Action.* Washington, D.C.: Urban Institute Press.

————. 1994. "The Rise of the Nonprofit Sector." *Foreign Affairs* 73 (4, July–Aug.): 111–24.

————. 1995. *Partners in Public Service: Government-Nonprofit Relations in the Modern Welfare State.* Baltimore: Johns Hopkins University Press.

————. 1997. *International Guide to Nonprofit Law.* New York: John Wiley and Sons, Inc.

Salamon, Lester M., and Helmut K. Anheier. 1993. *The Third Route: Subsidiarity, Third-Party Government, and the Provision of Social Services in Germany and the United States.* Paris: OECD.

————. 1996. *The Emerging Nonprofit Sector.* Vol. 1 of the Johns Hopkins Nonprofit Sector Series, edited by Lester M. Salamon and Helmut K. Anheier. Manchester, U.K.: Manchester University Press.

————. 1997a. *Defining the Nonprofit Sector: A Cross-National Analysis.* Vol. 4 of the Johns Hopkins Nonprofit Sector Series, edited by Lester M. Salamon and Helmut K. Anheier. Manchester, U.K.: Manchester University Press.

————. 1997b. "The Civil Society Sector." *Transaction* 34 (2, Jan.–Feb.): 60–5.

————. 1998a. "The Third Route: Government-Nonprofit Collaboration in Germany and the United States." In *Private Action and the Public Good,* edited by Walter W. Powell and Elisabeth S. Clemens (151–62). New Haven, Conn.: Yale University Press.

————. 1998b. *The Emerging Sector Revisited: A Summary.* Baltimore: Johns Hopkins Institute for Policy Studies.

————. 1998c. "Social Origins of Civil Society: Explaining the Nonprofit Sector Cross-Nationally." *Voluntas* 9 (3): 213–48.

Salamon, Lester M., Helmut K. Anheier, and Wojciech Sokolowski. 1996. *The Emerging Sector: A Statistical Supplement.* Baltimore: Johns Hopkins Institute for Policy Studies.

Sen, Siddhartha. 1998. "The Nonprofit Sector in India." In *The Nonprofit Sector in the Developing World,* edited by Helmut K. Anheier and Lester M. Salamon (198–293). Manchester, U.K.: Manchester University Press.

Spiegelhalter, Franz. 1990. *Der Dritte Sozialpartner.* Bonn: Lambertus.

Starr, Paul. 1992. "The Limits of Privatization." *Proceedings of the Academy of Political Science* 36 (3, 1987): 124–37.

Taylor, Marilyn. 1997. *The Best of Both Worlds: The Voluntary Sector and Local Government.* York, U.K.: Joseph Rowntree Foundation.

Thränhardt, Dietrich. 1983. "Ausländer im Dickicht der Verbände: Ein Beispiel verbandsgerechter Klientelselektion und korporatistischer Politikformulierung." In *Sozialarbeit und Ausländerpolitik,* edited by F. Hamburger et al. Neuwied, Darmstadt, Germany: Luchterhand.

Ullman, Claire F. 1998. "Partners in Reform: Nonprofit Organizations and the Welfare State in France." In *Private Action and the Public Good,* edited by Walter W. Powell and Elisabeth S. Clemens (163–76). New Haven, Conn.: Yale University Press.

Weisbrod, Burton. 1977. *The Voluntary Nonprofit Sector: An Economic Analysis.* Lexington, Mass.: D.C. Heath.

Wistow, Gerald, Martin Knapp, Brian Hary, Julien Forder, Jeremy Kendall, and Rob Manning. 1996. *Social Care Markets: Progress and Prospects.* Buckingham, U.K.: Open University Press.

The World Bank. 1997. *World Development Report 1997: The State in a Changing World.* New York: Oxford University Press.

Yamamoto, Tadashi. 1998. *The Nonprofit Sector in Japan.* Vol. 7 of the Johns Hopkins Nonprofit Sector Series, edited by Lester M. Salamon and Helmut K. Anheier. Manchester, U.K.: Manchester University Press.

ABOUT THE EDITORS

Elizabeth T. Boris is the director of the Center on Nonprofits and Philanthropy at the Urban Institute in Washington, D.C. She is the author of many research publications and articles on philanthropy and nonprofits, including "Philanthropic Foundations in the United States: An Introduction," published in 1992 and revised in 1998. She was the founding director of the Nonprofit Sector Research Fund at the Aspen Institute from 1991 to 1996.

C. Eugene Steuerle is a senior fellow at the Urban Institute and author of a weekly column, "Economic Perspective," for *Tax Notes Magazine*. He is the author of 7 books, more than 125 reports and articles, and approximately 500 columns and 40 congressional testimonies or reports. His research on charity and philanthropy include studies on the patterns of giving by the wealthy (for the Council on Foundations), the effect of taxes on charitable giving, payout rates for foundations (for the Filer Commission), unrelated business income taxes, and ways of simplifying and reforming tax rules for charitable contributions and charitable giving.

Alan J. Abramson is director of the Nonprofit Sector and Philanthropy Program at the Aspen Institute in Washington, D.C. In this capacity, he oversees the Nonprofit Sector Research Fund, the Nonprofit Sector Strategy Group, and other Aspen Institute initiatives on the nonprofit sector and philanthropy. He is also a longtime consultant to Independent Sector and serves on several advisory committees and boards in the nonprofit field. He is the author and coauthor of numerous books and papers.

Evelyn Brody is an associate professor of law at the Chicago-Kent College of Law, Illinois Institute of Technology, where she teaches tax courses, and is an associate scholar of the Urban Institute. She writes and lectures on a variety of legal, economic, and social issues affecting individuals, businesses, and nonprofit organizations.

Joseph J. Cordes is a visiting fellow at the Center on Nonprofits and Philanthropy at the Urban Institute while on sabbatical from George Washington University, where he is professor of economics and director of the graduate program in public policy. He is a member of the American Economic Association and the National Tax Association, where he currently serves as coeditor of the *Encyclopedia of Taxation and Tax Policy*. He has published numerous articles on tax policy, government regulation, and government spending. He is a coeditor of *Democracy, Social Values, and Public Policy* (Greenwood-Praeger), and he has been a contributor to several edited volumes, including *Readings in Public Policy* and *To Profit or Not to Profit*.

Carol J. De Vita is senior research associate in the Center on Nonprofits and Philanthropy (CNP) at the Urban Institute. She oversees CNP's work on faith-based organizations and a study of community organizations and neighborhood networks in three low-income neighborhoods in the District of Columbia. She also is developing a national study of nonprofit organizations in an era of welfare reform.

John H. Goddeeris is professor and chairperson of the Department of Economics at Michigan State University. His primary research interests are in the economics of health care and government finance. He has published numerous articles in journals such as the *Journal of Political Economy*, *Economic Inquiry*, the *Journal of Health Economics*, and the *National Tax Journal*, as well as a number of chapters in various books. His work with the Governor's Task Force on Access to Health Care in Michigan led to an edited volume, *Access to Health Care: What Can States Do?*

Virginia A. Hodgkinson is a research professor of public policy at the Center for Voluntary Organizations and Service at the Georgetown University Public Policy Institute. She is the author and editor of numerous articles and papers on the nonprofit sector, including *The Nonprofit Almanac: Dimensions of the Independent Sector 1996–1997.* She has coauthored six volumes in the *Jossey-Bass Publishers Nonprofit Sector Series* and served as associate editor of the *Nonprofit and Voluntary Sector Quarterly* from 1985 to 1990.

Elizabeth J. Reid is part of the adjunct faculty at the Corcoran School of Arts in Washington, D.C., teaching courses in political and economic affairs. She currently teaches "Artists and Communities," a course she designed to help students and emerging artists explore their relationship with the arts community. She has 20 years of experience in labor and community organizations, grassroots political education, leadership training, and involvement in civic and political affairs.

Lester M. Salamon is a professor at the Johns Hopkins University and director of the Johns Hopkins Center for Civil Society Studies. His 1982 book, *The Federal Budget and the Nonprofit Sector*, was the first to document the scale of the American nonprofit sector and the extent of government support to it. He is also the author of *Partners in Public Service: Government-Nonprofit Relations in the Modern Welfare State*, *America's Nonprofit Sector: A Primer*, and *The Emerging Sector*, which examines the international nonprofit sector.

Steven Rathgeb Smith teaches at the Graduate School of Public Affairs at the University of Washington, where he directs the nonprofit management program. He is the coauthor of *Nonprofits for Hire: The Welfare State in the Age of Contracting* and *Adjusting the Balance: Federal Policy and Victim Services* and coeditor of *Public Policy for Democracy*. His current research focuses on the privatization of social welfare services, the role of community partnerships and coalitions in building and rebuilding local communities, and the impact of welfare reform and devolution on faith-related service agencies. He is currently the editor of *Nonprofit and Voluntary Sector Quarterly*.

Burton A. Weisbrod is John Evans Professor of Economics at Northwestern University. He is the author of numerous books and articles on nonprofits and economics. Recently, he edited and cowrote several chapters in the 1998 book *To Profit or Not to Profit: The Commercialism Transformation of the Nonprofit Sector*, and he coedited *The Urban Crisis: Linking Research to Action* in 1997.

Robert Wuthnow is the Gerhard R. Andlinger '52 Professor of Social Sciences and director of the Center for the Study of Religion at Princeton University. His recent books include *Loose Connection: Joining Together in America's Fragmented Communities* (1998) and *After Heaven: Spirituality in America since the 1950s* (1998). He is currently conducting research on religion and the arts.

Dennis R. Young is professor of nonprofit management and economics at Case Western Reserve University. He is founding editor of the journal *Nonprofit Management and Leadership* and current president of the Association for Research on Nonprofit Organizations and Voluntary Action (ARNOVA). His research interests include the management, organizational structure, and economics of nonprofit organizations. He is author or coauthor of several books, including *Economics for Nonprofit Managers* (with Richard Steinberg) and *Corporate Philanthropy at the Crossroads* (with Dwight Burlingame).